NARRATING TRAUMA

THE YALE CULTURAL SOCIOLOGY SERIES
Jeffrey C. Alexander and Ron Eyerman, Series Editors

NARRATING TRAUMA

ON THE IMPACT
OF COLLECTIVE SUFFERING

EDITED BY
RON EYERMAN,
JEFFREY C. ALEXANDER, AND
ELIZABETH BUTLER BREESE

 Routledge
Taylor & Francis Group

LONDON AND NEW YORK

First published 2011 by Paradigm Publishers

Published 2016 by Routledge
2 Park Square, Milton Park, Abingdon, Oxon OX14 4RN
711 Third Avenue, New York, NY 10017, USA

Routledge is an imprint of the Taylor & Francis Group, an informa business

Library of Congress Cataloging-in-Publication Data

Narrating trauma : on the impact of collective suffering / edited by Ron Eyerman, Jeffrey C. Alexander, and Elizabeth Butler Breese.
    p. cm. — (Yale cultural sociology series)
 Includes bibliographical references.
 ISBN 978-1-61205-346-2 (Ebook)
 1. Suffering—Social aspects. 2. Suffering—Political aspects. I. Eyerman, Ron. II. Alexander, Jeffrey C., 1947–. III. Breese, Elizabeth Butler. IV. Title. V. Series.

 BF789.S8N37 2011
 303.6—dc22

                                                                          2011008244

Designed and Typeset by Straight Creek Bookmakers.

ISBN 13: 978-1-59451-886-7 (hbk)
ISBN 13: 978-1-59451-887-4 (pbk)

To Neil Smelser,
with admiration and affection.

Contents

Preface

The ideas presented in this volume were developed by each author or author pair and they were crucially nurtured and challenged in two intense, face-to-face meetings over the course of two years.

In May 2008, the contributors to this volume met in New Haven, Connecticut, sponsored by Yale's Center for Cultural Sociology, for a day-long workshop. In this meeting, we introduced one another to our cases and our methods for studying them.

One year later, in June 2009, we met in Athens, Greece. This meeting was patiently and generously organized by Nicolas Demertzis and Evangelos Liotzis. Over two days, we presented our works-in-progress and collectively refined our analyses of the cases, and we considered together the concept of cultural trauma. We came away from this meeting quite eager to share our ideas.

Thanks to the hard work of many people, those ideas are now contained in the pages of this book. Inge Brooke Schmidt and Hiro Saito attended the first meeting in New Haven, and Radim Marada attended both meetings. Although they were not able to participate in this book, each of these scholars added richly to our conversations, and we thank them for contributing to this project.

We wish to thank Katerina Koronaki for sitting in on our meeting in Athens and issuing a report on our progress in the 2009 *Newsletter for the International Sociological Association's Historical and Comparative Sociology Thematic Group*. In addition to thanking Nicolas Demertzis and Evangelos Liotzis for their organizational contributions, we wish to thank Nadine Amalfi at the Center for Cultural Sociology for organizing the meetings and for helping to coordinate the publishing details.

On Social Suffering and Its Cultural Construction

Jeffrey C. Alexander and
Elizabeth Butler Breese

This book deals with social suffering; with exploitation and violence; with war and genocide; the massacre of innocents; and intense and often grue-some religious, economic, ethnic, and racial strife. These formidable top-ics do not in themselves render our book distinctive. What distinguishes the contributions that follow is how they approach social suffering's causes and effects. While they are deeply sensitivity to the materiality and pragmatics of social suffering, they reject materialist and pragmatic approaches for one centered inside a cultural sociology.

Material forces are, of course, deeply implicated in social suffer-ing, and the practical considerations surrounding traumatic events have significant effects on social organization. Here, we are concerned, how-ever, to trace the manner in which these causes and effects are crucially mediated by symbolic representations of social suffering and how such a cultural process channels powerful human emotions. We demonstrate how symbolic-*cum*-emotional forces are carried by social groups and how together they create powerful, history-changing effects in the worlds of morality, materiality, and organization. Intellectuals, artists, and social movement leaders create narratives of social suffering. They project these as new ideologies that create new ideal interests. Such ideologies and interests can trigger significant repairs in the civil fabric or instigate new rounds of social suffering in turn.

We approach this process of symbolic-*cum*-emotional representation as a collective, sociological process centering on meaning-making. The construction of collective trauma is often fuelled by individual experiences of pain and suffering, but it is the threat to collective rather than individual identity that defines the kind of suffering at stake. The pivotal question becomes, not "who did this to me?" but "what group did this to us?" Intellectuals, political leaders, and symbol creators make different claims about collective identity, about the nature of the wound and what caused it, about the identity of victim and perpetrator, and about what is to be done to prevent the trauma from happening ever again. Conflicting accounts weave protagonist and antagonist into powerful accusatory narratives and project these to audiences of third parties.

Which narrative wins out is not only a matter of performative power. It is also a matter of power and resources and the demographics of the audiences who are listening. Who can command the most effective platform to tell the trauma story? Some stories are repressed, while others are materially sustained. Some stories are enriched by long-standing traditions; others seem so counterintuitive as scarcely to be believed. Some trauma narratives find willing, able, and homogeneous audiences; other stories are received by fragmented or constricted audiences; still others simply fall on deaf ears.

The emotional experience of suffering is critical, but it is not primordial. To find the meaning of suffering, it must be framed against background expectations. Individual suffering is of extraordinary human, moral, and intellectual concern; in itself, however, it is a matter for psychologists and psychoanalysts, not for the sociological contributors to this book. We are concerned with traumas that become collective, and they can become so only if they are conceived as wounds to social identity. This is a matter of intense cultural and political work. Suffering collectivities—whether dyads, groups, societies, or civilizations—do not exist simply as material networks. They must be imagined into being.

When social processes construe events as gravely dangerous to groups, social actors transform individual suffering into a matter of collective concern, of cultural worry, group danger, social panic, and creeping fear. Individual victims react to traumatic injury with repression and denial, gaining relief when these psychological defenses are overcome, bringing pain into consciousness so they are able to mourn. For collectivities, it is different. Rather than denial, repression, and working through, it is a matter of symbolic construction and framing, of creating a narrative and moving along from there. A "we" must be constructed via narrative and coding, and it is this collective identity that experiences and confronts the danger. Perhaps thousands of people have been killed. Individuals have lost their lives, experiencing intense suffering and pain. These are individual facts. Beyond this point, collective processes of cultural framing decide: Are the massive deaths seen as sacrifices for a legitimate war? Americans who sent soldiers to triumphal victory in the World Wars I and II did not experience collective trauma, despite the tens of thousands of deaths to men and women they loved and lost. Neither did Germans during their early Blitzkriegs. The reason was that these lost lives, far from endangering American and German collective identities, actually reinforced them. It is when narratives of triumph are challenged, when individual deaths seem worthless or polluted, when those who have fallen are seen not as sacrificing for a noble cause but as wasted victims of irresponsible chicanery, that wars can become traumatic indeed (Giesen 2004).

To transform individual suffering into collective trauma is cultural work. It requires speeches, rituals, marches, meetings, plays, movies, and storytelling of all kinds. Carrier groups tie their material and ideal interests to particular scripts about who did what to whom and how society must respond if a new collective identity is to be sustained. Historical episodes of social suffering have the potential to trigger dangerous group conflict, but also ameliorating reconciliation. Lost wars; economic depressions; mass murders of every conceivable ethnic, racial, and religious stripe—such social events can be understood according to drastically varying accounts and can be made to imply sharply antithetical social prescriptions. This cultural work produces spirals of symbolic signification, signifying processes that are mediated by institutional structures and uneven distributions of wealth and power. Are we struggling over the nature of collective trauma in the field of party conflict, in a court of law, in the mass media, or on a theatrical stage? Do the cultural entrepreneurs' stories have access to the means of symbolic production? Even the most compelling trauma narratives must reach outside themselves. Power and resources are terribly important here, even if they alone will not decide.

In an earlier work, *Cultural Trauma and Collective Identity,* the senior editors of this volume helped work out a foundational theory of collective trauma (Alexander et. al. 2004). We invited contributors to the present volume to elaborate and apply this theory to new social contexts and to revise and change it in their own distinctive ways. Our earlier work generated some controversy, both in its insistence on differentiating collective from individual trauma and in its suggestion that emotional experience is channeled via cultural processes relatively independent of the trauma's social origins.

We believe these foundational positions are sustained in the case studies that follow, even as new propositions are proffered, theoretical territory extended, and new conceptual connections are forged.

Individual Suffering Is Separate from Collective Representation

In their chapter on the controversial bombing war against German cities during World War II, Volker Heins and Andreas Langenohl vividly demonstrate that massive suffering of many individuals does not create collective trauma. They open their account by providing an overview of magnitude of the suffering of the German people, both soldiers and civilians:

> More than five million soldiers were killed, most of them on the eastern front. Those who survived the war in the east were often wounded, half-crazed, or frostbitten, and were further decimated by the harsh conditions in Soviet POW camps. British and American bombers attacked more than one hundred German cities and towns, reducing many of them to a sea of rubble, killing around six hundred thousand civilians, and making many more homeless. Millions of ethnic Germans who had settled in Poland or Czechoslovakia fled the onslaught of the Red Army, or were expelled by the newly established communist governments. On their way to Berlin and in the fallen capital itself, Soviet soldiers raped altogether perhaps one and a half million women.

In the immediate postwar period, and indeed for many years afterward, individuals recorded these massive sufferings in photographs, in personal diaries, and in family conversations, and often made these public. In heavily bombed cities such as Hamburg, the bombardment was commemorated in local official ceremonies. Their painful experiences were not silenced, as some have claimed. Yet, these representations of the bombings never amounted to an authoritative representation orienting collective political and moral perceptions.

Why was it that the suffering experienced by Germans in this period—their individual traumatic experiences—did not become a cultural trauma? The explanation Heins and Langenohl offer is simple and clear: commemorating air raids as a trauma for the national collectivity would have conflicted with the trauma narrative postwar Germany constructed when it was occupied by those who had perpetrated the injuries. The trauma construction in postwar Germany centered on the harm that the Germans had done to others. The Holocaust-centered, war-guilt narrative became even stronger after the occupation, forming the core of democratic Germany's collective identity in the decades afterward, right up until today. It was this new moral frame that allowed German national identity to rise from the ashes of World War II, and it did not allow the individual injuries that millions of Germans suffered at the hands of the Allies to become the nation's collective narration. Once German identity was tied to a perpetrator identity, neither individual Germans nor their nation could be portrayed as victim. It was the nation's mass murder of the Jews, not the German people's own deaths, which needed constituting as the primary injury at stake.

> Germans saw their own misery filtered through a sense of what had been done to others in their name … The memory of the bombing war has not been turned into a national or "cultural trauma" … Germans learned to connect their own suffering to the suffering of others. They remember that their cities were firebombed and often completely flattened by identifiable actors, but it is not this fact in itself that is remembered and commemorated as a psychologically searing, identity-changing event … Germans felt no longer entitled to speak of themselves as victims … The Allied bombing of German cities during World War II—that has not become a cultural trauma, *not even for the successive generations of the victim group.* (Original italics)[1]

Yet, while such a refusal laid the groundwork for moral redemption, it was neither sociologically determined nor socially consensual. Many Germans commemorated their soldiers' suffering at the Battle of Stalingrad well into the 1960s; it was only the rise to preeminence of Holocaust memory that made such trauma construction of German military sacrifice impossible. In the eastern city of Dresden, so horribly destroyed by the infamous firebombing, controversial efforts by left and right to sustain anti-American and anti-British narratives of German World War II suffering continue today; however, as Heins and Langenohl argue, these narratives will not rise, in the foreseeable future, to the level of symbolic condensation necessary for a cultural trauma to emerge.

Total war, an objective event of staggering empirical significance, demands the countless loss of individual life and enormous expenditure of national treasure. Its narration as triumph or trauma depends, however, on whether these sacrifices are deemed to have contributed to collective glory or to have been wasted in vain. As in post-Nazi Germany, postwar Japan considered its national society to have been gravely wounded by defeat. Japan's postwar storytellers did not, however, separate the new nation from the old trauma in Germany's radical and insistent way. In her account of Japan's trauma process, Akiko Hashimoto, using a concept proposed by Eyerman (2004), insists that empirical referent does not determine signification:

> The horrendous event emerges as a significant *referent* in the collective consciousness, not because it is in some way naturally ineffaceable but because it generates a structure of discourse that normalizes it in collective life ... Wars, massacres, atrocities, invasions, and other instances of mass violence can become significant referents for subsequent collective life not because of the gruesome nature of the events *per se*, but because people choose to make them especially relevant to who they are and what it means to be a member of that society. Some events therefore become more crucially significant than others, because we manage to make them more consequential in later years for our understanding of ourselves and our own society. (Original italics)

Hashimoto devotes attention to the supra-material symbolization of Japanese defeat. "August 15, 1945, has come to represent not strictly the end of a military conflict," she writes, "but the cultural trauma of a fallen nation, the collapse of the nation's social and moral order, and the failed aspirations of an East Asian Empire." Yet, even while "epitomizing a rupture of national history rather than the strictly military event"—a rupture that allows a "radical departure from a stigmatized past"—who exactly were the traumatic event's perpetrators and who its victims are not determined by simply establishing such a narrative break. The autonomy of representation and referent means that the characters of a rupture narrative can be filled in sharply different ways, "The war was wrong, but there is also sufficient elasticity here in assigning the blame to different agents and causes, from the emperor and colonial aggression to incompetent military strategists and self-serving Western powers."

When Rui Gao investigates Maoist reconstructions of Chinese suffering, her account also demonstrates that individual wounds and collective representations are not by any means necessarily intertwined. Why did Maoism largely ignore what Chinese people suffered at the hands of Japanese armed forces during World War II? The lack of cultural construction cannot be attributed to the dearth of painful experience.

Certainly, the latter was sufficiently massive and horrible to trigger trauma on a large scale:

> The millions of Chinese people who had the misfortune of living through the War of Resistance Against Japan (hereafter "the War") experienced nearly unbearable trauma and pain. From 1937 to 1945, during the eight years of the War, China lost three million lives in combat, and civilian casualties were estimated to be about twenty million. The heinous nature of the war atrocities committed by the invading army must have left indelible marks on the consciousness of millions of war victims. Indeed, the notorious Nanjing Massacre, the crimes of Unit 731 Special Forces, and the conscription of "comfort women" are but three particularly atrocious cases of trauma inflicted by the Japanese army.

To explain Maoism's silence about these massively painful experiences, Gao traces symbolization, more precisely the lack thereof. "Such vivid and massively shared suffering and injustice," Gao writes, "remained ultimately private and individual. For many years after the building of the People's Republic of China, this suffering seldom found its way into the public sphere of expression."

To understand why millions of brutal individual experiences were not translated into collective representation, Gao examines the carrier group of postwar Chinese trauma, the nation's revolutionary and newly triumphant Communist party. She finds its ideal interests lay elsewhere. Rather than create a national narrative pitting Chinese victims against war-mongering Japanese, the ruling party focused on its own suffering and on the pain experienced by the class that it fought to sustain. According to the revolutionary trauma narrative of Maoism, it was Chinese ruling class who inflicted collective pain, not the Japanese, and it was the party and the proletarian who were the victims, not the Chinese people *per se.* These New China storytellers projected "the intense trauma drama of class struggle … That is, perpetrators in the old society epitomized an absolutely evil class enemy." If this alternative trauma story were successful, it would justify the leadership of the communist party: the "suffering of the proletarian victims" could be "represented symbolically and emotionally as suffering shared by a broad group of people, united regardless of national boundaries in a new universal class collectivity." The riddle of Maoist silence can now be solved. It is because the "the experience of the War … does not fit with this grand narrative of 'class trauma'" that the "emergence of the War as a collective trauma was effectively inhibited by the trauma of class struggle."[2]

Ivana Spasić similarly separates Serbians' actual experience of the "trauma of Kosovo" from its symbolic figuration. "If asked what distinguishes them as a nation," Spasić writes, "most Serbs would tell you it is the memory of the Battle of Kosovo, fought between the Serbian army and the forces of Ottoman Turks in 1389." It is from this "Kosovo 'sore,' 'wound,' or 'pain,' as it is usually called" that "the sorrowful but proud feeling of tragedy, death, and loss engendered by remembrance" that are "generally held to be the foundation of Serbian identity" is sustained. For her part, Spasić questions whether that earlier traumatic event ever actually happened, at least as Serbians have remembered it. To understand the Serbian experience of trauma, she argues, requires a cultural turn, moving "from 'blood' to 'referent.'" "When referring to 'Kosovo,'" she explains, we are speaking of "the symbolic, abstract meaning, not Kosovo as a real place."

Viewed as narrative rather than event, "Kosovo" is far from straightforward. Describing "the symbolism of Kosovo" as "ambiguous and open-ended," Spasić finds "many gaps, loops, double-entendres and other discursive plays."

> Trauma may be seen as a speech act, a continually discursively produced condition that stands in mutually constitutive relations with the contextual circumstances. In this sense, it is present as a cultural meaning-structure, Eyerman's "referent" or Živković's "entrenched story."

It is the myth's rhetorical success rather than Serbians' actual experiences of pain that is "responsible for the myth's enduring power." Spasić challenges the idea that "trauma is actively *felt* by people, that it is located somehow within them, that it affects them uniformly and unavoidably" (original italics). Collectively constructed, trauma is located inside of cultural structures, and it is these narratives, not the actual experience of real events, that has the capacity to inflict collective pain, "Over the centuries, the thematic cluster of Kosovo has become a (potentially) traumatizing interpretive framework readily available to Serbs for making sense of their collective experiences."

For contemporary Serbians, the paradox and tragedy of the Kosovo myth derives from this chasm between individual experience and collective construction. In their "more personalized and private discourse," Spasić contends, Serbs display a "rationalism and open-mindedness" that could lay the basis for more "realistic" foreign relations. Today, however, "with the verbal stakes rising, it has become all but impossible to talk about Kosovo, real as well as symbolic, in anything but the most elevated tone." The result is that, while "people harbor all kinds of doubts and grudges against the symbolic prevalence of Kosovo and its impingements on current Serbian politics," they "feel extremely uncomfortable expressing them in public, or even to themselves, because the sacredness of the topic has been so extremely enhanced."

The distinction between private experiences of suffering, shame, and defeat and the public expression, signification, and symbolization of trauma stands at the core of Nicolas Demertzis's history of the social and political aftermath of the Greek civil war in 1944–1949 (though, as Demertzis advises, this periodization is controversial). The suffering brought about by the bloody war among members of the same national and ethnic community, Demertzis explains, was linguistically, emotionally, and politically difficult—and for a time impossible—to publicly express in Greece. Regarding individual, psychological trauma, we speak of the repression of memories and experiences. Cultural traumas, as not only Demertzis but also Bartmanski and Eyerman in their chapter on the Katyn Massacre explain, may follow such periods of silence, exclusion, and oblivion. Private pain and loss can be excluded from the public realm and silenced by the state, as in the case of the Katyn Massacre. In Greece, however, "the veil of silence was socially imposed but not directly enforced by a repressive state apparatus." The social forces imposing the "veil of silence" were effective nevertheless. The conflict was not given a name, was not even signified in the weakest sense. Without a public vocabulary or public recognition, individuals experienced shame and confusion within their most intimate spheres: their families.

Demertzis's chapter begins with a moving account of his "hardworking" and "honest" father's inability to answer the opaque yet crushing accusations of previously committed sins leveled by his elder son. In the cultural trauma of the Katyn Massacre, too, Bartmanski and Eyerman explain, the family plays a crucial role. The family is the site of grieving for a lost father, brother, or husband, and it is a unit isolated from society; the truth of the identity of the perpetrators, known to most if not all of the families, was aggressively distorted by the state and concealed in public life. Families who lost a member in the Katyn Massacre and participants in the Greek civil war hold memories and emotions as individuals and as families that may become part of the cultural collective trauma once the political or social climate allows for public symbolization and wider signification. The period of silence, exclusion, and oblivion is not only a period of being "on hold"; such prevention of more public narrations may become part of the broader social trauma itself. Indeed, Bartmanski and Eyerman find their title in the words of the daughter of a man killed at Katyn, "the worst was the silence." As both Bartmanski's and Eyerman's and Demertzis's studies make clear, it was not certain in either case that individual and family experience would become traumas for the broader collectivity. Not all silences become spoken; not all personal anguish becomes collective trauma.

The chapters about trauma construction in Colombia and South Africa reveal the same independence of collective construction from personal experience, a separation that allows not only for moral reckoning but also for these lessons to be pushed in more inclusive or more reactionary directions.

In Colombia, writes Carlo Tognato, the battle waged by the left-wing FARC against the Colombian state constitutes the longest-standing guerilla conflict in the world, and it is largely financed from kidnappings that have imposed extraordinary individual suffering on the Colombian people. "Just between January 1996 and June 2008," according to Tognato, "approximately twenty four thousand people have been kidnapped," and "by June 2008, almost three thousand were still in the hands of their captors and almost fourteen hundred had died in captivity." Yet, despite these extraordinary afflictions, "Colombians have been traditionally quite indifferent to the suffering of the kidnap victims."

> In a letter to his family one of the kidnapped, Coronel Mendieta, writes: "It is not physical pain that paralyzes me, or the chains around my neck that torment me, but the mental agony, the evil of the evil and the indifference of the good, as if we were not worth anything, as if we did not exist."

It is not inevitable that massive individual suffering will produce a collective trauma process, much less an ameliorating social narrative to repair social fragmentation. "The Colombian case bears witness," Tognato observes, "to the fact that the view of human suffering does not automatically trigger solidarity for the victims." Yet, while not automatic, it remains possible. Tognato describes how dramatic new symbolic performances by antikidnapping demonstrators and civil activists have challenged Colombia's desperate political situation in progressive and democratic ways.

In his examination of refugees in South Africa, Ari Sitas addresses the pain Africans have suffered in postcolonial societies. "Since 1994, a stream of refugees has arrived in South Africa from a number of conflict zones on the African continent," and they have "fled from frightening scenes of violence and war in their countries." Sitas conceptualizes the most outspoken and politicized among these refugees as, at least potentially, an intellectual carrier group. He interprets their discourse as an effort to give meaning to the suffering of their fellow citizens, reading their political demands as efforts to repair the searing strains that undermine peace in the nations from which they flee. In their speeches and writings, members of this carrier group in *status ascendi* speak of "*isikhala*—a polysemic word that borders almost on the Marxian concept of alienation, of homelessness, pain and suffering." As Sitas understands it, however, this discourse about pain, "is not [about] a personal experience," not about "what happened to the individual ... as such." Instead, "the performance listed general details—the kind of misdeeds, rapes, hackings, stabbings, burnings, shootings, bombs that happened." Yet, even as "the killer neighbor ... was invoked" in a generalized and abstract manner, there is "a question left hanging." It is this: "Who put the knife in his or her hand?"

When their narration comes to this question, the refugees' trauma constructions veer sharply away from the actual experiences of victims and the actual actions of perpetrators. The spiral of signification is deflected by the long-standing trauma framework that fuelled the African anticolonial movement in an earlier day. Rather than pointing to postcolonial African perpetrators, refugees refer to "the vintage formulation" of Africa "as a continent of humanism, sociality and equality before the European pillage." With Africa entering the collective imagination as pure victim, the refugees tell a story whose "key trauma [is] constructed around slavery, racism and, after the late nineteenth-century imperial scramble for its resources, colonialism." According to Sitas, narrating the old white-man-as-perpetrator story—of "the transatlantic experience of slavery and into the forms of forced/corvee labor on the continent of mines and plantations—it was about the suffering of servitude and about real and metaphorical bondage"—misses what must be the contemporary point.

> The acknowledgment of suffering then slid invariably toward the White Man as a perpetrator in the imaginary—nothing specific—"he" as a trans-historical entity, a Manichean counterpoint. Nothing about the *Interhamwe* on Rwandan lips, of Mobutu or the various factions of the Congo, of the Derg or the Amharas, of the warlords was ever mentioned—only a broad context of the White origins of a suffering.

Sitas finds this "a disturbing construction" because so imagining perpetrator and victim avoids addressing the African sources of postcolonial suffering and prevents, at the same time, a cosmopolitan resolution. It "asserts an 'unassimilable otherness' from the rest of the world," homogenizing the imaginary of a terribly divided continent and making wider solidarity with outsiders impossible. Trauma, victim, and perpetrator are identified and interrelated in a distorted and particularistic rather than realistic and morally responsible manner. While "the interviewees agree that the agencies of violence and of conflict are African and African-led," Sitas explains, "the cohorts, power-elites, [and] rulers who come to benefit from it are seen as 'corrupt' or better, 'the corrupted.'" In this rhetorical construction, there is an abdication of responsibility.

> The inflection is important as corrupt is not so much a personal at-tribute as the result of pressure from external forces. In this way, the problem of corruption is not owned but instead fingers are pointed at inflictors of the problem—not corrupt, but corrupted. It refuses to own "the" problem. "They" have been victims of external forces and/or internal servants of external forces.

This narrative points to "remote-control colonialism" as having "spawned tribalism and ethnic strife," ignoring Africa's own selfish and misguided elites, the groups that are actually responsible for the most recent impositions of trauma and pain. Such constricted trauma con-struction closes off the social space for attacking contemporary African suffering, to demand the kinds of social changes that would reconstruct African societies in more civil manner—the kind of radical change that Sitas himself has advocated throughout his own intellectual-*cum*-activist career.

That processes of symbolic representation establish and mediate the nature of collective suffering is the ground bass of cultural trauma theory. From it follows a series of more specific sociological propositions: cultural agents are central, collective trauma dramas are performed rather than simply described, and trauma dramas have material repercussions.

Cultural Agents Are Central

Meanings do not come out of thin air. Webs of signification are spun by culture creators. Here, we mean most centrally to point to the work of novelists, painters, poets, movie directors and television producers, comic book scribes, journalists, and intellectuals. The category of cul-tural agent would also include other kinds of publicly oriented speech acts as well, for example, the factual claims making of lawyers, forensic scientists, academics, and politicians. We mean to highlight not the epistemological status of truth claims but the agency with which every claim to reality, whether ostensibly factual or fictional, must be made.

From a cultural-sociological perspective, the difference between factual and fictional statements is not an Archimedean point. Cultural trauma theory is post-foundational. Yet, while the spiral of signification is not rational, it is intentional. The spiral is spun by individual and group carriers. It is people who make traumatic meanings, though they do so in circumstances which they have not themselves created and which they do not fully comprehend.

The more conservative and heroic version of postwar Japanese trauma discourse, Akiko Hashimoto tells us, was crystallized by Yoshida Mitsuru's best-selling nonfiction memoir *Requiem for Battleship Yamato*. One of the few survivors of a tactically dubious suicide sortie only months before Japan's defeat, Yoshida dramatically recounted the naval officer Captain Usubuchi's emotional framing of imminent defeat as patriotic sacrifice, not only his own and his 3,000 crew members but of Japan itself. "We will lead the way," the captain is purported to have proclaimed; "we will die as harbingers of Japan's new life." While acknowledging defeat and drawing a sharp line in historical time, such trauma narration does not actually make Japan's war regime impure, as Hashimoto explains, "In Yoshida's rendering, the courage and discipline of the men facing certain death are emphasized, without blame or resentment directed toward the state leadership that ordered the tactically dubious special attack mission with no fuel to return home." Hashimoto traces how this conservative pattern of trauma signification, crystallized in a best-selling book, spiraled along the aestheticized pathways of popular culture and into the political sphere, with immense social and political significance.

Progressive Japanese countered this conservative, justificatory trauma reconstruction via narratives of equally dramatic coloration. The aesthetic power of such leftist counter-narratives made them massively popular. "At the height of the Vietnam War," Hashimoto recounts, "an artist of the wartime generation penned mortifying stories that would become some of the most iconic antiwar literature in postwar Japan." Nakazawa Keiji's semi-autobiographical comic *Barefoot Gen* told the story, not of heroic defeat in military battle but of the tragic nuclear obliteration of a city, Hiroshima. The narrative constructs a civil rather than military protagonist, telling the story from the perspective of a family's day-to-day survival after the atomic bomb:

> Gen's father and sister died in the nuclear blast under [their] collapsed house, but Gen, his mother, and brothers narrowly escaped. His mother was pregnant and gave birth to Gen's sister on the day of the blast amid the wreckage. Thereafter, for ten volumes, Gen survives hunger and

poverty, loss of his mother and sister, humiliation and fear, illness and discrimination, exploitation and crimes.

Nakazawa's comic novel graphically portrays the physical suffering of individuals—"charred bodies; people with torn skin hanging from their faces and limbs, and eyeballs dangling from their sockets; maggots hatching on corpses; and heaps of burned dead bodies in the river and elsewhere all over the scorched flattened city." Yet *Gen* depicts the national antagonists responsible for this suffering as forces of a decidedly collective kind, groups whose militarist politics must be defeated for peace to once again reign. "In Nakazawa's rendering," writes Hashimoto, "the war was brought on recklessly and unnecessarily by the Japanese military and the Imperial state that heartlessly and ineptly misled civilians to deathly destruction and suffering." *Gen*'s father, Hashimoto explains, "serves as a spiritual background of the story," because he represents the possibility of a clear-eyed comprehension and rejection of the Imperialist forces that invited the violence upon its own people. This left-wing political understanding is not made didactically via truth claims but aesthetically, via narrative resolution. Psychological identification with an esteemed moral protagonist allows the civil antiwar argument to be made and a new, more critical moral position to be extended.

Gen's symbolic reenactments of trauma drama inside the popular imagination were "the most influential and iconic antiwar literature to reach successive postwar generations and shape popular consciousness about the horrendous consequences of militarism in the past four decades." The manga volumes became the "vehicle for intergenerational transmission of antiwar sentiments." Hashimoto sees *Gen* as a Japanese "equivalent of Anne Frank's story," an immensely influential work "that mobilizes empathy and pity" and whose "reinforcement effect works over the generational cycle."

In their study of "what came to be called the Katyn Massacre," Bartmanski and Eyerman carefully detail the tangled, distorted, and fraught history of the killing of 14,500 Polish military officers and over 7,000 other Polish citizens—representing a significant segment of the elite, professional class of Polish society—by the Soviet army in April 1940. Three years later, when some of the corpses were discovered, the Soviets blamed the Germans for perpetrating the mass killing. This is the basic story the Soviets would claim for decades, with various levels of tenacity, official decree, and threats to the families involved. In the meantime, most if not all of the families knew the truth: Members of the Soviet army had killed their husbands, fathers, brothers, sons, uncles, and nephews. Knowledge of the truth needed to remain unspoken, under threat of losing access to education, jobs, and a public life without harassment in Poland. It remained, for several decades, a personal sorrow and burden rather than a trauma that could be collectively felt and talked about. They write, "Cultural trauma became possible only when the directly affected individuals and communities were able to express themselves, verbally and visually, in a sustained way and project their personal tragedies onto the larger moral screen of the nation." Literal screens—ones that display films—as well as literature played a crucial role in the extension of the trauma of the massacre and of the distortion of the truth from the affected families to the Polish people and beyond.

The transformation of "Katyn" from an occurrence known to a few to a symbol of Polish collective suffering depended on families becoming cultural agents "creating and sustaining the trauma narrative" and on "intellectuals/politicians" who, after official suppression ended, could also create, sustain, and spread the symbolization of "Katyn." One of the most prominent of these intellectual carriers is the well-known film director Andrzej Wajda, who depicted Katyn in a film in 2007. Bartmanski and Eyerman write that "Wajda (2008) emphasized the importance of '*showing* Katyn to the world'" and aimed at triggering moral and cultural shock. The film's plotting technique moved from the actual victims of the Soviets' mass murder to the suffering of their families, especially the wives and the sisters of the victims. Bartmanski and Eyerman elaborate:

> Wajda, whose father was among those murdered in Kharkov, visualizes this aspect and reveals through it the cold-blooded destruction of a particular life-world. By shifting the attention from the soldiers themselves to those who loved them and whose loss was publicly unrecognized, he makes the extension of sentiments and identification possible, and thereby reveals the existential depth of the Katyn trauma. Staging the women as Antigones can be seen an instantiation of intertextuality that renders the story potentially generalizable.

The performance of trauma via theatrical staging is the focus of Elizabeth Breese's examination of performances of *Waiting for Godot* in the devastated urban settings of New Orleans and Sarajevo. While acknowledging that "claims to fact" are indeed performative assertions that may not themselves "correspond to something 'real,'" Breese distinguishes between factual and aesthetic trauma claims. Breese concentrates on how "carrier groups and social actors use art, in addition to claims to fact, to construct claims to trauma" to illuminate the inner workings of dramatic performance.

Through expressive and artistic performance, social actors represent elements of their experience and construct them as traumatic. Painting, dance, song, film, and drama do not accuse in the political or juridical realm; social actors use artistic productions to represent, to speak for, and to construct trauma ... The productions of *Waiting for Godot* in Sarajevo and New Orleans are social performances whose "success" is not achieved in the register of factual truth. Like Picasso's *Guernica* and other artistic constructions and claims to trauma, the success, or re-fusion, of the social performance of trauma through *Godot* is achieved in the register of expressive aptness.

For Breese, *Godot* becomes a laboratory in which to examine how the dramatic logics of cultural traumas get formulated; how their crystallization separates symbolic retellings from their actual point of origin; how such dramatic narrations subsequently are evoked in other, not precisely similar, situations; and how these iterations have the potential to make concretely different situations seem the same, giving meaning to collective wounds via an iconic drama's performative effect. Working inside this laboratory of aesthetic innovation, Breese can offer a new reading of Becket's most famous play. It was "born out of Beckett's personal trauma" of exile during Nazi occupation, she suggests, and from "the mood of collective trauma in Paris following the war." The master-slave pairing of Pozzo and Lucky, and the coupling of the desperate but ever-hopeful Vladimir and Estragon, were "rendered and read in Paris as a reference to the collective trauma of Parisians at the time." Instead of *Godot* as absurd drama without reference, Breese sees Beckett's "famously meaningless play" as something utterly different—an artistic rendering of the trauma-filled twentieth century.

Beckett's trauma-text gained worldwide fame for aesthetic reasons that were social at the same time. By its spare and careful plot, oblique dialogue, and minimalist staging, the play moves from the specifics of a concrete situation to the essential tensions of the human condition. Yet, like every trauma narrative, to gain traction in a particular trauma situation *Godot* must be implanted in a concrete time and place. Here, Breese gives to audience an active role.

Audiences and producers insert meanings ... by specifying victims, perpetrators, and the nature of their trauma ... The audiences to these productions of *Waiting for Godot* pronounced the performances a success or failure based on the performances' ability to express and depict the experiences of the residents in each city ... Audiences expected the actors to embody Vladimir and Estragon, sure, but there was an expectation that they personify the residents of the city as well.

In New Orleans and Sarajevo, Breese demonstrates, successful performances of *Godot* "turned theater performance into social performance of trauma." This is, of course, exactly what every cultural creator hopes their performance will be.

Trauma Dramas Are Performed, Not Described

Collective traumas are reflections neither of individual suffering nor actual events, but symbolic renderings that reconstruct and imagine them in a relatively independent way. This spiral of signification is the work of culture creators, who create scripts that answer the four "w" questions: What happened? Who were its victims? Who were its perpetrators? And what can be done? These scripts are not descriptions of what is; they are arguments for what must have been and, at least implicitly, of what should be. The truth of cultural scripts emerges, not from their descriptive accuracy, but from the power of their enactment. Trauma scripts are performed as symbolic actions in the theaters of everyday collective life. In Serbia, the crisis of the 1980s began with Milosevic's supposedly factual and certainly highly expressive, virulently nationalist speech commemorating the Serbia's defeat by the Islamic forces in a largely mythical war. In postwar Germany, a turning point in trauma construction arrived with the sentimental but compelling fictional television series *Holocaust.* In the wake of the Sabra and Shatila massacres after Israel's 1982 Lebanon War, it was not only the public war of words between right-wing Likud officials and their Peace Now critics that allowed the Holocaust narrative to be extended to Palestinians for the first time. It was the extraordinary and unprecedented ritual of the "400,000 protest," the spectacle of hundreds of thousands of patriotic but outraged Israelis massively protesting in a Tel Aviv square (see Alexander and Dromi's chapter in this book).

Rui Gao's analysis of China's "Speaking Bitterness" campaigns provides a particularly vivid illustration of trauma texts in their performative mode. From the early 1950s onward, the CCP's narrative of interclass trauma were consummated in what Rui Gao describes as an "ubiquitous performative mechanism where the drama was not only written and read but also performed and recited by real people on a daily basis."

Consecutive national campaigns demanded "struggle meetings," rituals of confrontation that were "enacted at all levels up from the local communities." In a "Speaking Bitterness" performance, "the drama could be literally put on show and the bitterness reenacted on a stage." The trauma script of bitterness "rose beyond cognitive argument and demanded the acute physical presence, emotional involvement and performative action of the audience." In the 1960s, Chinese junior high school textbooks contained what purport to be descriptions of the actual proceedings of a bitterness ritual called "Struggling Han Lao Liu." In her interpretation of this event, Gao emphasizes the salience of "the absolute coding and weighting of the chief antagonist, the target of the struggle, landlord Han."

> When the meeting began, the landlord was brought to the center of the courtyard where a certain kind of stage was set for the struggle, and one by one, people who felt that they had been wronged, oppressed, or persecuted by the landlord came up to the stage to give a public testimony to the unforgivable sins of the evildoer. The ritual started as the first figure, a young man named Yang San, stepped onto the central stage. He testified that Han had once attempted to force him [to work] as a slave laborer for the Japanese colonizers, and when he refused and ran away, Han retaliated by sending his mother into prison, where she eventually died. "'I want to take revenge for my mum today!' as Yang San bellowed with anger," the chapter goes; "people around all cried out, 'Let's beat him to death!' and started to push forwards with sticks to the center of the courtyard." "Their chorus," the text went on, was like "the thunder of spring roaring in the sky" .... When the last bitterness speaker finished her story by yelling "give me back my son!" the text described that "men and women all pushed forward, crying that they want their sons, husbands, fathers, brothers back. And the sounds of weeping, crying, beating and cursing all mixed together." Indeed, the scene was so intense and moving that Xiao Wang, a young member of the land reform team who came from outside the village, "kept wiping his tears with the back of his hand."

In their study of Greek identity and the partition of the island of Cyprus, Roudometof and Christou address what Hashimoto calls "intergenerational transmission" of trauma constructions. They ask: How is it that people yearn to return to a home and a homeland which they themselves have never known? The question itself reveals that the experience of displacement of Greek Cypriots from the north of the island to the south is not an individual trauma, but a collective one. Roudometof and Christou describe the commemorative practices, especially within Greek Cyrpiot schools, which serve to introduce children to the trauma of separation from their homeland and narrate it as the trauma of all

Greek Cypriots, for those who moved from their homes to the southern part of Cyprus as well as for successive generations. "For Greek Cypriots," Roudometof and Christou write, "the experience of uprootedness and the vision of a mythical day of return are the two major characteristics of the '1974' cultural trauma." The collective trauma of leaving behind their original lands—always remembered as beautiful, fertile lands—and the hope of returning to them is integrated into many facets of school, from classroom decorations to school assemblies; "the whole curriculum," Roudometof and Christou explain, "is infused with references to the problem of occupation." In the Greek Cypriot school curriculum, as in religious rituals and in popular culture, the partition of Cyprus is not merely described as a problem of politics or property; it is performed as a problem of Greek Cypriot identity.

In Colombia, purely textual narrations of the trauma suffered by the thousands of innocent kidnap victims seemed largely without performative effect. A 33-year old computer science engineer named Oscar Morales responded with horror and sympathy to an iconic representation of the suffering—a ghostly image of Ingrid Betancourt, the French victim of FARC guerillas, photographed in the jungle chained to a tree. Morales created a Facebook page called "One Million Voices against the FARC," calling for a protest march that eventually drew ten million people into the streets in 115 cities around the world. An even more dramatic portrait of the narrative enactment of trauma in Colombia is the story Tognato tells about Gustavo Moncayo, the 55-year-old high school teacher who in 2006 began publicly to wear chains at his writs and neck to protest FARC's kidnapping of his son. A year later, after FARC assassinated eleven regional congressmen in captivity, Moncayo set out on foot for Bogotá in what became a nationally arresting pilgrimage of protest.

> He started his march in the middle of a generalized neglect and without support of any institution—social, political, religious or economic. But then he managed to catch public attention. The media would accompany him along the track. People impatiently awaited his arrival. They applauded him, hugged him, touched him, took photos with him, asked for autographs, dedicated local folk songs to him, donated money, and offered food.... Toward the end of his march, his arrival [in Bogotá] was announced on the radio, and schools would stop their classes. The march lasted forty-six days. Even the FARC acknowledged that his gesture was "valiant." When he got to Bogotá, Moncayo met with the president and the mayor of the city. At the end of 2007, he was awarded the National Peace Prize. Though his painful march did not manage to obtain the liberation of his son, he managed ... to command

the attention and the solidarity of broad and diverse segments of the Colombian society.

Trauma Dramas Have "Material" Repercussions: Polarization or Reconciliation?

The relative independence of collective narration of trauma from individual experience and historical event, the intervening agency of culture creators, the performative impact of textual enactment—these social facts explain why and how trauma dramas have such extraordinarily powerful effects on the organization and structure of our social worlds. Would Germany have engaged in such democratic and pro-Western politics if the Allies' wartime city bombs rather than the Holocaust had become central to its postwar collective identity? Would an economically empowered Japan have chosen to remain undermilitarized if its own postwar trauma dramas, from nationalist to cosmopolitan, had not enshrined war in such a polluted way? Would Maoism have achieved such sustained legitimacy, despite its political repression and disastrous economic policies, if class trauma had not been so strenuously narrated and so relentlessly performed? Would Serbia have invaded its neighbors and so threatened its Islamic minority if the Kosovo Myth had not aligned its struggle for collective identity in such a xenophobic and militaristic way? Simply to ask these questions is see how the cultural constructions of trauma often play out in world-historical ways.

Trauma dramas can be consensual or polarizing. In the former, they may lead to social reconciliation; in the latter, to divisive conflict and traumatic injury on a wider scale. Institutionalizing a dominant trauma narrative is a singular social accomplishment. It stabilizes not only collective memory but also the contemporary sense of social reality, pointing the way forward in a confident way. Unfortunately, this seems to be the exception rather than the rule in the history of injuries that has afflicted humanity's collective life.

Perhaps more than any other bloody event in the last century's dark history, the Holocaust would seem to qualify as an event whose meaning cannot be open to doubt or contestation. Yet, while the Holocaust was certainly experienced as an indelible horror by its Jewish victims, its collective configuration has been contingent and shifting. For the Western non-Jewish community, the Nazi mass murder was initially understood within the context of World War II as perhaps the most brutal but still representative incident of that worldwide midcentury war. Over time, symbolization began shifting from a war crime rooted in a particular time and space to a universal event of such singular evil that it moved beyond history and territory to become a moral lesson "for all mankind." The legendary status of the Holocaust as a sacred evil inspired international human rights laws, new restrictions on national sovereignty, and newly powerful moral strictures against ethnic and racial cleansing.

Yet, even as this markedly universalizing construction became ever more deeply institutionalized in Western Europe and North America, the Holocaust came to be configured in a radically particularistic manner in Israel and the Middle East. For Arab nations neighboring the new Jewish nation, for occupied Palestinians inside Israel or in exile, and for radical Islamicists the world wide, the Holocaust's reality was fiercely challenged and the extraordinary nature of Jewish trauma ridiculed and denied. Meanwhile, inside the boundaries of the Jewish state, religiously conservative Jews and politically right-wing Zionists came to understand the Holocaust as a tragedy that was unique to the Jewish people, not as a tragedy of our times. This Israeli version of the Holocaust trauma drama reinforced ethnic and religious boundaries rather pointing to the necessity for transcending them. Because it would be foolish for Jews to trust the world, they would need their own state, and they must exercise eternal vigilance against Arabs, Islamicists, and especially Palestinian Arabs, whose very existence constituted a permanent threat to the Jewish state from the outside. Jeff Alexander and Shai Dromi describe "a self-justifying, narrowly particularistic, and deeply primordial reconstruction of the Holocaust trauma, one that continues to exert great influence up to this day." In this narrative, the Jewish fighters who founded Israel and continue to defend it are cast as protagonists.

> Arrayed against them is the long list of their historical antagonists: the Germans and their accomplices; the British, who stood between Jewish refugees and the soon-to-be-Israelis; the Allied Forces, who intervened too late and failed to save European Jews from the Final Solution; Arab-Palestinians and the surrounding nations, who opposed the establishment of the Jewish State; and Europeans, who resented the Jewish survivors and greeted their return to their original residences with several postwar *pogroms*... [This] Jewish-Israeli narrative reinforces the militaristic and exclusionary aspects of Zionism. Foreign nations have proved to be untrustworthy. Israel can rely only on the resources of the Jewish people and its own military strength to defend itself.

Such trauma construction inspired Israelis' reluctance to share "their" land with Palestinians, and it fuelled intense investments in military over diplomatic strategy.

The autonomy of event and referent, however, also allowed the relation between Holocaust and Israel to be reconfigured in a sharply different way. Alexander and Dromi show how much more moderate versions of Zionism gradually emerged. Less exculpatory narratives and their performative enactments challenged the particularistic construction of Jews as primordial victims. Eventually, post-Zionist narratives crystallized assigning Israelis a perpetrator role in a Middle Eastern trauma drama and Palestinians victim status. These more universalizing symbolic constructions were, no doubt, partly responsive to Israeli military reversals and the PLO's mobilizing success. "The new post-1973 context," Alexander and Dromi write, "allowed the tragic construction of the Holocaust trauma to provide a different kind of script, one that could connect Jewish Israelis with Palestinian suffering." But these new trauma narrations were not determined by situational events. Cultural agency and performative enactment took pride of place. Novelists, filmmakers, and painters created new fictions that mandated pity and sympathy for the Palestinian plight. After the Sabra and Shatila massacres, Amos Oz, a leading Israeli author of fiction and nonfiction, wrote an open letter to Prime Minister Begin.

> Often I, like many Jews, find at the bottom of my soul a dull sense of pain because I did not kill Hitler with my own hands. [But] tens of thousands of dead Arabs will not heal that wound ... Again and again, Mr. Begin, you reveal to the public eye a strange urge to resuscitate Hitler in order to kill him every day anew in the guise of terrorists.

In the years following, revisionist Israeli historians challenged one-sided accounts of the birth of their nation. An Israeli peace movement emerged that put land for peace on the table. As the occupation continued for decades, a new generation of righteous intellectuals and activists indignantly exposed Israeli complicity in Palestinian suffering, sometimes drawing bitter analogies between reactionary Jewish political and military leaders seemingly bent on Palestinian destruction and Nazis responsible for the traumatic destruction of European Jews in the century before.

We hope this brief introduction substantiates our initial claim that the following contributions amplify propositions about cultural trauma and collective identity we developed in our earlier work.[3] They depart from that earlier foundational theorizing, however, in two ways, one historical, the other civilizational.

Cultural Trauma and Collective Identity was researched and written in the decade that followed the end of the Cold War, a period marked by progressive narratives, widespread hopes for a new world order, and what now appears to have been mostly wishful thinking about the dawn of a new day. The intellectual efforts comprising the current volume are published in a decidedly less hopeful time. Even as we wrote this book, an earthquake wreaked unprecedented destruction—of human lives, of institutions, of the built environment—in Haiti. A plane carrying the president of Poland and other dignitaries crashed on its way to commemorate the massacre in the Katyn Woods; no one on board survived the crash. And, in Tucson, a member of the United States Congress was shot at close range, along with several of her constituents. Tragic events all, we cannot yet know how cultural agents will code these events as traumas—deepening and exposing social and cultural wounds and chasms—or as ultimately triumphant episodes in the life of a collective, the life of a nation.

The studies in this volume largely conceptualize and explain a recent history that has been marked by the return of the same kinds of heinous events and social suffering that scarred the century before. As a result, the outcomes of cultural trauma traced in this book have less to do with overcoming schism and civil repair and more to do with how trauma construction so frequently crystallizes polarizing narratives, exacerbates conflict, and leads to even more suffering in turn. Many of the chapters that follow explain how cultural traumas can continue without closure. Moncayo's son returned home in 2010 almost three years after Moncayo's march, but thousands like him have not, and many will not, return home, and Colombians increasingly experience this as an affront not only to families but also to society. The island of Cyprus remains divided, and Greek Cypriots wish for homelands from which they are ever more temporally, though not emotionally, removed.

The second distinctive difference of the present volume is that its case studies are devoted more to the "East" and the "South" than to the "North" and the "West." Our earlier work examined slavery in the United States and the Holocaust trauma in America and Western Europe, with some discussion of post-Communism as well. Contributors to the present volume look at trauma processes in China and Japan, in Colombia and South Africa, in Cyprus and Greece, in pre-1989 Poland, and in Serbia and Israel. This empirical variation gives us more confidence that cultural trauma theory is not ethnocentric, that it captures the significant processes that mark a class of powerfully affecting, if historically bounded, social facts.

Neither greater empirical variation nor increased theoretical strength, however, produces an increment in normative terms. The moral benefit of cultural trauma is not to be found in the starlight of the scientific firmament, but in ourselves.

Notes

1. In *Doctor Faustus,* symbolically situated and actually written in the waning years of World War II and published just after its conclusion, Thomas Mann (1997 [1947]) contests the right of Germans to protest against the "earth-shaking, plummeting havoc" that not only killed hundreds of thousands of Germans but also ended its claim to represent *kultur*: "We have experienced the destruction of our venerable cities from the air—an act that would scream to the heavens were not we who suffer it ourselves laden with guilt. But since we are[,] the scream dies in the air and, like King Claudius's prayer, can 'never to heaven go.' How strange that lament for culture, raised now against crimes that we called down upon ourselves, sounds in the mouths of those who entered the arena of history proclaiming themselves bearers of a barbarism that, while wallowing in ruthlessness, was to rejuvenate the world" (p. 184).

2. For how this trauma process prevented the Nanjing Massacre from becoming a postwar focal point in local and global discussions of genocide, see Alexander and Gao, "Remembrance of Things Past: Cultural Trauma, the 'Nanking Massacre' and Chinese Identity" (Alexander, Eyerman, and Smith forthcoming).

3. These contributions also support the series of subsequent works that have appeared between our initial collaboration in 1998–1999 and the present volume. See, e.g., Eyerman 2001, Giesen 2004, Goodman 2009, Eyerman 2008, and Alexander 2009.

Works Cited

Alexander, Jeffrey C. 2009. *Remembering the Holocaust: A Debate.* Oxford: Oxford University Press.

Alexander, Jeffrey C., Ron Eyerman, Bernhard Giesen, Neil J. Smelser, and Piotr Sztompka. 2004. *Cultural Trauma and Collective Identity.* Berkeley, CA: University of California Press.

Alexander, Jeffrey C., and Rui Gao. Forthcoming. Rememberance of Things Past: Cultural Trauma, the "Nanking Massacre" and Chinese Identity. In *The Oxford Handbook of Cultural Sociology,* eds. J. Alexander, R. Eyerman, and P. Smith. New York: Oxford University Press.

Eyerman, Ron. 2001. *Cultural Trauma: Slavery and the Formation of African American Identity.* Cambridge: Cambridge University Press.

————. 2004. Cultural Trauma: Slavery and the Formation of African American Identity. In *Cultural Trauma and Collective Identity,* eds. J. Alexander, R. Eyerman, B. Giesen, N. Smelser and P. Sztompka. Berkeley: University of California Press.

————. 2008. *The Assassination of Theo Van Gogh: From Social Drama to Cultural Trauma.* Durham, NC: Duke University Press.

Giesen, Bernhard. 2004. *Triumph and Trauma.* Boulder, CO: Paradigm Publishers.

Goodman, Tanya. 2009. *Staging Solidarity: Truth and Reconciliation in a New South Africa.* Boulder, CO: Paradigm Publishers.

Mann, Thomas. 1997 [1947]. *Doctor Faustus: The Life of the German Composer Adrian Leverkuhn As Told by a Friend.* Translated by John E. Woods. New York: Alfred A. Knopf.

Wajda, Andrzej. 2008. Pokazałem światu Katyń (I have showed Katyn to the world). *GW,* February 26.

PART 1

National Suffering
and World War

1

A Fire That Doesn't Burn?

The Allied Bombing of Germany and the Cultural Politics of Trauma[1]

Volker Heins and Andreas Langenohl

A lot of seriously bad things happened to Germans during and immediately after World War II. More than five million soldiers were killed, most of them on the eastern front. Those who survived the war in the east were often wounded, half-crazed, or frostbitten and were further decimated by the harsh conditions in Soviet POW camps. British and American bombers attacked more than one hundred German cities and towns, reducing many of them to a sea of rubble, killing around six hundred thousand civilians, and making many more homeless. Millions of ethnic Germans who had settled in Poland or Czechoslovakia fled the onslaught of the Red Army or were expelled by the newly established communist governments. On their way to Berlin and in the fallen capital itself, Soviet soldiers raped altogether perhaps one and a half million women, often "in the presence of their menfolk, to underline the humiliation" (Evans 2009, 710).

This list of horrors is, of course, deliberately one-sided in that it ignores not only the endless suffering inflicted by Germans on their non-German victims, including their own Jewish fellow-citizens, but also questions of causal and moral responsibility. Historians like Richard Evans have shown that such questions have not only been asked in hindsight but were already on the minds of many ordinary people during the war itself. To some degree at least, Germans saw their own misery filtered through a sense of what had been done to others in their name. Given the context that has shaped the experience of suffering especially of German civilians, we believe it is interesting to explore how they have represented their own suffering, how these representations have been transmitted into the collective and national memory, and to what extent the political culture has been shaped by war-related memory projects.

In his influential lectures *On the Natural History of Destruction,* the German-born writer W.G. Sebald notes that some of the occurrences of the war, in particular the mighty air raids against German cities "left scarcely any trace of pain behind in the collective consciousness" (Sebald 2004, 4). We suggest to rephrase this statement by saying that the memory of the bombing war has not been turned into a national or "cultural trauma." This is not to deny that the defeat of Germany set the stage for a trauma process in the course of which Germans began to fundamentally redefine themselves. Yet this process was successful precisely because Germans learned to connect their own suffering to the suffering of others. They remember that their cities were firebombed and often completely flattened by identifiable actors, but it is not this fact in itself that is remembered and commemorated as a psychologically searing, identity-changing event. The question we try to answer is why this particular collective experience of suffering has not, in spite of its horrifying proportions, given rise to a cultural trauma. The answer given by Sebald (2004, 11) is that there has been a "taboo" on speaking about the devastation and suffering caused by the Allied air war. What is implied is that Germans felt no longer entitled to speak of themselves as victims as they increasingly accepted their image of being perpetrators of war crimes and the Holocaust. We believe that this answer is flawed. For one, the term "taboo" insinuates that Germans should finally break the silence and lay claim to their own suffering, something they have done all along. In modern societies, calling something a taboo does not end a conversation but, on the contrary, introduces issues into the public debate in a sensationalist way. Sebald's claim also implies that there is something fundamentally wrong with German war memories. Yet, we argue that there is considerable controversy, incoherence, and awkwardness but nothing pathological or repressed about the way in which most Germans remember and commemorate the devastation of their cities and the death of civilians during the war.

In developing our argument, we not only agree with but also wish to bolster Jeffrey Alexander's and Ron Eyerman's point that a cultural trauma does not directly flow from historical occurrences, however horrible they may have been. Rather, cultural traumas are socially constructed through narratives and other forms of representation. For Sebald, the absence of almost any trace of pain in the memory of the bombing war is something "paradoxical" (Sebald 2004, 4) because he assumes that there is a positive correlation between the magnitude of suffering experienced by a collectivity and the intensity of memories transmitted from one generation to the next. For us, such a correlation exists only to the extent in which a social and political consensus on the meaning of the relevant historical instance of suffering can be constructed and effectively communicated. Yet it is also true that a recognizable instance of massive suffering is always the raw material of cultural trauma. In fact, the most prominent examples of sociological trauma theory have so far been American slavery (Eyerman 2002) and the Holocaust (Alexander 2003, 27–84). Slavery in the antebellum South was an instance of collective suffering that has been turned into a cultural trauma for successive generations of the same victim group of Afro-Americans. The Holocaust was an instance of collective suffering that has been turned into a cultural trauma of successive generations of the victim group, Jews, as well as for successive generations of (non-Jewish) Germans and other national membership groups who were the perpetrators and bystanders of the Holocaust. Our case study breaks new ground by focusing on an instance of collective suffering—the Allied bombing of German cities during World War II—that has not become a cultural trauma, *not even for the successive generations of the victim group.* This points to the crucial argument that the trauma drama must not be conflated with the traumatizing event itself. As a cultural trauma may be constructed even if the society in question is deeply divided about the meaning of the traumatizing events (see Chapter 8, "Extending Trauma Across Cultural Divides: On Kidnapping and Solidarity in Colombia"), so it conversely may fail to materialize even under conditions of a supposedly coherent social body.

In what follows, we give a short overview of the ways in which the air war has been remembered, memorialized, and commemorated in postwar Germany. We begin by rejecting the widespread claim that the memories of German victims, in general, and of civilian bombing victims, in particular, were actively silenced in postwar Germany. Instead, we sketch out the memory matrix that in our view has underpinned and constrained practices of remembrance of the *Bombenkrieg.* We then turn to three case vignettes to shed light on the reasons why the bombings have not given rise to a cultural trauma. First, we highlight the case of

Hamburg, which among German cities was hit the hardest by British bombers in 1943. More specifically, we are interested in how the rise of the Holocaust trauma has rendered the remembrance of the firebombing of Hamburg more complex, inconsistent, and ultimately nontraumatic. Second, we look at attempts to draw analogies between the high-altitude bombing of German cities and the bombing of other places, in particular Baghdad in the Second Gulf War (1990–1991). These attempts have displayed the deep historical embeddedness of bombing memories in Germany without, however, indicating the belated beginning of a trauma process. Third, we briefly explore the memory and commemoration of the 1945 bombings of Dresden, in which neo-Nazi extremists, who would like to redefine the memory of the bombings as the new cultural trauma of post-reunification Germany, play a major role. The final section summarizes the reasons why we believe that memory projects aiming at the establishment of a cultural bombing trauma in Germany are unlikely to succeed anytime soon.

The German Bombing War Memory Matrix

Since the reunification of Germany in 1990, every major broadcast or publication on the bombing of the country during World War II has been pitched as taboo-breaking. However, there has never really been a taboo on representing the suffering of Germans. In fact, this is a rumor or legend so ubiquitous that it requires explanation. Still, like all rumors and legends, the idea of a taboo on representing Germans as victims is based on a small kernel of truth.

Our main point is that what has been forgotten is not the bombing war itself but its many traces in the memories of those who survived and documented it. Artists, in particular, began drawing, painting, carving wood, writing about, and photographing the destruction often literally as soon as the dust had settled after the air raids. Ignoring an official ban imposed by the Nazi government, which was later renewed by the Soviet military authorities, more than thirty "rubble photographers" emerged in Dresden alone, some of whom like Kurt Schaarschuch and Richard Peter quickly rose to fame (Kil 1989). As early as 1949, Peter published a much-reprinted collection of photographs under the title *Dresden, eine Kamera klagt an* (*Dresden: A Camera Accuses*). There were early bestsellers such as Axel Rodenberger's memoir *Der Tod von Dresden* (*The Death of Dresden*) and a whole new genre of German "rubble films" depicting the destruction of cities in flashbacks (Shandley 2001). German studies scholars such as Jörg Bernig (2005), Thomas Fox (2006), and Ursula Heukenkamp (2001) have offered overviews of the range of artistic representations of the bombing war experience, listing novels, memoirs, anthologies, films, poems, plays, song texts, and audio recordings that have escaped the attention of those who claim that the air war has fallen into oblivion.

Thus, what we have seen after the war was not a taboo on the remembrance of suffering but rather an irrepressible zeal to give meaning to the harrowing experiences of the recent past. Ulrike Heukenkamp has observed that writers often did not use a vivid, authentic language to describe the experience of being bombed, not because they forgot what had happened but because part of that experience was a sense of panic, of emptiness, of loss of self that led authors to use clichéd metaphors such as "hell," "inferno," or "Judgment Day" to fix the meaning of the bombings (Heukenkamp 2001, 470–472). She also points out that talking was less easy for the civilian survivors of the bombing war than for the exhausted, defeated, and disillusioned soldiers who returned from the front lines of what they saw as the "real" war. The soldiers were often compulsively loquacious and have left detailed descriptions of their war experiences in the memories of families as well as in literary texts. To the extent it was real, the silencing of civilian bombing victims, a majority of them being women, was the result of the restoration of the patriarchal family order in which men decided about what counts as an experience worth telling and transmitting (Heukenkamp 2001, 470).

Apart from the perceived lack of authenticity in literary representations and the dominance of the memory of front soldiers over the memory of women, there is a third factor that has contributed to the notion of silence surrounding the human consequences of the bombing war. West Germans, in particular, were eager to rebuild their cities and their economy and felt that they had no time to look back. Sebald mentions "the unquestioning heroism with which people immediately set about the task of clearance and reorganization" (Sebald 2004, 5). This is something very different from a taboo, although it may as well have had a silencing effect on memories.

That the immense suffering caused by incendiaries and high-explosive bombs dropped from the sky was not forgotten does, however, not imply that this particular memory fit easily into a larger, agreed-upon frame of public remembrance of World War II. In fact, all the controversies and struggles in recent decades have been about this problem: how to insert the memory of the air war into the larger process of meaning-making in a way that is in harmony with the self-description of Germany as a liberal Western democracy. Before we delve into the political struggles over the memory of the bombings, we want to outline the memory matrix that has guided activists and audiences in their attempts to represent those occurrences as broadly meaningful and significant.

We suggest distinguishing four basic positions in recent German memory struggles. Three of these positions share the implicit assumption that there was no alternative to the defeat of Germany and the Axis Powers by the combined military forces of the Allies. Obviously, neo-Nazis beg to differ on this point. But we are not aware of a position saying that the German people were able or willing to overthrow the government of Hitler on its own. There is thus a widely shared conviction that Germany had to be defeated militarily. A classical early statement of this consensus can be found in the preface to the first edition of Franz Neumann's *Behemoth*, "A military defeat is necessary ... More and better planes, tanks, and guns and a complete military defeat will uproot National Socialism from the mind of the German people" (Neumann 1942, ix). Note that Neumann wrote before the emergence of a transnational Holocaust trauma, which in retrospect has made the imperative to destroy Nazi Germany by military means even more compelling. Today, German historians and democratic politicians across the board basically agree on the connection that existed between defeating Germany and ending the mass extermination of Jews and others groups (see, e.g., Nolte 2008 and White 2002). Differences among the following first three discursive positions emerge only against the backdrop of this taken-for-granted consensus. The fourth position is an outlier, at least for now.

A *just-war position* has been articulated by military historians in Britain and the United States and continues to influence in particular left-wing memory activists in Germany to this day. This position states that the air bombing of German cities contributed to the defeat of National Socialism and was therefore by definition legitimate.[2]

The *moderate anti-Machiavellian position* says that, in pursuing highly legitimate war aims, the Allies employed illegitimate means such as the indiscriminate bombing of entire cities. Moderate anti-Machiavellians usually refrain from using the term "crime" to describe the bombings. They are often members of the liberal academic and political elites in Germany and have called for reconciliation and for strengthening international humanitarian law.[3]

A *radicalization of the anti-Machiavellian position* can be observed among those groups who claim that the air bombing of cities did not serve its alleged military purpose. There has been, it is argued, a growing disjuncture between ends and means in the final stages of the war. Radical anti-Machiavellians use the term "crime" to describe the bombings. Yet these groups, too, call for reconciliation and for a moralization of international affairs that goes beyond legal reforms.[4]

A *revisionist right-wing position* has been adopted by those who claim that the bombings were not meant to serve a limited military purpose but were launched to commit genocidal crimes against the Germans. These groups, some of which should be called neo-Nazis, are against reconciliation with the former victors and in favor of bringing them to what they call "justice."

The foundational moment and organizing principle of this memory matrix is the Holocaust. Although the notion that the bombing of cities might appear legitimate, given the unrelenting aggressiveness of Nazi Germany, had been formulated earlier, as the example of Neumann shows, knowledge about the unprecedented crimes committed in Auschwitz or Treblinka dramatically propelled this argument. In fact, the split that divides the memory matrix between those who acknowledge the military necessity of pain inflicted upon civilians (if to different degrees) and those who indiscriminately reject the air bombings as crimes is congruous with the cleavage between those who in principle acknowledge German responsibility for the consequences of the Holocaust and those who deny it. Thus, the memory of the air war on German cities is closely intertwined with struggles over the representation of the Nazi past, and in particular of the Holocaust.

The Bombing of Hamburg and the Rise of the Holocaust Trauma

Hamburg suffered one of the most devastating air raids in the entire war on Nazi Germany when the British Bomber Command under General Sir Arthur Harris launched Operation Gomorrah on July 24, 1943. This attack consisted of a coordinated series of "city-busting" night raids, which were supplemented by a smaller number of U.S. Air Force daylight raids against shipyards and submarine pens. Altogether, more than thirty-four thousand people were killed within a couple of days (Thiessen 2007, 12).

Explicitly taking issue with Sebald, the young German historian Malte Thiessen has demonstrated that the postwar memory of the bombing raids, far from being suppressed, served in fact as an important symbolic resource for creating a new sense of togetherness and local pride among the citizens of Hamburg. While immediately after the war even democratically elected officials continued to use Nazi propaganda terms such as "air terror [*Luftterror*]" (Thiessen 2007, 98) to characterize the bombings, the perpetrator-centered frame was quickly replaced by an almost exclusive focus on victims. From early on, political representatives from all parties, including the Communist Party, called for mourning a generously defined group of victims, which included all the civilians killed by bombs but also German soldiers and the inmates of Hamburg's concentration camp in Neuengamme, where many more people were killed than in Operation Gomorrah (about fifty thousand). Significantly, this emotional and semantic shift from the accusation of perpetrators to the mourning of victims was in no way driven by the British occupying forces in Hamburg, although the German desire to regain a minimum of recognition and good will from their former enemies played a role (Thiessen 2007, 176–177). What is also important is that most Hamburgers did not harbor any resentment toward Britons, a fact that was already noted by Nossack, who was an eyewitness to the air raids (Nossack 2004, 34; see also Evans 2009, 466). A perpetrator-centered framing of the bombings would therefore not have resonated with the public.

At the local level, at least, a vibrant culture of remembrance emerged that garnered significant public attention. Unsurprisingly, the early memory of the air war was constructed in such a way as to suppress simmering collective feelings of guilt. Germans defined themselves as victims not just of the bombing assault and other horrors but also as victims of the "hypnotic influence" of Hitler, as a former mayor of Hamburg has put it (quoted in Thiessen 2007, 109). What is indeed surprising and unsettling is that apparently there has not been a one-directional movement toward enlarging the circle of victims to be mourned. Thiessen (2007, 173–174) shows that until 1950, the inmates of Neuengamme, many of whom were shot, starved to death, or sent to extermination camps in the east, were included in various commemorative performances and discourses, whereas later, only German city dwellers were considered worth the tears and thoughts of Germans. This narrowing of the collective memory can be described as a consequence of the early Cold War, which led to the marginalization of communist groups, who previously had played a crucial role in keeping the memory of the concentration camps alive, although without any reference to what was later called the Holocaust.

The Cold War pattern of remembering with its heavy emphasis on local bombing victims combined with an inhibition to discuss the motives and strategies of those who were in charge of the air war changed with the rise of a new generation that no longer had any direct experience of the bombings. The new generational memory began to crystallize in the early 1970s. For the first time, officials interpreted the bombing of their city not in the context of the "collapse" of the Third Reich but as a harbinger of the "liberation" of Germany (Thiessen 2007, 203 and 388). This new moral term immediately brought back the memory of Neuengamme, a memory that at that time was already embedded in a much broader narrative about the Holocaust. The Holocaust as a defining memory icon and signifier for what Theodor Adorno (1998, 89) characterized as "a horror that one hesitates to call ... by name" emerged in West Germany only in the course of the 1970s.[5] Once established, the Holocaust narrative and the narrative of the liberation of Germany by the Allies reinforced each other, forming a new web of meaning.

In Hamburg, this shift in the mode of remembrance was to a large extent spearheaded by the regional Evangelical Lutheran Church whose leading representatives tried to marry two different narratives. The first insisted on the innocence of the German bombing victims who were described as having been sacrificed and even "crucified," as the Austrian artist Oskar Kokoschka said, who contributed a mosaic (*Ecce Homines*) to the St. Nikolai Church memorial in Hamburg (Thiessen 2007, 230). The second narrative represents German civilians not merely as victims but also as (knowing or unknowing) accomplices to the evil that ruled Germany. In a speech given on the occasion of the inauguration of the memorial in 1977, the bishop of Hamburg reminded the audience of a plaque hanging at some distance from Kokoschka mosaic, "Open your mouth for the mute, for the rights of all the unfortunate" (Proverbs 31: 8). Germans, the bishop continued, did not heed the call and ignored the plight of "those people for which we did not open our mouth" (quoted in Thiessen 2007, 232). This way of interpreting the past gave a new twist to the perception of the bombings as some kind of divine "punishment"—a perception that was already prevalent among some eyewitnesses (Nossack 2004, 12–14).

Occasionally, this dual innovation of representing the perpetrators of the air war as also being liberators and the victims as also being accomplices of the same forces Germany had to be liberated from took the form of what we have called the "just-war position." For instance, in 1993 the editor of the influential liberal weekly *Die Zeit*, Gerd Bucerius, described his jubilant mood at the sight and sound of the bomber squadrons. "'Finally,' I kept shouting, 'finally.' In my view, the Allied had waited much too long before battling the world's enemy Hitler" (quoted in Thiessen 2007, 327). To be true, this was quite an exceptional statement that did not resonate with many in Bucerius's generation. Yet throughout these years, the liberation motif had to compete with a radicalization of anti-Machiavellian positions whose advocates claimed that the air war was not an immoral means to a moral end but did not contribute at all to the moral end of defeating Nazi Germany (see Thiessen 2007, 272–273, 400, 406).

As a result of these trends, the post-reunification period after 1990 offers a mixed picture. Partly in response to the contextualization of the air war and the enlargement of the circle of victims who have been included in the collective memory, public intellectuals and the media rediscovered the "taboo" on remembering German bombing victims. Since then, the term "taboo" has been used in different ways. Some usages are benign. Sebald, for example, only wanted writers to express themselves in an adequate language and the public to be aware of the horrible things that happened on the ground as a result of the bombings. More often, however, the interjection of "taboo" into controversies over collective memory is an expression of resentment against the inclusion of non-German victims in the collective memory and a response to the growing difficulties of constructing an imagined homogeneous community of victims out of the ruins left behind by the Royal Air Force. Yet, if there was a silencing of memories of the air war in Germany, it was because of the presence of POWs returning home and subsequently dominating public discourse with the memories of their suffering.[6]

The "taboo" vocabulary is paralleled by a return of the "terror" vocabulary that can be regarded as a response to the consolidation of the Holocaust trauma and the increasing moral difficulty of rejecting the Allied war effort *per se*. Once the Holocaust was memorialized as "sacred-evil" (Alexander 2003, 50), victory over its perpetrators became sacred, too. Thus, if Germans wish to avoid being symbolically polluted by the evil of the Holocaust, they have to phrase their opposition to the war by rejecting the means chosen by the Allies, or by questioning the relations of means and ends. This is precisely what happened in the 1980s in Hamburg's tabloid papers and later in national mainstream media such as the news magazine *Der Spiegel*, which in January 2003 published a series of articles on the "terror attacks against Germany," calling the assaults on Hamburg and Dresden "climaxes of *Luftterror*" (Thiessen 2007, 400–401).

Yet, although these terms are taken straight out of the dictionary of the Nazi Ministry of Propaganda, we wish to emphasize that the recent critique of the Allied "air terror" has undergone a process of semantic de-Nazification in the sense that it is no longer part of a strategy to create a harmonious community of heroic sufferers based on the radical exclusion of the other. The indictment of the Western Allies as perpetrators of terror attacks has not weakened the desire of the city of Hamburg, the vast majority of Germans, and mainstream media to be on most friendly terms with the alleged perpetrator nations and to be recognized as a member in good standing of the Western Alliance and the European Union. The return of a perpetrator-centered frame focusing on the "terror" spread by the Allies did not, for example, affect the planning for the fiftieth anniversary of Operation Gomorrah in 1994, which was organized in close coordination with the British Ambassador to Germany in a "spirit of peace, reconciliation, and friendship," as the mayor of Hamburg was eager to emphasize. When Prince Charles of Wales gave an appropriately fair-minded and conciliatory speech at the commemoration, about thirty thousand enthusiastic Hamburgers gathered to celebrate him, waving small Union Jack flags and wearing "Prince Charles" buttons (Thiessen 2007, 372–374).

The Air War as Bridging Metaphor

When the United States–led coalition launched a massive air campaign against Iraq on January 17, 1991, kicking off the Second Gulf War, many Germans drew an analogy between Germany's past and Iraq's present. For instance, visitors to the town of Giessen near Frankfurt could see messages sprayed on official city signs that read "Giessen = Baghdad." During World War II, Giessen offered many industrial targets and was an important link in the German transport system, which is the reason why the city was bombed and almost completely destroyed on the night of December 6, 1944, by American B-17 bombers.

The sprayed message in Giessen was symptomatic for a much broader phenomenon that was new at least in the Western part of the country. Several voices from the peace movement against the Gulf War employed allusions to the German experience of being bombed by the Western Allies as a "bridging metaphor" (Alexander 2003, 67–76) to make sense of and mobilize against the Iraq war. There had, of course, been other American air wars before, most notably the Vietnam War, which was also opposed on a global scale. However, the public controversy over the Vietnam War unfolded without any appropriation of specifically German war memories. Indeed, the perception of this particular war was still (or already) shaped by the fundamental perpetrator/liberator ambiguity that was about to dominate the public discourse on the World War II bombings of German cities.

In hindsight, the peace movement turned out to be a political actor whose contribution to the ongoing process of German memory-making has been much more salient than its effects on global politics, although spokespersons of the movement attempted to combine precisely these two areas. The popular psychoanalyst Horst-Eberhard Richter, for example, argued that Germany had a special right and duty to push for strictly pacifist policies in the international arena because this country had been the source as well as the site of mass atrocities during World War II. Although the bombing of German cities did not figure explicitly in his argument, Richter gave a telling list of impressions about what he perceived to be the immediate results of the Gulf War, "The enormity of the sacrifice in blood of soldiers and civilians, the misery of those who have been bombed out as well of hundreds of thousands of refugees, the destruction of cities and the landscape, the poisoning of the sea and the toxic oil well plumes engulfing hundreds of kilometers" (Richter 1991, 15). When reading such descriptions, it is hard to miss the vague similarity with accounts of what happened to Germany during World War II. This vagueness and ambiguity of Richter's lament was symptomatic for many other texts published in the context of the peace movement at that time.

What is most striking in Richter's account is the blurring of the distinction between victims and perpetrators in the context of the Holocaust and World War II. On the one hand, he clearly distances himself from any attempt to question the historical guilt and the political responsibility of Germans for the Holocaust; on the other hand, he uses German war memories to seize the moral high ground for Germany as an international actor. Because Germans have suffered so much, so the argument goes, they are uniquely well positioned to speak up against any war, whereas those who have suffered less are still caught up in nationalist and militaristic mindsets. From the memories of German suffering and victimhood, Richter distils a spirit of moral superiority that distinguishes Germany from other, allegedly more traditional nations. The implication of this rhetorical move is that the blurring of the line between victims and perpetrators is matched by an equally problematic blurring of "temporal and spatial boundaries," as Andreas Huyssen (2003, 163) has pointed out. Like many other Germans, members of the peace movement continued to define their identity largely in *temporal* terms, based on the difference between the democratic present and an ominous, highly charged, antidemocratic past. At the same time, however, this repudiation of the past was *spatialized* and turned into powerful rhetorical stances against contemporary nations such as the United States.[7]

Our reading of the ambiguities of the German peace movement was already reflected by some of the protagonists themselves, who felt that the movement was maneuvering in murky waters. Thus, Jörn Böhme, who had been an activist of the peace movement in the 1980s, argued that the attitudes of the German peace movement during the Gulf War were fraught with "dilemmas" (Böhme 1991, 215) of the kind discussed previously. Every attempt to define an unambiguous pacifist position in Germany, Böhme argued, was marred by an unconscious desire to escape those dilemmas. While mapping out a complex field of mutually contradictory loyalties and self-canceling positions, he also mentioned the memory of the air war, wondering "to what extent the bombing of Dresden and other cities has been tabooed among young Germans, on the ground that the older generation used Dresden to repress Auschwitz, with the consequence that now perhaps the lack of mourning is projected collectively on the people of Iraq as an innocent victim of 'the Allies'" (Böhme 1991, 223). It is important to stress that Böhme talks about the memories of the bombings in strictly psychological, nonconstructivist terms of a "return of the repressed." The intrusion of bombing memories into the public discourse is described not as the result of a lifting of a communicative taboo but as the result of an allegedly natural psychic dynamic.

We reject this interpretation as much as we have rejected the taboo thesis. As far as the public sphere is concerned, memories of the bombing of German cities did not "return" like a jack-in-the-box jumping at us. Rather, these memories were consciously revived by activists, although under inherited symbolic circumstances shaped by previous memory projects. In the early 1980s, for example, activists and the media began to circulate the slogan of the "nuclear holocaust" (Thiessen 2007, 256) to associate the memory of the destruction of Hamburg and other cities with two other evils at once: the Cold War threat of nuclear war and the systematic extermination of the European Jews captured by the rising Holocaust symbol. The fact that this analogy vanished together with the Soviet Union and the Cold War constellation, which again makes clear that it is misleading to speak of a past forcing itself onto the present.

Dan Diner (1991) was probably right when he interpreted the protests against the Second Gulf War as an expression of both continuity and change in the parameters of political protest in post-reunification Germany. On the one hand, he commended the peace movement, not the least for the ability of some of its representatives to reflect upon the movement's inherent anti-American ideological grounding. On the other hand, he was concerned about what began to take shape as an effort to mobilize memories of German victimhood in the protest against the U.S. campaign in Iraq, a campaign that should have been judged and criticized on its own terms. In 1990 and 1991, this mobilization was still very much dominated by the ideological debates within the West German left and the peace movement that grew out of it. Twelve years later, on the occasion of the protests against yet another Unites States–led war in Iraq, however, the memory symbol of "Dresden" could no longer be found occupying a particular position at one end of the ideological left-right spectrum. In hindsight, the German peace movement has indeed earned the dubious credit of having turned the bombing war on Germany into a free-floating symbol that allowed the public to understand and rally against the successors of the same Allies who had devastated but also liberated Germany in World War II.

At the same time, though, this symbol, precisely because it is free-floating, should not be regarded as pointing toward an underlying cultural trauma, because it is not really connected to issues of collective identity. Memories can be mobilized in conflicts over the self-definition of the collectivity as well as referred to in struggles over resources that have no inner connection to the issues resurrected from memory. Although most conflicts over memory have both strategic and identity dimensions, from the point of view of cultural trauma theory, the crucial question is whether memory offers a narrative that is directed toward the in-group in such a way as to shape its collective identity (Eyerman 2002, 70). The "achievement" of the peace movement has been the creation of a token of symbolic capital out of the memory of the bombings that now can be used for the public dramatization of issues and for adding moral weight to political arguments and positions, but which cannot be regarded as having any identity-constitutive meaning of its own.

Dresden and the Clash of Memories

More consequential for German memory struggles than any American-led war in recent decades has been the reunification of Germany itself. To be sure, this event did not fundamentally reconfigure what we have called the bombing war memory matrix. In fact, the institutionalization of the Holocaust trauma continued. More memorials to Nazi crimes were unveiled, the most spectacular of them being the Memorial to the Murdered Jews of Europe in central Berlin, which was inaugurated and opened to the public in 2005. Also, empirical research shows that contemporary Germans of all age groups continue to identify Nazism with evil and recognize the Holocaust as "the superlative historical genocide" (Langenbacher 2008, 65). At the same time, however, the inclusion of the former German Democratic Republic strengthened certain forces and trends that were already visible in West Germany. In the communist east, the memory of the bombing war was omnipresent and consciously evoked by the state. Many cities bore the scars of the war into the 1980s, with wastelands of rubble and facades of buildings pockmarked by bullet holes that served as constant reminders of the past. While the relative slowness of reconstruction made sure that popular war memories lingered on, the official public discourse politicized those memories in accordance with the binary Cold War logic.

From the mid-1950s onward the East German discourse on the bombing of Germany focused on the eastern city of Dresden, which was destroyed on February 13 and 14, 1945, by a highly controversial air campaign called Operation Thunderclap. The bombing of Dresden was the most catastrophic attack on a German city since Hamburg. Twenty-five thousand people were killed. Dresden had been a city that prided itself on its rich culture but was also a Nazi stronghold and an important hub for moving military personnel and supplies to the east. Because of its strategic position, the campaign was planned in London as a way to ease the Red Army's advance in Germany (Taylor 2004, 190–192). However, from our perspective, the most intriguing aspect of this horrible bombing is that it almost instantly morphed from a military fact into a powerful moral signifier of evil. As the British historian Frederick Taylor writes, the destruction of Dresden began "to exercise an independent power of its own, one that could not but affect the Allies' claims to absolute moral superiority" (2004, 372). According to Taylor, this transformation must partly be credited to the efforts of Joseph Goebbels and his Ministry of Propaganda that lost no time manipulating the figure of the dead (by adding a zero) and denouncing the raids as a "barbarian" terror attack on an innocent city that represented the epitome of European "culture" without having any military value.

Much of this straightforward coding of the events survived the end of Nazism with only minor permutations. Intellectuals and the government of East Germany offered a narrative of the bombing of Dresden that was based on a small set of symbolic equivalences between National Socialism and the Western Allies. The perpetrators of the bombings were analogically associated with the Nazis, and victims were represented in analogy to the victims of Nazism (although the Jews were not named). East Germans also perpetuated the myth of the innocence of Dresden as a place of no military or industrial importance where people loved the arts and kept themselves aloof from the demands of politics. Hence the trope of the "senselessness" of the air raids (see, e.g., Kil 1989, 19). For Cold War propaganda purposes the attackers were also called "Anglo-Americans," although in this particular case the U.S. Air Force had only been a junior partner in a largely British and Commonwealth operation. However, the role of the United States was seen as particularly frightening in light of the even worse fate that could have befallen Dresden: becoming the target of the first atomic bomb. According to a widely believed story line offered by Communist Party intellectuals, this possibility was thwarted only by the fast advancing Red Army, which saved the people of Dresden. Although empirically unsubstantiated, this doomsday scenario became a centerpiece of the East German collective memory of the air war (Taylor 2004, 454–456; Widera 2005). In short, the East German discourse lifted the assault on Dresden out of the overall context of the war, invested it with immense moral significance, and created a salvationary narrative that idolized the Red Army while polluting the British and American air forces as apocalyptically evil.

After reunification, this narrative entered the mainstream of German public culture, where some of its aspects such as the savior role attributed to the Soviet Union have been submerged, while other aspects have affected the collective memory. It is worth noting, though, that the East German discourse did not contradict the core assumption of the West German memory matrix that Germany had to be liberated by foreign armies. On the other hand, the Holocaust did not figure prominently, if at all, in East German memory. The place of the sacred-evil had remained empty in East Germany, even if the communist propaganda tried for some time to assign this place to the imperialist West. Yet this assignment was predicated on the changing geopolitical situation and was thus inherently unstable.[8]

After reunification, both Dresden and the province of Saxony, of which Dresden is the regional capital city, were governed by the liberal-conservative Christian Democratic Party (CDU). The new ruling political elite was, of course, determined to promote reconciliation with the West and made sure that the annual commemoration was organized and scripted accordingly. One of the early steps taken by the city of Dresden was the decision of reconstruct the eighteenth-century Lutheran *Frauenkirche* (Church of Our Lady). This decision was controversial because the heap of ruins to which the cathedral had been reduced by the 1945 air raids was conserved under communist rule as a war memorial, similar to the ruins of Coventry Cathedral in England, which was destroyed by German bombers. Supporters of the reconstruction, who were aware that the removal of the ruins would be interpreted by some as a "sacrilege" (Blaschke 1990), nevertheless argued that it was more important to allow people to forget and to leave behind the horrors of the past of which the dark stones of the ruins were a vivid reminder.

Today, the reopened cathedral is being touted by German as well as British representatives as a transnational symbol of "reconciliation" between former enemies. "Reconciliation" is indeed one of the key words of an official commemorative discourse that no longer differs significantly from the discourse on the bombing of Hamburg. In both cities, we have seen two different narratives of the air war in recent years. The first one describes the air raids as a symbol of the madness of war in general, or even as a symbol of the destructiveness of modernity as such. A former mayor of Dresden, for example, used the rhetorical device of metonymy to contextualize the memory of the bombing. The attack on Dresden was said to be "senseless" and "barbarian" but no more senseless and barbarian than "the entire war," which was started by Germany before taking on a life of its own.[9] This narrative amalgamates the different tactics and strategies used by the Allied and the Axis Powers, as well as their human consequences, into one single emblem of absurdity. In 2005, the city held an event where messages written by victims of war from Dresden, Baghdad, Guernica, New York, Hiroshima, Grozny, and other places were read out in public to evoke the idea of a global "community of victims." Around the same time, the mayor of Hamburg gave a commemorative speech in which he interpreted the firebombing of his city not as a consequence of decisions taken by countries that had been attacked before but as the result of a breach of "the dams of our civilization" that led Europe to abandon herself to the destructive potentials of technology and modernity (quoted in Thiessen 2007, 421–422; for the "dams of civilization" metaphor, see Freud 1953, 178).

A second narrative is based on the conviction that historical occurrences such as the bombing of cities should be explained not as expressions of a self-propelling modernity that got out of control but as consequences of motivated human action. Since the 1980s, much of the memory work done in Hamburg, for example, has been inspired by a causal story which regarded Nazi Germany as the source of a violence that finally boomeranged. Hosea 8: 7 ("For they have sown the wind, and they shall reap the whirlwind") was therefore much quoted. This way of distributing causal and moral responsibilities across different actors is by no means alien to the public discourse in Dresden. In February 2009, Helma Orosz, who had been elected mayor only a few months previously, addressed a crowd at the city center emphasizing that "like Dresden, thousands of other human places had to sink to ashes before the criminal Nazi racket that started the war could be stopped."[10] Other representatives of the city have called on the citizens to remember their former Jewish fellow-citizens who were persecuted and deported from Dresden like everywhere else in German-ruled territories. Recalling specifically the fate of Victor Klemperer, a Jewish citizen and professor of literature who survived the Nazi period in hiding, former mayor Lutz Vogel mentioned that Klemperer had barely escaped Hitler's henchmen, saying, "The air raid on February 13, 1945, had saved his life!"[11] Civic groups including a survivors' association have also invoked the double image of German civilians as victims/accomplices, which corresponds to the perpetrator/liberator ambiguity in the perception of the Allies including their bomber pilots.[12]

The crucial difference between east and west, Dresden and Hamburg, can be gleaned from the fact that there is virtually no commemorative speech by a democratic politician in Dresden that does not address the pervasive counter-discourse produced by extreme right-wing groups in society and their political parties. At the heart of this memory discourse is no longer what Adorno (1998, 90) ridiculed as the "quite common move of drawing up a balance sheet of guilt ... , as though Dresden compensated for Auschwitz." Instead of only minimizing the Holocaust by pointing to alleged crimes of the Allies, the new revisionist discourse directly analogizes "Dresden" to the Holocaust by calling the Allied bombing of German cities a "bombing holocaust." This new trope does not deny the Holocaust (doing so is a criminal offense in Germany) but rather treats it as a floating signifier that becomes truly meaningful only when attached to the memories of the air war. But it is precisely this floating that prevents that trope from becoming a point of crystallization for a clearly demarcated identity. For instance, Jörg Friedrich's bestselling book *The Fire: The Bombing of Germany, 1940-1945* establishes two equivalences: He calls the British Bomber Command and the aircrews dropping bombs over Germany *Einsatzgruppen*—the official name of the German death squads who rounded up and killed Jews and other groups throughout Europe, and he equates the basements where people died during the air attacks with "crematoria" (Friedrich 2006). Still, Friedrich does not see himself as a right-wing author. He believes that the Allied air war was a unique crime and should not be compared to more recent American wars. Thus, while drawing an analogy between the Holocaust and military actions that were (rightly or wrongly) believed to contribute to the defeat of the regime responsible for the Holocaust, Friedrich dissociates other, more recent bombing campaigns from the one launched against Germany. He mentions, in particular, that he supported the 2003 war in Iraq (see the "Afterword for American and British Readers" in Friedrich 2006, 483). This suggests that the rhetorical equation "Dresden = Auschwitz" hardly has the potential of rallying a broad coalition of political forces.

The right-wing manner of remembrance is passionately rejected by the democratic political parties as polluting the founding ideals of reunified Germany including its newly democratized eastern provinces. It is seen as "disgracing" Dresden and "sullying the memory of its dead."[13] Whereas in Hamburg we have seen a notable decline of public controversies over the meaning of the air raids on the city as well as over the appropriate mode of remembering them (Thiessen 2007, 457), Dresden has become a veritable cauldron of memory wars. In 2009, the annual "commemorative march" organized by local right-wing extremists attracted more than 6,000 like-minded people from all over Germany and some neighboring countries. Even official events held by the city of Dresden are hijacked by these groups. Their countless wreaths, for example, completely drown out the wreaths laid by ordinary citizens or German and British dignitaries at the Heath Cemetery. Unsurprisingly, this disturbing situation has triggered a cycle of counter-mobilizations by left-wing radicals who have begun to stage their own performances on the occasion of the anniversary of the bombings. Some of these groups adopt a provocative, almost carnivalesque version of the just-war position that is perhaps best illustrated by the slogan "Bomber Harris Superstar—Thanks to You from the Red Antifa [Antifascist Action]."

None of the actors involved in the annual Dresden bombing re-membrance spectacle achieves what Alexander (2004) calls a "fused performance" that would be characterized by the presence of an audi-ence identifying with the actors and by cultural scripts appearing to be true. Understandably, many citizens simply stay physically away from a scene dominated by radical memory activists from the opposite ends of the political spectrum, monitored by helicopters hovering over the city and kept in check by thousands of police officers in riot gear. The mayor of the city of Dresden has meanwhile organized a dialogue with citizens about how future commemorations of the past should look like in a situ-ation where there is little consensus neither about the symbolic text of the commemoration nor about the ways of transforming this text into a convincing and effective performance. Nothing could be more different from this situation of utter cluelessness than the state of affairs in Ham-burg where the memory of Operation Gomorrah has been "normalized" (Thiessen 2007, 457) and drained of explosive emotions.

Toward a New Cultural Trauma?

We wish to summarize the findings of our case study with a view to some of the more general issues in the debate on cultural trauma. The Allied bombing of Germany clearly represents a historical instance of massive collective suffering that was deliberately inflicted on civilians by identifiable actors. There is no question that these occurrences have been traumatic in the clinical and psychological sense of the term. Still, memory projects attempting to translate this original experience into a cultural trauma have failed. The psychological trauma of being bombed has not been transformed into a cultural trauma of "the" bombed. The remembrance of the destruction of Hamburg, Dresden, and many other German cities and towns does not point to an ongoing cultural trauma process that fundamentally shapes the collective identity of modern-day Germans. Rather, the memory of the bombing war is a function of another memory: the memory of the Holocaust.

This does not mean that the Holocaust memory has repressed that of the air war or put a taboo on it. The evidence presented in this chapter indicates that images of the bombings and their human consequences are deeply ingrained in the political culture. Our point, however, is that the meaning of the bombing war for the nation cannot be established independently from memory discourses on the crimes of Nazi Germany. The public discourse on the bombings is not about the obvious fact that Germans, too, have been victims of the war; it is rather about whether they deserve a place in the sun of virtuous victimhood, which would rule out that they have been perpetrators or accomplices to evil as well. Whenever Germans during World War II are obliquely represented as virtuous victims, we do witness not a return of repressed memories but a strategy to exonerate Germans from their responsibility for the Third Reich.

The memory of the Holocaust, not the memory of the air war, entered the core of the identity of Germans as a cultural trauma. This social fact constrains and conditions present and future memory projects. The memory matrix of the bombings is thus organized around a reference point external to the debate over the bombings. Political struggles over the public commemoration of the bombing victims, including all the historically incomprehensible analogies between "Dresden" and "Baghdad," always take place against the backdrop of the Holocaust as the negative foundational myth of contemporary Germany.

A cultural trauma serves as filter and organizing center of political perceptions and value-statements, which, in turn, fuel processes of collective mobilization and identity construction. Far from being such a symbolic resource, the memory of the air war in Germany has been more of a ghost light in an ideological swamp. Of course, there is nothing about this memory that makes it impossible to reconstruct the facts of German suffering in such a way as to initiate a cultural trauma process. Alexander overrates the importance of the fact that by winning the war the Allies gained control over the "means of symbolic production" (Alexander 2003, 32–33) so that they could portray the existence of German-controlled extermination camps in a certain fashion. The Allied victory in no way guaranteed that one day West Germans would accept the Holocaust as a defining national memory icon, and there is no transcendental guarantee—given that the means of symbolic production are quite evenly distributed today—that Germans (or others) will one day abandon this particular memory. However, the obstacles are formidable.

Let us look at the example of the "bombing holocaust." Apart from being obscene, this fairly successful trope highlights the fact that the same groups who deny or minimize the Holocaust have to refer to and affirm it as a sacred-evil to denounce the bombing of German cities. The much less extreme example of Friedrich's *The Fire* also shows that even a drastic and simplified account of Germans as innocent victims of evil perpetrators draws its persuasive power from the Holocaust narrative. Far from making a first step toward replacing or eroding this foundational narrative, Friedrich has actually strengthened what will remain for a long time the central symbol of evil in the Western world.

Obstacles to constructing a new cultural trauma abound as we move from the margins to the center of the public debate. A cultural trauma "demands reparation" (Eyerman 2008, 163). Thus, if the memory of the air war ever crystallized into a cultural trauma, Britain and, to a lesser extent, the United States would have to repair the damage, starting perhaps with a formal apology. But the refusal of British officials, including Queen Elizabeth II, to apologize for any bombing raid has not caused more than a minor and passing public outcry, not even in Dresden (Taylor 2004, 422). Leading German military historians have even argued that an "admission of guilt" on the part of Great Britain would be inappropriate (Müller 2004, 230). Thus, there are no indications of a memory project that is going to replace the double image of German civilians as victims/accomplices that corresponds to the perpetrator/liberator perception of the Allies, with the kind of polarizing discourse that is required to establish a cultural trauma.

Notes

1. Many thanks to Sulamith Gräfenstein for her assistance, as well as to the Press and Public Relations Office of the city of Dresden for providing documents.

2. See, e.g., U.S. Air Force Historical Division, "Historical Analysis of the 14–15 February 1945 Bombings of Dresden." Available at http://www.airforcehistory.hq.af.mil/PopTopics/dresden.htm. The case for the effectiveness of the Allied bombing campaign has been made, for example, by Gregor (2000). Rolf-Dieter Müller (2004, 229) of the German Military History Research Institute reckons that the air attacks have shortened the war by at least one or two years.

3. The origins of the anti-Machiavellian position can be found in the moral scruples that surfaced in internal debates in Britain itself during the war, as Sebald (2004, 14–15) has indicated. For details, see Taylor (2004, 360–366 and 376–379).

4. German military historians seem to waver between moderate and radical anti-Machiavellian positions. In a landmark publication, Müller (2004, 231) speaks of "transgressions" during the Allied bombing campaigns but rejects the term "crime." Yet the multivolume history of World War II edited by his research institute concludes that the area bombings were a "crime against humaneness [*Verbrechen gegen die Menschlichkeit*]," although not illegal in terms

of international customary law (Boog 2008, 874–876). This ambiguity is shared by Commonwealth historians such as Randall Hansen (2009, 277 and 297).

5. The Auschwitz trials in Frankfurt in 1963–1965 focused the attention of the public more on the perpetrators than the victims. Michal Bodemann has argued that a major turning point in the perception of the Jews was the Six Day War in 1967, during which many Germans as well as mainstream media sided with Israel. Citizens in Hamburg, for example, donated blood for Israeli soldiers (Bodemann 2002, 48–49).

6. For instance, the anniversary of the battle of Stalingrad was being commemorated in German media right into the 1960s, before it became increasingly problematic due to the rise of the Holocaust memory as the organizing center of the German memory matrix.

7. The arbitrariness of these rhetorical stances became obvious when, in 1999, the German government successfully enacted a reversal of the analogical framework introduced by the peace movement by deciding to join the Kosovo intervention on the ground that Serbia was planning a "second Auschwitz" against Kosovo Albanians. Here, again, we saw the spatial localization of an evil retrieved from the collective memory and projected onto a real place which then was bombed by the German Air Force and others (Heins 2007).

8. As the Cold War was winding down in the 1980s, East German historians like Olaf Groehler softened their critique of the Allied bombing considerably (Fox 2006).

9. Address by Ingolf Rossberg, Dresden, February 13, 2006 (on file with authors).

10. Speech by Helma Orosz, Altmarkt Dresden, February 14, 2009 (on file with authors).

11. Speech by Lutz Vogel, First Mayor, Neumarkt Dresden, February 13, 2008 (on file with authors).

12. "At the same time the history of the city shows the co-responsibility also of the citizens of Dresden for the inhumane, criminal policies of the National Socialist power holders," says the mission statement of a group of local history activists called "13 February 1945."

13. Speech by Helma Orosz, Heidefriedhof Dresden, February 13, 2009 (on file with authors).

Works Cited

Adorno, T. W. 1998. The Meaning of Working Through the Past. In *Critical Models: Interventions and Catchwords,* trans. H. W. Pickford. New York: Columbia University Press.

Alexander, J. C. 2003. *The Meanings of Social Life: A Cultural Sociology.* New York: Oxford University Press.

———. 2004. Cultural Pragmatics Between Ritual and Strategy. *Sociological Theory* 22(4): 527–573.

Bernig, J. 2005. Phantomschmerzen: Die Gegenwärtigkeit des Bombenkrieges gegen die Deutschen. In *Die Zerstörung Dresdens: Antworten der Künste*, ed. W. Schmitz. Dresden: Thelem.

Blaschke, K. 1990. Die Trümmer des Krieges. *Frankfurter Allgemeine Zeitung*, February 13.

Bodemann, Y. M. 2002. The Uncanny Clatter: The Holocaust in Germany before Its Mass Commemoration. In *Remembering the Holocaust in Germany, 1945-2000*, ed. D. Michman. New York: Peter Lang.

Böhme, J. 1991. Der Golfkrieg, Israel und die bundesdeutsche Friedensbewegung. In *Nachgedanken zum Golfkrieg*, ed. G. Stein. Heidelberg: Palmyra.

Boog, H. 2008. Die strategische Bomberoffensive der Alliierten gegen Deutschland und die Reichsluftverteidigung in der Schlussphase des Krieges. In *Das Deutsche Reich und der Zweite Weltkrieg*, vol. 10.1, ed. M. Forschungsamt. Munich: Deutsche Verlags-Anstalt.

Diner, D. 1991. *Der Krieg der Erinnerungen und die Ordnung der Welt*. Berlin: Rotbuch.

Evans, R. J. 2009. *The Third Reich at War*. New York: Penguin.

Eyerman, R. 2002. *Cultural Trauma: Slavery and the Formation of African-American Identity*. Cambridge: Cambridge University Press.

———. 2008. *The Assassination of Theo van Gogh: From Social Drama to Cultural Trauma*. Durham, NC: Duke University Press.

Fox, T. C. 2006. East Germany and the Bombing War. In *Bombs Away! Representing the Air War over Europe and Japan*, eds. W. Wilms and W. Rasch. Amsterdam: Rodopi.

Freud, S. 1953. Three essays on the theory of sexuality. In *The Standard Edition of the Complete Psychological Works of Sigmund Freud*, vol. 7, trans. J. Strachey. London: Hogarth Press.

Friedrich, J. 2006. *The Fire: The Bombing of Germany, 1940-1945*, trans. A. Brown. New York: Columbia University Press.

Gregor, N. 2000. A *Schicksalsgemeinschaft*? Allied Bombing, Civilian Morale, and Social Dissolution in Nuremberg, 1942-1945. *The Historical Journal* 43(4): 1051–1070.

Hansen, R. 2009. *Fire and Fury: The Allied Bombing of Germany, 1942–1945*. New York: Penguin.

Heins, V. 2007. Crusaders and snobs: moralizing foreign policy in Britain and Germany, 1999-2005. In *Rethinking Ethical Foreign Policy: Pitfalls, Possibilities and Paradoxes*, eds. D. Chandler and V. Heins. London: Routledge.

Heukenkamp, U. 2001. Gestörte Erinnerung. Erzählungen vom Luftkrieg. *Amsterdamer Beiträge zur neueren Germanistik* 50(2): 469–492.

Huyssen, A. 2003. Air War Legacies: From Dresden to Baghdad. *New German Critique* 90: 163–176.

Kil, W. 1989. Dokumente und Argumente. In *Hinterlassenschaft und Neubeginn: Fotografien von Dresden, Leipzig und Berlin in den Jahren nach 1945*, ed. W. Kil. Leipzig: VEB Fotokinoverlag.

Langenbacher, E. 2008. Twenty-first Century Memory Regimes in Germany and Poland: An Analysis of Elite Discourses and Public Opinion. *German Politics & Society* 26(4): 50–81.

Müller, R. 2004. *Der Bombenkrieg 1939-1945.* Berlin: Ch. Links.

Neumann, F. 1942. *Behemoth: The Structure and Practice of National Socialism.* New York: Oxford University Press.

Nolte, H. 2008. Die andere Seite des Holocaust. *Die Zeit* (Hamburg), January 24.

Nossack, H. 2004. *The End: Hamburg 1943,* trans. J. Agee. Chicago: Chicago University Press.

Richter, H. 1991. Gegen das Vergessen und Verdrängen. In *Nachgedanken zum Golfkrieg,* ed. G. Stein. Heidelberg: Palmyra.

Sebald, W. G. 2004. *On the Natural History of Destruction,* trans. A. Bell. New York: Modern Library.

Shandley, R. 2001. *Rubble Films: German Cinema in the Shadow of the Third Reich.* Philadelphia: Temple University Press.

Taylor, F. 2004. *Dresden, Tuesday, February 13, 1945.* London: Bloomsbury.

Thiessen, M. 2007. *Eingebrannt ins Gedächtnis: Hamburgs Gedenken an Luftkrieg und Kriegsende 1943 bis 2005.* Munich: Dölling und Galitz.

White, J. R. 2002. Target Auschwitz: Historical and Hypothetical German Responses to Allied Attack. *Holocaust and Genocide Studies* 16(1): 54–76.

Widera, T. 2005. Gefangene Erinnerung. Die politische Instrumentalisierung der Bombardierung Dresdens. In *Alliierter Bombenkrieg: Das Beispiel Dresden,* eds. L. Fritze and T. Widera. Göttingen: Vandenhoeck & Ruprecht.

2

The Cultural Trauma of a Fallen Nation

Japan, 1945

Akiko Hashimoto

Every year on August 15, Japan turns to commemorating the end of World War II with events that have become fixtures on the national calendar. On that day, government leaders and dignitaries, veterans and bereaved, media commentators and observers participate in annual rituals of commemoration to remember the lost war and to "renew the nation's vow for peace." Citizens can turn on the television at noon to watch the state-sponsored *Memorial Service for the War Dead* broadcast live from Budōkan, one of Tokyo's largest events arenas. It is the focal official event of the memorial day attended by the emperor who formally conveys his words of mourning for those who died in the war, followed by a brief speech by the prime minister. The choreography of the one-hour ceremony is solemn, centered on a soaring tablet representing the soul of the war dead displayed in the middle of the stage and surrounded by a twin-peaked sculpture of yellow and white chrysanthemum. Many participants are attired in funeral black, including representatives of

27

all branches of government and over 5,000 representatives of bereaved families from all over the nation. Every year, this ceremony takes place at the same time and place; using the same stage, the same protocol, and the same address; and with the same funerary effects. This sameness year after year brings a certain familiarity and indelibility to war memory, as it reiterates an official memory that promotes a continuity of collective mourning. At the same time, it allows the state to reiterate its discourse of war, reconnecting it to the private narratives of loss and superimposing it on cultural templates of funerary dramaturgy.

On the same day, citizens can find commemorative editorials in their daily newspapers, usually recounting some tragic experiences of national failure and vowing to overcome them by pledging for peace. The somber themes of war and peace appear in most major national and regional papers, urging readers to carry on the war memory—by never forgetting the hardship, passing on the painful lessons, confronting the difficult history, and so on—with varied emphasis according to the paper's political persuasion.[1] In the evening, and throughout most of the month, audiences can find similar themes on television that feature commemorative documentaries, live debates, oral history interviews, live-action drama and reenactments, or feature films. During this month, scores of nationally circulated magazines also offer commemorative features molding and remolding the collective memory of war, while major book publishers also compete to sell war memory books and special editions that bring back memories of events and experiences, like oral history collections. They often draw attention to the colossal negative legacy with sensational headlines: *"Japan was Defeated," "Japan's Failure," "Causes of Japan's Defeat,"* and *"Why Did We Lose That War?"*[2]

These concerted acts of annual commemoration reveal how deeply war memory is embedded in contemporary life in Japan. At the same time, the cumulative effect of reproducing familiar war memory over and over in a concentrated timeframe—recounting suicide missions, deadly bombings, mortal danger, fear, starvation, violence, killings, deaths, and so on—is also to situate the hateful events in the past, on the other side of ruptured time symbolized by August 15, 1945. In a broader sense, August 15, 1945, has come to represent not strictly the end of a military conflict but the cultural trauma of a fallen nation, the collapse of the nation's social and moral order, and the failed aspirations of an East Asian Empire. Epitomizing a rupture of national history rather than the strictly military event, Japan's notion of "August 15, 1945" has come to represent an idea similar to the German "May 8, 1945" (the Zero Hour) that also emphasizes a radical departure from a stigmatized past. Japan's commemorative performances and debates act as discursive tools that demarcate the failures of 1945 from the present, while reinforcing the events as a cultural trauma for successive generations. These commemorative events can also conceal the wide dissension among the Japanese. Such multiple layers of consensus and dissent are not uncommon to cultures of defeat such as Japan's.

The establishment of August 15 as the commemorative day was many years in the making. As in most cases of invented tradition, what appears today to be long-standing custom is, in fact, not determined by historical imperative but constructed over time to symbolize, reinforce, and reinvent the political meaning of defeat. The official date of commemoration could have been August 14 (the date of signing the acceptance of the Potsdam Declaration) or even September 2 (signing of the instrument of surrender), but August 15 ultimately carried emotional resonance because it represented the ritual between the Emperor and his subjects, mediated by the radio broadcast, when the surrender was announced and emotionally accepted to be final. At the same time, there were also other coincidences for August 15, like *obon*, the day for honoring departed souls (Sato 2005, 32).

During the U.S. Occupation (1945–1952), no commemoration of August 15 took place. The Occupation had officially banned the Shinto memorialization of the war dead and commemorated Japan's surrender on VJ Day, September 2. It was only in 1952, after regaining sovereignty, that the Japanese government held a memorial service for the departed soldiers for the first time. This commemoration set in motion a process of memory-making focused on the emperor's announcement to end the war, rather than the capitulation to the victors (Sato 2005). In 1963, the government began the memorial service as an annual ritual broadcast on both radio and television, and by 1965, when the secular service moved to the Budōkan arena, the construction of war memory came into full swing, establishing the association between the deaths of *obon* and deaths of soldiers, fathers, and sons—all merged into one. Films, novels, television programs, and other cultural media dramatizing the events of August 15 rather than September 2 also accentuated it as the end of the Imperial era and the war (Sato 2002). Underneath this ritualization of the war's end, however, lies a deep social discord over the assessment of Japan's war. Some have resisted and protested the annual state commemoration by holding their own counter-memorial for Asians victimized by Japanese aggression, as the socialists did until 1993 (Hammond 1997, 120). Others attempt to elevate the status of annual commemoration beyond the state ceremony by campaigning for the prime minister to officially honor the war dead at the controversial Yasukuni Shrine. Because of these deep contestations over the commemoration of the controversial war, different groups have come to attach different meanings to August 15 today: for some, it is simply a day to pledge never to wage war again; for others, it is a way of mythologizing the emperor's connection to the people or to purify the tainted war; and for still others, it is an angry time to remember the untrustworthiness of the military and the evils of authoritarian leadership (Hammond 1997; Sato 2005, 61–63).

Examining how commemorative practices shape and are shaped by memory of difficult pasts reveals a great deal about why and how cultural trauma is continually sustained in national consciousness. A cultural trauma occurs "when members of a collective feel they have been subjected to a horrendous event that leaves indelible marks upon their group consciousness, marking their memories forever and changing their future identity in fundamental and irrevocable ways" (Alexander 2004a, 1). The horrendous event emerges as a significant *referent* in the collective consciousness, not because it is in some way naturally ineffaceable but because it generates a structure of discourse that normalizes it in collective life over time (Eyerman 2004). In the process, the memory of the event is made culturally relevant, remembered as an overwhelmingly damaging and problematic collective experience and incorporated as part of collective identity with strong negative affect (Smelser 2004, 36–42). Wars, massacres, atrocities, invasions, and other instances of mass violence can become significant referents for subsequent collective life not because of the gruesome nature of the events *per se* but because people choose to make them especially relevant to who they are and what it means to be a member of that society. Some events therefore become more crucially significant than others, because we manage to make them more consequential in later years for our understanding of ourselves and our own society.

Japan's national collapse in 1945 contributes a significant empirical case to the development of cultural trauma theory not only because it epitomizes an event of considerable scale and historical significance sustained in the national consciousness for many decades but also because it constitutes a case that embodies deeply contested meanings that are continually reworked in a divided society that has yet to develop a wide consensus view of the event. It reveals the cleavages in what is remembered, the contradictions in what is retold, and the tensions in what is disputed and negotiated. In a society that contends with divided sentiments, disputed assessments, and fragmented meanings of the war, this case study shows how cultural trauma narratives may develop a splintered discursive structure under particular conditions. The Japanese case shows the divergent memory of the traumatic event remains in constant and recurrent struggle, subject to flare ups of contestation, without resolution and closure, but nevertheless conditions the larger process of forging a collective identity polluted by a stigmatized past.

This chapter analyzes Japan's splintered narratives of cultural trauma. It builds on Bernhard Giesen's archetypes that illuminate the different constructions of moral trauma. His typologies are constructed along parameters between triumph and trauma, which emerge in different institutional arenas and include victorious heroes, tragic heroes, victims, and perpetrators (Giesen 2004, 6). I modify his schema to analyze Japanese narratives of war and defeat and suggest that the disparate, incongruent narratives of heroes, victims, and perpetrators express continuing unresolved tensions in Japanese society.

Some narratives emphasize the progress and amelioration after the war, representing the vision that defeat is the reason why Japan enjoys peace and material prosperity today. This "fortunate fall" argument, seen often in official speeches and commemorations, tends to justify and legitimate the sacrifices of the war dead, while, at the same time, diverting attention away from the culpability of the state in starting and losing the war. The focus on assigning positive value to the personal sacrifices of the heroic dead invokes a keen sense of indebtedness to them, while bracketing out the question of whether they fought the war for a legitimate cause. Thus, as long as those gallant soldiers' and civilians' sacrifices are emphasized, this narrative frame is elastic enough to allow the war itself to be either condemned or ennobled. The rationale that the destruction was somehow a necessary condition to attain fruitful ends is a strained logic to be sure, but it nevertheless satisfies a strong desire for elevating and dignifying failure.

Other narratives promote identification with tragic, suffering participants. This narrative frame emphasizes that the war wrought unimaginable tragedy to people who had to "bear the unbearable and suffer the insufferable."[3] The scale of violence and destruction in the total war is undisputable, and the only appropriate response as a nation is to make sure it will not happen again. Thus, those who were affected by this tragedy are duty bound to recount, warn of, and prevent repeating the mistake. The war was wrong, but there is also sufficient elasticity here in assigning the blame to different agents and causes, from the emperor and colonial aggression to incompetent military strategists and self-serving Western powers. These narratives often set a premium on Japan's victimization in Hiroshima, Nagasaki, and indiscriminate air raids and tend to cast war itself as an absolute evil.

Still others represent tragic narratives of violence and victimization of Asians during Japan's colonial aggression and military conflicts in China, Korea, and Southeast Asia. They stress the dreadful harm that Japan inflicted, with varied attribution of malicious intent, depicting brutal treatments of local populations by the Japanese military and colonial perpetrators. They depict violent military actions gone out of control: local combatants and civilians victimized by a military seen as sadistic, ill-equipped, incompetent, and indifferent to the value of human life.

These narratives of heroes, victims and perpetrators represent a triadic dynamic of discordant memory in a divided society that sustains and reworks the cultural trauma, awkwardly, inconsistently, and inconclusively. Their depictions and assessments of Japan's fall are incongruent, contradictory, and discrepant in their implications for Japan's war legacy and moral responsibility. Before exploring this trio of memory projects further, however, it is necessary to outline the context from which it emerged.

Divided Narratives in a Divided Society

Over the past decades, the trauma of 1945 and the national defeat have been recounted in many voices from a broad spectrum of perspectives. From personal accounts to commemorative speeches, and from media dramatizations to public controversies, the official and unofficial narratives of war and defeat have been inescapably present in national collective life. During this time, social groups of different persuasions have contended over the master narratives of the Asia-Pacific War. These groups—consisting of politicians, intellectuals, teachers, bureaucrats, business leaders, media entrepreneurs, labor activists, and students, who were themselves veterans, returnees, bereaved families, orphans, atomic bomb survivors, ethnic minorities, and so on—forged different narratives to interpret what the war meant and what went wrong. Broadly, their narratives used three different moral frames: some sought to triumph over the defeat ("defeat was the harbinger of peace"), while others relativized the war ("we were bad, but they were bad, too"), and still others condemned it ("we started an atrocious, reckless war"). Within these frames, individuals staked out different positions: tragic heroes caught in a bad war ("we had no choice"), victims of a brutal war ("we all suffered and paid heavily"), and perpetrators of an imperial war ("we wrought so much suffering in Asia"). These differences are brought together under a common denominator view that condemns war universally ("all wars are bad") and vows repentantly never to make the same mistakes again ("No more war! No more Hiroshima!"). Under this consensus, however, divisions persist, as do those who opt out altogether, preferring to bury their own memories in silence or conceal what, in psychiatric terms, would be called their post-traumatic stress disorder.

The triad of discordant memory projects emerges out of the broad range of disparate experiences in a total war whose phenomenal scope of death and destruction was unquestionable and recounted by many sources. The total death toll of World War II is estimated at 60 million, of which one-third occurred in Asia (Weinberg 2005). During the Japanese invasions, from China to Indonesia, the Philippines, and New Guinea, it is estimated that 20 million Asians died, not only from warfare but also from civilian raids, plunder, rape, starvation, and torture (Fujiwara 2001). In Japan, civilian death—from the atomic bombing of Hiroshima and Nagasaki to air raids in numerous cities—totaled approximately 1 million. In China, the civilian death toll is said to be around 16 million. In the United States, the total civilian dead numbered fewer than 2,000. One in every three Japanese soldiers died out of the 6 million who were mobilized. The death rate (38%, or 2.3 million dead) was higher than that of German soldiers (33%), and 19 times that of American soldiers (2%) (Yui 2005, 261). Because Japanese soldiers fought across the vast expanse of the Asia-Pacific region from north China to the South Pacific where supply lines were broken off especially toward the end of the war, approximately 60–70% of those soldiers died not from warfare but from starvation, disease, and abandonment. To date, only half of their remains have been repatriated, while the rest remain scattered throughout the far reaches of the region. Given the prohibition on surrender, a relatively small percentage was taken prisoner, and the last of them was returned in 1956. The repatriation of several million civilians and former soldiers took decades (Fujiwara 2001).

Shaping the narratives of the war began immediately after the surrender, as the U.S. Occupation set forth and imposed from above its version of events on the population. Perpetrator guilt was defined explicitly in the Tokyo war crimes tribunal (1946–1948) by the Allies, according to their version of "victors' justice" that pinned the blame for waging war on reckless, ambitious, and incompetent military wartime leadership who committed crimes against peace and other violations of war conventions. Among the war atrocities counted in the indictments were the Nanjing massacre and the Manila massacre (Fujita 1995). Thousands of perpetrators in the lower ranks who carried out those crimes in the battlefront were convicted in Class B and C war crimes trials that took place throughout East and Southeast Asia (1946–1951). However, national reckoning with a larger scope of guilt by untold, often lesser-known perpetrators remained elusive.[4] The emperor, who had by then renounced his divine status, was not held culpable for crimes against peace and escaped prosecution. The Japanese people at large were also held unaccountable, as they were said to have been misled by a deceptive militarist state. Tens of thousands were purged as collaborators of the wartime regime, but many were depurged even before the end of the Occupation as Cold War tensions intensified.

The contention among views of different stakeholders and custodians over the truth of Japan's war has endured ever since (Gluck 1993). Having experienced a complete inversion of the moral order by the U.S. Occupation who changed the right war to the wrong war, and the wrong war to the right war, it is not surprising that the wartime generation itself reacted with a measure of cynicism about the "truth" of historical accounts. Their children, in turn, learned that truth-building was malleable depending on who won the war when they were ordered to ink out passages of false history (Dower 1999). The name of the war itself also proved immensely malleable depending on which truth was evoked: called the Greater East Asia War and the Sacred War in wartime, it was then renamed the Pacific War by the U.S. Occupation that censored imperialist militarist language and deemphasized the significant role of China and East Asia in the conflict. While "the Pacific War" thus became a standard name for the state, the countervailing vernacular name used by Japanese progressive intellectuals and educators to overcome such Cold-War rhetoric also gained ground: "the Fifteen-Year War" recognized the salience of Japanese Imperial aggression in East Asia for a decade preceding the war in the Pacific. Subsequent designations used to sidestep such naming politics have been "the Asia-Pacific War," "the Shōwa War," "World War II," and, as people became weary of the political baggage that each name carried, the war ultimately came to be called "the last world war," "that war," and even "that unfortunate period of the past." With Japanese history so easily and frequently renamed, redefined, and reinterpreted, these experiences could not help but reinforce the awareness that historical truths were elusive and mutable, like the different accounts of the same event by *Rashōmon*'s protagonists in Kurosawa's film. The cynicism rooted in this experience left many to see the war through a lens of moral relativism that has become an integral part of Japan's culture of defeat. The truth, as they learned, could not be trusted. The distinction between true and false, right and wrong, heroes and villains was a convenient construction made in retrospect by different proponents.

The ensuing decades after the Occupation were characterized by disputes over the meaning of war, defeat, and collective identity as it affected different political agenda of the political right, left and center. After the conservative party (LDP) came to dominate the Japanese government in the mid-1950s, the economic imperatives of material growth and stability took priority over punishment for past deeds, while the political imperatives of security and alliance with the United States took priority over reconciliation with communist China and the Soviet Union (Dower 1999). As the conservatives stabilized their foothold as the stewards of unprecedented economic growth for the long haul in a nation determined to make up for the astronomical losses of the war, they gained institutional control over the official metanarrative of the war, which they sought to characterize as a tragic conflict fought reluctantly but bravely for national survival. In this narrative, the growth and prosperity enjoyed were the hard-won rewards built on this national tragedy.

The opposition, however, skeptical and distrustful of the conservative account of unmitigated progress, forcefully dissented and joined forces with myriad countervailing social groups and movements such as the teachers' union and various peace movements opposing the U.S.–Japan Security Treaty, nuclear tests, and the Vietnam War in the 1960s and 1970s. These groups, led by educators, intellectuals, journalists, and activists, claimed that the war was waged by ambitious leaders of an aggressive state who carried out reckless military invasions and colonization that resulted in myriad pain and suffering in Asia. Centrists, in turn, staked a narrower claim, emphasizing the domestic toll of total war inflicted on Japan like the atomic bombing of Hiroshima and Nagasaki and the thousands of air raids carried out by American forces. For them, the war was a tragic conflict fought foolishly by a dysfunctional military state, involving not only the military but also civilians at home and the whole nation, only to end in a monumental downfall.

The contentious politics of memory in the 1960s and 1970s nevertheless came to a point where the cultural trauma could be normalized as diverse stakeholders came to share a measure of agreement over remembering the Japanese side of the suffering. Even if they disagreed on who to designate as heroes, victims, and perpetrators and how to remember Asian suffering inflicted by Japan during the war, they shared a memory of their own losses and could not deny the visible hardship that was around them. As such, veterans and civilians, rich and poor, elite and downtrodden at least forged a common ground in their antipathy for war, ultimately developing into powerful antimilitary and antinuclear sentiments that became integral to the culture of defeat (Igarashi 2000, Orr 2001).

In the 1980s and 1990s, a global memory culture that had begun to coalesce around an emerging human rights movement that focused on redressing past wrongs refueled the triad of memory projects in different ways. Pressured by neighboring Asian nations and the international media, Japan's long-standing problem of reckoning with the past became an international concern that erupted on many fronts: disagreements over self-justifying history textbooks, struggles over official apologies, compensation suits filed by former colonial subjects and victims, controversial commemorations of the war dead and war criminals, disputes over museum exhibits, and others. A most significant case in point was the redress for former "comfort women," who were mobilized or coerced as sex workers to service Japanese soldiers during wartime and who began to break their silence and claim redress from the Japanese government. Emerging as a transnational feminist movement against sexual violence, the comfort women's case succeeded in bringing the world's attention to victimization of women in war, while also tarnishing the carefully crafted image of "innocent" Japanese soldiers. Such developments were catapulted not only by global trends but also domestic events that transformed the conditions of memory-making, such as the death of Emperor Hirohito, the end of the monopolistic rule of the Liberal Democratic Party, and the shattering of the bubble economy; and regional events, such as the rising political, economic, and cultural importance of East Asia. By the early 2000s, the culminating effects of change had also evoked a neo-nationalist backlash against the globalization of "the history problem" (Dudden 2008; Gluck 2007; Hashimoto forthcoming; Hein and Selden 2000; Seraphim 2005).

Today, six decades since defeat that ended the Asia-Pacific War, the Japanese are still deeply split in their evaluation of both the character and conduct of the war and its consequences (Makita 2000; Saaler 2005; Seaton 2007). A 2006 survey published by the largest Japanese national newspaper *Yomiuri*, headquartered in Tokyo, reveals an ongoing pattern of dissent where 34% believed that the Asia-Pacific War was a war of aggression, while 34% agreed that only the Japan-China War was a war of aggression but not the Pacific War. About 10% believed that neither conflict was a war of aggression, while 21% were undecided. A 2006 survey published by the second largest national newspaper *Asahi* showed that 31% of the respondents thought the war was a war of aggression, 7% thought it was a war of self-defense, while 45% thought it had elements of both, and 15% were undecided (Yomiuri Shinbun 2006; Asahi Shinbun 2006). At the same time, when asked in a national survey about whether they would fight for their country in case of war, the answer was emphatic: Only 15% of Japanese are willing to fight for their country, leaving Japan ranked fifty-ninth out of 59 nations (Takahashi 2003, 66). The fallen nation of 1945 has turned into a cultural trauma that has forged a dominant antimilitarism and antiwar culture in Japanese society.

The Trauma Narratives of a Fallen Nation

There are many examples of the urge to generate positive meaning in the aftermath of defeat in modern history, from the myth of the Lost Cause for the American Confederacy after the Civil War to the myth of the Fallen Soldier for German soldiers who died in World War I (Mosse 1990). The desire to search for positive meaning after defeat in war through a progressive narrative is often very powerful (Schivelbusch 2003; MacLeod 2008; Smith 2005). With the benefit of hindsight, people have often strained contradictory logic to find meaning even in tragic slaughters, attempting to reconcile the violence with virtue: "the soldiers killed to free people," "the bomb was dropped to save lives," "the war dead have brought peace," "the soldiers died to protect the future," and so on. Such meanings are often sustained and reworked by stories of legendary individuals who exemplify gallantry, pain, redemption and so on—rendering the reality palatable enough to speak to a mass audience. These stories are especially powerful when personified in individuals who invite broad identification and moral extension, like Anne Frank (Alexander 2004b). In this vein, I now turn to examine some well-known, popular stories of heroes, victims, and perpetrators that are reproduced and circulated in Japanese cultural media, to consider how the three dominant narratives of the cultural trauma are produced and reproduced as memory projects.

Narrating the Heroes

Attempts to turn national failure into motivation for building a better future are often found in efforts to come to terms with the enormity of the war dead. For example, public intellectuals like Nanbara Shigeru vowed in his tribute to the fallen as early as 1946 that they had not died in vain as they would serve as the foundation upon which peace would be built in the future (Dower 1999, 489). The anxieties about the futility of sacrifice for the state were often channeled into a narrative of hope for peace, which played a key role in reconfiguring the meaning for the deaths and devastation in the collective imagination. By blending together narratives of tragedy and messages for peace, defeat could be made into a more palatable experience, like the fortunate fall where destruction is supposedly instrumental to bringing about something better. The deaths of those men were rendered worthwhile by the claim that they managed to prevent a worse fate. They did not die in vain, because their death enabled the defeat which ended the atrocious violence. Regardless of where and how they died, this narrative allowed their deaths to be framed as an act of courage and selfless sacrifice, while relieving the guilt of the living. The emotional attachment to the valor of the fallen especially among conservative groups of the wartime generation has to be understood in this light (Takahashi 2005).

A discourse explicitly linking acts of sacrifice to achieving peace in a formula of national "progress" started to gain traction in national commemorations and national newspaper editorials especially in the 1960s, at a time that the ruling Liberal Democratic Party (LDP) consolidated power and claimed to guide Japan toward "prosperity and affluence" that would ultimately make it the second largest economy in the world (Akazawa 2005). The understanding of progress here referred to a broad range of ideas—peace, prosperity, democracy, justice, and security—that seemed to be preconditions for a society aspiring to a high standard of living without a state of war (Gluck 1993, 93; Igarashi 2000, 130–39). With such a broad and elastic definition of progress, the ameliorative narratives helped to energize and unite their proponents in a time of rapid uncertain social change; they also reassured that loyal sacrifice for the "greater good," such as the national-state or a business corporation, were meant to be amply rewarded.

One of the best-known examples used often in this heroic discourse of sacrifice for the greater good in Japan is the story of battleship *Yamato* and its 3,000 crew who died in the sea southwest of Japan. This patriotic tale recounts the last moments of those navy men in the largest battleship ever built, used for a tactically dubious suicide sortie only months before the defeat. One of its survivors, Yoshida Mitsuru, documented the tormented discussion among the young officers aboard who questioned the meaning of their impending death for a war that was certain to end in defeat. Yoshida recounts the now infamous phrase attributed to Captain Usubuchi desperately seeking answers moments before the ship sank under overwhelming bombardment by 700 American bombers. Finally, he finds a thought that renders his impending death worthwhile: his sacrifice would serve as an awakening, a rallying cry for a better national future.

> Japan has paid too little attention to progress. We have been too finicky, too wedded to selfish ethics; we have forgotten true progress. How else can Japan be saved except by losing and coming to its senses? If Japan does not come to its senses now, when will it be saved?
> We will lead the way. We will die as harbingers of Japan's new life. That's where our real satisfaction lies, isn't it?" (Yoshida 1985, 40)

What this twenty-one year old officer meant by "progress" here is vague enough so that it is possible to attribute different meanings like peace, justice, and prosperity. It is also easy to fault the logical contradiction of a young man claiming to contribute to a future that he will not experience. Yet this contradictory logic is at the core of the fluid idea of linking progress to sacrifice which engendered the collective belief that Japan could rebound and recover. In Yoshida's rendering, the courage and discipline of the men facing certain death are emphasized, without blame or resentment directed toward the state leadership that ordered the tactically dubious special attack mission with no fuel to return home. Instead, Yoshida's account is a requiem for the dead, a tribute that facilitates and legitimates the idea that the deaths were heroic and also somehow a catalyst for progress. However, this popular story also works as a cautionary tale against war not only because of the futility of 3,000 deaths in a no-win mission but also because those men hailed from the Imperial Navy, which is the arm of the Japanese military on record for opposing the war against the United States in the Pacific. So they are more readily cast as seekers of peace in war, and their stories of heroism can still be framed in terms of opposition to war. This allows the narrative to both align neatly with the search for innocence in these men who have committed no evil and also harmonize with the pacifist collective identity. The protagonists are cast not as killing machines but tragic heroes of a country going through a national catastrophe. Thus the *Yamato* story also serves to mitigate condemnation of the protagonists as also perpetrators of an aggressive war (Fukuma 2007, 56).

The nationalist appeal of this tale of sacrifice is obvious, even if it never quite fulfills even those who survived the Yamato catastrophe like Yoshida, much less the veterans embittered by this and other cases of military ineffectiveness (Yoshida 1986, 2003a; Iida 2008). The story of the *Yamato* has been made into action-packed feature films from 1953 to 2005, and it has also inspired numerous fictive accounts espousing ideals that range from nationalism and anti-Americanism to supranationalism and pacifism (e.g., the popular graphic comic manga and anime series *Space Battleship Yamato* and *Silent Service*). The statement of sacrifice attributed to Usubuchi itself has been cited often in language arts textbooks, and recounted in a variety of political speeches, such as the Speaker of the Diet's recent official speech on August 15, 2006, on the sixty-first anniversary of the end of the war, and voted by scores of viewers as one of the top five favorites in a popular history program in national public television in 2007 (NHK's *Sonotoki Rekishiga Ugoita— That's When History Changed*). The appeal and the usefulness of this story of loyalty and selfless devotion especially for the state and the conservative business sector is evident, and at the same time, the theme of tragic heroes caught in a bad war cannot avoid promoting to successive generations a revulsion for a military defeat that killed so many promising young men.

Narrating the Victims

Just as the conservative power elite developed a heroic narrative genre with alluring personal stories, the progressives and centrists also successfully produced a powerful antimilitary narrative genre involving widely known, popular characters. These stories tended to depict tragic protagonists—civilian and military—caught in hopeless cycles of violence and paying a heavy price physically, emotionally, and materially. For example, at the height of the Vietnam War, an artist of the wartime generation penned mortifying stories that would become some of the most iconic antiwar literature in postwar Japan. Nakazawa Keiji's semi-autobiographical comic *Barefoot Gen* (1973–1987) offers a tragic narrative of the obliteration of Hiroshima, through an intimate family portrayal of day-to-day survival after the atomic bomb. Interweaving personal history and world history, it tells the horrific effects of the nuclear blast and radiation with unmistakable rage, agony, grief, and despair. The graphic details of the atomic blast are depicted to maximum effect: charred bodies; people with torn skin hanging from their faces and limbs, and eyeballs dangling from their sockets; maggots hatching on corpses; and heaps of burned dead bodies in the river and elsewhere all over the scorched flattened city. The tragic plot and logic are straightforward. Gen's father and sister died in the nuclear blast under the collapsed house, but Gen, his mother, and brothers narrowly escaped. His mother was pregnant and gave birth to Gen's sister on the day of the blast amid the wreckage. Thereafter, for ten volumes, Gen survives hunger and poverty, loss of his mother and sister, humiliation and fear, illness and discrimination, exploitation and crimes (Morris-Suzuki 2005, 160; Nakazawa 1994; Spiegelman 1994).

In Nakazawa's rendering, *Barefoot Gen* unequivocally indicts the war as absolute evil. Moreover, the war was brought on recklessly and unnecessarily by the Japanese military and the Imperial state that heartlessly and ineptly misled civilians to deathly destruction and suffering. In this perspective, all the suffering emanating from this atomic bomb could have been averted if only the war had been stopped earlier; if only the military state had the sense to accept the Potsdam Declaration sooner. *Barefoot Gen*'s message is clear: Authorities like the state, the military, the emperor, the American military, and American doctors are evil and cannot ever be trusted again (Dower 1999, 243–244 and 248–249). Thus, even as the story progresses from obliteration to rebuilding new life, it carries a bitter undertone, since nothing can really undo the permanent damage to people's lives and bodies, and the culprits are not brought to justice. Although the story ends when Gen is a preteen, readers can sense that the radiation disease that claimed his mother and sister, the last of his surviving biological family, may also eventually catch up with Gen himself.

Widely used in schools and easily accessible, *Barefoot Gen* is argu-ably the most influential and iconic antiwar literature to reach succes-sive postwar generations and shape popular consciousness about the horrendous consequences of militarism in the past four decades. It is a popular vehicle for intergenerational transmission of antiwar senti-ments, and many have attested to the psychological trauma of learning about Hiroshima in childhood first from *Barefoot Gen* (Ito 2006, 152). It is available in most school libraries, shown in peace education classes, broadcast in commercial television, and released in cinemas. It has been reprinted several times (1975, 1988, 1998, 2000, and 2001), has sold 10 million copies, and has been translated into 11 languages (Fukuma 2006, 29; Mainichi Shinbun 2009). It has been made into an animation film, live action features, a musical, and television broadcasts, the most recent of which was shown as a two-part live action story on prime time television in August 2007 and earned a high rating of 19.3% (Fuji Television 2007). As a social equivalent of Anne Frank's story that mobilizes empathy and pity, its reinforcement effect works over the generational cycle: People read *Barefoot Gen* in manga, then reencounter it later in anime, then again as an adult on TV, and then watch it with their own children. The generational transmission has now reached the point that grandparents report watching *Barefoot Gen* with their grandchildren (Fuji Television 2007). The significance of such vernacular tales in forging cultural trauma and promoting antiwar identity cannot be overestimated. The message is clear: We must take control of our own lives and have the strength to say no to war and nuclear weapons, so as to never become such victims again (Dower 1999; Nakazawa 1994).

One of the most important ingredients for *Barefoot Gen*'s endur-ing success is its ability to offer a clear alternative political identity in the father figure who serves as a spiritual backbone of the story, even though he dies at the beginning by the impact of the atomic blast, crushed excruciatingly under the roof of his house. Gen's principled father, the source of Gen's strength, was a down-to-earth, clear-thinking artist who opposed the war and saw the deception of the military and imperialist government for what it was. He was tortured by the police for expressing his misgivings. Nakazawa was five when his own father was tortured for being critical of the war, and this greatly influenced his political views.

This father is the antithesis of the common postwar excuse of the wartime generation that claimed "we were all deceived." Gen's father therefore represents the possibilities of courage to fight, resist authority, and oppose the war (Napier 2001, 168).

Although *Barefoot Gen* is influential in encouraging people to learn about the destructive power of nuclear weapons and the value of civic courage, it rarely takes a wider look at the victims of the entire war. No connection is made between the bomb and the 15 Year War that preceded the blast, even though Hiroshima was a military city (Yoshida 2006). As the primary response of the young audience who watch this horrendous inferno is shock and horror, they often seem too overwhelmed to even ask how the war came about, why the Americans did it, or why the Japanese military did not prevent it. Among those who watched the August 2007 television broadcast, the overwhelming response was "never again," but they were unable to say why or how (Fuji Television 2007). While the shock tends to induce a fear of victimization in the audience, they gain no insight from *Barefoot Gen* that much of invaded Asia welcomed the atomic bombs dropped on Japan at the time (Ōnuma 2007, 223) and little sense that the work is largely rejected by Korean audiences (Yamanaka 2006). For the most part, Gen's has become a tale of victims of a brutal war, extolling the theme of suffering that came at a very high price. For some, that suffering and price negates Pearl Harbor, or even the Japanese atrocities in Asia. For others, they give way to a moral superiority otherwise deficient in a defeat culture. The mobilization of victimhood succeeds in feeding into the larger cultural trauma of the fallen nation and emerges not as an anti-American sentiment but as an antimilitary sentiment.

Narrating the Perpetrators

Perpetrator narratives are the most complicated and controversial type of war memories because of implications for individual guilt, criminality, and moral and legal responsibility. Historians, journalists, novelists, and public intellectuals who have written about perpetrator narratives have therefore taken more risks of defamation and libel suits than those in the preceding memory projects. One of the most influential figures to shape the critical public discourse on the war in postwar Japan is historian Ienaga Saburō, a prolific scholar of war history and war responsibility (Ienaga 1978, 1985, 1986). He is the well-known plaintiff who waged the longest legal battle against the state over how to teach the tainted national past. Motivated by a sense of remorse at having been a passive bystander during the wartime regime, Ienaga devoted himself to asserting the right to publish perpetrator history in school textbooks, claiming that the state had specific culpability and responsibility for the mistaken judgments and decisions regarding its entry into and conduct during the war (Nozaki 2008, 154). His three lawsuits over the course of 32 years (1965–1997) claimed the right to freedom of speech and challenged the constitutionality of the Ministry of Education textbook certification system, which demanded extensive revisions for Ienaga's textbooks. Importantly, the speech that he sought to protect and keep alive in the public discourse by filing those lawsuits is the critical narrative of national history, especially the dark chapters of World War II, from the invasion of China, rapes and plunders in China, the biological experiment Unit 731, and the Nanjing massacre to the forced labor of colonial subjects and POWs and the Japanese civilian victimization in Okinawa (Nozaki and Inokuchi 2000, 116).

Ienaga's narrative of perpetrator history was unmistakably an indictment of the Japanese government. He represented the viewpoint that the war was an illegal war of aggression in violation of international conventions, driven by Japan's economic and political ambitions to control north China as it culminated in a 15-year conflict, starting from the Manchurian Incident in 1931, through the Marco Polo Bridge Incident in 1937, Pearl Harbor in 1941, the invasion of southeast Asia and the south Pacific, and ultimately ending in 1945. He does not spare the state:

> … the fifteen-year war was an unrighteous, reckless war begun with unjust and improper goals and means by the Japanese state, and … starting the war and refusing to end the war in a timely fashion were both illegal and improper acts of the state …" (Ienaga 2001, 148)[5]

In turn, the Ministry certification officials countered with statements like, "Japan was not unilaterally bad," "do not write bad things about Japan," and "eliminate the description that Japan caused suffering in China and Asia" (Nozaki 2008, 22). As these disputes over the texts were publicized over time, Ienaga's lawsuits raised public awareness about the perpetrators' side of the war and spurred citizens' movements and civic organizations to support his ongoing efforts. A favorable verdict for his second lawsuit emboldened other history textbook writers to increase their coverage of perpetrator history in the 1970s and 1980s. Furthermore, following a dispute with South Korea and China in 1982, the Cabinet Secretary of the Japanese government announced that Japan would promote a more diplomatically sensitive framework to depict war in history textbooks. By 1993, another court challenge was underway by an Okinawa educator Takashima Nobuyoshi to continue the pressure on the state certification system that sought to reduce perpetrator narratives in textbooks (Aramaki 2003, 233; Takashima 2003).

The political climate that Ienaga and other educators, intellectuals, and activists helped to open fostered a growing public awareness and vernacular understanding of Japan's colonial war on the continent. Along these lines, scores of popular history books, novels, documentaries, even manga cartoon history books for school libraries, and other cultural media developed robust narratives of Japanese perpetration in Asia during the colonization and war. For example, the 20-volume manga history of Japan published by Shūeisha, a premier publisher of children's books, has included accounts of the Nanjing Incident, atrocities, forced labor, and the biological warfare Unit 731 over many years (Matsuo 1998). Graphic artist Ishinomori Shotarō's 55-volume opus on Japanese history is also not shy about offering pages on Japanese oppression and aggression in China, Korea, Taiwan, Singapore, and elsewhere (Ishinomori 1999). As teachers, activists and the media routinely recounted and disseminated these stories, they exposed children to Japanese acts of perpetration more than in the past, thereby reproducing the cultural trauma of the war for the next generation.

Acts of public defiance and advocacy such as Ienaga's directly fuelled antimilitary and antistate sentiments, and also inspired peace movements, NGOs, and civic actions that sought a new collective identity based on ideas of peace, freedom, democracy, and rights of citizens (Nohira 2003; Yoshioka 2008). Journalists, novelists, and public intellectuals were crucial in shaping a critical public discourse and generating public awareness, though these trends have also sparked fierce disputes over the years. In 1972, journalist Honda Katsuichi wrote *Journey to China,* a widely-known chronicle of Japanese atrocities based on Chinese testimonies, around the time Japan resumed diplomatic relations with China in 1972 (Honda 1972). Bestselling novelist Morimura Seiichi wrote *Devil's Gluttony* about the Japanese biological warfare experiments in 1982, and the book sold a million copies within a year (Morimura 1983). However, such public reckoning with perpetrator history has also often been dogged with fierce rebuttals and libel suits by those who took issue. For example, the defamation suit against Ōe Kenzaburo, the Nobel winner whose *Okinawa Notes* in 1970 refers to the involvement of the Japanese military in the mass suicides of Okinawan civilians, ended only in 2008. Although the antagonisms surrounding these writings have been fierce—often involving questions about the authenticity of witness testimonies and validity of evidence that point to blame—the media storm highlighting them has kept the stories patently visible in the public discourse.

Elusive Closure in a Divided Society

In defeat cultures where heroes, victims, and perpetrators can be often made up of the same people, attempts to conceptualize them, to separate them as discrete groups of people, are always fraught with ambiguities, which in turn greatly complicate constructing and sharing national identity. The incongruent and discordant narratives of heroes, victims, and perpetrators and the ambiguous boundaries they embody shed much light on Japan's struggle to define collective identity today. This complicated entanglement of memory projects was set in motion by an inversion of the moral order imposed from above by the U.S. Occupation. Memories of war and defeat were superimposed on a foundation of guilt defined by the war crimes trials, condemnation of the Japanese military by the victors, and a constitution and social systems reconstructed to conform to Western democracy. These memories thereby came to be normalized in the national consciousness, but in disparate ways for different people. At a minimum, the three narratives converged in legitimating the sentiments of the "peace nation" embodied in Article 9 (the constitutional article that renounces the right to wage war and maintain military capabilities), and in an antimilitarism of the kind that is opposed to war, belligerence, and aggression. As a result, a "peace and antiwar" identity has served as an umbrella construct for the nation—for the political left, center, and right, from official discourse to kitchen talk, and across generations— and infused Japanese collective identity with antiwar ideals, working to present a face of Japan as a repentant pacifist nation. Beneath the surface, however, this peace has meant different things and entailed different moral categories and judgments about the past events to different people. Thus the trifurcated narratives of the fallen nation have often reignited conflict and controversy in the public discourse, which in turn, have kept the cultural trauma alive. As Neil Smelser notes, such contests are chronic and "never come to a point of consensus over meaning, appropriate affect and preferred coping strategy," and therefore there is no "completely official version of the collective trauma, but rather a continuing counterpoint of interested and opposing voices" (2004, 42, 49–50).

When people in a defeated nation face new questions of dying for the country, sacrificing for the country, or killing for the country, it is not surprising that they have to encounter their long-standing distrust for the military that had led them astray in the past. Thus different assumptions about heroes, victims, and perpetrators from the militarist past erupt to the surface in proxy political disputes. One example of such proxy political disputes is the Diet resolution of remorse that sought to institutionalize a definitive statement on war culpability at the fiftieth anniversary of the end of war in 1995, when anxieties about national standing in the world community became entangled with concerns about sullying the memory of those who heroically fought for the wrong war, and about legal liabilities. Another example is the revision of the Basic Law of Education that brought patriotism back to public school curricula in 2006 but which raised fears for some, and hope for others, that Japanese children may be induced to believe again that dying for the country was a worthy goal. When North Korea's missile launches and 9/11 set in motion the enactment of a series of new security legislation, the disputes were intertwined with fears of giving too much power to the Self Defense Force (SDF), as Japan's *de facto* military is known, and whether military leaders could ever again be trusted. After the Gulf War, when sending the SDF overseas for the first time to join the U.N. Peace Keeping Operations was disputed, the question of whether any Japanese soldier could harm another foreign national again was indisputably present. In the wake of these controversies, then, the state shifted its definition of pacifism from "love for peace" to the potentially more active "contribution for peace." These struggles and concerns were not merely tussles between political hawks and doves but also shook the core of antiwar national identity produced by the cultural trauma of defeat (Berger 1998; Katzenstein 1996; Koseki 2002; Oros 2008).

Although developing along different lines, and serving different— even contradictory—ends, the three memory projects are multiple pathways into the core postwar identity that espouses "never again" as the political and moral outcome of the war. Importantly, as long as Japan doesn't wage another war, there is no chance that it will ever have to experience another defeat. Hence, while divergences persist, antimilitarism and antiwar emerged as a significant common denominator in the trauma process that followed the fall of 1945.

Notes

1. Cited from editorials of August 15, 2002. "Heiwa na seiki o tsukuru kufū o: Shūsen kinenbi ni kangaeru (Creating a peaceful century: Reflections on commemorating the end of war)" (*Asahi Shinbun*); "Rekishi o sunao ni minaoshitai (Revisiting history honestly)" (*Yomiuri Shinbun*); "Genten wa kiyoku mazushiku yume ga atta (At the beginning, we were poor and pure, and we had a dream)" (*Mainichi Shinbun*); " 'Haisen' kara nanimo manabitoranai kunino higeki (The tragedy of a nation that learns nothing from 'defeat')" (*Nikkei Shinbun*); "'Chi' o ikashita saishuppatsu—Tsuginaru kokuminteki gōi o kangaeru (Making a prudent fresh start: Reflections on the next national consensus)" (*Sankei Shinbun*); "Shūsen kinenbi heiwaga nanika kangaeru hi

ni (Commemorating the end of war as a day to reflect on peace)" (*Okinawa Times*).

2. "Nihon yaburetari (Japan was defeated) " *Bungei Shunjū,* November 2005; Matsumoto, Ken'ichi. *Nihon no shippai: Daini no kaikoku to daitōa sensō (Japan's failure: The second opening and the Greater East Asia War).* Tokyo: Iwanami Shoten, 2006; Komuro, Naoki. *Nihon no haiin: Rekishiwa katsutameni manabu (Causes of Japan's defeat: Learning from history to win).* Tokyo: Kōdansha, 2001; Handō, Kazutoshi et al. *Ano sensō ni naze maketanoka (Why did we lose that war?).* Tokyo: Bungei Shunjū, 2006.

3. A well-known phrase used by the emperor in his radio broadcast to the nation on August 15, 1945.

4. Almost 5,700 men were prosecuted and over 4,400 indicted in Class B and C war crimes trials across East and Southeast Asia after the war. Seven were executed as Class A war criminals, and 920 were executed as Class B and C war criminals. See Dower 1999 and Fujita 1995.

5. Originally in "Jūgonen sensō ni yoru shi o dō kangaeru ka (Reflections on the war dead of the Fifteen Year War)," *Rekishi tokuhon* (expanded issue, March 1979); in *Ienaga Saburō shū (Ienaga Saburō collected works),* vol. 12, 260); cited and translated by Richard Minear in *Japan's Past, Japan's Future: One Historian's Odyssey.* Lanham, MD: Rowman and Littlefield, 148.

Works Cited

Akazawa, S. 2005. *Yasukuni jinja: Semegiau "senbotsusha tsuitō" no yukue (Yasukuni Shrine: The struggle over "mourning the war dead").* Tokyo: Iwanami Shoten.

Alexander, J. C. 2004a. Toward a Theory of Cultural Trauma. In *Cultural Trauma and Collective Identity,* ed. J. C. Alexander et al., 1–30. Berkeley: University of California Press.

———. 2004b. On the Social Construction of Moral Universals: The "Holocaust" from War Crime to Trauma Drama. In *Cultural Trauma and Collective Identity,* ed. J. C. Alexander et al., 196–263. Berkeley: University of California Press.

Alexander, J. C., R. Eyerman, B. Giesen, N. Smelser, and P. Sztompka, eds. 2004. *Cultural Trauma and Collective Identity.* Berkeley: University of California Press.

Aramaki, S. 2003. Jiyū, heiwa, minshushugi o motomete: Musubini kaete (In search of freedom, peace, and democracy: A conclusion). In *Ienaga Saburō no nokoshita mono hikitsugu mono (Ienaga Saburō's legacy and beyond),* eds. T. Ōta, H. Oyama, and K. Nagahara, 233–240. Tokyo: Nihon Hyōronsha.

Asahi Shinbun Shuzaihan. 2006. *Sensō sekinin to tsuitō: Rekishi to mukiau 1 (War responsibility and mourning: Confronting history 1).* Tokyo: Asahi Shinbunsha.

Berger, T. 1998. *Cultures of Antimilitarism: National Security in Germany and Japan.* Baltimore: Johns Hopkins University Press.

Dower, J. W. 1999. *Embracing Defeat: Japan in the Wake of World War II*. New York: W.W. Norton.

Dudden, A. 2008. *Troubled Apologies Among Japan, Korea, and the United States*. New York: Columbia University Press.

Eyerman, R. 2004. Cultural Trauma: Slavery and the Formation of African American Identity. In *Cultural Trauma and Collective Identity*, ed. J. C. Alexander et al., 60–111. Berkeley: University of California Press.

Fuji Television. 2007. Hadashi no Gen: Bangumi messeeji (Barefoot Gen: Program messages). Tokyo, at http://www.fujitv.co.jp/gen/message_yomu.html. Accessed January 28, 2008.

Fujita, H. 1995. *Sensō hanzai towa nanika (What are war crimes?)*. Tokyo: Iwanami Shoten.

Fujiwara, A. 2001. *Uejini shita eireitachi (The fallen heroes who starved to death)*. Tokyo: Aoki Shoten.

Fukuma, Y. 2006. Genbaku manga no mediashi (The media history of "atomic bomb manga comics"). In *'Hadashi no Gen' ga ita fūkei: Manga, sensō, kioku (The landscape of 'Barefoot Gen': Manga comics, war, and memory)*, eds. K. Yoshimura and Y. Fukuma, 10–58. Matsudo-shi: Azusa Shuppansha.

———. 2007. *Junkoku to hangyaku : "Tokkō" no katari no sengoshi (Martyrdom and resistance: A postwar history of the tales of suicide attack)*. Tokyo: Seikyūsha.

Giesen, B. 2004. *Triumph and Trauma*. Boulder: Paradigm Publishers.

Gluck, C. 1993. "The Past in the Present." In *Postwar Japan as History*, ed. A. Gordon, 64–95. Berkeley: University of California Press.

———. 2007. Operations of Memory: "Comfort Women" and the World. In *Ruptured Histories: War, Memory, and the Post-Cold War in Asia*, eds. S. M. Jager and R. Mitter. Cambridge: Harvard University Press.

Hashimoto, A. Forthcoming 2011. Divided Memories, Contested Histories: The Shifting Landscape in Japan. In *Cultures and Globalization: Heritage, Memory, Identity*, vol. 4, eds. H. Anheier and Y. R. Isar. London: Sage.

Hammond, E. 1997. Commemoration Controversies: The War, the Peace, and Democracy in Japan. In *Living With the Bomb: American and Japanese Cultural Conflicts in the Nuclear Age*, eds. L. Hein and M. Selden. Armonk, NY: M.E. Sharpe.

Hein, L., and M. Selden. 2000. The Lessons of War, Global Power, and Social Change. In *Censoring History: Citizenship and Memory in Japan, Germany, and the United States*, eds. L. Hein and M. Selden. Armonk, NY: M.E. Sharpe.

Honda, K. 1972. *Chūgoku no tabi (Journey to China)*. Tokyo: Asahi Shinbunsha.

Ienaga, S. 1978. *The Pacific War, 1931-1945: A Critical Perspective on Japan's Role in World War II*. New York: Pantheon Books.

———. 1985. *Sensō sekinin (War Responsibility)*. Tokyo: Iwanami Shoten.

———. 1986. *Taiheiyō sensō (The Pacific War, 1931-1945)*. Tokyo: Iwanami Shoten.

———. 2001. *Japan's Past, Japan's Future: One Historian's Odyssey*, trans. R. Minear. Lanham, MD: Rowman and Littlefield.

Igarashi, Y. 2000. *Bodies of Memory: Narratives of War in Postwar Japanese Culture, 1945–1970*. Princeton: Princeton University Press.

Iida, S. 2008. *Jigokuno nihonhei: Nyūginia sensen no shinsō (The Japanese soldier in hell: The true story of the New Guinean front)*. Tokyo: Shinchōsha.

Ishinomori, S. 1999. *Manga nihon no rekishi: Nitchū sensō—Taiheiyō sensō (History of Japan in manga comics: The Japan-China War—The Pacific War)*, vol. 53. Tokyo: Chūō Kōronsha.

Ito, Y. 2006. "Hadashi no Gen" no minzokushi: Gakkō o meguru manga taiken no shosō (A cultural history of "Barefoot Gen": The manga experience in schools). In *"Hadashi no Gen" ga ita fūkei: Manga, sensō, kioku (The landscape of "Barefoot Gen": Manga comics, war, and memory)*, eds. K. Yoshimura and Y. Fukuma, 147–181. Matsudo-shi: Azusa Shuppansha.

Katzenstein, P. J. 1996. *Cultural Norms and National Security: Police and Military in Postwar Japan*. Ithaca: Cornell University Press.

Koseki, S. 2002. *"Heiwa kokka" Nihon no saikentō ("Peace nation" Japan reconsidered)*. Tokyo: Iwanami Shoten.

Macleod, J. 2008. *Defeat and Memory: Cultural Histories of Military Defeat in the Modern Era*. New York: Palgrave Macmillan.

Mainichi Shinbun. 2009. Mangaka "Hadashi no Gen" Nakazawa Hiroshi san Intai (Manga artist Nakazawa Hiroshi of "Barefoot Gen" retires), at http://mainichi.jp/select/today/news/20090916k0000m040041000c.html?link_id=RTH05. Accessed September 15, 2010.

Makita, T. 2000. Nihonjin no sensō to heiwa kan: Sono jizoku to fūka (Japanese attitudes toward war and peace: continuity and change). *Hōsō Kenkyū to Chōsa (Journal of Broadcasting Research)* 50: 2–19.

Matsuo, T. 1998. *Gakushū manga nihon no rekishi: Ajia Taiheiyō sensō (Study manga comic history of Japan: The Asia-Pacific War)*, vol. 18. Tokyo: Shūeisha.

Morimura, S. 1981. *Akuma no hōshoku: "Kantōgun saikinsen butai" kyōfu no zenbō (The devil's gluttony: The fearsome truth of the "Kwangtung army's biological warfare unit")*. Tokyo: Kōbunsha.

Morris-Suzuki, T. 2005. *The Past within Us: Media, Memory, History*. London: Verso.

Mosse, G. L. 1990. *Fallen Soldiers: Reshaping the Memory of the World Wars*. New York: Oxford University Press.

Nakazawa, K. 1982. *Hadashi no Gen (Barefoot Gen)*. Tokyo: Chōbunsha.

———. 1994. *"Hadashi no Gen" jiden ("Barefoot Gen" Autobiography)*. Tokyo: Kyōikushiryō Shuppankai.

Napier, S. 2001. *Anime from Akira to Princess Mononoke: Experiencing Contemporary Japanese Animation*. New York: Palgrave.

Nohira, S. 2003. Piisubōto no funatabi o tōshite (On the journey aboard Peace Boat). In *Ienaga Saburō no nokoshita mono hikitsugu mono (Ienaga Saburō's legacy and beyond)*, eds. T. Ōta, H. Oyama, and K. Nagahara, 229–231. Tokyo: Nihon Hyōronsha.

Nozaki, Y. 2008. *War Memory, Nationalism and Education in Post-war Japan, 1945–2007: The Japanese History Textbook Controversy and Ienaga Saburo's Court Challenges*. London and New York: Routledge.

Nozaki, Y., and H. Inokuchi. 2000. Japanese Education, Nationalism, and Ienaga Saburo's Textbook Lawsuits. In *Censoring History: Citizenship and Memory in Japan, Germany, and the United States*, eds. L. Hein and M. Selden, 96–126. Armonk, NY: M.E. Sharpe.

Ōe, K. 1970. *Okinawa nōto (Okinawa notes)*. Tokyo: Iwanami Shoten.

Ōnuma, Y. 2007. *Tokyo saiban, sensō sekinin, sengo sekinin (The Tokyo trial, war responsibility, and postwar responsibility)*. Tokyo: Tōshindō.

Oros, A. 2008. *Normalizing Japan: Politics, Identity, and the Evolution of Security Practice*. Stanford: Stanford University Press.

Orr, J. J. 2001. *The Victim as Hero: Ideologies of Peace and National Identity in Postwar Japan*. Honolulu: University of Hawaii Press.

Saaler, S. 2005. *Politics, Memory and Public Opinion: The History Textbook Controversy and Japanese Society*. Munich: Iudicium Verlag.

Sato, T. 2002. Kōfuku kinenbi kara shūsen kinenbi e: Kioku no media ibento (From commemorating defeat to commemorating end of war: The memory of media events). In *Sengo nihon no media ibento 1945–1960 (Media events in postwar Japan 1945–1960)*, ed. T. Tsuganesawa, 71–94. Kyoto: Sekai Shisōsha.

———. 2005. *Hachigatsu jūgonichi no shinwa: Shūsen kinenbi no mediagaku (The myth of August 15th: Media research on war commemorations)*. Tokyo: Chikuma Shobō.

Schivelbusch, W. 2003. *The Culture of Defeat: On National Trauma, Mourning, and Recovery*. New York: Metropolitan Books.

Seaton, P. A. 2007. *Japan's Contested War Memories: The "Memory Rifts" in Historical Consciousness of World War II*. London and New York: Routledge.

Seraphim, F. 2006. *War Memory and Social Politics in Japan, 1945–2005*. Cambridge: Harvard University Press, Asia Center.

Smelser, N. J. 2004. Psychological Trauma and Cultural Trauma. In *Cultural Trauma and Collective Identity*, eds. J. C. Alexander et al., 31–59. Berkeley: University of California Press.

Smith, P. 2005. *Why War?: The Cultural Logic of Iraq, the Gulf War, and Suez*. Chicago: University of Chicago Press.

Spiegelman, A. 1994. Foreword: Comics after the Bomb. *Barefoot Gen 4: Out of the Ashes (A Cartoon Story of Hiroshima)*, K. Nakazawa, v–viii. Philadelphia: New Society Publishers.

Takahashi, T. 2003. *Nihonjin no kachikan: Sekai rankingu (Japanese attitudes: World rankings)*. Tokyo: Chūōkōronshinsha.

———. 2005. *Kokka to gisei (The nation-state and sacrifice)*. Tokyo: NHK Books.

Takashima, N. 2003. Ienaga kyōkasho saiban o hikitsugu Takashima kyōkasho saiban (Ienaga textbook trials are passed on to Takashima textbook trials). In *Ienaga Saburō no nokoshita mono hikitsugu mono (Ienaga Saburō's legacy and beyond)*, eds. T. Ōta, H. Oyama, and K. Nagahara, 122–128. Tokyo: Nihon Hyōronsha.

Weinberg, G. L. 2005. *A World at Arms: A Global History of World War II*, 2nd ed. New York: Cambridge University Press.

Yamada, A. 2005. Heishi tachi no ni'chū sensō (The soldiers' perspectives on the Japan-China War). In *Iwanami kōza Ajia-taiheiyō sensō: Senjō no shosō (Iwanami lectures on the Asia-Pacific War: The Battlefront)*, ed. A. Kurasawa et al., 33–58. Tokyo: Iwanami Shoten.

Yamanaka, C. 2006. Yomare enai "taiken," ekkyō dekinai "kioku": Kankoku ni okeru "Hadashi no Gen" no juyō o megutte (Unreadable "experience" and uncrossable "memory": The demand for "Barefoot Gen" in South Korea). In *"Hadashi no Gen" ga ita fūkei: Manga, sensō, kioku (The landscape of "Barefoot Gen": Manga comics, war, and memory)*, eds. K. Yoshimura and Y. Fukuma, 211–245. Matsudo-shi: Azusa Shuppansha.

Yomiuri Shinbun. 2006. *Kenshō: Sensō sekinin I (Verification: War responsibility I)*. Tokyo: Chūōkōronshinsha.

Yoshida, K. 2006. "Hadashi no Gen" o yomitoku shiten: Higai to kagai no puroburematiiku (Reading "Barefoot Gen": The victim-perpetrator problematique). In *"Hadashi no Gen" ga ita fūkei: Manga, sensō, kioku (The landscape of "Barefoot Gen": Manga comics, war, and memory)*, eds. K. Yoshimura and Y. Fukuma, 294–298. Matsudo City: Azusa Shuppansha.

Yoshida, M. 1985. *Requiem for Battleship Yamato*, trans. R. Minear. Seattle: University of Washington Press.

———. 1986. Sanka no sedai (The perished generation). In *Yoshida Mitsuru chosaku shū: gekan (Yoshida Mitsuru collected works, volume 2)*, 32–45. Tokyo: Bungei Shunjū.

———. 2003. Ichi heishi no sekinin (A soldier's responsibility). In *Senkan Yamato (Battleship Yamato)*, 166–184. Tokyo: Kadokawa Shoten.

Yoshioka, T. 2008. Experience, Action, and the Floating Peace Village. In *Another Japan is Possible: New Social Movements and Global Citizenship Education*, ed. J. Chan, 317–322. Stanford: Stanford University Press.

Yui, D. 2005. Sekai sensō no nakano ajia-Taiheiyō sensō (The Asia-Pacific War in the context of the world war). In *Ajia-taiheiyō sensō 1: Naze, ima ajia-taiheiyō sensō ka (Asia-Pacific War 1: Why now Asia-Pacific War)*, ed. R. Narita et al., 235–274. Tokyo: Iwanami Shoten.

3

Revolutionary Trauma and Representation of the War

The Case of China in Mao's Era

Rui Gao

The millions of Chinese people who had the misfortune of living through the War of Resistance Against Japan (hereafter "the War") experienced nearly unbearable trauma and pain. From 1937 to 1945, during the eight years of the War, China lost three million lives in combat, and civilian casualties were estimated to be about twenty million.[1] The heinous nature of the war atrocities committed by the invading army must have left indelible marks on the consciousness of millions of war victims. Indeed, the notorious Nanjing Massacre, the crimes of Unit 731, and the conscription of "comfort women" are but three particularly atrocious cases of trauma inflicted by the Japanese army. Such vivid and massively shared suffering and injustice, however, remained ultimately private and individual. For many years after the building of the People's Republic of

China (PRC), this suffering seldom found its way into the public sphere of expression.[2]

Why was this the case? Indeed, few scholars have questioned the absence of public representations of this massive suffering.[3] Mostly, the peculiar absence of publicly acknowledged traumatic memories was regarded as the default "suppression" stage that preceded what many assumed to be a powerful resurgence of "new remembrance" in the post-Mao era (Coble 2007; Cohen 2003; Mitter 2003; Waldron 1996; etc.). This lacuna in interest is revealing in itself, for it points out both the elusive nature of the problem and a lack of efficacious theoretical tools to frame the question. It is more difficult to study, and even to identify, a lack of public representation than its presence. Before the question of why no shared trauma narrative developed can be addressed, the question of "what?" needs to be adequately defined.

Scholars of this era in Chinese history seek to explain the nature of remembering as well as amnesia within a framework of geopolitics in the East-Asian area, focusing on the Sino-Japanese relationship, the political and military tension between mainland China and Taiwan, and the domestic ideological needs for legitimacy-building within the PRC. The importance of political exigencies may be a significant factor in collective memory and collective silence or forgetting, but studying the instrumental actions of social actors and the political framework alone can hardly capture the complexity of the issue. In particular, it cannot adequately explain why traumatic memories of the War, which could have potently strengthened the solidarity of the nation, did not play a central role in the grand narrative of Mao's new republic.

A chief goal of this chapter is to delve into this curious phenomenon and seek to explain it from a cultural sociological point of view. The theory of cultural trauma will help define the phenomenon and articulate what needs to be explained. I argue that the horrendous misery and mass destruction brought by the War were never translated into a collective trauma for the newly built PRC. In other words, a cultural trauma process never took place. Thus what I seek to explain is the absence of the collective trauma of the War in those years.

In addition, trauma theory illuminates powerfully the question of "why?", as it brings to the fore the explanatory autonomy of culture and sheds light on the relationship between various cultural structures in the process of trauma formation. The absence of the trauma of the War should be understood not merely as a consequence of political necessity; it should be contextualized and comprehended within the web of meanings woven by powerful cultural structures that predominated in the public sphere at the time. To a certain degree, particularly dominant and potent cultural structures could powerfully influence the formation of other contemporaneous cultural structures; the dominant one may enable other cultural structures when their logic complies with its own but may constrain or preempt them when their innate rationale presents a conflict. In fact, I argue in this chapter that the case of the War trauma seems to fit with the constraining scenario, as the War trauma narrative was blocked and inhibited by the universal cultural trauma of class struggle that formed in Mao's China.

My tasks in this chapter are therefore twofold. First, I trace in Mao's era the successful construction of a cultural trauma that sought to form a new collectivity. I argue that the intense trauma drama of class struggle occupied the core of this era's cultural trauma. That is, perpetrators in the old society epitomized an absolutely evil class enemy. Further, the unspeakable suffering of the proletarian victims was represented symbolically and emotionally as suffering shared by a broad group of people, united regardless of national boundaries in a new universal class collectivity.

My second task is to examine how the experience of the War fits, or, rather, does not fit with this grand narrative of class trauma. Tracing representation of the War in the public sphere around the time, I argue that the emergence of the War as a collective trauma was effectively inhibited by the trauma of class struggle. More specifically, I argue that as class trauma gathered momentum in the newly built republic, it became a rhetorical juggernaut that left little symbolic space for alternative trauma claims to emerge. When the fundamental conflict of the War threatened to contradict the intrinsic logic of class trauma, the compelling force of the narrative of class conflict dictated that the narrative of the War bend to it. The narrative of class conflict blurred the national distinctions (Japanese/Chinese, us/them, perpetrator/victim) that would be crucial to constructing a collective trauma of the War.

The Symbolic Birth of the New Nation and Its Traumatic Past

As communities of memories, modern nations, from the moment of their birth, were defined by collective memories, on which they built their collective identities and national grouping. Since memories of oppression and suffering have even more bonding potential than memories of a glorious past (Schwartz 1995, 267), it is not surprising to find that the founding myth of a nation often consists of a grand narrative built on the cornerstone of a collective trauma in which "members of a collectivity feel they have been subjected to a horrendous event that leaves indelible marks upon their group consciousness" (Alexander et al. 2004, 1).

This seemed to be exactly the case of the founding of the People's Republic of China. In an opening speech given immediately before the building of the PRC, Chairman Mao Tse-tung drafted an authoritative narrative that recounted the new nation's origins and where it was destined to go. The founding myth was characterized by an ascending narrative that endowed the symbolic birth of the new nation with a sense of millennial salvation, which, it explicitly pointed out, must be understood as a radical rectification of what had gone horribly wrong in the past. In this speech, Mao powerfully argued that it was only after a long and "unyielding struggle" that the nation was redeemed from the fate of being subjected to over a century of "insult and humiliation" (Mao 1949, 4).[4] When Mao solemnly claimed that the Chinese people must overthrow the enemies "or be oppressed and slaughtered by them, either one or the other, there is no other choice" (Mao 1949, 3), he further coded the birth of the nation as a battle of life and death for the Chinese people. The building of the new state, in other words, was the last chance for the nation to be saved from its horrendous fate.

The elements of "birth trauma" in Mao's speech—namely, the positive construction of a sacred new that would become possible only after a transcendental leap from the profane old—reverberated everywhere in the public discursive field of post-revolutionary China. While both the old and new played important roles in shaping the emergent collective identity, ultimately the evil old society assumed disproportionately greater symbolic significance. It was established clearly as the very "polluting" signifier that denoted all that had gone wrong before 1949.[5]

A quick glance at contents of school textbooks of the time, for instance, could yield an inexhaustible list of how "old society" was fervently painted with a profane brush: the old society seldom, if ever, appeared as a single phrase without being prefixed by a series of virulent derogatory adjectives such as *Wan E* (characterized by tens of thousands of evil) and *Hei An* (dark and sinister). The old society was perennially portrayed as a hellish "jungle" where, as one author claimed, the only possible option left for human beings was to "exploit and subjugate each other" (Editorial Division for Chinese Course, People's Education Press 1960, Book 5, 17).[6] The pain suffered by ordinary people under the stifling oppression was crystallized in a series of speech genres which evoked macabre visual images of agony, such as *Shui Shen Huo Re* (being constantly drowned in the depth of the water, and burned in heat of fire) (Alexander and Gao 2007). To further expose the horrendous nature of the evilness, it was claimed that cannibalism characterized the entire history of the old society, or "eat people," as the paranoid protagonist in one of the most widely read short stories in modern China concluded (Lu 1951 [1918]).[7] In fact, the signifier "the old society" assumed such a sacred-evil status that it started to possess the ability to pollute by means of mere association, as editors for music textbook who adapted folk songs from the old society into the course had to apologetically justify their choice by summoning up the sacredness of the folk culture of proletarian people.[8]

With the past being represented as a period so traumatic that it was capable of consuming human flesh and engulfing anything in its symbolic vicinity, the suffering that characterized the birth trauma of the nation seemed to have been fully established. However, it would soon become evident that the trauma involved in the past was more than a simple birth trauma that served merely to precede a better and brighter future. Rather, class conflict was a trauma that demanded perpetual return and identification, a drama that was constantly reproduced and reenacted at every basic social units of Maoist China.

The Genre of "Remembering the Bitterness" and the Cultural Trauma of Class Struggle

The predicament and suffering people used to have in the past would have remained abstract had there been no symbolic identification to bridge the temporal and psychological gap between the new and the old eras. Such symbolic extension and emotional identification was success-fully achieved among the public in Mao's China because the traumatic representation of the past was extensively and consistently dramatized in various types of cultural products. In fact, a new literary genre was created for such a purpose, which was known as *Yi Ku Si Tian,* literally, "appreciating the sweetness of today by remembering the bitterness of the past" (hereafter "remembering the bitterness" genre).

Serving as a transcendental mechanism that bridged the happy present with the traumatic past, the genre was designed specifically to facilitate the symbolic identification of a wider public with victims in the old, bad society. Works of this genre therefore usually adopted the form of memoirs, biography, or autobiography, in which the distressful life story of a specific victim was poignantly re-created; this lent much authentic-ity and truthfulness to the genre. A prototype of this genre can be found in the lyric of a song titled "Mum's Story." Selected in music textbooks for elementary school students, the melodious song is still popular with young kids of today. The song starts with a brief portrayal of the blissful new life and then goes on with a reconstruction of the traumatic past in which Mum, a landless and impoverished peasant, had suffered unspeakable misery at the hands of avaricious landlords:

> At that time, Mum was landless and all she had was her hands and labor,
> Toiling in the field of the landlord, the only food she could get was wild herbs and husks,
> The blizzard of harsh winter howling like wolves, mum had barely anything on except for her pieces of rug,
> She fainted at the side of the road out of hunger and coldness, being on her way to sew a fur robe for the landlord's wife.

It is not hard to notice that the painful experience suffered in the old society was successfully personalized here because the victim took the image of one's most intimate family member. This undoubtedly made a psychological identification much easier. But more than anything else, what we cannot miss in these lyrics is that the major conflict was explicitly developed along a class line where the victim, the mother, represented the impoverished proletarian class, and the perpetrator, the landlord, obviously served as a metonymy for all exploitative classes. This highlighted the fact that the profanity of the old society was principally constructed via the dramatic struggle between class antagonists and was thereby inseparably coupled with the trauma of class struggle. In fact, the following discussion would testify that "remembering the bitterness" genre played a crucial role in building the trauma drama of class struggle, which, in turn, became the core component in the overall traumatic representation of the past.

With two of the essential elements in trauma claim thus explicitly defined, the victims being the proletarian people and the perpetrators exploitative classes,[9] the unspeakable torment and grief that had been the ubiquitous motif in public discourse was thus shed in a different light. The trauma of the old society was no longer simply a birth trauma that could be and had been once and forever transcended, thoroughly resolved, or happily dismissed; instead, it was a perpetual pain that must be re-created and re-experienced in current time. Indeed, it seemed that only through a constant cycle of reconstruction and remembering of the darkness of the old evils could the new collectivity come into being. As the protagonist in another illuminating example, after recounting his miserable suffering in the past to his daughter, exclaimed at the end, "What a society that was! What a miserable life! We must inscribe them line by line upon our heart! Even when we are one-hundred years old, when we are enjoying a happiness that is equivalent to paradise, we must not let these marks erode!" (Editorial Division for Chinese Course, People's Education Press 1964, Book 4, 83).[10]

The perpetual return to a traumatic past takes on a universal dimension when one takes into account the wider community of suffering that went beyond national borders, as identified and facilitated by the genre of "remembering the bitterness." In fact, one major group of articles in this genre, as demonstrated by articles selected into Chinese textbooks for junior high school in the 1950s, were dedicated to depicting wretched life suffered by proletarian people in other countries at the hands of their similarly ruthless exploitative class. The public was constantly reminded that two-thirds of the world proletarian people were still "living the bitterness" day by day. This extended and reinforced the trauma claim to a universal community. Through such an emphasis on ubiquity, the shared bitterness became the expanded boundary of solidarity, building a broad class identity that was deeply entrenched in internationalism; as proletarian people of different nations united by a sacred universal victimhood, the world and its conflict was simplified into an unbridgeable demarcation along the horizontal line of class chasm, where any other social differentiation or conflict—including conflict of nation against nation as in the War—ought to be and could be overlooked and transcended.

Four Genealogies, the Deepening of the Nature of Suffering, and the Building of the Sacred Evil of Class Enemy

By the beginning of 1960s, the genre of "remembering the bitterness" had surged with such momentum that, in the *General Catalogue of Publication* compiled by the central government, there appeared a new column named "Four Genealogies," namely, genealogies of factories, of the People's Liberation Army, of people's communes, and of villages, which were exclusively composed of "bitterness" works published nationwide. The choice of the new term, "genealogy," conveyed a significant message; while having a genealogy used to be "the privilege of reactionary ruling class," as an editor explained in the prologue of one representative book series, "under the leadership of CCP, we, the revolutionary people are endowed with the privilege ... to write genealogy of proletarians" (Editorial Division for *Red Genealogy*, Xinhua Daily Press 1964 vol. 1, 1; vol. 2, 2). The new terminology was thus chosen purposefully to reinforce the class boundary of bitterness works, and thereby to further intensify the focus on class struggle.

Reading through stories with the label of "genealogy," it is not hard to notice that, while they shared with other "remembering the bitterness" works the endeavor to reach out for breadth of audience and for creating a symbolic collectivity, they distinguished themselves by an acutely heightened fixation on efforts to deepen the evilness of the perpetrators, to make the wound on the collectivity more painful and the scar on the memory more indelible. Indeed, in comparison with other bitterness works, genealogies seemed much more articulate and intent on constructing a drastically tragic trauma drama for the proletarian collectivity, a process that entailed two building blocks.

The first one was to showcase the incredibly broad extent and the tremendous volume of the sufferings of the people. This was successfully achieved with the large-scale and prominent publication of stories and memoirs under the column of genealogy in the 1960s.[11] All of these stories seemed to adopt the same framework of plot and narrative development, and their protagonists represented people from all walks of life. In the prologues, epilogues, or editors' words of genealogy publications, all editors seemed to be focused on building the universality of the anguish and afflictions experienced by proletarian class in its entirety. They would not only justify the production of their own collections by emphasizing how "class grievances are just endless to speak" (Editorial Division for *Red Genealogy*, Xinhua Daily Press 1965a, 40) but also apologize for being able to present only such a tiny part of all "emblematic cases." Indeed, the most frequently quoted Chinese idioms in these texts was perhaps the term, *Qing Zhu Nan Shu*, literally meaning that "(the horrendous agonies inflicted on us) were so tremendous and so profound, that even if all the bamboos (an ancient Chinese substitute for paper) in the world were exhausted, we still could not finish writing them." The overwhelming amount of publicity given to the tragic experiences of poor people in the old society not only magnified the sufferings of individuals and increased the enormity of the evil doings of the perpetrators but also elevated traumas that would have remained in the privacy of personal memories onto a public sphere, so that the pain and agony of a worker or a peasant became the sufferings of an entire collectivity.

The second building block involved the heightened weighting of all symbolic codes and the deepening of the emotional involvements of the audience. Browsing over the titles of genealogy works from 1960 to 1965, one would be struck by how dramatically gory and sentimental language had been used to present a general image that was tinted with violence and blood. Take the collection titled *The Red Genealogy* as a revealing example. The titles, or subtitles, of the memoirs in this collection, echoing the general trend, were full of words and expressions that were capable of reenacting grisly visual images that would heighten the level of people's alertness and emotional response. In one article titled "The Surge of Indignation Avenged the Feud of the Fishers' Family," for instance, the first section was subtitled "The Yangtse River was a River of Blood and Tears" (Editorial Division for *Red Genealogy,* Xinhua Daily Press 1964, vol. 1, 35). In another article titled "The Killing Ground of the Imperialists" (Editorial Division for *Red Genealogy,* Xinhua Daily Press 1965b, 21), the title of a section read "Before the Liberation, A Drop of Milk Was Produced with a Drop of Blood of the Workers." The extensive use of words like "feud," "hatred," "blood," "tears," and "killing" alerted readers that what awaited them in these stories were not simply some ordinary offense or usual incidents of oppression, but tragedies of greater consequence, situations where people's blood was spilled.

In fact, just as these titles indicate, all genealogy stories aimed to show "a debt of blood that went as deep as the ocean," a collective trauma of the proletarian people, who, according to these stories, had not only been oppressed, starved, tortured, persecuted, humiliated, trampled on, and relentlessly exploited but also murdered, massacred, and carnally destroyed. It seems to be the rule that in every genealogy story there must be at least one victim whose life was deprived by various evil perpetrators. One very representative piece came from the memoir of a nurse, titled "From a Slave to a Fighter in White Dress" (Editorial Division for *Red Genealogy,* Xinhua Daily Press 1964, vol. 2). In the memoir, she recalled the tragic fate that befell many of her young female colleagues before 1949: one was raped by a high-ranking government official; one was forced to marry a rich businessman as his concubine; another committed suicide soon after being sold to a brothel by her rogue husband. In case this was not adequate to make things traumatic, she continued to expose more horrendous details she witnessed in medical practice. According to her story, hospitals in the old society would deliberately admit poor patients who could not afford the expenses for the secret purpose of medical experiments, and many of these poor people were killed during the process of being treated (93).

Obviously, "death" and "blood" functioned as the transcendental mechanism through which common sad stories about how good people suffer were elevated to a more dramatic level where innocent and sacred people were being slaughtered. Through this transcendental mechanism, the nature of the trauma was endowed with a grave symbolic weight, and such deepened weighting of perpetration was perfectly matched by the portrayal of perpetrators who took proportionally dreadful forms in various contexts. Many times, the perpetrators were compared to marauding and cannibal predators. To expose the equally savage nature of all oppressors, for example, it was rhetorically asked in one article "can you find a tiger in the world that does not eat people?" (Editorial Division for *Red Genealogy,* Xinhua Daily Press 1964, vol. 1, 67). In another memoir, the author compared the Kuomintang reactionaries to "beasts that eat human fleshes without even spitting out the bones" (Editorial Division for *Red Genealogy,* Xinhua Daily Press 1964, vol. 2, 24). Yet, it seemed that even the most predatory beasts could not hold up to comparison with the evilness of the exploitative classes. Therefore, more widely adopted than the figuration of animals was the comparison of class enemies to the ultimate embodiment of cruelty in traditional Chinese culture. One most frequently employed symbol was *Yao Mo,* the Chinese word for "devils" and "fiends," as shown by a subtitle in one article, "The Reactionary Forces Are a Group of Devils and Fiends Who Stank with the Odor of Blood" (38). Another group of popular symbols could be found in the nicknames that local peasants attributed to rapacious landlords. One particularly devilish landlord in a village was called "*Yan Luo* in human world" (Editorial Division for *Red Genealogy,* Xinhua Daily Press 1964, vol. 1, 67), meaning the god of Yama, or the god in Chinese folklore who was in charge of hell and was famous for taking pleasure in inflicting pain upon people. *Ba Pi,* which literally means the "person who strips people's skin," is another most frequently employed metonymy typically reserved for bad landlords who are notoriously rapacious and exploitative.

Speaking the Bitterness and the Trauma Drama of Class Struggle

The "remembering the bitterness" genre, with the surge of genealogy stories as its climax, offered a very efficient narrative mechanism through which the cultural trauma of class struggle was successfully built in Mao's China. By huge-scale distribution, witness-perspective storytelling and dramatically heightened weighting of the symbolic codes attributed to the nature of sufferings and the perpetrators, such narrative construction successfully re-created a universally shared experience of class victimhood. What complemented such narrative construction and consummated the success of the trauma drama was the ubiquitous performative mechanism where the drama was not only written and read but also performed and recited by real people on a daily basis.

Since the early 1950s, various nationwide campaigns were carried out consecutively that not only necessitated but also facilitated struggle meetings and other types of rituals to be enacted at all levels up from the local communities.[12] Among these rituals, "speaking the bitterness" was perhaps the most universally adopted and exerted the most profound impact on people, as it offered an efficient mechanism where the drama could be literally put on show and the bitterness reenacted on a stage. In other words, "speaking the bitterness" was to certain extent the performative embodiment of "remembering the bitterness;" only that it was much more compelling as it rose beyond cognitive argument and demanded the acute physical presence, emotional involvement, and performative action of the audience.

To observe how the ritual works and to understand its powerful impact on participants, we now turn to works that actually record the proceedings of such a ritual, a text titled "Struggling Han Laoliu," found in a Chinese textbook for junior high students in the 1960s (Editorial Division for Chinese Course, People's Education Press 1964, Book 3).[13]

What became salient from the very beginning was the absolute coding and weighting of the chief antagonist, the target of the struggle, landlord Han. It was described that even before the ritual began, women and kids had started to sing a folk *Yang Ge* song that they improvised on the spot. The lyrics go like this: "Thousands of years of hatred, and tens of thousands of years of scores, can only be cleared when the Communist Party comes! Han Laoliu, Han Laoliu, people today will cut you to pieces!" The rancorous sense of animosity illustrated here made it lucid that the evilness of the landlord had been weighted to such a level that he deserved to be killed in a most relentless way.

When the meeting began, the landlord was brought to the center of the courtyard where a certain kind of stage was set for the struggle, and one by one, people who felt that they had been wronged, oppressed, or persecuted by the landlord came up to the stage to give a public testimony to the unforgivable sins of the evildoer. The ritual started as the first figure, a young man named Yang San, stepped onto the central stage. He testified that Han had once attempted to force him working as a slave laborer for the Japanese colonizers and when he refused and ran away, Han retaliated by sending his mother into prison, where she eventually died. "'I want to take revenge for my mum today!' as Yang San bellowed with anger … people around all cried out, 'Let's beat him to death!' and started to push forwards with sticks to the center of the courtyard. … Their chorus," the text went on, was like "the thunder of spring roaring in the sky" (61).

The text shows that the ritual of speaking bitterness was also a production of trauma drama, where the tragedy that victims had to suffer individually and privately was dramatized on the stage and publicized to an audience who shared with victims their pain and hatred toward the common foe. If the bitter story told by each victim comprised one independent act of the drama, the momentum of each act would accumulate and eventually reach a climax when a collective effervescence was achieved and a stronger solidarity created among the community. Such a dramatic process could be found in the final act of the struggle described in the chapter.

When the last bitterness speaker finished her story by yelling "Give me back my son!" the text described that "men and women all pushed forwards, crying that they want their sons, husbands, fathers, brothers back. And the sounds of weeping, crying, beating and cursing all mixed together." Indeed, the scene was so intense and moving that Xiao Wang, a young member of the land reform team who came from outside the village, "kept wiping his tears with the back of his hand" (63).

It is interesting to note that at this moment, when Xiao Wang emotionally identified with the victims of the village, readers of the chapter would also have relived the trauma drama that occurred in the all-evil old society that they may or may not have experienced personally. So what we observed here was a dual process that paralleled two mechanisms working at two distinct levels: one on the micro level of the local communities, where rituals, physical presence, and intensified emotions produced a concrete and tangible collective effervescence that bonded individuals together into a collectivity; and the other on the macro level of the wider "imagined community," where the powerful textual re-creation of a common trauma produced widely spread symbolic identification and emotional extension among readers who were tightly united by both the past anguish that they believed they had shared, and the new proletarian class identity that emerged from the collective trauma.

What has been demonstrated up to this point is that the national collectivity of new China was determinedly shaped by a powerfully established cultural trauma of class struggle. Via cultural structures such as the "remembering the bitterness" genre, and particularly the broad distribution and popularity of genealogy stories, the trauma was personalized and dramatized extensively and consistently in various cultural products. The textual re-creation of a shared trauma was also performed and embodied by rituals as struggle meetings that exponentially add to the force of impact. Through a constant reproduction of the trauma drama in texts and in rituals, the class enemies were firmly crucified as an absolute evil, whose only befitting fate was to be perpetually struggled and condemned, and the bitterness that characterizes the sufferings of poor people in the traumatic past was being consciously revisited and relived by a broad public, which was continually traumatized in class struggle and all too willing to identify with the victimized proletarian brothers and forge a class solidarity that also served as the very foundation of the new national collectivity.

The question now turns to the relationship between such a powerfully built cultural trauma and representation of the War around the time. Indeed, how had the War been narrated and memorized within a cultural context where class trauma predominates with such compelling force? It is my argument in the following sections that the trauma of class struggle contributed to the absence of the collective trauma of the War through a process of inhibition that involves two cultural and symbolic dimensions. First, as I demonstrate in previous sections, the successful construction of class trauma has been achieved with such sweeping scale and engrossing depth that, to the extent that the trauma grew to be the very symbolic anchor around which social meanings of the new Chinese nation were organized, the likelihood of the emergence of other trauma claims is largely determined by their relation to the central structure of class conflict and trauma, for other trauma constructions would inevitably compete for symbolic resources and media venues. Those trauma claims that are not symbolically aligned with class trauma, like the War, which entails a different and conflicting central binary of victim and perpetrator and nature of suffering, would be left with little symbolic space and their narratives would be significantly colonized.

Second, because the logic of class trauma dictates that the world be structured along a horizontal boundary of class and collective identity that transcends other borders posed by race, ethnicity, and nation, neither the perpetrator nor the victim group of the War are allowed to be identified as legitimate collectives or categories, as both are polluted by an awkward and dangerous hybrid between the sacred and the profane. The potential Japanese perpetrators are inconveniently composed of poor proletarian brothers, and the potential Chinese victim category unfortunately includes members of the exploitative class. In other words, because the fundamental conflict of the War, basically defined along a vertical boundary of national difference, runs counter to the innate logic of class trauma, it thereby poses an inconvenient symbolic problem. The overwhelming force of class conflict dictates that both the collective significance of the War suffering is decreased and that the identification of its perpetrators and victims be put in a symbolically ambiguous light so as not to jar with class line.

Remembrance of the War: Absent-Minded Commemoration in Public Sphere

To substantiate my argument that a collective trauma of the War was blocked from emerging by the overwhelming force of the trauma of class conflict, we should observe what happened in 1965, the twentieth anniversary of victory in the War. Fully two decades after the end of the War, with the benefit of hindsight, one might imagine that sufficient time had passed to reflect on what happened and transform the profound sense of trauma that still seared on the minds and bodies of millions of individuals into a collective trauma. Yet this did not come to pass. A general survey of publications in 1965 indicates that none of the necessary elements that might contribute to the emergence of a collective trauma based on the War ever appeared in the public sphere; what is more, the institutional commemoration activities convened by the central government appeared to be rather limited in quantity and absent-minded in intention.

Browsing briefly through the *General Catalogue of Publication* of 1965, one would be surprised to find that besides two monographs that were listed respectively in the "Politics and Social Life" and "Military" columns, and a collection that comprises four books listed in the "News Features and Profile Stories" section in literature, hardly any special works published were explicitly dedicated to the commemoration of the War. The lack of commemorative attention is even more pronounced when we consider the section following the commemorative collection—the lengthy column of "Four Genealogies" includes 109 books whose titles cover six and half pages (Library of the Administration Bureau for Publication, Ministry of Culture 1966, 127–133).

Another telling piece of evidence can be found in *Selected Editorials of People's Daily 1965*, compiled and published by People's Daily Press (People's Daily Press 1965, vol. 1–5; 1966, vol. 6). Among all six volumes, not a single piece was dedicated to the commemoration of the War, powerfully revealing what little historical significance the War had in the public sphere at the time. The very fact that *People's Daily* is the mouthpiece of CCP and editorials from it are meant to serve as a policy guide for the provincial governments and local people makes such an absence more pronounced and the meaning more illuminating.

While the absence is striking, the contents of what had been published on the War prove more rewarding to explore. In what follows, I demonstrate the ubiquity of three semiotic and narrative features that are salient in most of the texts that represent the War in Mao's era: first, the semiotic hierarchy that is shown in the identification of the enemy camp between the conspicuous and the true; second, the symbolic ambiguity that is embodied in the sacredization of the conspicuous enemy; and the third, the rosy romantic narrative in which the War was being represented. I show that these features not only testify to the absence of a traumatic representation of the War but also illuminate the concrete mechanisms through which significance of the War was overshadowed by the dominant trauma of class struggle and the construction of the War past was subsumed and filtered through the framework of a revolutionary struggle between the oppressed proletariat and the sacred evil of their class enemy.

Semiotic Hierarchy: Conspicuous Enemies vs. True Enemies

One way that the narrative of the War was colonized by the central trauma of class struggle is that the role of the "conspicuous enemy," that is, the Japanese Imperial Army, was greatly downplayed so that that the army is meaningful only as a blurred backdrop image, whereas the "true evil" of all time, class enemies—often epitomized by Kuomintang—were exposed and brought back into the dazzling light on the central stage. Indeed, it seems the rule that the Japanese were seldom constructed as the sole offenders without the accompanying demonization of Kuomintang forces; often, Kuomintang reactionaries were not only singled out as the main devil, but the profane code assigned to them carried heavier symbolic weight.

A very representative case can be found in Vice Chairman Lin Piao's 1965 commemoration article (Lin 1965). Examining the entire sixty-eight pages of the monograph, one would be curious to find that not a single war crime or brutality committed by the Japanese forces was mentioned, and except for the word "barbarous" (8), used once when the nature of the war was being discussed, no characterization stronger than this was attributed to the conspicuous enemies of the War. In contrast, the profanity of the leading antagonists in this narrative, Chiang Kai-shek and his Kuomintang reactionaries, seems hard to redeem. It was, as claimed in the monograph, the Kuomintang reactionaries who "had betrayed the revolution, massacred large numbers of Communists and destroyed all the revolutionary mass organizations" (26) after the First Revolutionary Civil War; it was the Kuomintang who, when the CCP called for a national united front, were engaged in "passive resistance to Japan and active opposition to the Communist Party" (15); and it was Chiang Kai-shek again, "our teacher by negative example," who launched a "surprise attack" on part of CCP-led forces in 1941 and "slaughtered" many of "our heroic revolutionary fighters" (17). Portrayed explicitly as "treacherous," "brutal," and "ruthless," the "massacre" and "slaughter" committed by Kuomintang was obviously coded as more unforgivable than the "barbarous" attacks by the Japanese troops.

Another telling piece can be found in *The East is Red,* a song and dance epic of the Chinese revolution.[14] Preceded by a vehement condemnation of the murderous besiege on "our base areas" launched by Kuomintang reactionaries, the artistic re-creation of the conspicuous enemy in the fourth episode of the performance, which was dedicated to the depiction of the War, is completely absent. During the only dance piece that was meant to represent CCP's battle with Japanese troops, the enemy figures never materialized on the stage, and the theme forcefully focused on the demonstration of the superior tactics of Chinese guerilla soldiers and the merit of the People's War. This virtual shunning of the representation of Japanese enemy figures clearly consummated the effort to build a hierarchy in the identification and coding of the profane camp. The message seems clear: No matter who else might be put into the conspicuous enemy camp under different historical circumstances, the dark title of "true enemy" was perpetually reserved for class antagonists.

The semiotic hierarchy testifies to the constraining effect of the trauma of class struggle on War narratives. The absolute evil of class enemies and the enormity of their crimes, as established in class trauma, thoroughly deprived the Kuomintang regime of likelihood for symbolic redemption and left them transfixed on the pillar of shame in a just war, which they not only fought as the incumbent government but to which they also contributed enormously in winning. Via such a hierarchy, the structure of War narration was tailored to match with that of class struggle, and the role of the conspicuous Japanese enemy was reduced to a piece of stage setting and the Imperial Army's atrocities factually covered up and largely dismissed as unworthy in comparison.

Symbolic Ambiguity: Victimization of Japanese Proletarian Soldiers and Their Symbolic Redemption

The semiotic hierarchy that constructed the Japanese enemy as the lesser evil was strengthened by a symbolic ambiguity that made the distinction between the conspicuous enemy and the true enemy a qualitative leap, instead of just quantitative difference. Unlike the true enemy, forever condemned and denied a redemptive opportunity, the conspicuous enemy was always endowed with a potential for symbolic transcendence. In fact, more than just being portrayed as redeemed former enemies, many Japanese figures in literary works were identified as "retrieved brothers" who were "rescued" from fascist poisoning imposed by the imperial class enemy. One such figure can be found in a popular novel of the 1950s that uniquely took Japanese POWs as its protagonists (Ha 1951). Portrayed as being a miner before being forced into the army, the figure of Matsuyama was intentionally created to represent Japanese soldiers who were members of "Japanese proletariat that had suffered miserably" (18).

The wretched life Matsuyama and his family led in Japan was given a lengthy and detailed depiction, as he himself recounted during his interrogation. Reading his story, it would be hard not to recognize immediately the salient pattern of the "remembering the bitterness" genre. Indeed, there is the debt of blood (the death of his mother and physical injury of his father), the inhuman treatment and merciless exploitation of proletarian people (starvation, meager salary, long working hours, and poor child labor), and ruthless political persecution (being sent to prison for potential political involvement)—all of which were attributed to the evil exploitative class and its representative agency, the imperial regime.

The presence of the "remembering the bitterness" genre demonstrates that the figure of Matsuyama was emphatically constructed as a typical victim of class oppression instead of a perpetrator of war crimes. And befitting such a class identity, his bitter grievance was bound to cleanse him of whatever sin he might have committed by joining the Imperial Army, mightily bond him with brothers and sisters of Chinese proletarians, and quickly confer on him the certificate for reentry into the sacred camp of camaraderie. In fact, it was portrayed in the novel that even before the interrogation was brought to an end, Wang Ming, the eighth route army cadre, "deeply touched by the adversity suffered by this Japanese class brother," (22) had already generously granted Matsuyama his symbolic redemption, to which the latter responded with enthusiasm. Both held hands "like old friends for many years" (24).

The case of Matsuyama and other enemy-turned-comrade Japanese figures especially illuminate how representation of the War was powerfully engulfed by the symbolic juggernaut of class trauma. As implied by the logic of the latter that solidarity must be extended to Japanese proletarians, the majority of Japanese soldiers, instead of being constructed as merciless perpetrators of war crimes, were to be more often than not identified as innocent victims subjected to the poisoning and exploitation of the Jingoist ruling class. Their victimized status as proletarians significantly eclipsed their identity as perpetrators in the War and thereby further confounded identification of the central binary that had already been skewed by the aforementioned semiotic hierarchy. With class perpetrators constructed as the true enemy, with the conspicuous enemies of the War depicted as sacred War victims, and with Chinese War victims (as I will show in the following section) being fiercely constructed as dauntless resistant heroes, all the essential components of a potential War trauma claim were dislocated and thereby dismissed. The nature of the struggle was effectively shifted back into the framework of class trauma.

Romanticization of the War: Denial of Chinese Victimhood and Sufferings

As conspicuous enemies were overshadowed by the dazzling darkness of class enemies and further established as class victims, a traumatic narrative of war atrocities and victims was largely preempted; in its place, the War was narrated in a rosily romanticized and fiercely heroic pattern, which is characterized by an exaggeratedly empowering construction of heroes and caricaturization of enemy figures.

One very convincing case comes from the lyrics of "The Song of Guerillas," which accompanied the aforementioned dance in *The East is Red*. In the song, the guerilla soldiers are portrayed as being capable of conquering any possible adversities and finding ways to triumph regardless the dangers and difficulties they face, as one paragraph claims:

> We are sharpshooters, wipe out one enemy by each bullet; we are pilots, no matter how high the mountain and how deep the water is; in the tight forest, comrade's camp is all over; on the high mountains, there's unlimited numbers of our brothers. If we haven't food and clothes, enemy will give us; if we haven't weapon, enemy will supply us ...[15]

No one would have missed the thoroughly cheerful construction of heroic protagonists here; they were empowered with a superman-like capabilities and seemed to be injected with a symbolic immunization against feelings of pain, loss, or distress. Such a romantic portrayal, with the heroes covered with an impregnable armor of an undaunted spirit, would intrinsically inhibit the enactment of victimhood in the role of Chinese guerilla/civilians. In other words, the only central binary that could emerge in the narrative of the War is that of the "David versus Goliath" genre—absolutely not the "helpless victim versus ruthless perpetrator" set.

The picture of the War as depicted through chapters selected from literary works proves to be equally incurably rosy.[16] In fact, it almost seems a rule that any conflict between the CCP-led forces and the Japanese invading armies must end with a thorough triumph of the former, with Chinese victory usually coming at little or no cost of lives or blood.[17] More often than not, the right thing happens at the right time in the right place so that all conducible elements coincide to contribute to the eventual triumph of the people. A text titled *Troops on the Yanling Ridge* (People's Education Press, Book 4 1954, 16–22)[18] for instance, tells how a small guerilla dispatch team thwarted a round of attacks made by a Japanese water force, and the defeat of the enemy was portrayed as simple: As soon as the enemy characters appeared in the scene, they fell into the trap prepared by the guerilla soldiers, and their fate was inexorably doomed. Predictably, the battle scene barely started when all the dozens of Japanese soldiers were erased with a light brush, and their much more advanced weapons and the impressive modern steamboat became the booty of a boisterous crowd of guerilla soldiers.

The incredible prowess and good fortune of Chinese people as depicted in these chapters is juxtaposed sharply with the portrait of their Japanese antagonists, always constructed as being ridiculously weak, absurdly stupid, and incredibly unfortunate. Indeed, though they were most frequently referred to as *Guizi*, the Chinese word for "the devils," their images as portrayed in these chapters were usually so deprived of evil characters that the signifier instead took on a certain comic connotation.[19] To demonstrate this point, let us turn to the text titled *At the Baiyang Lake*,[20] where *Guizi* were more vividly portrayed than in the other pieces.

At the beginning, several *Guizi* soldiers, who came to attack Baiyang village, were depicted as being obsessively engaged with their petty pursuit of catching a rooster to give themselves a treat; as their very awkward and frantic chase was successfully thwarted by the rooster, which was personified as brave and tactful as its Chinese guerilla master, they came across three young Chinese women who hid themselves in huge piles of grass. As *Guizi* happily cried to each other that they found some "young pretty women," they quickly met with their premature death by a grenade thrown by one of the Chinese girls. It was quite manifest that *Guizi*, as portrayed in this text, are not capable of doing any serious harm; not only were they not able to pose any formidable threat to young civilian girls, who on the contrary were portrayed as merciless soldiers miraculously equipped with heavy arsenal at the critical moment, but the way *Guizi* soldiers fell to their tragic demise was so convenient that one could even pity these pathetic figures. After all, their cardinal sin in this work—the desire for food and women—makes them somewhat sympathetic as human beings.

The romanticized representation of the War, with unfailing triumphs that always come with little cost, and the rosy binary construction that reminds us of childhood tales in which bad rascals are always defeated by good people, maximally covered up the traumatic sufferings inflicted by the War and powerfully relativized its enormity. By virtually shunning the re-creation of war atrocities, it mitigated the symbolic weighting of the nature of suffering and further marginalized the significance of the War. In this rosy picture, unlike the oppressed, trampled, and massacred proletariat as constructed in the trauma of class struggle, which by principle also includes the majority of Japanese soldiers, the identification of war victims was curiously yet thoroughly evaded, turned into a nonidentity or nonexistence. In its place, as the aforementioned cases so vividly illustrate, any potential war victims would have been constructed as heroic warriors of resistance, intrinsically rejecting enactment of victimhood.

Combined with the absent-minded and scanty commemoration of the War in the public sphere, these features characterizing representation of the War help to highlight the salient absence of a collective trauma-making process; such an absence, as argued in this chapter, was the result of an inhibition process where representation of the War was overshadowed, subsumed, and shaped by the ubiquitous and compelling force of the hugely successful trauma of class struggle.

The conspicuous perpetrators of the War, comprised of an awkward heterogeneity that does not necessarily fit within one class, were always portrayed in an ambiguous light where their perpetration appeared as not worthy of consideration in comparison with the ultimate vileness of the Kuomintang regime, and their symbolic significance was largely dwarfed by the dark sacred evilness of true class enemies. The horrible War atrocities, factually yet inconveniently committed by Japanese soldiers of all class origins, were effectively shunned and replaced with the romantic narration of proletarian triumph. Millions of Chinese war victims were virtually left out of the picture as the class victimization of Japanese proletarian soldiers commanded more symbolic significance, and the unabashedly empowering construction of resistant Chinese heroes cleansed the victory of blood and suffering. It is thus that some of the most important elements for a potential trauma claim on the War were preempted from emerging, and in their place, representation of the War was adeptly tailored to become just another episode seamlessly fitting with the sweeping trauma of class struggle. After all, in comparison with a landlord who would not hesitate to strip your skin and who therefore must be eliminated without mercy, a Japanese soldier, not capable of doing any serious harm and usually also a victim of class oppression himself, is a much more amicable figure and embodies greatly more potential for redemption.

Notes

1. There has probably never been an accurate statistic of the loss of lives and numbers of casualties caused by the War in Chinese society since 1945. The number here came from estimate from the Nationalist (or Kuomintang) government in Taiwan, as written by Chiang Kai-shek's son in an article memorializing the ex-president who led the War.

2. There is a wide consensus, especially among Western scholars on China, that the initial decades after the building of PRC were characterized by a "cultural amnesia" toward the War (Chang 1997; Coble 2007; Cohen 2003; Li 2000; Mitter 2003; Waldron 1996). As I will argue here, while "amnesia" may not be an accurate description, it certainly captured the relegated status of its representation in the public sphere. In terms of the international community, however, as Western scholars have long argued, the historical truth of the atrocious war crimes committed in China by the Japanese imperial army indeed has been subjected to virtual oblivion ever since and remains "the best kept secret about World War II."

3. With the exception of perhaps two recent papers that focus on the suppressed collective memories of the Nanjing Massacre (Alexander and Gao 2007; Xu and Spillman 2010), both addressing why "one of the worst instances of mass extermination" was largely ignored and excluded from the central official memories in the communist era of PRC.

4. This is the opening address Mao gave at the First Plenary Session of the Chinese People's Political Consultative Conference held on September 21, 1949. It was selected in *Chinese* (Junior High School), Book 5 of the 1960 edition. (Editorial Division for Chinese Course, People's Education Press 1960). The English translation can be found at http://www.marxists.org/reference/archive/mao/selected-works/volume-5/mswv5_01.htm.

5. I drew my data extensively from sources like Chinese and history textbooks; commemorative articles and reports in newspapers; mnemonic sites such as museums; and cultural products such as novels, films, and dramas.

6. The text was selected from an article written by Zhu Tao titled *Being Steadfast for Revolution*. It was originally published in 1959 in a journal by CCP Guangdong Province Committee titled *Shang You*.

7. Refers to Lu Xun's *A Madman's Diary*, first published in 1918 in *New Youth* and was later selected into the book *Na Han*. While this story was not selected into school Chinese textbooks, it, as well as the book, are perhaps some of the most widely read and well known literary works in modern Chinese history. Within the writer's lifetime (he died in 1936), the book *Na Han* had been reprinted twenty-two times. And after the building of the PRC, thirty-two pieces of works written by the writer were selected into Chinese textbooks during the so-called seventeen-year-period (1949–1966), including the preface of the book *Na Han*. According to Bo (2006), no other Chinese writer in modern history has ever enjoyed such a popularity in the field of education and textbook compilation in the PRC.

8. Indeed, the editors appeared eager to justify why folk songs that were composed "in the old era" should be known and learned by the students at all. For instance, the editors kept saying that folk songs, because of their "profound ideas, their rich expressiveness and their authentic emotionality," are "extremely beneficial teaching materials" (Zhang [ed.] 1957, 28). It was also emphasized that folk songs were created collectively by the proletarian people and therefore were the crystallization of the wisdom and talents of the mass people over time.

9. It was evident in the public discourse of Maoist era that, while class enemies include imperialism, feudalism, and bureaucratic-capitalism, it was always their "general representative" (as Mao defined in his opening speech) the Kuomintang reactionary that served as the scapegoat for all in the construction of the class enemy. Such epitomized embodiment status bore fatal consequences on the construction of the regime in the representation of the War; its absolute evil status determined that it were to outrank the Japanese troops as the true enemy even in a war they fought on the just side.

10. The title of this text is *New Watch,* and in the Chinese textbook, footnote number one of this text explains that this was selected from a work, most probably a book, titled *Sparkles of Hatred,* yet offers no information of the author or publication of the original work.

11. While no official statistics seems to exist regarding the number of publication on "Four Genealogies," an article written on the development of oral history in contemporary China points out that the collection of genealogy was part of the nationwide campaign directly advocated by Chairman Mao and therefore "huge amount of people's life experience was collected and preserved" via the means of oral history (Song 2006, 73–74). To a certain extent, the very fact that "Four Genealogies" was singled out as a major column in the *General Catalogue of Publication* in the 1960s was in itself a testimony to the significance and scale of the publication.

12. Other daily rituals include "asking for instructions in the morning and reporting back in the evening;" quoting Chairman Mao's words at the beginning and the end of each speech, conversation, and text; reciting Chairman Mao's "Three Old Pieces" every day; the ritual of criticizing and self-criticizing, and so on.

13. The text was selected and adapted from Chapter Seventeen, Book One of a novel titled *The Hurricane (Bao Feng Zhou Yu)* written by Libo Zhou (1948).

14. The performance debuted in Beijing in October 1964. In celebration of the fifteenth anniversary of the founding of the new republic, the epic performance presents a vivid depiction of Chinese revolution in forms of songs, dance, opera, and ballet and thus offers an ideal text for interpreting how the nation represents its own past and defines its collective identity to the public, including the construction of the War in public arena.

15. The English translation was revised by the author, based on a version available at http://en.wikipedia.org/wiki/Guerillas'_Song.

16. These refer to excerpts and chapters of novels or other literary works on the War that had been selected into Chinese textbooks for senior elementary

and junior high schools in the 1950s and 1960s. Altogether, there were eight such texts, all written by writers under the leadership of CCP and published during the 1940s to late 1950s.

17. Only in samples of Chinese textbooks was this the case. It cannot be denied that, in the majority of novels written about the War, there was usually loss of innocent lives and some brutalities, but as I have shown to certain extent, the immaculately heroic image of the martyrs who were killed and the excessively caricaturized image of the Japanese enemies served as the main mechanism to inhibit a sense of trauma. Instead, there emerged a strong collective sense of righteousness and efficacy, and the highlight was always focused onto the eventual outcome of triumph.

18. The text was excerpted and adapted from a famous novel written on the War, titled *New Story of Heroic Sons and Daughters (Xin Er Nv Ying Xiong Zhuan)* (Yuan and Kong 1954).

19. This does not mean, of course, that they were not unequivocally coded as evil or bad. But as I have demonstrated in this chapter, the deepening of such an evil seldom occurred. And this, in a self-reinforcing way, further strengthened the semiotic hierarchy that ranked class enemies over *Guizi* soldiers.

20. The article was selected into two major editions of Chinese textbooks for junior high school in the 1950s and 1960s, book 4 published in 1952 and book 1 published in 1963. It was excerpted and adapted from Li Sun's selected stories written on life and fights of people in the CCP-led base areas during the War (Sun 1958).

Works Cited

Alexander, J., R. Eyerman, B. Giesen, N. Smelser, and P. Sztompka. 2004. *Cultural Trauma and Collective Identity.* Berkeley: University of California Press.

Alexander, J., and R. Gao. 2007. Remembrance of Things Past: Cultural Trauma, the 'Nanking Massacre' and Chinese Identity. In *Tradition and Modernity: Comparative Perspectives,* K. Sun and H. Meng, 266–294. Beijing: Beijing University Press.

Bo, J. 2006. On the Teacher's Reference Guide for Lu Xun's Works during the Seventeen-Year Period (1949–1966). *Lu Xun Research Monthly* 12: 46–51.

Chang, I. 1997. *The Rape of Nanking: The Forgotten Holocaust of World War II.* New York: Basic Books.

Coble, P. M. 2007. China's "New Remembering" of the Anti-Japanese War of Resistance, 1937–1945. *The China Quarterly* 190: 394–410.

Cohen, P. A. 2003. *China Unbound: Evolving Perspectives on the Chinese Past.* London: Routledge Curzon.

Editorial Division for Chinese Course, People's Education Press. 1960. *Chinese* (Junior High School). Books 5–6. Hangzhou: People's Education Press in Zhejiang.

———. 1963. *Chinese* (Junior High School, newly edited in 1963). Books 1–2. Beijing: People's Education Press.

────. 1964. *Chinese* (Junior High School, newly edited in 1964). Books 3–4. Beijing: People's Education Press.

Editorial Division for *Red Genealogy,* Xinhua Daily Press. 1964. *Red Genealogy,* vol. 1–2. Nanjing: People's Press of Jiangsu.

────. 1965a. *The Battle Song at the Cotton Mill: A Collection on Genealogy of Villages.* Nanjing: People's Press of Jiangsu.

────. 1965b. *The Indignant Surge at the River: A Collection on Genealogy of Mines and Factories.* Nanjing: People's Press of Jiangsu.

Ha, H. 1951. *Asano Sanbuloo (Qian Ye San Lang).* Shanghai: New Literature and Art Press.

Li, P. 2000. The Nanking Holocaust Tragedy, Trauma and Reconciliation. *Society* 37(2): 56–65.

Library of the Administration Bureau for Publication, Ministry of Culture. 1966. *General Catalog of Publication 1965 (for internal reference).* Beijing: Book Bureau of China.

Lin, P. 1965. *Long Live the Victory of People's War! In Commemoration of the 20th Anniversary of Victory in the Chinese People's War of Resistance Against Japan.* Beijing: Foreign Language Press. First published in *People's Daily,* September 3, 1965.

Lu, X. 1951 [1918]. A Madman's Dairy. In *Na Han,* ed. Memorization Committee of Mr. Lu Xun, 13–27. Beijing: People's Literature Press.

Mao, T. 1949. The Opening Address at the First Plenary Session of the Chinese People's Political Consultative Conference (September 21, 1949). In *Important Documents of the First Plenary Session of the Chinese People's Political Consultative Conference,* 1–6. Beijing: Xin Hua Bookstore.

Mitter, R. 2003. Old Ghosts, New Memories: China's Changing War History in the Era of Post-Mao Politics. *Journal of Contemporary History* 38(1): 117–131.

People's Education Press. 1954. *Chinese* (Junior High School). Books 1–6. Shenyang: People's Education Press.

────. 1955. *Chinese* (Senior Elementary School). Books 1–4. Beijing: People's Education Press.

People's Daily Press. 1965. *Selected Editorials of People's Daily 1965,* vol. 1–5. Beijing: People's Daily Press.

────. 1966. *Selected Editorials of People's Daily 1965,* vol. 6. Beijing: People's Daily Press.

Schwartz, B. (1995) Deconstructing and Reconstructing the Past. *Qualitative Sociology* 18(2): 263–170.

Song, X. 2006. A Study of Contemporary Chinese History and Oral History. *Collected Papers of History Studies* 5: 70–75, 80.

Sun, L. 1958. *The Baiyang Lake (Bai Yang Dian Ji Shi).* Beijing: China Youth Press.

Waldron, A. 1996. China's New Remembering of World War II: The Case of Zhang Zizhong. *Modern Asian Studies* 30(4): 945–978.

Xu, X., and L. Spillman. 2010. Political Centres, Progressive Narratives and Cultural Trauma: Coming to Terms with the Nanjing Massacre in

China, 1937–1979. In *Northeast Asia's Difficult Past: Essays in Collective Memory,* ed. B. Schwartz and M. Kim, 101–128. Hampshire, UK: Palgrave Macmillan.

Yuan, J., and J. Kong. 1954. *New Story of Heroic Sons and Daughters (Xin Er Nv Ying Xiong Zhuan).* Shanghai: New Literature and Art Press.

Zhang, L., ed. 1957. *Pedagogical Guidance Book for Junior High School Music Teachers.* Beijing: People's Education Press.

Zhou, L. 1948. *The Hurricane (Bao Feng Zhou Yu).* Harbin: North East Bookstore.

PART 2

Ethnic Suffering and Civil War

4

The Trauma of Kosovo in Serbian National Narratives

Ivana Spasić

If asked what distinguishes them as a nation, most Serbs would tell you it is the memory of the Battle of Kosovo, fought between the Serbian army and the forces of Ottoman Turks in 1389. Serbs lost the battle, and their prince was killed. The event marked the collapse of the medieval Serbian state and beginning of the long Ottoman domination. The Kosovo "sore," "wound," or "pain," as it is usually called in the "stories Serbs tell themselves about themselves" (Živković 2001), that is, the sorrowful but proud feeling of tragedy, death, and loss engendered by remembrance of the Kosovo catastrophe 600 years ago is generally held to be the foundation of Serbian identity, part of the very essence of being a Serb. Yet this thesis is precisely what needs to be examined. The present chapter seeks to describe how this claim has come to look so self-evident.

Interest in the Kosovo myth received a strong impetus from the wars in former Yugoslavia during the 1990s. The widespread perception of Serbs as the main culprits for Yugoslavia's bloody collapse and chief perpetrators of atrocities prompted many to look for causes of such behavior in the Serbian cultural past and to find a pivotal point in the Kosovo myth. An unbroken line was established extending from the late fourteenth century through nineteenth-century Serbian nationalism to the present day. Serbs were never able to overcome the traumatic memory of the Kosovo failure, the argument went, and this unhealed wound spurred them to aggression, expansionism, trampling on others' rights, and finally, genocide (e.g., Anzulović 1999; Sells 2002; Vetlesen 2005; Volkan 1996 and 2002; Šuber 2006).

In the literature, the Kosovo myth is most often presented in a misleadingly univocal manner, as conveying invariably a single message over the centuries.[1] It is striking how two opposing discourses have converged in producing this impression: a critical outsider perspective and a celebratory Serbian nationalist one. For both, the mythicized collective remembrance of the trauma of Kosovo is indelibly imprinted on the minds of Serbs, founding their identity and actively shaping their actions. Also, both discourses exoticize Serbs, arguing that this special relation to their trauma makes them radically different from others and, crucially, somehow immune to modernity. Finally, both homogenize Serbs, assuming an overly consensual reception of the Kosovo legacy, disregarding internal multiplicity of voices.

But all three points may and ought to be questioned. First, the traumatic effect of Kosovo for Serbs is not a fact but a social process, an "ongoing practical accomplishment" as ethnomethodologists would put it. Second, Serbs' radical alterity is better understood as part of their self-posturing than a naturally occurring condition.[2] Third, homogenization has been widely used in the Serbian political arena for purposes of exclusion, undermining the development of genuine pluralism. By challenging these three points, I hope to show that the symbolism of Kosovo is actually much more ambiguous and open ended. It contains many gaps, loops, double-entendres, and other discursive plays that I believe are mainly responsible for the myth's enduring power. The apparently unitary Kosovo myth has operated within a number of vastly different ideological-political programs in modern Serbian and Yugoslav history. This contextual variation has been enabled by a basic ambiguity within the Kosovo tradition, that of particularism versus universalism, a sliding back and forth between a more narrow and constricted and a more expansive and inclusive interpretation.

My theoretical terrain can be delineated by comparing two seemingly similar sentences. One is by two Serbian-American scholars, who claim that "Kosovo is many diverse things to different living Serbs, but they all have it *in their blood*" (Dragnich and Todorovich 1984, 4). The other is used by Eyerman (2002, 18) writing about a different but theoretically related case, of slavery in forging of African American identity;

"[s]lavery has meant different things for different generations of black Americans, but it was always there *as a referent*" (both emphases added). It is from "blood" to "referent" that I wish to move in this chapter, retracing the path by which the latter turned into the former. Kosovo is the main Serbian "entrenched story"—the narrative a community comes to be stuck with, which becomes ever more entrenched even as it is bitterly contested, for any new reference only serves to make it associatively richer (Živković 2001, xii–xiii). As such, it is a good example of how cultural structures operate within the dynamically unfolding historical contexts, in constant tension between the semiotic resistance of patterned cultural meanings, on one hand, and the contingencies of political, economic, and military circumstances, on the other.

Two reservations are in order here. First, I will only deal with Kosovo as a *Serbian* symbolic referent. Albanians, who make up the overwhelming majority of inhabitants of Kosovo as a real territory and newly independent Balkan country, also feel Kosovo to be "more than" just a piece of land. For them, too, Kosovo has sacred attributes, and this sacralization is similarly based on suffering and heroism. Though it would be fascinating to examine the parallels between Albanian and Serbian constructions of Kosovo as trauma, such discourse must remain beyond the scope of this chapter.[3] Second, when referring to "Kosovo," I mean the symbolic, abstract meaning, not Kosovo as a real place, unless I specifically indicate so. I will not deal with the more directly political, legal, or security issues involved in the Kosovo crisis since the late 1980s, because they are far too complex to be dealt with summarily. Kosovo as territory has been a bone of contention between Serbs and Albanians for the last one hundred and fifty years. For Serbs, Kosovo is a sacred symbol not only because of the Battle but also for the presence on the soil of real Kosovo of precious cultural monuments, most notably medieval monasteries. Thus when Serbs claim Kosovo is the "cradle of Serbhood," they ambiguously refer to both the embodied place and the sacred idea, and the dynamic between an abstracting, de-territorializing symbolization and recurrent re-territorialization of "Kosovo" has been quite important in the cultural history of the notion.

Story and (Its) History

The Beginnings

The Kosovo legend was spun over several centuries from elements originating in orally transmitted folk epic poetry, religious writings (sermons, eulogies, hagiographies), and early secular works (chronicles, biographies, travelogues). The battle itself took place on a field near present-day Pristina, on June 15, 1389.[4] The Christian side was led by the Serbian prince Lazar Hrebeljanović and the Ottoman army by Sultan Murad. Like all medieval battles, it was not, strictly speaking, fought by "Serbs" and "Turks" in national terms, although it was redefined as such later on. It was, however, felt at both sides to be a clash between Christianity and Islam. Though the battle's immediate outcome is not clear, it was an important step in Serbia's loss of statehood and independence to the Ottomans, whose rule would continue until the beginning of the nineteenth century. Whatever the relative merits of pre-Kosovo Serb kingdoms and the post-Kosovo Ottoman reign—in conventional Serbian historiography fondly referred to as "five centuries of Turkish yoke"—the conquest meant a historical rupture, and the Kosovo legend emerged as part of the collective effort to make sense of it.

The narrative is organized around two foci, one Christian and martyrial and the other epic and heroic. They are personified by two towering figures, Prince Lazar and Miloš Obilić. Lazar was canonized as a saint shortly after the battle, and every year, a memorial service has been held in Serbian Orthodox churches honoring him as a Christian martyr, who earned the entrance to eternal life by deliberately embracing death "in defense of the Holy Cross." In this way, Lazar, like Jesus Christ, reversed the outcome: a worldly defeat became spiritual triumph. Folk tradition elaborated on this symbolic baseline laid out by the church. Before the battle, Lazar, in a series of powerfully bleak images, threw a curse on all Serbs who failed to show up at Kosovo to perform their sacred duty. Then, confronted by God's messenger with a choice between an earthly and a heavenly kingdom, he chose the latter, although he knew he had to die for it together with all his men. Lazar's choice of death as redemption would become known as the "Kosovo covenant" or "Kosovo pledge."

Miloš Obilić is not a historical personality. In the legend, he is a brave soldier and Lazar's son-in-law who at the supper before the battle— modeled in folk poetry after the Last Supper—was unjustly accused of imminent treason. To prove his loyalty, the next day he penetrated into the Ottoman camp, killed the Sultan, and was killed himself. Miloš's figure became preeminent within the legend toward the end of Ottoman rule and, nowadays, is the very symbol of selfless heroism and epitome of Serbhood, especially of its militant, warrior variety.[5]

The cast is completed by the third, negative character. If Lazar was Jesus Christ, someone had to be Judas. Vuk Branković, in historical reality the only Serbian feudal lord who continued resisting the Ottomans after Kosovo, became in the legend the despicable traitor who went over to the enemy side and contributed to Serbian defeat. How Vuk Branković got into this role is not entirely clear, but both political intrigue and demands of narrative cogency played their parts.

Serbian Modernity

There was nothing very exotic in the early formative drives that helped shape the Kosovo Myth: medieval Christian hagiography and liturgical literature, chivalric ethics and heroic poetry—perhaps even the broader Indo-European epic pool (Loma 2002; Popović 1998, 71–87)—and the heavily fictionalized early histories, all partook of the cultural dynamics of the times and connected Serbian culture with the outside world. Similarly, the moment when the myth was rounded off in the early 19th century, was precisely the moment when Serbia was getting (back) into European modernity. This was launched by two uprisings (1804–1813 and 1815) against Ottoman rule, opening the long process of acquiring independence that would last until 1878 (see Roudometoff 2001, 101–129).

The Kosovo legacy lived into the late eighteenth century as a collection of interrelated bits and pieces. In Bakić-Hayden's apt phrase, it was the First Serbian Uprising that "tied into the knot of collective awareness many loose strands of a long epic memory" (2004, 31). In the preceding decades, the cult of Kosovo had become more alive than ever before, centering on the heroic figure of Miloš Obilić rather than the Christ-like Lazar. The main site of the cult was not in Serbia proper but among the Serb diaspora in the Habsburg Empire. These settlers, having arrived from Ottoman territories in successive migration waves,[6] developed an entrepreneurial middle class and were the only modernized Serbs at the time. They were crucial inspirers of the myth's first direct political use and played an invaluable role in providing Serbian nationhood with an intellectual background. In the same period, the ethnographer and language reformer Vuk Karadžić recorded, compiled, and published folk poetry, including the central "Kosovo Cycle" of epic poems.[7]

From the very beginning, the nation-builders felt that the Kosovo legacy could be used for political mobilization. At first, the mobilization was quite literal, and the leader of the first uprising, Karađorđe, nicknamed "the Avenger of Kosovo," called "every Serb to arms, so that we may take revenge on the Turks, and in the name of God cast off the yoke that the Serb has carried since Kosovo to this day" (quoted in Antonijević 2007a, 142). On the other hand, the folklore collected by Karadžić, presented as a living expression of Serbian "national spirit," was used to win outside support for the national cause. In the epoch of the Romanticist craze for "authentic" folk culture, Serbian poems were warmly received by some of the great Western intellectual figures of the day. This was of utmost importance for Serbs, who hardly had anything else to substantiate their claims to nationhood and political independence. So, ironically, the final form of the Kosovo myth, nowadays taken as the badge of Serbian antimodern exclusivity, was fruit of the Serbian desire to construct a modern national culture that will be part of the Western world (Bakić-Hayden 2004, 32).

Around the middle of the century, the Montenegrin poet-ruler Petar Petrović Njegoš published his epic drama *Mountain Wreath,* which enormously popularized the Kosovo themes. In Serbia, the painstaking state-building process included the establishment of public education to improve the abysmally low literacy rate. Collections of folk songs immediately became part of the curriculum, and the importance of the educational system in inculcating the Kosovo legacy in subsequent generations can hardly be overestimated. The government was putting together a standardized version of the Kosovo symbolism as the founding myth of the emerging nation-state and dynastic rule. As Roudometoff points out, religious categories were redeployed to build a new secular national identity (2001, 101).

The central national tradition was being invented at both official/political and unofficial/social levels (Hobsbawm 1983). The ideas of European liberal and national revolutions of 1848 resonated strongly among Serbian youth, especially students, both in the Principality of Serbia and in the Habsburg lands. Midcentury literary Romanticism was particularly passionate in reviving the Kosovo myth, emphasizing heroism and self-sacrifice for the nation. Student societies, clubs, and associations idolized the Kosovo heroes and emulated folk singers in the poetry they themselves wrote.[8] In their ideological outlook, these young radicals were similar to their comrades in Italy, Hungary, or France. They were nationalist and cosmopolitan at the same time. They wanted their people to join the family of free European nations, and the Kosovo legacy was seen not as an obstacle but a support on that road, as the specific Serbian gift to the colorfulness of the world. Finally, the nationalist youth often clashed with authoritarian Serbian governments on issues of internal policy. While calling on the government to "redeem Kosovo"—the region remained under Ottoman control until 1912—they were also asking for freedom of the press and constitutional checks on the power of the prince. The authors who wrote most enthusiastic poems about the "bleeding sore" of Kosovo were also the ones who wrote the first liberal political programs.[9]

The Serbian Orthodox Church, for its part, opposed such thorough secularization of the Kosovo legacy. While definitely sharing in the nationalism of other elites, the high clergy tried to preserve the more conservative and traditional ways of celebrating Kosovo. The controversy over *Vidovdan* is a good case in point. This folk name for the day when the Battle of Kosovo happened is the Serbianized form for Saint Vitus day. Although June 28[10] was commemorated by increasingly extensive secular manifestations since the mid-nineteenth century, the Church refused to include it as a holiday in its official liturgical calendar until as late as 1892, on the grounds that Saint Vitus was not a saint recognized by the Orthodox. The defenders of *Vidovdan* did not care much about Saint Vitus, either: For them, it was an occasion to celebrate the heroes of Kosovo and, through them, venerate the nation itself.

Around the five hundredth anniversary of the battle (1889) the first professional historical studies of the event were published. Two rationalist, critical historians, Ilarion Ruvarac and Ljubomir Kovačević, sifted through what was believed to be facts and exposed most of it as products of poetic imagination and political fabrication.[11]

A significant re-territorialization of Kosovo symbolism took place in the second half of the nineteenth century. The (real) Kosovo was still in Ottoman hands, and Serbia proclaimed the incorporation of the province a major national goal.[12] At the same time, Albanians were creating their own national movement.[13] Like never before, Serbian and Albanian collective aspirations began to diverge and conflict. Mutual victimization of the two groups began to feed back into the already existing traumatizing framework of the Serbian Kosovo narrative.

By the end of the nineteenth century then, the Kosovo Myth was completed as a cultural structure: A narrative was there, with its cloud of recognizable symbolic associations and its presumed centrality for national identity. Simultaneously, in this period, different social actors pursuing various and often-conflicting goals reached for Kosovo as an inspiration, a call to arms, a spiritual reminder, an emotional bond with their fellows, or a scourge to chastise them. This multidimensionality and pragmatic versatility of Kosovo would remain its basic, though largely unacknowledged, feature.

From Serbia to Yugoslavia and Back

At the turn of twentieth century, sentiments favoring the unification of the South Slavs were revived. For Serbs in this period, the "Kosovo pledge" was ubiquitous as an inspiration, artistic as well as political and military, but many non-Serb artists, too, found it appealing as an expression of South Slavic unity and shared longing for freedom from alien oppression. Distinguished Croatian writers Ivo Vojnović and Vladimir Nazor wrote on Kosovo themes, combining traditional folk motifs and sophisticated modernist literary form. The best-known Croatian sculptor, Ivan Meštrović, designed the (never-realized) project for a spectacular Kosovo Temple, and individual sculptures embodying characters from the legend brought him international fame.[14]

Serbia finally liberated, or occupied, the region of Kosovo in the Balkan Wars (1912). In 1918, a common state of the South Slavs was created, the Kingdom of Serbs, Croats and Slovenes (renamed Kingdom of Yugoslavia in 1929), under the Serbian Karađorđević dynasty. King Aleksandar felt it necessary to develop an ideological underpinning to his rule over the newly united subjects. His project of "integral Yugoslavism" was based on the idea that Serbs, Croats, and Slovenes were one and a single people, divided in three tribes. A Yugoslavized Kosovo legend was supposed to act as its founding myth. Thus the Kosovo theme figured prominently in many manifestations of this political-cultural outlook, which was officially promoted in the 1920s and much of the 1930s.

Within the then-fashionable disciplines of ethnopsychology and national characterology, the importance of Kosovo for the "national soul" had already been stressed by the Serbian geographer Jovan Cvijić. In his typology of Serbian characters, Cvijić described as clearly superior the so-called Dinaric Highlander, a warrior and state-builder, whose spiritual pillar is the memory of Kosovo and the upholding of the Kosovo covenant. In the works of a major exponent of integral Yugoslavism, the Croat Vladimir Dvorniković, Kosovo became Yugoslav rather than just Serbian. For him, folk epics, especially the central "Kosovo Cycle," are the true expression of the "people's psyche," the essence of the Yugoslav soul. It is "ethically higher" than the lore of other nations, since it represents a stance of "struggle, resistance and ultimate sacrifice" (Dvorniković 1939, 537).

World War II provided many opportunities for using and abusing Kosovo motifs. At the outbreak of the war in Yugoslavia, the protagonists of the British-backed putsch of March 27, 1941 overthrowing the government that two days earlier had signed the Tripartite Pact, referred to the Kosovo covenant as their inspiration. During the war itself, the Kosovo theme became one of the stakes in the intra-Serb strife between the communist-led partisans, the forces loyal to the exiled king (the Chetniks), and the quisling government installed by the Germans. All sides used Kosovo as symbolic capital and claimed to be the legitimate heirs to Kosovo heroes; all sullied their opponents by identifying them with Vuk Branković (Emmert 1990; Ćosić 2004; Žanić 1998).

After the establishment of the communist regime in 1945, the Kosovo legacy was not wiped out, as has sometimes been claimed. Though public celebrations of *Vidovdan* were banned, the communists knew how to incorporate the legacy of Kosovo into their ideology. In a somewhat modified form, purged as much as possible of its religious content, and with its Serbian character played down, it remained an obligatory part of the school curricula.[15] Communists presented the Kosovo legend as part of the tradition of "our peoples," which they took as the basis of their cultural legitimacy. Nevertheless, Kosovo would soon resurface as Serbian trauma.

The Production of Trauma

The 1980s was a decisive decade for Kosovo as both a real place and a symbol. The ethnic Albanian majority in the province increasingly demanded more autonomy, that is, the status of a full-fledged republic within the Yugoslav federation.[16] Political unrest was suppressed by force, and no dialogue was opened. On the other hand, Kosovo Serbs began to complain they were being harassed by the Albanians and forced to move out. Hostility between the two peoples was growing rapidly, and their political projects were becoming totally incompatible. The Serbian republic authorities were not particularly receptive to Kosovo Serbs' grievances, so these were taken up first by the Serbian Orthodox Church[17] and then by such institutions as the Association of Writers and the Serbian Academy of Sciences.[18] This unofficial nationalism made ample use of the discourse of trauma in depicting Serbian distant and recent history. It established a continuity of Serb suffering since 1389. It used elements of the existing Kosovo legacy, in its most traumatic version possible, to make sense of contemporary developments and vice versa—a traumatic interpretation of present-day events was used to reinforce a traumatic reading of the traditional Myth.

The Bards

In her interesting typology of nationalisms, Ramet (1995) takes Serbs as the example of "traumatic" nationalism, one that draws its energy "from a reinterpretation of Serbia's history in terms of suffering, exploitation, pain, and injustice" (1995, 103). Yet her claim that this dates back only to the late 1980s is unacceptable. The trauma was not, and could not have been, invented from scratch. By then, it had already had a lengthy history. Those youngsters of the 1860s did not wail for nothing. But in one thing Ramet is right, and that is the major role of the Serbian Orthodox Church, and other agents of unofficial nationalism of the 1980s, in constructing an especially insistent, and occasionally quite morbid, traumatic version of Kosovo symbolism.[19] Some crucial trauma-producing publications appeared at this time, written by apparently nonpolitical actors—priests, theologians, and poets. But what turns out only upon closer inspection is to what extent these works, too, in all their traumatizing impact, played on the particularist/universalist theme.

Let us begin with the simplest, because the most overt, case of Matija Bećković, the foremost poetic bard of the new nationalism. His collection of poetic essays entitled *The Service* (1990) is a veritable compendium of traumatic themes. "Kosovo is the most expensive [or 'most precious,' 'dearest'] Serbian word," says Bećković. "It was paid for by the blood of the whole people" (1990, 47). The Battle of Kosovo mystically instituted Serbs as a collectivity; they have nothing but this traumatic legacy; "Kosovo is the deepest sore, the longest memory, the most vivid recollection, the most beloved ashes of the Serbian people" (68). At the same time, Kosovo is Serbs' sole accomplishment; "[It is] the heritage and bequest of Serbian art and spirit to the humankind" (49). True, this is poetic discourse, but Bećković's book has functioned as a political statement since the moment it appeared.

The other major work, although written decades before, became known to the general public only in its 1980s edition: *Kosovo and Vidovdan* (1988) by Nikolaj Velimirović, an anticommunist Orthodox bishop active before World War II who died in emigration. Velimirović is a controversial figure; he is much revered by the Church for his theological writings and for his presumed suffering in the hands of the Nazis and communists,[20] while at the same time, he's heavily criticized by liberals for his anti-Semitism and antidemocratic conservatism (Byford 2008). In his book, the operation of a rhetorical dialectic between the universal and the particular is much more visible than in Bećković. Its main note is Christian humbleness and martyrdom, and open aggression is almost absent, which certainly makes its messages—however decoded—more acceptable. The martyrdom at Kosovo is described as necessary because self-deserved by Serbs' alienation from God; this-worldly death and destruction are a price to pay for spiritual redemption. "Wrong are those who argue that Kosovo stopped the wheel of our history … On the contrary, it was Kosovo that made us a great people" (69). Serbs are here presented in the universalistic Christian key of redemption through suffering. The more exclusionary effects are accomplished by a detour: Suffering earns Serbs a sort of moral absolution in advance. Whatever they do will be right, provided their "entire social and stately, cultural and political life is penetrated by the idea of the superiority of the heavenly over the earthly" (103). (But how do we measure this "penetration," one feels compelled to ask?) "*Vidovdan* demands purification from hate, selfishness and vanity," and, while "inebriating with love of Christ," it also "thunders with damnation against the traitors of the people's faith and people's mission" (114). (How do we recognize them?) These are some early examples of a discursive move that would become common from the 1980s on: a rhetorical depoliticization of Kosovo to wage quite political battles by ostensibly metaphysical means. A rhetorical sacralization of politics opens up a dangerous space of arbitrariness. The precise content of the "Kosovo covenant" and, therefore, of its possible political operationalizations are kept utterly vague. Elimination of shared and testable criteria of political performance invites the intrusion of self-appointed interpreters of what actually *is* the fulfillment of the covenant. In the superb formula of ethnologist Ivan Čolović (2001, 195–197), Kosovo then becomes "the Golden Bough of Serbian politics."

The arguably most powerful trauma-engendering book of the period was *From Kosovo to Jadovno* written by the active Orthodox bishop Atanasije Jevtić (2007 [1987]). Its chapters, first published in the early 1980s as a series of articles in the Patriarchate's official newspaper, document instances of victimization of Serbs at the hands of others—most prominently, Kosovo Albanians in the present day and the Croatian fascists during World War II.[21] The vacillation between universalizing and particularizing thrusts, between Orthodox/Christian/human and Serbs-as-a-special-people provides the basic dynamic of the text and is propelled by sustained doubletalk taking place between the textual surface and the implied, half-buried messages—or sometimes in a single sentence: "This speaks to us about Lazar's, and all our people's, commitment to the Heavenly Kingdom as the enduring and imperishable, eternally meaningful substance of human life and history" (389). Like in Velimirović, political implications are treated with strategic open-endedness, "We Orthodox Serbs ... are fighting simultaneously for the earthly and the heavenly kingdom and in both cases it is one and the same spiritual battle that we are waging" (387). At the explicit level, aggression is rejected.[22] But it is at least potentially present, in the relentless production of trauma by the sheer quantity of gory detail, by insistence on crimes against Serbs (without ever remotely mentioning crimes committed by them), and by the simple placing side by side of the accounts of two very different settings, as if they were intimately connected by the metaphysical logic of Serbian suffering.

Milošević's Failed Reconquista

It is in this atmosphere, and thanks to it, that Slobodan Milošević took power in Serbia in 1987. In his triumphant march first through the structures of the Serbian Communist Party and then of the republic government, he aligned himself with the unofficial nationalism but always retained some rhetorical distance from it, as if a sort of division of labor were in force: trauma for the priests and the writers, victories and a bright future for the government.

Milošević was lucky enough to be given the occasion to celebrate the six hundredth anniversary of the Battle of Kosovo at the height of his charisma. In his memorable speech delivered at the huge rally held at Gazimestan, the site of the battle, on June 28, 1989, he referred to the heroes of 1389 and their virtues, drawing direct parallels with the present. Earlier that year, Milošević had curtailed the autonomy of the Province of Kosovo by constitutional redesign, provoking Albanian protests whose violent suppression resulted in dozens of casualties. In the Gazimestan speech, he presented this as a fulfillment of the Kosovo covenant—not, of course, by explicitly boasting of the dead but by arguing that Serbia had reclaimed its dignity.

Milošević's recasting of the Kosovo story was much less traumatic than that of the cultural nationalists. Actually, his 1989 speech comes closest to a "progressive narrative" of the Kosovo trauma. It is full of optimism, problems solved, difficulties left behind, and new challenges bravely taken. Ironically of course, his version only led to new traumas, definitively antagonizing Albanians and destroying the last chances for a peaceful settlement. But it is important to bear in mind that Milošević took pains to fashion his rhetoric in such a vague way as to enable different readings of his messages. He did not attack Albanians directly or openly arouse Serbian aggressive nationalist feelings; the aggression was there, but implicit. What was promised explicitly was national rebirth, peace, and prosperity, all in idyllic multiethnic coexistence. True, Milošević also promised to regain "our" Kosovo, but who exactly "we" were was not fully specified. And his notorious mention of "battles" was so ambiguous that an ordinary listener could easily choose to ignore the violent undertone.[23]

Milošević's true concern in this speech was to threaten his political opponents by invoking the treason of Vuk Branković and the "disunity" among Serbs as the "evil fate throughout their history."[24] In this way, the old epic tradition was used to legitimate the wholly communist practice of "differentiation," that is, a purge of dissenters, and to underwrite a forced unity of mind and action.

Trauma as a Speech Act

Rather than attempting to give a clear-cut answer to whether Kosovo *is* or *is not* Serbian trauma, we are now in a position to approach the question in a more fruitful way. In the language pragmatic perspective, both can be true at the same time. Trauma may be seen as a speech act, a continually discursively produced condition that stands in mutually constitutive relations with the contextual circumstances. In this sense, it is present as a cultural meaning-structure, Eyerman's "referent" or Živković's "entrenched story". But this does not imply that Trauma is actively *felt* by people, that it is located somehow within them, that it affects them uniformly and unavoidably, or that there is some mysterious connection between being Serbian and the trauma.

Over the centuries, the thematic cluster of Kosovo has become a (potentially) traumatizing interpretive framework readily available to Serbs for making sense of their collective experiences. Though to call it a "master narrative" would be stretching it too far, the Kosovo legend has certainly been the most widespread, familiar, habitual and easily usable story Serbs have had to explain things to themselves. This framework, although not absolutely conditioning, did facilitate a traumatic rendering of a series of collective events, especially during the nineteenth and early twentieth centuries, and then again in the last three decades, that is, whenever Albanian-Serbian rivalry over real-life Kosovo re-territorialized the myth. These events in turn provided empirical fodder that reinforced the traumatic strand in the myth.

But it is good to keep in mind that official discourse, inevitably privileged in historical record and social scientific analysis alike, is not all there is. While in governmental, academic, journalistic, or religious ways of talking about Kosovo, the trauma is constantly referred to as the undisputable center of Serbian identity,[25] there is ample evidence that the vernacular receptions have not always conformed. For instance, in the early 1990s, a team of ethnologists studying the actual presence of the Kosovo myth in rural Serbia found that it had largely been lost (Bandić 2001).[26] More examples follow.

Serbhood as Victimhood

Although multivocal, the Kosovo tradition does tend to funnel Serbian collective self-construction along certain paths. Two of such paths are especially prominent. One, which has an elective affinity with the traumatic weave in the Kosovo myth, especially in the versions reviewed previously, is self-identification as victims, and the other is verbal grandiosity.

That "we" have always been victims of evil others is, of course, not an exclusively Serbian idea. But Serbs seem to have developed it rather elaborately and to keep to it with much enthusiasm (Jansen 2000). The most troubling consequence is the tendency to think of "us" in morally righteous terms, to routinely assume one's own moral superiority presumably wrought by suffering. A corollary is a difficulty to engage in collective soul-searching, self-criticism, and self-censure.[27] The double-edged nature of the Kosovo story, deriving from the original reversal of defeat into victory, has made it usable for "having it both ways," as it were: for being at once a *victim* and a *winner,* and claiming moral capital on both counts by virtue of suffering and of coming out on top. Or, in Giesen's (2004) terms, Kosovo seems to be available as *both* triumph and trauma, even though Giesen presents the two as mutually exclusive.

Furthermore, claim on victimhood often turns into a monopolization of it. Especially in strained, trauma-favorable periods, the circle of legitimate victims tends to be restricted to "us." Instead of broadening the category of victims and expanding the circle of the "we" that Alexander (2004, 1) sees as an important part of the trauma process, here we have a contrary trend of *shrinking* of the "we." The solidarity of others is not sought, perhaps it is even discouraged. This seems to be going on right now, with a perceived "lack of understanding" for Serbs on the part of the West fuelling further alienation and allowing some to sink deeper into an exclusive-victimhood language of identity.

Claiming moral superiority on the basis of the supposed purifying effects of suffering may be read as an assertion of particularism through reference to some kind of universal standards. Another paradoxical move of this kind is asserting Serbian specialness by insisting on the megalomaniac exceptionalism of Kosovo. Statements such as "[h]ow to present this spiritual meaning of Kosovo for Serbs to the public opinion, when there is no analogous example in the world heritage?" (a 1998 newspaper article, quoted in Čolović 2001, 208), or "[s]ix centuries ago, nothing on the globe happened more important than the battle at the Kosovo Field" (Bećković 1990, 47) are not at all uncommon, in spite of their extravagance, and could easily be heard even from ordinary people.

This is connected with the second path along which the Kosovo legacy tends to channel Serbian narratives: the tendency of grandiloquence when the nation is concerned. Somehow, Serbs have developed the belief, or at least the habit, that when talking about matters of nation and state only lofty and pompous terms are in order. A down-to-earth language of Serbian patriotism is mostly lacking. The "great" (read "national") has been decoupled from the "small," the petty things of everyday life, work, ordinary human effort, and patient building of an ordered life. Of course, Serbs have been doing all these things, just as anybody else, but this sort of endeavor has been kept at the side of the profane, at a distance from the sacrality of the nation. It is not easy to verbally perform as a good Serb talking about daily, this-worldly matters; there is no "sacralization of the everyday" in a Weberian sense. The problem is that this contributes to a devaluation of Serbia's civilian accomplishments during the two centuries of its modern history and hinders the recognition of national interest in a democratically defined common good.

The Trauma, a Trauma, and the Importance of Registers

In 1998–1999, the symbolism of Kosovo was rather brutally terrestrialized again, with the outbreak of armed conflicts between the Albanian Kosovo Liberation Army and the Serbian state forces. In March 1999, NATO intervened and bombed Serbia for two and a half months. The trauma as a cultural script was now confronted with a real-life, palpable trauma of being victimized by the high-technology weaponry of the world's most powerful military machinery. What is more, the immediate trauma was directly connected with Kosovo as the site of the original trauma, and the victimization was widely perceived as thoroughly unjust because, as the prevailing opinion went, "we are just trying to keep what is ours." All the reasons were there to expect that the trauma of NATO bombardment would be experienced and narrated in a framework heavily determined by trauma.

But two sets of data collected at roughly the same time (the end of the 1990s through the early 2000s) reveal vastly different, even contrary, ways of talking about the matter. Between 1998 and 2000, ethnologist Saša Nedeljković (2007, 52–66) collected two hundred written compositions by Belgrade University students, mostly in the ethnology department, on the topic of "Serbhood." Although Kosovo was not a required theme, most respondents wrote about it. It was discussed in emotional rather than intellectual terms, and a lot of mythical rhetoric was used.[28] These constructions are in evident contrast with the ethnographic data collected only several years before by Bandić. The explanation lies partly in the differential educational levels of the two samples, but not in the direction social scientists would expect: The almost illiterate peasants were *less* colonized by the mythical discourse than the urban college students. This is another indication of the importance of the educational system in inculcating the allegedly inborn Serbian trauma.

The other set of data was collected in 2001 and 2002 within a research project dealing with popular experience of the fall of Milošević in 2000 and Serbia's future prospects.[29] One question concerned the issue of (real) Kosovo and the 1999 NATO bombing, and in this conjunction, many respondents referred to Kosovo as symbolic legacy. Although for most (but by no means all) of them the events of 1999 were in various ways traumatic, it is remarkable how much this was *not* couched in the language of mythical trauma. People were familiar with the symbolic tradition and generally ready to respect it, but also tried not to let it determine their political stands. They seemed to be caught between demands of rational positioning in the real world and moral sentiments of pride and justice that are so strongly associated with the Kosovo theme. The result was a perplexed and contradictory but open attitude, an honest attempt to think through a difficult topic. Well-known tropes, like "Kosovo is the Serbian cradle," were often employed in a casual, even ironic manner. The discussion often started from a simple assertion that "Kosovo is ours," referring not to any kind of metaphysics but rather to political and legal, though hardly more commendable, "ownership" of Kosovo by Serbs as the entitled nation. Another general trend was for interviewees to acknowledge, with a sort of aggrieved resignation, that Kosovo was "lost."

So how do we account for the difference between the extensively mythicized discourse in the first data and uneasy realism in the second? The main reason lies, I believe, in the different framings of the discussion, resulting in two different registers people were employing in response to these framings. Nedeljković's assigned title, "Serbhood" (srpstvo), framed the issue in a way that invited mythologization: srpstvo is a very loaded word, abstract and general, with a flavor of artificiality, and never used in daily speech (not even when talking "grand" of the nation). The other data were obtained with a questionnaire that provided a very different frame—rational, concrete, and personal and discouraging of generalized proclamations. Thus different discursive registers produced divergent ways of talking about the same things.

A Common Language in Which to Disagree

The long history of the Kosovo trauma as a cultural structure has produced the layered character of its meanings. Yes, Kosovo means something to most Serbs, probably even matters to them. But the contents are highly diverse. What is more, the layered meanings are only partly expressible in words. They may also involve a whole range of vague feelings of uneasiness, discontent, and shame, provoked by the recent collective experiences. So within the seemingly singular trauma some meaning layers may be closer to the surface and more readily articulable, and others buried, tacit, and possibly activated only in the mode of Herzfeldian (Herzfeld 1997) "cultural intimacy" (or not even then). This amounts to more than just different meanings, to profoundly different emotional and moral import, including possibly outright irrelevance of the trauma to an individual Serb. What remains, and what really functions as connective tissue among Serbs, is the identical language they are all familiar with, the "entrenched" symbolism of Kosovo that rhetorically brings all of these differences together without admitting them. The name remains the same, providing the impression of stability, and making it possible to ostensibly revive the myth, while in fact, the name is just turned into "a useful cliché or linguistic stereotype, a 'reference' and argument in ideological use" (Đerić 2005, 30).

The tropes of the Kosovo legend, especially in its epic guise, have been used as political devices for condemning and morally polluting political opponents since the mid-nineteenth century. This practice has been so widespread in Serbian political life that the function of *internal exclusion* may qualify as an even more prominent pragmatic function of the trauma than aggression toward others, currently foregrounded in critical outsider accounts. Nevertheless, mechanisms of exclusion may be more subtle than the explicit pollution of the opponent by identifying him/her with the treacherous Vuk Branković. An excellent instance of this more oblique deployment was provided in 2006 by then-Prime Minister Vojislav Koštunica, a democratic but conservative nationalist. Speaking at the symbolically highly charged site of the ancient Serbian monastery of Hilandar in Greece, in the midst of a political campaign, Koštunica said, "Everybody knows what Kosovo means to us." Let us have a closer look at this phrase. If "everybody" knows it, then those who feel they do *not* know exactly what Kosovo means to them, or to others, cannot help feeling excluded or better, completely obliterated (since they do not even belong to the "everybody"). If everybody "knows" something, there is no need at all to articulate, discuss, and argue this something. Finally, who the "us" refers to is similarly unclear. (Serbs? All of them, or only some? Maybe just the patriots, or the Orthodox, or the members of Koštunica's party?) Hence, by a short and seemingly innocuous phrase, all those who do not recognize themselves in it are excluded from the community. But this is done implicitly, which makes the move less conspicuous and harder to challenge: One would not really know how to protest it. The main paradox involved in both "simple" and "complex" strategies of exclusion is that the trauma, presented as what binds Serbs together, is used to produce internal and self-inflicted traumatization of the national polity, by deepening cleavages within and preventing their pacification.

The period after 2000 has been characterized by a series of new twists and turns on the Kosovo theme. After the war of 1999 and installment of international administration in (real) Kosovo, the region's status remained unresolved. This has been conducive to a mood in Serbia in which it is quite easy to score political points by raising the rhetorical stakes concerning Kosovo. While the unofficial, more personalized and private discourse, as shown above, has been characterized by a general rationalism and open-mindedness, the discourse produced by political elites has sought a re-traumatization of Serbian attitude to Kosovo. Instead of being gradually replaced by more rational and realistic, policy-oriented suggestions, the tropes of the Kosovo Myth in its traumatic version have been liberally employed by elite actors, trying to outdo one another in upholding the sanctity of Kosovo. With the verbal stakes rising, it has become all but impossible to talk about Kosovo, real as well as symbolic, in anything but the most elevated tone. A whole range of positions on the issue have been rendered discursively unavailable or excessively costly.[30] On the other hand, uttering or supporting empty phrases like "Kosovo is Serbia!", "We shall never give up Kosovo!", "Kosovo is our sacred land!" and so on, costs nothing and can even bring some profit—if anything, the profit of showing that one is not sticking out. So many people choose to repeat these phrases, without much thinking. At the same time, people harbor all kinds of doubts and grudges against the symbolic prevalence of Kosovo and its impingements on current Serbian politics and feel extremely uncomfortable expressing them in public, or even to themselves, because the sacredness of the topic has been so extremely enhanced. This private and subdued attitude of weary irritation is almost impossible to pin down: one may feel it in muttered remarks, half-voiced comments, and grumbles overheard, on people's faces, and in the tone of their voices.

These ambivalences came out in elections. The year 2008 was hot with passions, with (real) Kosovo's proclamation of independence in February, ensuing protests turned riots in Belgrade, the raiding and burning of the U.S. embassy, sudden icing of Serbia's relations with Western countries, and so on. The public sphere reverberated with innumerable invocations of Lazar's oath and the bequest of the Kosovo heroes, particularly in the campaign of the ultranationalists. Nevertheless, in February 2008, the incumbent democratic president Boris Tadić was reelected, and in parliamentary elections held in May, the democratic coalition marked a convincing victory.[31] True, Tadić and his democrats, just like almost everybody on the Serbian political scene, consider Kosovo's independence illegal and fight it as they can, but whatever one may think of their Kosovo policy, it is not extremist. Pointing in the same direction, polling data show that, when asked to list the most important problems Serbia is currently facing, people place (the status of real) Kosovo below "unemployment," "low living standard," and "corruption" (SMMRI 2008).[32]

Referring to the theoretical framework, I hope to have shown how the concept of cultural trauma, with its emphasis on stories, debate, and discursive struggle within actually existing civil societies, helps avoid the impasse of having to choose between equally unacceptable poles. On one hand, arguing that traumas found collective, especially national identities, pushes one almost irresistibly toward one or another kind of essentialism: in the form of a dangerous biologism of the national "soul," "nature," or "being," or of the easy psychologism of postulated (but empirically im-provable) collective pain and wounds on the communal psyche. On the other hand, the only way to avoid these antisociological musings seems to be shedding off "culture" altogether, as inconsequential and specious. The analysis presented in this chapter makes clear that beyond these two nonoptions there is a way to see how "national" stories, if successful, and having been told and retold thousands of times, stick to the nation and become its second, cultural nature. And their inherent ambiguity is a necessary condition for this to happen. The Serbian case also points to the ironies of symbolic exchange between inside and outside. It has been described how critical observers, aiming at denouncing the reprehensible actions of a community and thus pricking the balloon of its self-conceit, are unwittingly drawn in by the semiotic force of the existing narratives and end up reinforcing the very chimera of a unified national essence that democracy wants to see dissolved.

So, finally, is there a Kosovo trauma for Serbs? The answer may be "yes" provided that we understand its proper location: it does not dwell *in* Serbs, but in the discursive space *between* them. And the trauma itself involves a whole knot of entangled traumas, not necessarily those that bards of the trauma strove to inculcate. The deceptive simplicity of the noun, *Kosovo,* might also hide traumas of the Yugoslav wars, including the "trauma of perpetrators" (Giesen 2004); the trauma of being caught in an irresolvable conflict with a neighboring people, Albanians; the trauma of Serbia's exclusion from European integration; the trauma of living in a faulty democracy and continuing economic stagnation. And also, perhaps, the trauma of being forced into a traumatic identity and lacking the language in which to express one's dissent without being called a traitor.

Notes

1. Works that acknowledge the changing meanings of the myth with-out dismissing its relevance are quite infrequent. Good examples are the brief analyses by Bieber (2002), focusing on the political aspects, and Bakić-Hayden (2004), with a more cultural-hermeneutical approach. Zirojević (2000) provides a condensed account of the historical background.

2. Sometimes this posture happily coincides with a researcher's post-modernist abdication of social science, like in Van de Port (1999).

3. See Vickers 1998, Luci and Marković 2008, Zdravković 2005, and Duijzings 2000. On recent symbolizations of Kosovo Albanian victimhood, see Di Lellio and Schwandner-Sievers 2006.

4. See Emmert (1990) and Vucinich and Emmert, eds. (1991), for detailed discussions of the historical event and the legend.

5. Ironically, in the Albanian legend the same character, called Millosh Kopiliq, is Albanian (Di Lellio 2009).

6. In the so-called Great Migration of 1690, Serbs leaving Kosovo for southern Hungary took with them the earthly remains of the Holy Prince Lazar, thus moving the symbolic center of religious-national identity.

7. Given the specific nature of oral literature, where there is no "original" or "true" version, it is significant that the Kosovo poems were written down precisely at the moment of revolutionary turmoil. The circumstances certainly colored the versions that were recorded and thereby fixed for posterity as *the* Kosovo lore. Moreover, a few of the key poems in the "Kosovo Cycle" are known to be, to a certain degree, authorial creations of specific individuals, the well-known singers of the day.

8. The Battle of Kosovo was the *Leit-motiv* of Serbian poetry of the 1860s, with literary magazines swarmed by poems entitled *Kosovo, At Kosovo, Oh Kosovo* and full of wailings such as "Kosovo—my bloody wound!", "Woe Kosovo!" and so on (Skerlić 1925, 155).

9. In the same period, the Kosovo myth was sometimes found to be instrumental to ideologies broader than Serbian nationalism. The Pan-Slavists in the Habsburg Empire felt they could use it for promoting Slavic unity. The Illyrians, members of the Croatian National Revival movement, read Kosovo as a symbol of South Slavic, not just Serbian, national pride and a promise of future liberation. See Wachtel (1998) on this model of language-based cultural unity of South Slavs, and Banac (1984) for a more critical discussion.

10. The difference in dates is due to the fact that the Serbian Church uses the old, Julian calendar which is 13 days behind the Gregorian, accepted internationally as well as by the Serbian authorities.

11. But with all their rationalism, their motivation in courageously deconstructing national myths, against much opposition, was firmly patriotic: they wanted to rid Serbian glory, which they did not doubt the least, of harmful lies and mystifications. Today, this ideological combination would look curious indeed.

12. On Garašanin's "Memorandum" (1844), which set expansionist national policy in terms of a resurrection of the medieval Serbian state, see Roudometoff (2001, 117–118).

13. For Albanian political development in this period, see Vickers 1998 and Malcolm 1998; a Serbian view is presented in Bogdanović 2006.

14. On these three artists and their relation to the ideology of Yugoslavism, see Wachtel 1998 and Banac 1984.

15. From my personal experience as a pupil in Serbian schools in Titoist times, I know many hours were devoted to the Kosovo folk poems and large chunks of them had to be learned by heart. *That*—by having learned the poems

for homework—is how most Serbs become familiar with the characteristic topoi of the Kosovo legend, and not because they "have it in their blood."

16. After 1945, Kosovo had been established as an autonomous province within the Republic of Serbia, one of the six republics comprising the Socialist Federative Republic of Yugoslavia.

17. In 1982, twenty-one priests signed an "Appeal for the Protection of Serb Inhabitants and Their Holy Places in Kosovo."

18. The activities of these three institutions are analyzed in the respective chapters in Popov, ed. 2000. For a more general discussion of the Serbian intellectual opposition and its "nationalization" in the 1980s, see Dragović-Soso 2002.

19. A weird example of explicit traumatization for political purposes took place in 1988, when the remains of Prince Lazar were taken on a long journey through Serb-populated regions, being displayed, hailed, and mourned in many towns and villages before arriving at the Gračanica monastery in Kosovo on the eve of the Battle's six hundredth anniversary. The organizer was the Church, while the Milošević authorities benevolently condoned.

20. He spent three months in Dachau during World War II. In 2003, Velimirović was canonized as a Serbian saint.

21. *Jadovno,* the name of a pit where the *Ustasha,* Croatian fascist militants, were throwing bodies of slain Serbs, is a metonymy for all *Ustasha* crimes against Serbs.

22. For example, "God is our witness that we do not wish any evil to the Albanians" (120). The book's preface, written by another publicly visible nationalist bishop, Amfilohije Radović, argues that the book is not an appeal to revenge and hate, but "an evangelical appeal to repentance and sober rationality."

23. In what is probably the most often-quoted passage from this speech Milošević says, "Nowadays, six centuries later, we are again in battles and facing battles. They are not armed ones, although such cannot be ruled out either." This sounds belligerent indeed, but the very next sentence reads, "Our main battle today refers to the achievement of economic, political, cultural and generally social prosperity. For approaching more rapidly and successfully the civilization humans will live in [the] twenty-first century." Quoted from www.uio.no/studier/emner/hf/ilos/BKS4110/Eksamensoppgaver/BKS4110%20V07.doc.

24. See the analysis in Naumović (2009, 227–239) and Antonijević (2007b, 127–8).

25. A volume purporting to offer a conclusive historian's view of the battle (Tasić and Đuretić, eds. 1991) is a good source of illustrations: for the contributors, Kosovo is "*undoubtedly* the most important event in the entire history of the Serbian people" (7); "not just the national idea but that inner trait that makes a Serb a Serb" (14); "part of our destiny ... built into the foundations of our consciousness and our culture ... Battle of Kosovo, this is *us*" (49; all emphases added).

26. Informants did not have much to say about Prince Lazar, only that he had died at Kosovo; many didn't even know which kingdom he had chosen (Bandić 2001, 462).

27. Čolović (2002, 7–9) provides an ironic summary of what, to paraphrase Malkki (1995), might be called Serbian "mythico-history," revolving around victimhood and moral purity.

28. Kosovo is "the only true core of truth, … the heart of Serbia" where "one is stunned into silence, and time comes to a halt … Kosovo is the insistent strong pain in the soul, … Serbia's cancer" (Nedeljković 2007, 60–61).

29. The project's title was "Politics and everyday life" (Golubović et al. [eds.] 2003; Spasić 2008). Three hundred semistructured interviews were conducted with ordinary people throughout Serbia.

30. When in 2007 prominent journalist Boško Jakšić argued in his column in the *Politika* daily for Serbia's recognition of an independent Kosovo, this provoked public uproar that lasted for weeks.

31. The coalition Democratic Party/G17 won 38.40 percent of the vote (102 seats in Parliament), while the ultranationalist Serbian Radical Party came second with 29.45 percent (78 seats) (RZS 2008).

32. In 2005–2008, the percentage of respondents placing Kosovo among chief problems ranged on the average between 20 and 30 percent, rising to 40 percent only around February 2008. In November 2008, it was 13 percent. "Unemployment" scored consistently between 45 and 60 percent, and "low living standards" 35 to 45 percent (more than one priority could be listed).

Works Cited

Alexander, J. 2004. Toward a Theory of Cultural Trauma. In *Cultural Trauma and Collective Identity*, J. Alexander et al. Berkeley: University of California Press.

Antonijević, D. 2007a. *Karađorđe i Miloš: Između istorije i predanja (Karađorđe and Miloš: Between History and Legend)*. Beograd: Etnološka biblioteka.

———. 2007b. *Karađorđe i Miloš: Mit i politika (Karađorđe and Miloš: Myth and Politics)*. Beograd: Etnološka biblioteka.

Anzulović, B. 1999. *Heavenly Serbia: From Myth to Genocide*. New York: New York University Press.

Bakić-Hayden, M. 2004. National Memory as Narrative Memory: The Case of Kosovo. In *Balkan Identities: Nation and Memory*, ed. M. Todorova. New York: New York University Press.

Banac, I. 1984. *The National Question in Yugoslavia: Origins, History, Politics*. Ithaca: Cornell University Press.

Bandić, D. 1997 [1990]. *Carstvo zemaljsko i carstvo nebesko (Heavenly and Earthly Kingdom)*. Beograd: XX vek.

———. 2001. Tajni život kosovskog mita (The Secret Life of Kosovo Myth). In *Zbornik Etnografskog muzeja u Beogradu: 1901–2001*, ed. J. Bjeladinović-Jergić. Beograd: Etnografski muzej.

Bećković, M. 1990. *Služba (The Service)*. Beograd: SKZ.

Bieber, F. 2002. Nationalist Mobilization and Stories of Serb Suffering: The Kosovo Myth from 600th Anniversary to the Present. *Rethinking History* 6(1): 95–110.

Bogdanović, D. 2006 [1985]. *Knjiga o Kosovu (Book on Kosovo)*. Beograd: SKZ.

Byford, J. 2008. *Denial and Repression of Anti-Semitism: Post-Communist Remembrance of the Serbian Bishop Nikolaj Velimirović*. Budapest: CEU Press.

Cvijić, J. 1992 [1931]. Dinarski, centralni i panonski tip. In *Karakterologija Srba (Characterology of Serbs)*, ed. B. Jovanović. Beograd: Naučna knjiga.

Čolović, I. 2001. *Dubina (Depth)*. Beograd: Samizdat B92.

——. 2002 [1997]. *The Politics of Symbol in Serbia: Essays in Political Anthropology*, trans. C. Hawkesworth. London: Hurst.

Ćosić, D. 2004. *Kosovo*. Beograd: Novosti.

Di Lellio, A. 2009. *The Battle of Kosovo 1389: An Albanian Epic*. London and New York: I.B. Tauris.

Di Lellio, A., and S. Schwandner-Sievers. 2006. The Legendary Commander: the Construction of an Albanian Master-Narrative in Post-War Kosovo. *Nations and Nationalism* 12(3): 513–529.

Đerić, G. 2005. *Pr(a)vo lice množine (Speaking [of the] We)*. Beograd: IFDT/ Filip Višnjić.

Dragnich, A., and S. Todorovich. 1984. *The Saga of Kosovo: Focus on Serbian-Albanian Relations*. Boulder, CO: East European Monographs.

Dragović-Soso, J. 2002. *Saviours of the Nation?: Serbia's Intellectual Opposition and the Revival of Nationalism*. London: Hurst.

Duijzings, G. 2000. *Religion and the Politics of Identity in Kosovo*. London: Hurst.

Dvorniković, V. 1939. *Karakterologija Jugoslovena (Characterology of Yugoslavs)*. Beograd: Geca Kon.

Emmert, T. A. 1990. *Serbian Golgotha: Kosovo 1389*. New York: Columbia University Press.

Eyerman, R. 2002. *Cultural Trauma*. Port Chester, NY: Cambridge University Press.

Giesen, B. 2004. The Trauma of Perpetrators: The Holocaust as the Traumatic Reference of German National Identity. In *Cultural Trauma and Collective Identity*, J. Alexander et al. Berkeley: University of California Press.

Golubović, Z., I. Spasić, and Đ. Pavićević, eds. 2003. *Politika i svakodnevni život: Srbija 1999–2002 (Politics and Everyday Life: Serbia 1999–2002)*. Beograd: IFDT.

Herzfeld, M. 1997. *Cultural Intimacy: Social Poetics in the Nation-State*. New York: Routledge.

Hobsbawm, E. 1983. Mass-Producing Traditions: Europe, 1870–1914. In *The Invention of Tradition*, eds. E. Hobsbawm and T. Ranger. Cambridge: Cambridge University Press.

Jansen, S. 2000. *Victims, Underdogs and Rebels:* Discursive Practices of Resistance in Serbian Protest. *Critique of Anthropology* 20(4): 393–419.

Jevtić, A. 2007 [1987]. *Od Kosova do Jadovna (From Kosovo to Jadovno)*. Trebinje/ Vrnjci: Manastir Tvrdoš/Bratstvo sv. Simeona Mirotočivog.

Loma, A. 2002. *Prakosovo: slovenski i indoevropski koreni srpske epike (Pre-Kosovo. Slavic and Indo-European Roots of Serbian Epics)*. Beograd: Balkanološki institut SANU.

Luci, N., and P. Marković. 2009. Events and Sites of Difference: Marking Self and Other in Kosovo. In *Media Discourse and the Yugoslav Conflicts*, ed. P. Kolstø. Farnham: Ashgate.

Malcolm, N. 1998. *Kosovo: A Short History*. New York: New York University Press.

Malkki, L. 1995. *Purity and Exile: Violence, Memory and National Cosmology among Hutu Refugees in Tanzania*. Chicago and London: University of Chicago Press.

Milošević, S. 1989. Milošević's Gazimestan Speech, at www.uio.no/studier/ emner/hf/ilos/BKS4110/Eksamensoppgaver/BKS4110%20V07.doc.

Naumović, S. 2009. *Upotreba tradicije u početkom i javnom životu Srbije na kraju 20. i poÕetkom 21. veka (The Use of Tradition in Serbian Political and Public Life at the Turn of 21st Century)*. Beograd: IFDT/Filip Višnjić.

Nedeljković, S. 2007. *Čast, krv i suze (Honor, Blood and Tears)*. Beograd: Zlatni zmaj/Odeljenje za etnologiju i antropologiju Filozofskog fakulteta.

Popov, N., ed. 2000. *The Road to War in Serbia: Trauma and Catharsis*. Budapest: CEU Press.

Popović, M. 1998. *Vidovdan i časni krst (Vidovdan and the Holy Cross)*. Beograd: XX vek.

Ramet, S. P. 1995. The Serbian Church and the Serbian Nation. In *Beyond Yugoslavia: Politics, Economics, and Culture in a Shattered Community*, eds. S. P. Ramet and Lj. S. Adamovich. Boulder: Westview Press.

Roudometoff, V. 2001. *Nationalism, Globalization, and Orthodoxy: The Social Origins of Ethnic Conflict in the Balkans*. Westport, CT: Greenwood Press.

RZS. 2008. Parliamentary elections of May 11, 2008. Beograd: Republički zavod za statistiku, at http://webrzs.stat.gov.rs/axd/izbori200805.htm.

Sells, M. A. 2002. The Construction of Islam in Serbian Religious Mythology and Its Consequences. In *Islam and Bosnia: Conflict Resolution and Foreign Policy in Multi-Ethnic States*, ed. M. Schatzmiller. Montreal and Kingston: McGill-Queen's University Press.

Skerlić, J. 1925. *Omladina i njena književnost (1848–1871). Izučavanja o nacionalnom i književnom romantizmu kod Srba (Youth and Its Literature [1848–1871]. Studies in National and Literary Romanticism among Serbs)*. Beograd: Napredak.

SMMRI. 2008. Attitudes concerning Kosovo. Monthly Omnibus Survey, Strategic Marketing Research. Belgrade, December.

Spasić, I. 2008. Serbia 2000–2008: A Changing Political Culture? *Balkanologie* 11(1–2), at http://balkanologie.revues.org/index1282.html.

Šuber, D. 2006. Myth, Collective Trauma and War in Serbia: A Cultural-hermeneutical Appraisal. *Anthropology Matters Journal* 8(1): 1–9.

Tasić, N., and V. Duretić, eds. 1991. *Kosovska bitka 1389. i njene posledice (Kosovo Battle of 1389 and its Consequences)*. Beograd: SANU.

Van de Port, M. 1999. "It Takes a Serb to Know a Serb": Uncovering the Roots of Obstinate Otherness in Serbia. *Critique of Anthropology* 19(1): 7–30.

Velimirović, N. 1988. *Kosovo i Vidovdan (Kosovo and Vidovdan)*. Šabac: Glas crkve.

Vetlesen, A. J. 2005. *Evil and Human Agency: Understanding Collective Evildoing*. Cambridge: Cambridge University Press.

Vickers, M. 1998. *Between Serb and Albanian: A History of Kosovo*. London: Hurst.

Volkan, V. D. 1996. Bosnia-Herzegovina: Ancient Fuel of a Modern Inferno. *Mind and Human Interaction* 7: 110–127.

———. 2002. Bosnia-Herzegovina: Chosen Trauma and Its Transgenerational Transmission. In *Islam and Bosnia*, ed. M. Schatzmiller. Montreal and Kingston: McGill-Queen's University Press.

Vucinich, W. S., and T. A. Emmert, eds. 1991. *Kosovo: Legacy of a Medieval Battle*. Minneapolis: University of Minnesota Press.

Wachtel, A. B. 1998. *Making a Nation, Breaking a Nation: Literature and Cultural Politics in Yugoslavia*. Stanford: Stanford University Press.

Žanić, I. 1998. *Prevarena povijest (Tricked History)*. Zagreb: Durieux.

Zdravković, H. 2005. *Politika žrtve na Kosovu (The Politics of Victim in Kosovo)*. Beograd: Etnološka biblioteka.

Zirojević, O. 2000. Kosovo in the Collective Memory. In *The Road to War in Serbia: Trauma and Catharsis,* ed. N. Popov. Budapest: CEU Press.

Živković, M. 2001. Serbian Stories of Identity and Destiny in the 1980s and 1990s. Unpublished PhD dissertation, Department of Anthropology, University of Chicago.

5

Trauma Construction and Moral Restriction

The Ambiguity of the Holocaust for Israel

Jeffrey C. Alexander and Shai M. Dromi

"Yad Vashem Fires Employee Who Compared Holocaust to Nakba"

Yad Vashem has fired an instructor who compared the trauma of Jewish Holocaust survivors with the trauma experienced by the Palestinian people in Israel's War of Independence. Itamar Shapira, 29, of Jerusalem, was fired before Passover from his job as a docent at the Holocaust Martyrs' and Heroes' Remembrance Authority, after a teacher with a group of yeshiva students from Efrat made a complaint. Shapira had worked at Yad Vashem for three and a half years....

Shapira confirmed, in a telephone conversation with *Haaretz*, that he had spoken to visitors about the 1948 massacre at Deir Yassin. He said he did so because the ruins of the Arab village, today a part of Jerusalem's Givat Shaul neighborhood, can be seen as one leaves Yad Vashem. "Yad Vashem talks about the Holocaust survivors' arrival

107

in Israel and about creating a refuge here for the world's Jews. I said there are people who lived on this land and mentioned that there are other traumas that provide other nations with motivation," Shapira said. "The Holocaust moved us to establish a Jewish state and the Palestinian nation's trauma is moving it to seek self-determination, identity, land and dignity, just as Zionism sought these things," he said.

The institution's position is that the Holocaust cannot be compared to any other event and that every visitor can draw his own political conclusions ... "Yad Vashem would have acted unprofessionally had Itamar Shapira continued his educational work for the institute," [Yad Vashem spokeswoman Iris] Rosenberg said. Yad Vashem employs workers and volunteers from the entire political and social spectrum, who know how to separate their personal position from their work, she said.

Shapira said Yad Vashem chooses to examine only some of the events that took place in the War of independence. "It is being hypocritical. I only tried to expose the visitors to the facts, not to political conclusions. If Yad Vashem chooses to ignore the facts, for example the massacre at Deir Yassin, or the Nakba ["The Catastrophe," the Palestinians' term for what happened to them after 1948], it means that it's afraid of something and that its historical approach is flawed," Shapira said.

—Haaretz, April 23, 2009

"Gaza: Cleric Denounces Possible Holocaust Education"
A Hamas spiritual leader said Monday that teaching Palestinian children about the Nazis' murder of six million Jews would be a "war crime." The leader, Yunis al-Astal, lashed out after hearing that the United Nations Relief and Works Agency was considering the introduction of Holocaust lessons in some of the 221 schools the United Nations [runs] in Gaza. Adding the Holocaust to the curriculum would amount to "marketing a lie and spreading it," Dr. Astal wrote in a statement. An Israeli government spokesman, Mark Regev, said the comments were "obscene." A United Nations official said no decision had been made on Holocaust education Gaza.

—New York Times, September 1, 2009

These disheartening reports, appearing in two of the world's most sophisticated, liberal, and democratic newspapers, illustrate the idea at the core of this collective research project. References to trauma, and representations about it, are not just individual but social and collective. Who was responsible for a collective trauma, who were its victims, and what was the trauma's moral lessons for our own time? These are not simply theoretical or empirical issues for professional social scientists.

They are fundamental concerns of everyday life, matters for reporting in daily newspapers and web sites, and they powerfully affect contemporary conflicts at the individual, institutional, national, and global levels.[1]

As these reports also demonstrate, however, the manner in which collective traumas are presented in everyday life is naturalistic, to the point of being intellectually naïve. Traumas are spoken about as if they are simply historical facts, as things that happened, clearly understood events, empirical things that can either be recognized or ignored. How we choose to react to the facts of trauma is presented as if it were simply a matter of personal, individual reflection.

According to the cultural-sociological approach, however, neither of these latter suppositions is correct. Collective traumas are not found; they are made. Something awful usually did occur, but how it is represented remains an open question, subject to whirling spirals of signification, fierce power contests, simplifying binaries, subtle stories, fickle audiences, and counter-narrations. Individuals do not respond to traumas but to trauma constructions. How they come to reflect upon them is certainly a matter for individual conscience, but it is also a massively collective thing. Individuals experience the pain and suffering of defeat, and the hopes for future emancipation, in terms of collective stories that engulf and instruct them, sometimes in positive, sometimes in frightening, ways.

Earlier work on the Nazi murder of six million Jews[2] explored how the representation of this horrendous event shifted, in the half-century after it transpired, from "war crime" to "Holocaust" (Alexander 2004). As a heinous event associated with Nazism, the mass murder was initially contextualized inside the culture structures that had framed the World War II, a civilization-versus-barbarism binary, on the one hand, and a progressive narrative of modern amelioration, on the other. For two decades afterward, this binary and narrative frame allowed Western nations to keep the mass murder of the Jews, even as it remained ferociously stigmatized, as an event very much relegated to the past. In the postwar period, people looked to the future and engaged in reconstruction. They saw themselves as building a new, modern, and civilized society, one in which Nazi genocide would never be allowed to happen again. These efforts at civil repair were not illusory. Democracies were reconstructed from dictatorships, and millennia-long anti-Semitic barriers were overcome. Nevertheless, in the course of the 1960s, this grand narrative of postwar progress, which had sequestered racial, religious, and ethnic mass murder in a distant past began to be vulnerable and to change.

Collective traumas are complex symbolic-*cum*-emotional constructions that have significant autonomy from, and power over, social structure and interests in the more material sense. At the same time, however, trauma constructions are affected by the kinds of social groups that promote them, by the distribution of resources to broadcast them, and by the institutional structure of the social arenas in which their construction takes place. With the rise of anti-Western, anticolonial movements abroad, and the emergence of antiwar movements and racial and ethnic movements of liberation at home, the postwar protagonists of the progressive narrative were profoundly challenged. Their purity became polluted by association with their own ethnic, racial, and religious massacres, and their ability to maintain the civilization-barbarism binary destroyed. Rather than being seen as carriers of universalism, they were accused of being primordial and particularistic themselves. It was as these new understandings developed that the shift from "war crime" to "Holocaust" emerged. Rather than being relegated to the past, the dangers of massive racial, ethnic, and religious domination, and even mass murder, moved forward into the present. They became part of modernity. For contemporaries, the Holocaust shifted from a progressive to a tragic narrative. It became a story about hubris and punishment, a trauma drama that evoked sorrow and pity; its victims became objects of universal identification, and its perpetrators were now constructed as representing humanity rather than any particular national group. Its bathetic denouement provided a drama of eternal return to which contemporaries felt compelled to return over and over again. The Holocaust came to be seen as the singular representation of the darkness of the twentieth century, the humbling lesson on which was erected postmodern doubt. Yet, this humbling and tragic lesson also opened up the possibility for judging present and future humankind by a new, more universal moral standard.

This research on Holocaust and trauma construction was conducted in the late 1990s. It was a time of cautious optimism. The American and European intervention in Kosovo seemed to provide singular evidence for the universalizing power of the Holocaust effect. Dictatorships were still being turned into democracies, and there was a bubbling effervescence about the emergence of global civil society. It was a time to focus on the emergence of global narratives about the possibility of justice, among which there was no more surprising and inspiring story than the transvaluation of the Jewish mass murder from a historically situated war crime into tragic trauma drama whose moral lessons had become central to all modernity. In the words of Bernhard Giesen, a principal collaborator in that earlier project, this transvaluation process provided "a new transnational paradigm of collective identity" (Giesen 2009, 114), according to which the Holocaust became the "global icon of evil." As Alexander put it, "a specific and situated historical event" had become "transformed into a generalized symbol of human suffering," a "universal symbol whose very existence has created historically unprecedented opportunities for ethnic, racial, and religious justice, for mutual recognition, and for global conflicts becoming regulated in a more civil way" (Alexander 2004, 197).

We live now in a darker time, more divided, more violent, more tense. We have become much more cautious about the possibilities for a global civil society, more sensitive to the continuing festering of local wounds and their often explosive and debilitating worldwide effects. This is the time to explore the relationship between cultural trauma and collective identity in a different way, elaborating the theory so that it can explain not only more universalizing but also more particularistic and deleterious results. In this chapter, we return to the historical genealogy of the Holocaust, but connect it with the emergence of a radically different carrier group, a drastically divergent social setting, and spirals of signification that depart sharply in their symbolic meanings and moral implications. We connect Holocaust symbolization not to pluralist Western democracies but to a democracy bent on securing the foundations of a single religion, not to a postwar national context but to a nation founded in war, facing challenges to its very existence for decades, right up until today. For this Jewish nation, despite its progressive aspirations, the memory of the Jewish mass murder connoted tragedy from the outset, and the catharsis produced by iterations of the trauma drama sustained moral strictures of more particularistic and primordial than universal and civil kinds.

Tragic Dramas, Divergent Effects

Tragic narratives compel members of a collectivity to narrate and symbolically re-experience the suffering of a trauma's victims. If these victims are represented narrowly—as simply the storytellers themselves—the tragic trauma drama is unlikely to generate sympathy for those on the other side. It creates not identification with extended others but with the storytellers' own ancestors, those who share the same primordial identity as the victims' themselves. The tragic trauma drama produces catharsis, but it is not the enlightening pity that Aristotle once described. It is more self-pity, a sentiment that blocks identification and undermines the expansion of moral feeling that such contemporary neo-Aristotelians as Martha Nussbaum have prescribed. Rather than a universalizing love for the other, what emerges from such trauma work is a more restrictive self-love, a feeling that cuts imaginative experience short, encouraging emotional splitting and moral scapegoating.

In this emplotment, the moral implications of the drama of eternal return are inverted. Not being able to get beyond the originating trauma, feeling compelled again and again to return to it, reinforces rather than mitigates the particularistic hatreds that inspired the aggression and murder of that earlier time. Narrowing rather than universalizing in morality and affect, earlier hatreds are reproduced, not overcome. Rather than expanded human sympathy for the other, we have Hitler revenging the defeated German people, Serbia's ethnic cleansing, and India and Pakistan's bloody-minded struggles against Islamic and Hindu "intruders" today.[3] We also have the *Nakba*, the construction of the catastrophe that Israeli's founding is believed to have created for the Palestinian people, a trauma that inspires the violently anti-Jewish and anti-Israeli struggles by Palestinian people and Arab states against the Zionism and the Israeli state. These polarizing, trauma-inspired struggles have fuelled the tragic-*cum*-primordial narratives that prevent peace between Arabs and Jews in the Middle East today.

An Israeli Patriot's Lament

In the middle of 2007, David Remnick, the editor of the *New Yorker* magazine, published a controversial "Letter from Jerusalem." It was a conversation with Avraham Burg, once Speaker of the Israel Knesset and former chairman both of the World Zionist Organization and the Israeli Jewish Agency. Remnick's conversation with the now embittered Israeli leader points directly to the social processes we wish to illuminate here. "As of this moment," Burg observes, "Israel is a state of trauma in nearly every one of its dimensions." Insisting that this is "not just a theoretical question," he asks, "would our ability to cope with Iran not be much better if we renewed in Israel the ability to trust the world?" It is because Israelis identify the Holocaust with their betrayal by Christian Europe, Burg reasons, that they do not possess the necessary reserve of trust that could propel a process of peace. "We say we do not trust the world, they will abandon us," Burg explains. Seeing "Chamberlain returning from Munich with the black umbrella," Israelis draw the conclusion "we will bomb them alone" (Remnick 2007). It is because of this trauma construction, Burg believes, that so many Israelis feel they must go it alone. He finds this path deeply self-defeating. "Would it not be more right," he asks, "if we didn't deal with the problem on our own but, rather, as part of a world alignment beginning with the Christian churches, going on to the governments and finally the armies?"

In its early "optimistic years," Burg tells Remnick, Israel was different. Paradoxically, "the farther we got from the camps and the gas chambers, the more pessimistic we became and the more untrusting we became toward the world." As Burg sees it, this narrative shift has produced chauvinism and selfishness. Today, the Holocaust trauma fragments and divides, allowing conservative Israelis to justify oppressing Palestinians. It is because of their Holocaust consciousness, Burg insists, that his contemporaries are not "sensitive enough to what happens to others and in many ways are too indifferent to the suffering of others. We confiscated, we monopolized, world suffering. We did not allow anybody else to call whatever suffering they have 'holocaust' or 'genocide,' be it Armenians, be it Kosovo, be it Darfur." The Holocaust trauma is remembered in a manner that makes a significant swath of Israeli society impervious to criticism: "'Occupation? You call this occupation? This is nothing compared to the absolute evil of the Holocaust!' And if it is nothing compared to the Holocaust then you can continue. And since nothing, thank God, is comparable to the ultimate trauma, it legitimizes many things."

Jewish Dreams of Post-Tragedy

It might have seemed, from a more naturalistic perspective, that the Holocaust would be written directly on the body of Israel and its Jews, whether via first-hand experience or by primordial identification. From a cultural-sociological perspective, however, meaning-work is contingent. For Israel and its Jewish people, the meaning and message of the Holocaust has been up for grabs, crystallized in strikingly divergent ways. "The memory of the Holocaust and its victims," Yechiam Weitz observes, "was accompanied by unending political strife;" these debates "were always ... bitter, full of tension and emotional," and occasionally "violent and even deadly" (Weitz 1995, 130).[4]

The millennia-long sufferings of the Jewish people created an historical memory of persecution. These tragic iterations were ritualized in Jewish religious ceremonies, constituting a cultural legacy that seemed to demand not progress but eternal return. While the postenlightenment European emancipation of ghettoized Jews triggered a more progressive narrative, the backlash against Jewish incorporation that exploded in the last decades of the nineteenth century, and accelerated during the early twentieth, pushed European Jewry to look backward again. Zionism emerged in response to this stinging disappointment. It fought against not only anti-Semitism but also the fatalism and pessimism that so often had marked the Jewish tradition itself. It promised that, if a homeland were regained, the Jewish people would be landed and citied, and their history rewound. The story of the Jewish people could start over again in a healthy and "normal" way.[5]

Zionist Struggles, Holocaust Memories

This historic dream came to earth in a land peopled mostly by others. Israel's founding did instantiate the progressive narrative of Zionism, but in a decidedly triumphalist and militarized manner. From the late nineteenth and early twentieth centuries, growing Zionist settlement faced increasingly embittered antagonists, not only indigenous Palestinians but also better organized Arab Muslim populations.[6] The troubles escalated during the 1920s, reaching their first peak in the 1929 Palestine riots, which killed approximately 250 people and presaged the decades of wrenching conflicts that lay ahead (Gavish 2005).

Could the Zionists have understood their potential opponents in anything other than an antagonistic way? In fact, different sorts of relations were possible, and some were tried. Of course, the options narrowed substantially after the murder of six million. The heinous event gave an extraordinary urgency to the Jewish exodus from Europe, both inside and outside the Jewish community itself. The British folded up their Mandate and the United Nations declared a fragile, and almost universally unpopular, two-state solution. Even then, however, there was more than one path to take. Despite their territorial ambitions, the more left-wing, socialist, and democratic Israeli fighters conducted their struggles in less violent and pugnacious, more civilly regulated ways. Right-wing Zionists, epitomized by the notorious Stern Gang, were more aggressively violent, demonstrating much less concern for non-Jewish life, whether British, Arab, Palestinian, Muslim, or Christian.[7]

Amidst the chaotic conditions and competing ambitions of this postwar struggle, Israel declared its independence, the Arab states and Palestinians declared and acted upon their opposition, and the historical options narrowed further still. Zionist forces engaged in pitched battles against local Palestinian fighters and invading Arab armies. Jewish soldiers individually, and the emerging Jewish nation collectively, experienced this birth struggle as a matter of life or death. "We, the Jewish Israelis," the psychiatrist Dan Bar-On recalled, "saw ourselves as surrounded by enemies and having to struggle, physically and mentally, for our lives and survival" (Bar-On 1997, 90). Feelings of compassion for displaced Palestinians—who were equally endangered, and most directly by Israel's own army—were cast aside. Whether or not Israeli individuals and the nation collectively made an explicit analogy with the Holocaust—and we argue here that, by and large, they did not—there seems little doubt the only recently terminated and extraordinarily searing experience of racially motivated mass murder contributed to the emerging Jewish nation's sense of itself as uniquely a victim.

Trauma and Primordialty

The Israeli state, established on the blood sacrifice of its courageous but also often dangerously aggressive army, honored its soldier-martyrs and inscribed in historical memory the trauma-inspired lesson that only military strength could prevent Jewish defilement and murder from ever happening again.[8] For the new nation's first two decades, the historical record shows, the school textbooks of Israeli children were filled with deeply polluting descriptions of Arabs as savage, sly, cheat, thief, robber, provocateur, and terrorist. As one Israeli historian has suggested, during these early decades the national narrative hewed closely to the "tradition of depicting Jewish history as an uninterrupted record of anti-Semitism and persecution" (Podeh 2000, 75–76). The continuing Arab military campaign against Israel was represented inside this frame. Palestinian violence was analogized with pre-Independence "pogroms" against Jews, and Palestinian and Arab leaders were depicted as only the most recent in "a long line of 'oppressors' of Jews during the course of their history" (75–76).[9]

Insofar as this trauma-construction conceived Israeli's origin as an iteration of the Jewish Holocaust experience, an aggressive and military response to the "Palestinian problem" became the only conceivable "solution" to the subjective fears of Israelis and the objective dangers that a series of Arab attacks posed to their nation. And, indeed, so long as military power seemed a viable method of wiping the historical slate clean, even the progressive narrative of democratic Zionism was deeply compromised, linking bereavement and triumph in an inward-turning, particularistic way (Ben-Amos and Bet-El 1999, 267).[10] When Holocaust Day was officially declared in 1951, it was not considered a major event, its tragic narration sitting uncomfortably alongside Zionism's future-oriented founding myth. One effort at metonymic resolution placed Holocaust Day one week before the Memorial and Independence Day sequence, in the period that followed upon the Passover celebration of Jewish enslavement and emancipation.[11] The Holocaust holiday, in other words, pointed backward and forward at the same time and, in both directions, remained resolutely particularistic. In its tragic mode, it mourned "the modern attempt to annihilate the Jewish people;" in its progressive mode, it celebrated the Warsaw Ghetto uprising as "the heroic spark" that had reignited Israel's birth (Ben-Amos and Bet-El 1999, 272).

In fact, constructing parallels between the Holocaust and Israeli wars was more than a metonymic matter. Strong metaphorical resemblances were established between the holidays marking them as well. On the eve of both holidays, businesses, coffee shops and cinemas close early. Radio stations replace their regular broadcasting schedules with melancholic Israeli songs, and television channels feature documentaries about the Holocaust and the Israeli wars. Schools devote these holy days to commemoration and hold compulsory memorial ceremonies. Although these ceremonies are planned and conducted by representatives of the student body, they closely resemble one another, drawing from the same limited, iconic cultural corpus. Many of the same poems are recited; many of the same songs are sung; similar imagery is projected, and parallel dress codes are required. A state ceremony is broadcasted live through most public TV and radio stations on both days (Handelman and Katz 1990, 192–195). Another feature the holidays share is the sirens that provide temporal and moral demarcation. "On the appointed minute, and for one minute's duration, siren blasts shriek in every village, town and city in the land. Human life stands still, people stop in their tracks, vehicles stop in mid-intersection ... All is silent" (193). These sirens, which in other contexts and with different modulation serves as an air-raid warning, not only enforces the short period of shared commemoration but also emphasize the incorporation of the victims of the Holocaust into the Jewish-Israeli collectivity.[12] However, while creating an analogy between those who perished in Europe and those who died defending Israel, it also creates a clear hierarchy between them. While the former, the Holocaust victims, are commemorated by one siren blast on the morning of the Holocaust Memorial Day; the latter, the fallen soldiers, are commemorated by two blasts, one on the eve of Memorial Day and the other the following morning.

At the heart of the Independence Day ritual is a binary that contrasts the "passive Diaspora Jewry" of the pre-Holocaust period, "sheep to the slaughter," with the "active Zionism" of post-Holocaust Israel, "which had fought successfully for statehood." For its part, Holocaust Day ceremonies are often accompanied by a similar pairing. Such phrases as "from Holocaust to heroism" and "from Holocaust to revival/establishment"[13] signify a Zionist chronology that leads from Holocaust in the Diaspora to Jewish revival via the establishment of modern Israel. These binaries inspire a progressive narrative according to which "resistance fighters ... and soldiers in the War of Independence became the protagonists of the ceremony." It was via such a political-*cum*-cultural process that youthful Israel, in Bar-On's words, "crossed the fragile distinction from being morally right as a persecuted people"—or whom "persecution became imbedded in our internal representations throughout the ages of the Diaspora"—to being a dominant and aggressive military power, one which did not "attempt to include the relevant 'other' but rather to ignore or disgorge him" (Shamir, Yitzhaki-Verner, and Bar-On 1996, 195).

This construction of a causal relationship between the Holocaust and Israeli war was dramatized in a closely watched and influential television series. *Pillar of Fire* first aired in 1981 on what was then the nation's only television channel, the government-run Channel 1. This series narrates the history of the Jewish people in the first half of the twentieth century from a distinctively Zionist perspective, encapsulating what later came to be criticized as the hegemonic Israeli narrative (Shejter 2007). *Pillars of Fire* led the viewer from the tragedy of the Final Solution to the heroic Warsaw Ghetto uprising; from there to the Jewish Brigades, which volunteered to serve in the British army and assist the Allied forces in their war against Germany; then onward toward the struggle of the Zionist leadership against the British forces who prevented Jews from immigrating to Palestine; and it concludes with Israel's the declaration of independence and the ensuing war with the Arab nations.

This historical account rests on a self-justifying, narrowly particularistic, and deeply primordial reconstruction of the Holocaust trauma, one that continues to exert great influence up to this day. The Jewish fighters are cast as protagonists. Arrayed against them is the long list of their historical antagonists: the Germans and their accomplices; the British, who stood between Jewish refugees and the soon-to-be Israelis; the Allied Forces, who intervened too late and failed to save European Jews from the Final Solution; Arab-Palestinians and the surrounding nations, who opposed the establishment of the Jewish State; and Europeans, who resented the Jewish survivors and greeted their return to their original residences with several postwar *pogroms*. The binary of Jew and Gentile, a defining characteristic of most Jewish communities since biblical times, is thus reformulated inside the Zionist narrative. Instead of leading, as it did in earlier times, to social seclusion, on the one hand, and moral calls for a more just and universal order, on the other, the new Jewish-Israeli narrative reinforces the militaristic and exclusionary aspects of Zionism. Foreign nations have proven to be untrustworthy. Israel can rely only on the resources of the Jewish people and its own military strength to defend itself.

Shifting Constructions, New Sympathies

Only later, as Israel became more embattled and militarized Zionism stymied and wounded, did this ambiguous and narrow reconstruction of the Jewish nation's founding began to falter. It is revealing that Holocaust Day became more culturally significant as the trauma drama framing it became more insistently pessimistic. A series of symbolic developments contributed to this darkening before the social arena for the performance of militarized Zionism actually changed. For example, the trial of Adolf Eichmann, a Nazi official publicly tried for war crimes in 1961, exposed the Israeli public to a multitude of testimonies which brought to light the horrendous war experiences of Holocaust survivors. After more than a decade in which the personal stories were belittled in favor of the collective progressive narrative, these relived testimonies set in motion a new, more privatizing Holocaust memory. Not only a national disaster brought on by the passiveness of Diasporic Jewry, the Holocaust now became a collection of personal tragedies, to be sympathized with and commemorated, and also avenged.[14]

This turn toward tragedy deepened after the Yom Kippur War in 1973, when Israel barely escaped a catastrophic military defeat. With this event, the social arena for the performance of collective trauma was changed. The war experience allowed the particularistic approach to the identities at stake to be challenged in a subtle but powerful way. A newly experienced "feeling of dread," according to a contemporary Israeli observer, meant "diminished importance of the fighter as a Zionist role model" and the corresponding reconstruction of the Holocaust drama in a manner, complementary to the post-Eichmann privatization, that "placed a bolder emphasis on the suffering of the victims and focused greater attention on daily life in the ghettoes and camps." As a consequence, "a different type of bravery was now given prominence—one that was non-military, but involved survival under oppressive conditions" (Ben-Amos and Bet-El 1999, 270).[15] For many Israelis, the published photographs of Israeli prisoners during the 1973 war triggered familiar possibilities of Jewish destruction and defeat. Moshe Dayan, who was Minister of Defense at that time, spoke about his anxieties as evoking nothing short of the "collapse of the 'Third Temple'" (Karsh 2000, ix). Dayan iterates here the Jewish memory of the worst catastrophe of biblical times: foreign conquest of Jerusalem and expulsion of Israelites from their land. Until the Yom Kippur War, only the Holocaust was comparable to this founding trauma of "Rabbinic Judaism." Dayan's poignant metaphor draws on the power of these two traumas, equating military defeat in 1973 with the worst historical disasters in the Jewish historical imagination.

From this point onward, the enduring conflict between more particularizing and more universalizing constructions of the Jewish trauma
drama became crystallized inside Israeli society. Of course, a sense of
victimhood continued to permeate political discourse in Israel's third
decade. The Six-Day War of 1967, the 1967–1970 War of Attrition,
the Munich Massacre of 1972, the Entebbe Operation of 1976, and the
punctuating acts of terrorism undertaken by the Palestine Liberation
Organization left deep marks on Israeli society, becoming frequent
trauma-recalling and trauma-inducing features of public discourse.
Conservative Prime Minister Menachem Begin made prominent use
of Holocaust imagery in his political speeches, warning time and again
against the "return of Auschwitz" in reference to threats from the Palestinians and Arab nations. Begin was indeed one of the key figures in
the politization of the Holocaust in the political discourse of Israel. His
vision of an anti-Semitic world against which Israel stands alone was a
dominant theme in his speeches and writings.

> No one came to save us—neither from the East nor from the West. For
> this reason, we have sworn a vow, we, the generation of extermination
> and rebirth: Never again will we put our nation in danger, never again
> will we put our women and children and those whom we have a duty
> to defend—if necessary at the cost of our lives—in range of the enemy's
> deadly fire. (Segev 1993, 398)

But the conflation of Holocaust and Israeli enemies was not confined to the right-wing "Likud" side. Leading Labor politician Abba
Eban famously compared the option of a return to the pre-1967 borders
of Israel with a return to the borders of Auschwitz.[16] When speaking of
the Arab-Israeli conflict, soldiers and politicians frequently expressed
concerns about a Holocaust-like disaster looming over their heads.[17]
Such narrative inscriptions of Holocaust tragedy inside the long history
of Jewish suffering provided further justification for violent resistance
against those were perceived as purely external threats.

The new post-1973 context, however, also allowed the tragic construction of the Holocaust trauma to provide a different kind of script, one
that could connect Jewish Israelis with Palestinian suffering. An Israeli
peace movement emerged that put land for peace on the table, and a new
generation of critical historians righteously exposed Israeli complicity in
Palestinian expulsion. Leftist intellectuals introduced such new critical
concepts as "cognitive militarism."[18] More moderate observers spoke about
the decline of "collective commemoration" and the growth of a more individual centered, rights-based political culture (Bilu and Witztum 2000, 25).

Such "devaluation of the myth of heroism" intensified after the 1982 Lebanon War, whose military frustrations produced feelings of futility and whose massacres at Sabra and Shatila ignited feelings of humiliation (23). In their initial response to the massacres, conservative Likud government officials lashed out against accusations of Israeli complicity. They described them as "a blood libel against the Jewish state and its Government," framing them in terms of historical anti-Semitism against the Jewish people. In response to this defensive and narrowly primordial construction, hundreds of thousands of Israelis organized a massive protest in Tel Aviv.[19] This unprecedented expression of criticism and antiwar feeling triggered the creation of a Commission of Inquiry. Chaired by former Supreme Court Justice Yitzhak Kahan, the investigation produced sharply critical findings and made significant recommendations for reform. While it was Lebanese Phalangists who had carried out the massacre against Palestinians, the Kahan Commission found that the Jewish government had indirect responsibility and declared Ariel Sharon, then Minister of Defense, directly responsible for not preventing the massacre (Kahan Commission 1983). The events surrounding the Lebanon invasion and the self-critical reaction to it not only created more universalizing trauma constructions inside Israel but also triggered a global reaction that, according to one French observer, allowed the normative symbolization of the Holocaust "to be turned against those to whom it hitherto protected." For the first time, "large swathes of international public opinion distanced themselves from the policy of Israel" (Wieviorka 2007, 57). Two decades later, the Israeli feminist critic Ronit Lentin (2000) asserted that this new spiral of signification had made an expanded solidarity possible.

Only after Lebanon did the suffering of others, particularly of Palestinian children, not Jewish suffering, become a principal subject of Israeli literary and poetic discourses. For the first time, the death of Palestinians was described using *Shoah* images. Palestinian fate was equated with the fate of the Jews, as Israeli poets and playwrights reflected and compelled Jewish understanding of the suffering of the Palestinians (Lentin 2000, 145).[20] This new understanding went hand in hand with a weariness of Prime Minster Begin's Holocaust-driven militarism and criticism of the Holocaust's role in Israeli politics. In an open letter to the prime minister, Israeli writer Amos Oz remarked,

> Often I, like many Jews, find at the bottom of my soul a dull sense of pain because I did not kill Hitler with my own hands ... Tens of thousands of dead Arabs will not heal that wound ... Again and again, Mr. Begin, you reveal to the public eye a strange urge to resuscitate Hitler

in order to kill him every day anew in the guise of terrorists. (Segev 1993, 400)

Palestinian Counter-Narrative of Trauma

Throughout this period of symbolic reconstruction, the emergent Palestinian national movement played a significant role, creating new "realities on the ground" that provided a new dramatic field of performative possibilities. Its energetic and aggressive ideology, and often murderous tactics, presented undeniable evidence of a previously "invisible" nation and people, making it more difficult, though not of course impossible, to narrate a progressive story of emancipation on the Israeli side. Yet, the PLO's terrorism severely restricted its dramatic appeal. In the late 1970s, the world's best-known Palestinian intellectual, Edward Said, declared that, while "we have gained the support of all the peoples of the Third World," the "remarkable national resurgence" of the "Palestinian *idea*" had not yet succeeded, for "we have been unable to interest the West very much in the justice of our cause" (Said 1979, xi–x, italics in source). While acknowledging how much he resented "the ways in which the whole grisly matter is stripped of all its resonances and its often morally confusing detail, and compressed simply, comfortably, inevitably under the rubric of 'Palestinian terror,'" Said declared himself "horrified at the hijacking of planes, the suicidal missions, the assassinations, the bombing of schools and hotels." Said believed that this performative failure would have to be redressed. To attract a Western audience, the trauma drama of Palestinian suffering would have to be told in a different way. For there to be "some sense of the larger Palestinian story from which all these things came," Said explained, there must be a new and more compelling focus on "the reality of a collective national trauma [that is] contained for every Palestinian in the question of Palestine" (xii). A new progressive counter-trauma narrative was projected, describing Palestinian suffering, Western/Israeli domination, and a heroic anticolonial movement for liberation. It provided a new symbolic protagonist with whom a widening circle of Western citizens, and the developing group of self-critical Israelis, could identify, or at least ambivalently support. This possibility deepened among many Israelis in the wake of the first Intifada, the relatively nonviolent Palestinian uprising that began in 1987. It was this expanding structure of solidarity became powerfully institutionalized in the treaties and ceremonies marking the Oslo peace process in 1993.

Right-Wing Backlash

What has been described as the emergence of "post-Zionism" was constrained, though not entirely cut short, by the assassination of Prime Minister Yitzhak Rabin in 1995 (Cohen 1995). Rabin's cruelly calculated murder managed to short-circuit processes of civil repair that had, in no small part, been fuelled by the manner which the Holocaust trauma specifically, and Jewish suffering more generally, was being symbolically and morally recast. This murderous short-circuiting demonstrated the ambiguous and contradictory trauma constructions that emerged in response to Israeli's post-1967 history. While the earlier, more particularistic trauma drama had been challenged, much of its narrowly primordial power had certainly remained. Indeed, even as the Yom Kippur War and the difficulties that unfolded in its aftermath allowed the creation of a more universalizing tragic narrative, they also energized a much more particularistic kind of tragic story, one that was distinctively more anticivil than the Israeli nation's ambiguously progressive founding myth. And even as the emerging Palestinian movement provided opportunities for cross-national solidarity, it had an equal and opposite effect. Alongside and competing with the Palestinian protagonist with whom the left could identify, Palestinian actions offered the growing backlash movement a more sharply defined, polluted antagonist against whom to carry on Israel's long-standing primordial fight.

In 1977, the right-wing Likud party took power on a platform demanding continued occupation and usurpation of the "holy lands," its leaders and supporters fervently opposed to any Palestinian accord. During the course of this backlash movement there also emerged *Gush Emunim* (literally "Block of the Faithful") whose supporters began a decades-long, highly successful campaign to take Jewish possession of occupied Palestinian lands. The religious Zionist ideology initially inspiring *Gush Emunim* was not militarist. Emerging in response to the seemingly "miraculous" 1967 war, it narrated the military acquisition of Judea, Samaria and Sinai, which had taken just six days, as a millennial sign of the Jewish people's imminent salvation. In opposition to the traditional views of Orthodox Judaism, *Gush Emunim* viewed building, settling and developing—whether in prewar Israel or in the Occupied Territories—as a positively sanctioned commandment. The movement's activities soon generated intense opposition nonetheless. Illegal settlements were forcibly removed time and again, only to be reinstated by *Gush Emunim*. Public opinion remained largely unsupportive, the expected salvation did not arrive and the Egyptian-Israeli peace accord forced withdrawal from Sinai and the first massive settlement removal in 1982. Its messianic aspirations thwarted, *Gush Emunim* turned from messianic to militaristic narrations of expanded settlement.[21]

In the years that followed, "settler" became as ubiquitous a trope in conservative Israeli society as "survivor." Indeed, the former collective representation drew its symbolic strength from the latter. For the dominant factions of the Israeli right, Jews needed desperately to annex every inch of Palestinian land that surrounded them, for every non-Jewish person was a potential enemy.[22] They had learned this deeply anticivil lesson from their tragic, and primordial, reconstruction of the Holocaust trauma. Because they experienced the Jewish victimhood of those terrible days as never having gone away, they could glean no bridging metaphors from their re-experience of trauma. Instead, they felt compelled to frame every conflict with outsiders in a boundary-making way.[23]

When the Likud Minister of Education delivered her Holocaust Day speech on 2001, she proclaimed complete identification with the protagonists in the original trauma. "We shouldn't suppose," she insisted, "that we differ from our grandfathers and grandparents who went to the gas chambers." Rejecting a progressive narrative that would dramatize the distance between the situation of Jews then and now, she insisted "what separates us from them is not that we are some sort of new Jew." What has changed is not the opposition between Jew and Gentile but its asymmetry. The Jewish side can now be armed. The Minister explained, "The main difference is external: we have a state, a flag and army." During the historical Holocaust, by contrast, the Jews had been "caught in their tragedy, [for] they lacked all three" (cited in Feldman 2002, 1). The trauma drama points toward an ineluctable solution: Only power and violence that can save contemporary Jews from suffering their ancestors' fate.

Caught up inside this narrowly constructed trauma drama, the majority of the Israeli right has identified the peace process with Jewish annihilation. In the months before Yitzhak Rabin's assassination, ultra-orthodox and right-wing magazines attacked the general-turned-peacemaker as a "traitor" and "madman," suggesting he was "antireligious" and even "non-Jewish." He and his Foreign Minister, Shimon Peres, were depicted as members of the *Judenrat* and *Kapos,* the infamous Nazi-appointed Jewish leaders who had collaborated in the administration of the death camps. At the antigovernment demonstrations that grew increasingly aggressive in the months and weeks before his murder, Rabin was portrayed in posters wearing an S.S. uniform and cap (Lentin 2000, 148). These disturbing images point to the construction of a trauma drama that is increasingly radical and particularist. Mainstream Zionism casts Israeli Jews as protagonists and Arabs as antagonists. The new conception marks Israeli settlers as victims, and any political or military party that attempts to evict them as Nazis. This trauma rhetoric framed resistance to the first large-scale eviction of Israeli settlers from the Sinai, which was mandated by the peace agreement with Egypt in 1982. In the final clash between the settlers and Israeli military forces who forcibly removed them, the settlers placed yellow stars on their chests, echoing the emblems that European Jews had been forced to wear under Nazi occupation.

Since 1982, the settlement movement has grown considerably not only in size but in influence. In the 2005 Disengagement, Israeli forces withdrew unilaterally from the Gaza Strip and Northern Samaria, and 25 settlements were dismantled. These powerful challenges to the anti-Palestinian land movement triggered more intense invocations of the Holocaust trauma in response. Soldiers sent to forcibly evict settlements were met with sobbing children wearing yellow stars, asking with raised hands, "Have you come to take us to the gas chamber?" Settlers prepared Auschwitz-like uniforms to be worn on eviction day. Prosettlement activists broadly referred to soldiers and Israeli leaders as *Judenrat,* which drew censure from Holocaust survivors and antisettlement political activists alike (Maariv 2004, 2005; Yediot Aharonot 2005). The mainstream Zionist invocation of the Holocaust trauma drama justified anti-Arab and anti-Palestinian violence in the name of creating and defending Israel. The right-wing prosettlement variation on this theme understands such violence differently, as an act of defiance. As the Nazis obliterated Jewish communities in Europe, so should Israeli leaders destroy the Jewish communities in the Occupied Territories.

Left-Wing Inhibition

Faced with such powerfully reactionary trauma constructions, the response of the left would seem clear. Drawing on the relatively autonomous cultural power of Holocaust symbolism, it could challenge the social instantiations on which right-wing deployments of the narrative rest. Building on the earlier peace movement, it could broaden solidarity by identifying the Palestinians as the victims of a Holocaust-like disaster themselves. That such counter-narratives only rarely appear in the highly polarized political conflicts that mark contemporary Israel, even among fierce opponents of the settlement movement, is not only a politically debilitating but also an empirically perplexing fact.

Western critics of Israel's occupation policy, whether Jewish or not, do not share this difficulty. In the 2008 animated pseudo-documentary *Waltz with Bashir,* Israeli journalist Ron Ben-Yshay recounts his arrival at Sabra and Shatilla at the massacre's end. "Do you remember the photo from the Warsaw Ghetto? The one with the kid raising his hands?" he asks his interviewer. The next shot shows a group of Palestinian women and children raising their hands while being led by gun-bearing Phalangists to their certain deaths. The following shot is a close-up of one of this group of victims, a solemn child of approximately the same age as the Jewish child from the Warsaw Ghetto. This potently inverted analogy strongly appeals to critical audiences outside of Israel. *Waltz with Bashir* was nominated for an Academy Award. Such inversion, however, rarely surfaces inside Jewish-Israeli discourse itself.

Post-Zionist scholars have certainly deconstructed the once widely accepted causal relationship between the Holocaust and the establishment of Israel. They have challenged the Zionist founder's claim that the establishment of Israel was the only possible response to the Holocaust and the only feasible solution to the anti-Semitism of the Diaspora and have voiced criticisms of its political and militaristic appropriation (e.g., Zertal 2005). While these radical arguments have not been universally accepted among critical Israelis, they reveal the persisting identification of certain Israeli left-wing circles with the suffering of the Palestinians.

Yet, when speaking out publicly against the occupation, critical Israelis today rarely evoke rhetorical solidarity with Palestinians. When Holocaust imagery is employed, it is directed inward, toward Jewish-Israeli leaders and institutions, identifying them as anti-Palestinian "perpetrators." Philosopher Yeshayahu Leibowitz publicly called Israeli military units "Judeo-Nazis" (*New York Times* 1994). Historian Moshe Zimmerman asserted that his ability to study extremist settlers was limited because the Jewish children of occupied Hebron resemble Hitler Youth. The Leibowitz interview became notorious. Zimmerman was sued for libel (Nudel 1995; *Zimmermann v. Yedioth Communication* 2005). In a similar incident, scandal erupted and legal proceedings ensued over a letter addressed to a settler in "KZ Kiryat Arba," widely understood as "Concentration Camp Kiryat Arba," an identification that clearly equated Jewish settlement with Nazi Holocaust crimes. While acknowledging that "doubtlessly, the defendant intended to claim that the plaintiff is an evil man," the presiding judge in the case adamantly maintained that, no matter how evil the settler seemed, the defendant could not have intended to link him with Nazism: "He did not mean to say that the plaintiff is, God forbid, a Nazi." The judge's reasoning underscores the difficulty of universalizing the Holocaust trauma in Israel today. "As a Jew," he explained, "the plaintiff cannot be anything but a victim of the Nazis" (*Haetzni v. Tomarkin* 1986).

There are several reasons for this discursive inhibition. One undoubtedly is that Israel's inability to come to terms with the Palestinian question has produced increasing radicalism, violence, and anti-Israeli, often anti-Semitic stereotypes among a significant part of the Palestinian resistance. Another, less noted reason has to do with the centrality of the army in Israeli society. Most Israeli Jews, both men and women, have compulsory military duty of two to three years starting at the age of 18. Many voluntarily extend their service to gain benefits and professional development, and most men remain in reserve duty until the age of 40. To severely criticize the military by comparing it to the bitterest antagonist in modern Jewish history is to pollute not only the military *per se* but, indirectly, the whole of Israeli society. Institutional setting plays a vital role in trauma construction, filtering and tilting the spiral of signification.

Whatever the causes, the result of this constraint on the signification process has been to deprive Israeli critics of a potent political weapon. Because post-Zionists criticize the intertwining of Holocaust and national founding narrative as a forced marriage, they are compelled generally to avoid evoking the trauma drama in a political context. This allows the meaning of the Holocaust to be monopolized by nationalist and conservative forces.

Recently, however, there have been moves to appropriate the Holocaust in ways that allow parallels to be made. In 2009, after a mosque was burned down in a Palestinian village, most likely by Jewish settlers, the Chief Rabbi of Israel Yona Metzger paid a visit to the village elders and offered his condolences and support. "We, the people of Israel," Rabbi Metzger told them, "have a trauma from 70 years ago when the greatest destruction we have ever known, the Holocaust, started with the burning of synagogues on Kristallnacht" (Yediot Aharonot 2009). What is striking about this statement is that it came not come from the extreme left, but from the religious center, from one of the highest ranking religious authorities in the country. By polluting the arsonists and the group from which they were supposed to have emerged—the extreme factions of the settlers—as being antidemocratic or even anti-Jewish, Rabbi Metzger is creating a long-overdue bridge between Palestinian and Jewish suffering. Such new metaphoric associations, this recent event suggests, do not only originate in liberal democratic groups but also can derive from an identification between religions. Several days after the arson, a delegation of rabbis and religious representatives from the Jewish settlement of Tekoa presented a new Koran to the Palestinian village's elder to replace the one burned. "We want to create new conditions between Jews and Arabs," said a member of the delegation. "Jewish law also forbids damaging a holy place" (Haaretz 2009a).

Critical and even moderate Israelis have been increasingly concerned by the Holocaust's role in collective memory and contemporary policies alike. According to the Israeli right, to recognize the rights of Palestinians is to become an enemy of the Jewish people. Solidarity cannot extend beyond the boundaries of one's own group. It must be primordial, not civil. So reconstructed, the trauma drama of the Holocaust is a recipe for conflict without end. If this view should prevail, it would not only be severely destabilizing in geopolitical terms. It would assault the universalizing moral principles that the memory of the Holocaust calls upon us to sustain. Changing this symbolic constriction is a prerequisite if peaceful coexistence is ever to reign. A recent issue of the well established journal *Israel Studies* is entitled "Israelis and the Holocaust: Scars Cry Out for Healing."[24] We agree.

Notes

1. It should be noted that the complaint that caused Itamar Shapira to be fired from Yad Vashem came from a group of students from Efrat, a large settlement in formerly Palestinian, now Israeli-occupied territory. While this is revealing of the very divisions inside contemporary Israel, which we discuss below, the origins of the complaint are not significant in terms of the point we are making here. What we are emphasizing is not where the complaint came from, but how this central communicative institution in Israel reacted to it.

2. See also Alexander 2009, where that earlier piece is subjected to intense debate. The present chapter draws from, revises, and substantially extends Alexander's postscript to that volume.

3. In a series of influential studies, the psychiatrist Vamik Volkan has explored such narrowing and particularistic responses to trauma and the manner in which they fuel violence and revenge, e.g., Volkan 2001. From a historical and cultural sociological perspective, Volkan's work is limited by the individualistic and naturalizing assumptions that so often detract from psychoanalytic perspectives on collective life. These problems also affect, but in a less restrictive manner, the wide-ranging, politically engaged studies by Dan Bar-On and his colleagues, e.g., Shamir, Yitzhaki-Verner, and Bar-On 1996 and Bar-On 1997.

4. It is paradoxical that in her searching and original investigation, Idith Zertal (2005) insists on contrasting what she views as the truly "historical dimension of the events" with their "out-of-context use" in the new nation's collective memory, which she condemns for having "transmuted" the facts (4–5). The position that informs our own approach is that history is never accessible as such. To make it seem so is to provide resources for the kind of ideology critique in which Zertal is so powerfully engaged.

5. For an account of this emancipation, its fateful disappointments, and the rise of Zionism as one among several Jewish responses, see Alexander 2006, chapter 18. The idea of returning to Jerusalem had, of course, long been an essential idiom of Diasporic Judaism.

6. For an account of this situation, see Khalidi 1997.

7. For a synthetic account of the significant contrast between the mentalities and fighting strategies of the left and right-wing Jewish forces fighting for the creation of the Jewish state, see Bickerton and Klausner 2002, 100–115.

8. For many contemporary friends of Israel—and we certainly count ourselves among them—such a characterization will appear harsh. It seems to us, however, the ineluctable conclusion from two decades of Israel's own deeply revisionist, self-critical historiography. As such writers as Benny Morris (1987) and Ilan Pappe (1992) have documented in painstaking and painful empirical detail, the independence conflict involved not just Palestinian residents' voluntary flight but massive Israeli-instigated population transfers, pushing hundreds of thousands of Palestinians off their land and wiping out the Palestinian identities of hundreds of once-Arab villages. This is not to say that the historical events triggered by the U.N.'s two-state resolution were inevitable, nor is it to absolve the Palestinian and Arab parties of their own fateful responsibilities. For a collection of archival-based essays by Arab and Jewish scholars exploring this complex and deeply contradictory period, see Rogan and Shlaim 2001. That collection is also notable for Edward Said's "Afterword: The Consequences of 1948" (2001). In this, one of the radical Palestinian critic's last published essays, Said lashes out at the repressive, anti-Semitic, and militaristic conditions that, in his view, have marked so much of Arab and Palestinian political and cultural life during the post-independence period. For an insightful overview of the polarizing, if delayed, effects of Israeli's "history wars" over its collective identity—and an argument for it as psychologically overdetermined—see Brunner 2002.

9. This specifically Israeli-Jewish frame complemented the more broadly polluting binary of Western orientalism. Though sweeping and polemical, Said was not wrong when he suggested, thirty years ago in *The Palestinian Question*, that "between Zionism and the West there was and still is a community of language and of ideology [that] depends heavily on a remarkable tradition in the West of enmity toward Islam in particular and the Orient in general." Asserting that Arabs were "practically the *only* ethnic group about whom in the West racial slurs are tolerated, even encouraged," Said suggested that "the Arabs and Islam represent viciousness, veniality, degenerate vice, lechery, and stupidity in popular and scholarly discourse" (Said 1979, 26, italics in source).

10. See also Bilu and Witztum 2000, Bar 2005, Ofer 2000.

11. Zertal 2005, 39, and Handelman and Katz 1990. Handelman and Katz interpret this juxtaposition as having suggested that, for the Israelis, Holocaust Day signified an exit from the suffering of diasporic Jewry, framing the tragedy, in a progressive manner, as adumbrating the emergence of the Jewish state.

12. As Zertal notes, it has even been proposed that all six million Jewish casualties be granted Israeli citizenships (Zertal 2005, 3).

13. The phrase "From Holocaust to Revival" (in Hebrew *M'shoah L'tkuma*) is polysemic. The word *Tkuma* can be translated both as "revival" and as "establishment" (specifically regarding the establishment of the state of Israel).

14. For an elaborate discussion of the privatization of the Holocaust memory in Israeli society, see Shapira 1998.

15. Bilu and Witztum note, for example, that the psychiatric diagnosis of post-traumatic-stress disorder could only emerge in the wake of the Yom Kippur War, for it implied a weakening of the indomitable Israeli protagonist's military strength: "The myth of heroism, and with it the layers of disregard and denial that had hidden combat stress reactions from the public eye in the preceding wars, were extensively eroded in the 1973 War. Following the utter surprise and confusion at the onset of the war, the military defeats in the first days of fighting, and the heavy toll of casualties—more than 2,500 soldiers killed and about 7,000 wounded—the war was inscribed in the national consciousness as a massive trauma" (Bilu and Witztum 2000, 20).

16. For a detailed account of this change in the Israeli attitude toward the memory of the Holocaust, see Yablonka 2008.

17. A collection of testimonies and experiences from the Six-Day War provides numerous examples, see A. Shapira 1968.

18. Examples include Azarya and Kimmerling 1985–1986, Kimmerling 1993 and 1999.

19. While this protest is popularly known in Israel as the "400,000 protest," sources disagree on the exact number of demonstrators who participated. More conservative estimates put the number at half of that, while others claim that the square in which it was held, including the adjoining streets, could not have held even a third (Azaryahu 2007).

20. The empathy-creating possibilities of Holocaust memory is ignored by Zertal's reconstruction, whose cultural history has no place for the peace movement.

21. For an elaborate account of the first years of Gush Emunim and of the religious and political context out of which it had emerged, see Newman 1985. The turn from a messianic religious discourse to a militaristic discourse in the political culture of Gush Emunim is discussed in Taub 2010. If the polarizing effects of the Israeli trauma drama's shifting retellings were deepened by more "fundamentalist," and often more eschatological, versions of Jewish religion, the same can be said for the Palestinian trauma. More radical and rejectionist elements, publicly dedicated to the annihilation of Israel, increasingly experienced the sources of their trauma, and its possible resolution, through Islamicist faith. For this intertwining of the religious extremes, see Friedland and Hecht 1996, 168–170 and 355ff.

22. Due to the multipartisan structure of the Israeli political map, the definitions of "right-wing" and "left-wing" are rather slippery. Whereas political parties differ according to their socioeconomic policies, ranging from socialism to extreme liberalism, these positions do not necessarily align with their positions regarding the Arab-Israeli conflict. Further complications arise when one takes into account these parties' stances regarding the relations between religion and the state, which range from orthodoxy to extreme secularism, as well as minority parties.

23. It should be emphasized that not all Jewish residents of the territories conquered by Israel in 1967 are part of this movement. While the original postwar settlers were characterized by a religious and ideological commitment to the settlement project, a significant part of the Jewish migrants to these territories were motivated by economic considerations. The ideology described here represents the more audacious and activist "settlement movement" and does not extend to all Jewish residents of the occupied territories.

24. *Israel Studies* 14, no. 1 (Spring 2009).

Works Cited

Alexander, J. C. 2004. On the Social Construction of Moral Universals: The "Holocaust" from War Crime to Trauma Drama. In *Cultural Trauma and Collective Identity*, 196–263. Berkeley: University of California Press.

———. 2006. *The Civil Sphere.* Oxford and New York: Oxford University Press.

———. 2009. *Remembering the Holocaust: A Debate.* Oxford and New York: Oxford University Press.

Azarya, V., and B. Kimmerling. 1985–1986. Cognitive Permeability of Civil-Military Boundaries: Draftee Expectations from Military Service in Israel. *Studies in Comparative International Development* 20(4): 42–63.

Azaryahu, M. 2007. *Tel Aviv: Mythography of a City.* Syracuse, NY: Syracuse University Press.

Bar, D. 2005. Holocaust Commemoration in Israel during the 1950s: The Holocaust Cellar on Mount Zion. *Jewish Social Studies: History, Culture, Society* 12(1): 16–38.

Bar-On, D. 1997. Israeli Society between the Culture of Death and the Culture of Life. *Israel Studies* 2(2): 88–112.

Ben-Amos, A., and I. Bet-El. 1999. Holocaust Day and Memorial Day in Israeli Schools: Ceremonies, Education and History. *Israeli Studies* 4(1): 258–284.

Bickerton, I. J., and C. L. Klausner. 2002. *A Concise History of the Arab-Israeli Conflict*, 4th ed. Upper Saddle River, NJ: Prentice Hall.

Bilu, Y., and E. Witztum. 2000. War-Related Loss and Suffering in Israeli Society: An Historical Perspective. *Israel Studies* 5(2): 1–31.

Brunner, J. 2002. Contentious Origins: Psychoanalytic Comments on the Debate over Israel's Creation. In *Psychoanalysis, Identity, and Ideology: Critical Essays on the Israel/Palestine Case*, eds. J. Bunzl and B. Beit-Hallahmi, 107–135. Boston: Kluwer Academic Publishers.

Cohen, E. 1995. Israel as a Post-Zionist Society. *Israel Affairs* 1(3): 203–214.

Feldman, J. 2002. Marking the Boundaries of the Enclave: Defining the Israeli Collective through the Poland Experience. *Israel Studies* 7(2): 84–114.

Friedland, R., and R. Hecht. 1996. *To Rule Jerusalem.* New York: Cambridge University Press.

Gavish, D. 2005. *A Survey of Palestine under the British Mandate, 1920–1948.* London and New York: Routledge.

Giesen, B. 2009. From Denial to Confessions of Guilt: The German Case. In *Remembering the Holocaust: A Debate*, J. C. Alexander, 114–122. Oxford and New York: Oxford University Press.

Haaretz. 2009a. Rabbis Meet Yasuf Leaders to Calm Tensions after Mosque Arson, December 14.

———. 2009b. Yad Vashem Fires Employee who Compared Holocaust to Nakba, April 23.

Haetzni v. Tomarkin, 552/84 (Jerusalem District 1986).

Handelman, D., and E. Katz. 1990. State Ceremonies of Israel-Remembrance Day and Independence Day. In *Models and Mirrors: Towards Anthropology of Public Events*, D. Handelman, 191–233. Cambridge: Cambridge University Press.

Kahan Commission. 1983. *The Beirut Massacre: The Complete Kahan Commission Report.* Princeton, NJ: Karz-Cohl.

Karsh, E. 2000. Preface. In *Revisiting the Yom Kippur War,* ed. P. R. Kumaraswamy, ix–x. London and Portland, OR: Frank Cass.

Khalidi, R. 1997. *Palestinian Identity: The Construction of Modern Consciousness.* New York: Columbia University Press.

Kimmerling, B. 1993. Patterns of Militarism in Israel. *European Journal of Sociology* 34(2): 196-223.

———. 1998. Political Subcultures and Civilian Militarism in a Settler-Immigrant Society. In *Security Concerns: Insights from the Israeli Experience*, eds. D. Bar-Tal, D. Jacobson and A. Klieman, 395-416. Stamford, CT: JAI Press.

Lentin, R. 2000. *Israel and the Daughters of the Shoah: Reoccupying the Territories of Silence.* New York: Berghahn Books.

Maariv. 2004. Moving to a New Home is not Similar to Crematoriums and Gas Chambers (Hebrew), December 21.

———. 2005. The Difficult Scenes that will Never Relent (Hebrew), August 8.

Morris, B. 1987. *Birth of the Palestinian Refugee Problem, 1947–1949.* Cambridge and New York: Cambridge University Press.

New York Times. 2009. Gaza: Cleric Denounces Possible Holocaust Education, September 1.

———. 1994. Yeshayahu Leibowitz, 91, Iconoclastic Israeli Thinker, August 19.

Newman, D. 1985. *The Impact of Gush Emunim: Politics and Settlement in the West Bank.* London: Croom Helm.

Nudel, A. 1995. Prof. Moshe Zimmerman: The children of the settlers in Hebron are exactly like the Hitler Youth. *Yerushalayim*, April 28.

Ofer, D. 2000. The Strength of Remembrance: Commemorating the Holocaust During the First Decade of Israel. *Jewish Social Studies: History, Culture, Society* 6(2): 24–55.

Pappe, I. 1992. *The Making of the Arab-Israeli Conflict, 1947–51.* London: I.B. Tauris.

Podeh, E. 2000. History and Memory in the Israeli Educational System: The Portrayal of the Arab-Israeli Conflict in History Textbooks (1948-2000). *History and Memory* 12(1): 65–100.

Remnick, D. 2007. The Apostate: A Zionist Politician Loses Faith in the Future. *The New Yorker,* July 30.

Rogan, E. L., and A. Shalim, eds. 2001. *The War for Palestine: Rewriting the History of 1948.* Cambridge: Cambridge University Press.

Said, E. W. 1979. *The Question of Palestine.* New York: Times Books.

———. 2001. Afterword: The Consequences of 1948. In *The War for Palestine: Rewriting the History of 1948,* eds. E. L. Rogan and A. Shlaim, 206–219. Cambridge: Cambridge University Press.

Segev, T. 1993. *The Seventh Million: the Israelis and the Holocaust,* trans. H. Watzman. New York: Hill and Wang.

Shamir, S., T. Yitzhaki-Verner, and D. Bar-On. 1996. "The Recruited Identity": The Influence of the Intifada on the Perception of the Peace Process from the Standpoint of the Individual. *Journal of Narrative and Life History* 6(3): 193–233.

Shapira, A. 1998. The Holocaust: Private Memories, Public Memories. *Jewish Social Studies* 4(2): 40–58.

Shapira, A., ed. 1968. *Warriors' Discourse: Chapter in Listening and Meditation (Siyach Lochamim: Pirkey Hakshava Vehitbonenut).* Tel Aviv: Kvutzat Chaverim Tzeirim Mehatnua Hakibutzit.

Shejter, A. M. 2007. The Pillar of Fire by Night, to Shew them Light: Israeli Broadcasting, the Supreme Court and the Zionist Narrative. *Media, Culture & Society* 29(6): 916–933.

Taub, G. 2010. *The Settlers and the Struggle over the Meaning of Zionism.* New Haven, CT: Yale University Press.

Volkan, V. D. 2001. Transgenerational Transmissions and Chosen Traumas: An Aspect of Large-Group Identity. *Group Analysis* 34(1): 79–97.

Weitz, Y. 1995. Political Dimenstions of Holocaust Memory in Israel. In *The Shaping of Israeli Identity: Myth, Memory and Trauma,* eds. R. Wistrich and D. Ohana, 129–145. London and Portland, OR: Frank Cass.

Wieviorka, M. 2007. *The Lure of Anti-Semitism: Hatred of Jews in Present-Day France.* Leiden/Boston, Mass: Brill.

Wistrich, R., and D. Ohana, eds. 1995. *The Shaping of Israeli Identity: Myth, Memory, and Trauma.* London and Portland, OR: Frank Cass.

Yablonka, H. 2008. The Holocaust Consciousness in the Third Decade: From "There" to "Here and Now" (Hebrew). In *The Third Decade,* eds. Z. Zameret and H. Yablonka, 264–278. Jerusalem: Yad Ben Zvi.

Yediot Aharonot. 2005. The Settlers: We'll Greet the Soldiers in Auschwitz Uniforms (Hebrew), July 28.

———. 2009. Rabbi Metzger Brings Peaceful Message to Yasuf Village, December 14.

Zertal, I. 2005. *Israel's Holocaust and the Politics of Nationhood,* trans. C. Galai. Cambridge and New York: Cambridge University Press.

Zimmermann v. Yedioth Communication, 2313/00 (Tel Aviv-Jaffa District 2005).

6

The Drama of the Greek Civil War Trauma

Nicolas Demertzis

Introduction

I was born in Athens in 1958, a child of a working class family. Like many thousands of internal migrants throughout the 1950s, my family had moved to the Greek capital, abandoning their village in search of a better life. With limited material resources and social capital, their new urban environment and its promise of upward mobility required social adjustment, emotional energy, and much human cost.

One of my clearest childhood memories is of the many quarrels that took place between my parents and my elder brother. What struck me, or at least, what I now think struck me about those quarrels, especially when the topic was related to mobility or life chances, was my brother's fervent reply to my father, "the sins of the fathers visit upon their children!" On hearing this biblical reprimand, my father would become speechless, his facial expression showing embarrassment and desperation. All discussion was over. For many years, I was at odds with these repeated episodes. I could not understand or imagine what the sins of my beloved father might have been and how it was ever possible for that hard-working and honest man to commit any sin at all. Insinuation and silence did not help, but as I entered adolescence, I began to realize that the meaning of words rarely mentioned by my parents at home, such as "occupation," "resistance," "resistance fighter," and "exile," applied to my father. And with that realization, I felt no puzzle of wrongdoing, no sin committed. On the contrary, my father was a resistance fighter, sent to a detention camp shortly after liberation from the Axis.

Throughout my formative years, due to my self-identification with my parents, and despite the fact that my father hardly spoke about his past political doings or about politics in general, I found his detention unjust. In time, this sense of injustice drew me almost naturally to the community of the Greek Left, whatever the vagueness of that political description. But those quarrels, my father's shamed face, and the silence visited on him by biblical verdict, stayed with me, an unsettling reminder of a mystery in my mind.

In his later years, my father was somewhat more talkative about his experiences in the 1940s, and from our conversations, two central themes emerged: first, he was emphatic that he "did no harm to anyone" while in the resistance; second, the civil war was, for him, a tragic mistake. It did not escape my notice that even though he did not take part in the civil war, he felt that he bore some responsibility for it. His guilt and humiliation had kept him silent. Though he personally committed no wrongdoing, he identified himself with the defeated Left as a whole, a diminished imaginary community. The mystery was almost solved. My father's state of mind reflected the mentality of an entire generation; the generation of the civil war, whose experiences and memories condemned them to shame, fear, and silence. For reasons discussed below, those experiences and memories could never remain generationally specific. For while the aftermath of the Greek civil war appeared as personal trauma for those who took active part in it, it became a cultural trauma that would affect the entire social body for decades.[1]

In this chapter, I attempt to show when and how this cultural trauma emerged. As developed here and in other places in this volume, cultural trauma is similar to but not identical to historical trauma, mass trauma, national trauma, and collective trauma. Cultural trauma is not a state of affairs but an open and adversarial process of societal negotiation over the meaning, public representation and the memorization of past events which are represented and put forward by carrier groups as humiliating, improper and unjust to large parts of society or the entire social body itself (Alexander et al. 2004). I will apply the framework of cultural trauma to the Greek civil war, where the physical and emotional effects of that war, especially as experienced by the losing side, were excluded from public discussion for decades. It was the force of this repressed and excluded memory carried by those such as my father that eventually set in motion the discursive process we can identify as "cultural trauma."

The Event: Historical Context and Prime Political Cultural Consequences

Although its chronology is controversial (see below), it is officially accepted that the civil war in Greece started in December 1944 and ended in August 1949. The war was waged between the armed forces of the Left, comprised mainly of Greek-speaking Communists joined by a relatively small minority of Slavic-speaking Communists, on the one side, and the Right, composed of paramilitary fighters and the armed forces of the state, backed by British troops and American military aid on the other. The war was won by the latter side. The Greek civil war was a defining moment[2] of the Cold War as well as Europe's bloodiest military conflict between the end of World War II and the dissolution of Yugoslavia in 1992–1995. The Great Powers (primarily Britain and the United States but also the Soviet Union) had vested interests in it, since the outcome would consolidate the post–World War II status quo in the Balkans. The Greek civil war was also the first test of the newly formulated American containment theory and of that country's role as a world leader in the fight against Communism. The American agenda was to keep Greece (of all the Balkan nations) out of the Communist bloc and to stop the Soviet sphere of influence from reaching the Mediterranean. The confrontation with Greek Communists served as a model for later American interventions in Guatemala, Lebanon, Cuba, the Dominican Republic, and Vietnam (Kolko 1994, 373–395; Iatrides 2002).

Like any other, the Greek civil war sprang out of a host of sociohistorical and politicocultural roots: a national schism between republicans and royalists, the conflict between refugees who fled the lands of Asia Minor versus the autochthones, and Metaxas' dictatorship (1936–1941) and its anticommunist legislation (Close 1995, 1–7). In 1921, the irredentist Greek army undertook a major ill-fated expedition in Asia Minor; as a result, 1,500,000 refugees fled to Greece. This "catastrophe" put an end to the Greek irredentism but gave rise to a new tension, between refugees and autochthones. Moreover, the large influx of refugees set in motion a significant left-wing labor movement in urban centers and an acute problem of agrarian reform in the countryside. Due to the interwar economic depression and the persisting confrontation between royalists and republicans, parliamentary democracy was suspended in 1936 by the anticommunist, restrictive dictatorship of the dedicated royalist General Ioannis Metaxas.

From 1941 to 1944, Greece was occupied by the Triple Axis (Germany, Italy, and Bulgaria), which led to a breakdown of state and society (Close 1995, 60–67). To a certain extent, it can be argued that the roots and causes of the civil war stem not so much from the aforementioned cleavages but from the dissolution of Greek society itself during the Occupation and the antagonisms, animosities, and hostilities it gave rise to. For instance, the winter famine of 1941–1942 resulted in approximately 100,000 deaths (Hondros 1983; Fleischer 1986). Even today the common expression "Occupation syndrome" refers to precautions and proactive consumption based on the assumption that there might be no food in the near future.

The prewar ruling elites were almost totally discredited in view of their reluctance to undertake any serious resistance initiatives during the occupation. As elsewhere in Europe, a leftist, mass-based liberation movement, called *Ethniko Apeleftherotiko Metopo* (EAM or National Liberation Front), emerged and gained impressive results against the occupying forces. EAM and its own military branch, *Ethnikos Laikos Apeleftherotikos Stratos* (ELAS [pronounced "Ellas"—the name of the country itself] or Greek People's Liberation Army), was by far the largest and most powerful organization amongst these forces.

To be sure, the majority of people were not communists; EAM enjoyed wide support, "between a million and two million" (Clogg 1979, 150), including many women who were thus able to participate in forms of social life from which they had previously been excluded. Other resistance organizations such as *Ethnikos Dimokratikos Ellinikos Syndesmos* (EDES or National Republican Greek League), though initially liberal, soon developed an anticommunist orientation. Consequently, the resistance was internally divided from the beginning. Already in 1943, deadly battles took place in the countryside and the Athens area between EAM/ELAS and various nonleftist organizations. These would be the seeds of the civil war to follow. In December 1944, three months after liberation, a short but deadly battle occurred between ELAS and the British troops that patrolled the Athens area following the evacuation of the German forces and the newly formed Greek gendarmerie (staffed mainly by collaborators) (Close 1995, 137–41). This battle became known as the Battle of Athens or *Dekemvriana* (December events). At stake were the disarmament of ELAS and the formation of new national armed forces to be controlled by the coalition government of George Papandreou. This government included some ministers appointed by EAM itself. The battle was ignited by the unwarranted shooting of a dozen of left-wing demonstrators in the central square of Athens by the gendarmerie. The conflict lasted over a month and in the end the anticommunist camp prevailed and was able to impose its terms on the subsequent Varkiza Agreement, in February 1945. Part of this agreement was to pardon all offenses committed during the *Dekemvriana* except "common-law crimes against life and property which were not absolutely necessary to the achievement of the political crime concerned." This clause provided ultra-right wingers and royalists legitimacy in launching large-scale violence and terror against members, followers, and sympathizers of EAM/ELAS (Voglis 2000, 74–75).

Left-wingers and ex-guerilla fighters found shelter in the mountainous countryside, defending themselves in small and isolated bands. At the same time, the Communist Party was now free to participate in public life but was at pains to put an end to the "white terror" by peaceful political means. This was the case because the prewar elites sought to regain control of the country by eliminating left-wing forces; it was also an American demand for the consolidation of the Yalta Pact (according to which Greece belonged 90 percent to the Western bloc), which meant assuming a tough anticommunist stance. For these reasons and due to conflicts within its own leadership (hard-liners versus soft-liners), the Communist Party opted for armed confrontation rather than taking part in the general election at 1946. Much later, in the 1970s, the party would characterize its actions as a mistake.

For the good part of a year, the Greek Communist Party chose not to launch any large-scale military campaign, either because it used military pressure to reach an acceptable political compromise, or simply because it was not ready for a full-blown war. Only after September 1947, when supported by the Eastern bloc (especially Tito's Yugoslavia), did the Party engage in major military confrontation. This occurred for the most part in the mountainous northwestern region of the country and resulted in the defeat of the Left.

Physical Casualties

According to official estimates, by August 1949, there were about 40,000 dead; unofficial accounts place that number as high as 158,000 (Tsoukalas 1969, 89). It is also estimated that up to 60,000 members of *Dimokratikos Stratos Ellados* (DSE or Democratic Army of Greece), the successor of ELAS, crossed the northern borders of the country and migrated into the surrounding communist countries, where they remained for several decades. Those of Slavic ethnic origin are still barred from returning even today. Needless to say, material disaster was of a much larger scale. One has to add the unprecedented hardship the country faced from the moment it entered World War II until the eve of Liberation. From 1940 to 1944, almost 8 percent of the population was killed, and 34 percent of the national treasury was decimated (Tsoukalas 1969, 69). According to McVeagh, the American ambassador in Athens, in early 1946, two-thirds of Greece's population survived on only 1,700 calories per day (in comparison to the 2,850 calories of the British); almost 30 percent of the population suffered from malaria, while the incidence of tuberculosis was fifteen times higher than that in Britain. Just after the end of the civil war in 1949, almost 10 percent of the population (i.e., 700,000 people), were homeless refugees waiting to reinhabit their wrecked villages. Cumulatively, World War II and the civil war devastated the Greek economy and ravaged Greek society almost entirely.

All of this exacted a profound impact on the way people became accustomed to violence (Voglis 2002). One could argue that the civil war rested on a culture of violence inherited from the Occupation, a period of collective retaliation, mass execution, deportation of local populations (especially in the region of Eastern Macedonia occupied by Bulgarians), burning of villages, and public exposure of corpses, which was amplified by black (right wing) as well as by red (communist) terror (Kalyvas 2002). Cruelty and atrocity on both sides marked collective memories and hammered personal political identities and life projects in far-reaching ways.

Cleavages and Long-Term Repercussions

In general, the Greek civil war was a multifaceted phenomenon. First of all, it was a total war that involved military and civilian forces employing conventional and unconventional tactics. Second, it was marked by local particularities and exigencies that have only recently been recognized by scholars using new methodological tools (Marantzides 2002; Kalyvas 2000 and 2002). Often, events in a local context diverged from the large-scale politics of the decision-making at the government and the Greek Communist Party (KKE) headquarters; therefore, local politics, personal and kinship relations and hostilities were of primary importance in the conflict (Mylonas 2003). To be sure, these divisions were much less intense than the intersecting cleavages that fueled the Spanish civil war (regional/ethnic differences, Catholics versus anticlerical groups, class conflicts), or the Finnish civil war, which had a much more solid class basis (Alapuro 2002).

For 25 years the most overwhelming consequence of the Greek civil war in political culture was the cleavage between the so-called nationally conscious (*ethnikofrones*), healthy, clean, and first-class citizens on one side, and on the other the sick, non-nationally-minded miasma, second-class citizens comprised of defeated communists, leftists, sympathizers, and nonroyalists. This cleavage permeated not only the political realm but also every social, economic, and cultural arena; social, political, and economic marginalization was the common plight for the defeated left. As a result, the public sector was purged of any non-nationally-minded civil servant. This cleavage intersected with the previously mentioned interwar cleavage between royalists and republicans.

Until the end of the 1950s, the space for any strongly worded discourse challenging the post–civil war establishment was extremely narrow. Since the beginning of that crucial decade, the 1960s, that space widened as the Union of the Center party (*Ένωση Κέντρου*) challenged the dominance of ERE (the right-wing dominant party). In addition, economic development in the tertiary and manufacturing sector allowed for the rapid integration of domestic migrants into the labor market. There existed, however, an unbridgeable contradiction: while economic incorporation continued and created the conditions for social consensus and the gradual de-EAMification of the lower classes (Charalambis 1989, 196), the structure of the post–civil war state (monarchy, army, national consciousness, etc.) did not allow for their political incorporation. Those who were defeated in the civil war, already incorporated in the market and the consumerist way of life, also demanded moral recognition and political representation. In the new socioeconomic environment, their fear gradually gave way to resentful indignation and accumulated emotional energy, which led to large-scale social protest between 1963 and 1964.

Seemingly, this was a period where the post–civil war regime was about to loose its grip. Yet, facing the prospect of losing control in the parliamentary elections scheduled for May 1967, April's *coup d'etat* in effect blocked every outlet for the democratic incorporation of the non-nationally-minded in the political system. On top of the traumatic memory of the civil war, there now came the dictatorship, which led to a fatalistic belief in the inevitability of political inequality and marginalization for this group. Their humiliation was only accentuated by this course of events.

The main consequence of the dictatorship was that the contradiction between the demand for political and moral recognition and the powerlessness to achieve it, combined with a chronic reliving of endless vindictiveness, hostility, and indignation on the part of the excluded. This combination produced a deep-rooted *ressentiment* (Demertzis 2006). I regard *"ressentiment"* as an unpleasant moral feeling without a specific addressee, which is experienced as a chronic reliving of repressed vindictiveness, hostility, envy, and indignation—all of which stem from the subject's impotence in expressing himself or herself in social practice (Scheler 1961). To the extent that the dictatorship reversed the democratizing tendencies of the mid-1960s, it can be argued that a significant portion of predictatorial resentment in the form of moral indignation, was, during the dictatorship, dematerialized and transformed into *ressentiment*. The injustice of political marginalization and through it the post–civil war establishment, were perceived as an inescapable fate, a form of fatalism leading to an experience of impotence and inferiority. However, no sooner than the socialists took office in 1981 and the lower middle strata made up of those defeated in the civil war (the "nonprivileged" in Andreas Papandreou's populist rhetoric) suddenly found themselves integrated into the political system. In this situation *ressentiment* gave way to vengeance, precisely because it could be expressed and acted out publicly. Party mass clientelism (Lyrintzis 1984) and the "green guards" (cadres who dominated in trade unions, the public sector, and state mechanisms during Papandreou's rule) were offered as compensation for the stony years of political marginalization.

The Civil War as Collective Injury

No one celebrated in the streets when the civil war ended, as was the case in October 1944, time of the liberation from German occupation. Nor was its end celebrated in later years in any massive or popular way. In fact, the civil war was quickly almost purged from the official discourse of its primary actors, victors and defeated alike, something quite uncommon in the history of civil wars. With respect to historical/official memory the date of the end of the civil war (August 29, 1949), apart from the dictatorship years (1967–1974, which was discredited in any case), has never been elevated to the status of a National Holiday. Of course, the memory of the civil war was conveyed through a number of local celebrations and memorial services, for example, for the victims of the communists in emblematic sites where deadly battles occurred (e.g., Meligalas, Makrygiannis, Vitsi), but the end of the civil war as such was not commemorated in any substantial way. Similarly, for all the devastation incurred by World War II, May 8 is not celebrated in Greece to commemorate the end of that war. Instead, it is October 28, the first day of the victorious Greek-Italian war, which is celebrated as a National Holiday. As the end of World War II almost coalesces with the beginning of the civil war, the victorious national elite did not want to connect the two events (Voglis 2008). From 1950 to 1967, the anticommunist discourse did not much refer to the recently ended war or to "red violence," rather its focus was on the threat of the so-called "international communism."

A politics of oblivion was gradually put into effect, generating public as well as private silence around the civil war, the same painful silence my father had been harboring for two and a half decades. The post–civil-war Left embraced the catchword forgetting (of the past) to help alleviate its marginalization. Similarly, the official discourse of the Right in the period between 1950 and 1967 was built around forgetting in an effort to gain greater legitimacy over multiple constituencies. It is indicative that during the 1950s emergency measures and censorship prevented the Greek film industry from actually producing a single film that directly addressed the violence of the civil war. Instead, in a number of successful folklore films (e.g., *Astero, Sarakatsanissa, Gerakina*) we can observe allusions to the struggles of the civil war as a filial conflict, as well as a desire for reconciliation and social cohesion (Potamitis 2008, 132–134). Even during the dictatorship, which promoted a great number of propaganda films about the communist atrocities and treason in an attempt to blame the Left and define accordingly the public memory of the civil war, there were no explicit references to it; in public speeches and propaganda there were more indirect and metaphoric rather than straight and polemic references. Why this silence then?

Horrendous as its impact on the body social might be, I would argue that during the period from 1950–1974, the civil war was primarily experienced as a collection of private injuries that could not be accommodated into the societal symbolic universe. The tragic occurrence of the war was experienced as a perpetual shock inflicting numbness and silence, a defense mechanism of collectives and individuals alike. Had this aggregate of individual suffering been openly discussed, recognized, and signified in the public sphere, it would have then resulted in a cultural trauma. I shall deal with this a bit later on. For the time being, some further explanation is needed regarding the veil of silence about the war.

Affective Casualties

For the defeated Left, the emotional injuries were as widespread as the physical ones referred to above; in addition to the battlefield, a moral and emotional war was taking place. All detainees in prisons or places of exile were pressed to sign declarations of repentance, through which they recanted their political ideas and the Communist Party itself. This method of demoralization during the civil war developed into an industry of recantation. In several thousand cases, these declarations were signed after a long and painful process of physical and psychological torture. What is more, these declarations were widely publicized in the local and national press, as well as in the village communities; those who signed were forced to prove their true repentance by informing on comrades, sending public letters repudiating communism, and by joining the military police to arrest and torture their former comrades and friends. Through this mechanism people were "reformed," transformed into good citizens who denounced their past identity (Voglis 2000, 76–77). Some could not stand such humiliation and committed suicide; a very tough emotional cross-pressure was exerted on all those who signed but did not alter their beliefs about communism or the Left in general, as they were stigmatized by both the authorities and the Communist Party itself. Activating a reflex syndrome of suspicion, the party organization treated such people not as politically defeated and physically exhausted subjects but as sinful and compromised individuals who would not defend the moral superiority of the party.

For those who signed such declarations, my father included, the emotional cost cannot be fully understood except by reference to the political culture of Greek Communism, as well as the emotional *habitus* of the Left in the decades before the war. The political socialization of the Greek communists had been carried out in a *milieu* of self-asserted marginalization. Following the Bolshevik revolution, the KKE was founded in 1918. From early on, the party, as institution and through its individual members, in line with the Marxist-Leninist creed and the Third International, was at pains to comply with the official policies of the Greek state and public opinion. In 1920, the Greek Communist Party strongly opposed the irredentist war in Asia Minor denouncing it as imperialist and adventurous. In 1924, it supported a "unified and independent Macedonia and Thrace"[3] propagating the idea of a working class revolution in Greece and the Balkans. During 1929, the opening year of the Great Depression, in tandem with popular sentiment, it organized militant rallies and strikes which resulted in many casualties. In 1930, it unsuccessfully declared a general strike and advocated the establishment of the soviet regime in Greece.

The repressive state apparatus responded harshly to these political projects by prosecuting hundreds of party members. What is more, the 1936 Metaxas dictatorship declared the Communist Party illegal; almost 2,000 of its members were arrested or exiled, and they were forced to sign declarations of repentance. The entire network of its organization was for the most part demolished by the secret police. Those who remained free had to be very secretive in their contact with each other and in their private everyday life.

Given the quasi-religious adherence to the communist utopia, these experiences and practices contributed to the shaping of an emotional climate and a *habitus* of strong group-mindedness, suspiciousness against real or alleged police agents, of traitors and revisionists within the party ranks; in other words, a disciplinary solidarity as well as a sense of being a righteous or expiatory victim. By and large, this emotional *habitus* was reactivated during the years of resistance (1941–1944) and afterward. In effect, it was a defense mechanism for coping with disappointment and humiliation. This inherited emotional climate of mutual suspicion in tandem with the process of humiliating self-negation imposed by the postwar regime (Voglis 2000) contributed to the silencing of the civil war in the period between 1950 and 1974.

Designating the War

Hitherto, I have been referring to the Greek civil war through the use of the English words. Yet, one should bear in mind that in Greek there is no semantic equivalent to *civil war*; in fact, the Greek word which usually substitutes for *civil war* is *emphylios polemos* (internecine or filial war, war within the same race). The idea of a civil war is premised on the notion of civil society and civil sphere; it presupposes individualized citizens who are organized according to collective goals and/or interests, who are in conflict over the definition of a society's historicity. On the contrary, the Greek political discourse cannot linguistically support the idea of an inner-state war *qua* civil war, precisely because it is endowed with a variety of premodern and antimodern social significations. This is a result of the traditionally weak civil society in Greece and the consequent absence of a deeply rooted bourgeois culture (Mouzelis 1986; Charalambis and Demertzis 1993; Demertzis 1997).

For more than a century, Greek society evolved within the tenets of cultural nationalism and traditionalism rather than political and socioeconomic modernity, resembling what Riggs (1964) defines as a "prismatic society," that is, a society with limited differentiation and highly mixed structural functions. In other words, despite the modernization processes experienced since the last quarter of the nineteenth century and the emergence of a stillborn class politics and interest intermediation in the interwar period, the hegemonic political cultural setting within which the civil war took place was of a *Gemeinschaft* rather than a *Gesselschaft*. As in other Balkan and eastern European countries, the nation-state in Greece, as a posttraditional mode of domination, is supported by what has been called "cultural nationalism," that is, an ideological discourse according to which the nation is far from being an association premised on modernity's civic liberties, but a particularistic, *qua* horizontal brotherhood, an ethnocultural community of language, religion, tradition, race, habits, with romanticized historical memories (Kohn 1961, 329–330 and 457; Sugar 1969, 19–20, 34–35).

With an absent strong civil sphere and a communal *habitus* prevailing, it follows naturally that the armed conflict between Greeks in the mid-1940s was designated as internecine or filial conflict rather than a proper civil war. It was understood as a conflict within the same national family, between men and women of the same blood, namely between brothers and sisters, rather than between opposing life projects and mutually exclusive societal interests.

No wonder that although in 1943–1944 and 1945–1946 both the EAM and the anti-EAM bloc warned of an imminent civil war (*emphylios*), during the period of the long and large scale fighting (1946–1949) both sides were cautious enough not to use the word *emphylios polemos* to describe what was happening. Had they employed such a semantic designation, they would have discredited themselves as violators of the transcendental racial/national unity. To put it in another way, the constitutive civiclessness of the Greek civil war can be explained by the moral, if not sacred, character of national community, which by necessity precluded the actors from defining their actions according to the only available codification the universe of Greek political discourse could offer them:[4] an "internecine war."

Since the "civil war" *qua emphylios polemos* was excluded from public discourse early on, both sides spoke metaphorically about what was happening and in the process demonized each other. For the Right, *Dekemvriana* were considered a rebellion, and their opponents were rebels against the legal national government. For them, the 1946–1949 conflict was a war against bandits and outlaws (*symmoritopolemos*), a war against communist bandits who betrayed their country by pursuing a path of partial annexation to the Soviet bloc or the Slavs. Among others, the latter was premised on the anticipation that the DSE and its government (*Prosorini Democratiki Kivernisi*, Interim Democratic Government) would serve Bulgaria's geostrategic ambitions, after the Soviet Union's proposal at the Peace Conference of 1946 that western Thrace, actually a Greek territory, should be conceded to the then-socialist Bulgaria.

For the Left, the 1946–1949 innerstate conflict as well as the December events were described as a "people's liberation war," a "people's democratic struggle," "people's self-defense," "armed struggle of DSE," "armed struggle," or simply "struggle." The opponents of the Left were identified as monarchists-fascists and reactionaries who gave up the country to British and American troops, whose presence was no less than a "second occupation." This is why, in the countryside, those on the Left referred to the civil war as "second guerilla war" (*deftero andartiko*). However, with the ceasefire of 1949, these metaphors were no longer in public use. To be sure, in the subsequent years, until the 1980s, *symmoritopolemos* has been the typical right-wing designation in public speeches and political documents, and also in legislation and jurisprudence, to the extent that any reference to the war was made at all. After the mid-1950s, apart from the seven years of dictatorship, the ruling elites refrained from bringing the war onto the public agenda when they could. The prevailing stance was silence. Unlike the Katyn case, however (see Bartmanski and Eyerman in this volume), the veil of silence was socially imposed but not directly enforced by a repressive state apparatus. It was imposed as a win-win political choice as well as a spontaneous collective response to a horrendous event. Within such a complex situation, it has not always been easy to conduct academic research on the Greek civil war; for the long period of silence (1950–1974), the topic was a taboo, and in addition, scholars were reluctant to deal with it because of the difficulty in accessing archives prior to the early 1980s. Systematic scholarly work started after the political changeover in 1974.

From Collective Injury to Cultural Trauma

According to cultural trauma theory, an event, as destructive as it may be, will become or produce cultural trauma only when connected to the hermeneutic horizons of social action. A cultural trauma involves the realization (in both senses of the term) of a common plight. As such, it must be collectively defined to influence the systems of reference of an entire society or, at least, of a significant part of it and, the process, change established roles, rules, *habitus,* and narratives. In other words, a cultural trauma is a total social event and not just an aggregate of numerous individual experiences. A dislocating event, for example, a civil war, does not in itself constitute a "cultural trauma." To become one, such an event must undergo a process of social signification; namely, it has to be signified and become socially accepted and constructed as "trauma."

In the context of middle-range theory (Alexander et al. 2004), the notion of "cultural trauma" has been systematically formulated as a distinctive sociological concept referring to group identity, the constitution of collective memory and to forms of collective action. Formulated alongside the tenets of a weak social constructionism, cultural trauma refers to "a memory accepted and publicly given credence by a relevant membership group and evoking an event or situation, which is (a) laden with negative affect, (b) represented as indelible, and (c) regarded as threatening to a society's existence or violating one or more of its fundamental cultural presuppositions" (Smelser 2004, 44). According to Alexander (2004, 1) cultural trauma occurs when members of a collectivity feel that they have suffered a horrendous event that leaves indelible marks on their group consciousness, marking their memories forever and changing their future identity in fundamental and irrevocable ways. From an intergenerational point of view, a cultural trauma is a "chosen trauma" in the way Vamik Volkan (2001, 2005) puts it, that is, a large group's unconscious "choice" to add to its own identity a past generation's mental representation of a shared event that has caused a large group to face drastic losses, feel help-less and victimized by another group, and share a humiliating injury. The fundamental elements of cultural trauma theory are memory, emotion, and identity. In this respect, the theory joins hands with the subfields of memory, trauma, and disaster studies. It is a complex area of theory and research which straddles micro and the macro levels of analysis and the long and short duration of historical time.

As a totalizing social event the Greek civil war can be described as a cultural trauma because it affected collective memories, group con-sciousness, and the organizational principles of Greek society, redirecting its orientation for several decades. Yet, as already mentioned, this was a process which could not have happened in a straightforward fashion; as it is the process of social construction that transforms selectively a painful condition of many individuals into cultural trauma of a collec-tive, the Greek civil war is transfigured into an exemplary case of cultural trauma through a "trauma process," which fills the gap between event and representation (Alexander 2004, 11). The remainder of this section is about this process.

The seven year dictatorship collapsed in July 1974. This occurred through a combination of grassroots activism and international pressure, but mostly due to its own inefficacy to secure economic development after the 1973 oil crisis and the collapse of its nationalistic foreign policy toward the Cyprus issue (which led to the invasion and military occupation of the northern part of the island). The political changeover (the so-called *Metapolitefsi*) put an end to the post–civil-war regime and constituted a major turn in the political opportunity structure of the country and, retroactively, set in motion the Greek civil war trauma process. The Communist Party was legalized, new parties were formed, all civil rights and liberties were reinstated, and the monarchy was overthrown; at the same time, the country prepared itself to join the European Union. Given the absolute discrediting of *ethnikofrosini* (national-mindedness) and its advocates, an entirely new context for political culture opened up. This allowed for the reinterpretation of the official and collective memory and the experience(s) of the civil war itself.

The carving out of a democratic public space removed the veil of silence and made it possible for various carrier groups such as parties, intellectuals, political refugees and prisoners, media, journalists, academics, and artists to bring the civil war into focus as an issue whose meaning was publicly negotiated and symbolically processed. Although right and center-right claim-makers were active, it was ultimately the left and center-left advocates that gained hegemony in this trauma process. To put it differently, the subsequent transformation of the civil war from collective injury or group pain into cultural trauma was primarily launched as an internal affair of the Left.

Analytically, I would divide this trauma process into two phases: the phase of selective construction from 1974–1990, and the reflexive construction period from 1990 on. As in any other cultural trauma (Alexander 2004, 10–24), in both phases the trauma process was conveyed at different and yet interrelated instances, whose impact to the final outcome may vary: official and collective memory, group identity, institutional arenas (aesthetic, media, scientific, legal), and attribution of responsibility endeavors.

Selective Construction Phase (1974–1990)

In the era of *Metapolitefsi* (officially, the Third Greek Republic) another catchword was keenly embraced by the Left and the Right alike: "reconciliation." The cleavage between first-class and second-class citizens should be suspended once and for all, here and now. Such an almost universal demand was premised on a paradoxical act of "remembering to forget" (Bhabha 1991, 93); namely, on a highly selective process of restructuring the official and the collective memory of the 1940s. With some exceptions, the mnemonic community of the defeated Left is built around the Resistance rather than the civil war. Now, however, talk of the civil war was not condemned to silence but was deliberatively put aside, in accordance with the reconciliation imperative. Hence, at the first phase of the trauma process another kind of politics of oblivion was carried through by both sides, while, as usual in such cases, at the level of unofficial memory, the civil war was recollected antagonistically so that for a divided or even multifaceted collective memory to emerge (Halbwachs 1992, 172 and 182; Connerton 1989, 38–99; Aguilar 1996; Eyerman 2001, 5–22; Voglis 2008), at the level of official memory, the civil war was banished, placed under the shadow of the Resistance.[5] The newly constituted Third Hellenic Republic had to consolidate itself and was searching for a founding myth capable of cementing emotional energy. Among others, in the host of nonacademic bibliographies concerning the 1940s, comprised from propaganda material, veterans' memoirs, autobiographies, biographies, diaries, illustrated texts, congresses, and convention minutes which appeared after 1974 (Marantzidis and Antoniou 2004), as well as in party documents and political discourse, one could detect the emergence of this myth: Through bypassing the civil war, resistance against the Axis powers became the master narrative.

A defining moment in this process came shortly after the 1981 general elections, when Socialists (PASOK), led by Andreas Papandreou, took office for the first time in the country's history and supported the legal recognition of the resistance (Law 1285/1982) turning it into "National Resistance," a term never before used. Although without much enthusiasm, National Resistance has ever since been officially commemorated on November 25. On that day in 1942, a major offensive against the Axis was carried out by combined ELAS and EDES forces. Typically, recognition was conferred on individual resistance fighters, who were awarded an appropriate title and pension. Accordingly, the names of hundreds of streets and squares across the country were changed overnight to "National Resistance." In a prominent and historic square in the center of Athens a statue was erected and dedicated to "national reconciliation."

Clearly, a myth-making process had been taking place to the extent that the period of resistance (1941–1944) was cleansed of any disturbing stains of internecine conflict and radical, if not virtually all revolutionary, projects, subjugated entirely to the nationalist discourse.[6] In Greece and many other countries, a mythic all-embracing national resistance movement promoted a postwar collective admiration that expunged any taint of toleration and collaboration with the occupiers. Actually, unlike other European countries (Fleischer 2008, 235), in Greece the punishment for collaborators was extremely mild, and many survived precisely because they served the anticommunist cause (Haidia 2000). In addition, large parts of the newly formed postwar ruling class had been collaborators and black market dealers during the occupation or usurpers of Jewish property. Not surprisingly these facts have been suppressed. In effect, the *resistancialist myth* did not so much glorify the resistance, as it celebrated a people *in resistance,* a people symbolized without intermediaries, such as political parties, movements, or clandestine leaders (Rousso 1991, 18; Giesen 2004, 148).

Another defining moment in the memorization of the civil war came seven years later when a ritual of great significance for the "nationalization" of the Resistance and the promotion of "national reconciliation" took place on the fortieth anniversary of the end of the civil war. Hundreds of thousands of secret police files of the so-called "non-nationally minded" citizens were ceremonially burned over the objection of Greek historians. As a result, a precious and rich corpus of documents was forever lost. That ritual was performed after the 1863/1989 Law according to which the term *symmoritopolemos* was officially replaced by the term *emphylios polemos* whose duration was defined from 1944 to 1949. Also, the term "bandits" (*symmorites*) was replaced by "Democratic Army" (*Dimokratikos Stratos*). That law was enacted by the three-month coalition government of the right-wing party of *Nea Democratia* (New Democracy) and the left-wing and originally communist *Synaspismos* (Left Coalition) formed in 1989, the eve of the post–Cold War era, and apparently had great symbolic impact. In contradistinction, public commemoration of the civil war has been rare and sporadic, inflicting sometimes embarrassment and bitterness. Within this context, the mnemonic rituals of the Right and the commemoration of its victory over the Reds were denounced by the so called democratic camp as "hate rites."

The portrayal of the 1941–1944 resistance as a "chosen glory" (Volkan 2005), mingled imaginatively with the far less massive resistance against the military *hunta,* was supported by the performances of left-leaning artists, especially musicians like Mikis Theodorakis and Yannis Markopoulos, who delivered concerts in stadiums all over Greece attended by large crowds and were broadcast across state-owned TV channels. This artistic work focused on the heroic, enduring, and victorious people who defended the motherland despite its mistakes and misgivings. Prominent position in these performances was afforded to *andartika tragoudia* (guerilla songs), which were extremely popular for more than a decade.

This (cultural) politics of oblivion bears witness to two defense mechanisms: "displacement" and "projection" with regards to the attribution of responsibility and the rationalization of trauma (Smelser 2004).[7] The 1946–1949 conflict is here interpreted as the straightforward outcome of British and U.S. intervention in Greek political life.[8] The December 1944 events, let alone the 1943–1944 clashes between ELAS, EDES, and the Greek Security Battalions which were formed at 1943 under the auspices of the German occupation forces (Mazower 1993), are scarcely mentioned at all. Scapegoats, expiatory victims, and conspiratorial explanations of history have been more than frequently employed to identify the causes and consequences of the civil war. For instance, hundreds of KKE executive members who disagreed with the official decisions were physically exterminated by the party's death squads *Organosi Perifrourisis*

Laikou Agona (OPLA or Organization for the Protection of the People's Struggle); they were accused of spying and exhibiting a "reactionary" petty bourgeois mentality. As an aside, the acronym OPLA is also the Greek word for "arms," a living metaphor designating death.

Ever since the late 1950s, the self-representation of the Left has been that of an expiatory or pious victim. The public memory of the Left selected the innumerable atrocities it suffered by the so called "white terror" of the Right between 1945 and 1946 as well as the unbearable prosecutions they endured during and after the war (executions, exile, imprisonments, rapes, tortures, social marginalization, etc). To this end, films like *The Man with the Carnation* (1980) and *Stony Years* (1985) visualized retroactively the suffering of the Left, rendering it thus a pious victim. At the same time, however, numerous malpractices, atrocities, and responsibilities were repressed or even disavowed in the public memory of the Left.

Likewise, the 1974–1990 mnemonic community of the victorious Right has been equally embarrassed by the civil war since it is more than reluctant to remember that approximately 5,000 of its opponents were executed by the extraordinary court-martials and nearly 70,000 prisoners and exiles were convicted between 1947 and the early 1950s. This is nicely depicted in the 1977 Theo Angelopoulos film *I Kynigi* (*The Hunters*), which is about "non memory," that is, the negation of the Right to undertake the responsibility for its victims. Yet, the public memory of the Right selectively retains the "red terror" and communist crimes. In addition, a taboo topic concerns the Greek Security Battalions that collaborated with German troops. During the December 1944 events, they were the backbone of the anti-EAM forces, and most of their members joined the National Army against DSE soon after, in order to escape legal prosecution for war crimes.

The attribution of responsibility for the civil war to the British and the Americans is a classic example of a conspiratorial view of history, quite common in the Greek populist political discourse, either left or right.[9] Under these terms, Greeks *in toto* are the expiatory victims of the foreigners, an interpretive motive supported by the famous 1975 movie *O Thiasos* (*Traveling Players*) by Angelopoulos. Another similar defense mechanism is the double tendency of remembering and forgetting. For such a traumatic event as the Greek civil war, there is, on one hand, the demand to "leave everything behind us" in the name of national reconciliation; on the other, however, there is the injunction to "preserve our historical memory."

Either option leads to unsuccessful mourning and, paradoxically, in spite of being profound political options, they depoliticize the civil war itself by subsuming it into nationalistic discourse. The adversarial political identities of the opponents of the 1940s are symbolically transfigured to the extent that (a) any revolutionary or counter-revolutionary potential of the civil war has been systematically suppressed from public discourse and popular memory; (b) the opponents were discursively endowed with nonpolitical, nearly metaphysical, traits—noble defenders of race and nation on one side and selfless and benign patriots who hunt the reactionary servants of imperialism on the other. Even the bridging of the opposition described as "reconciliation" instead of "compromise" bears its own significance; actually, "reconciliation" is the counterpart of filial war as it presupposes two formerly homogenous parts that have only temporarily parted. On the contrary, devoid of any moralistic overtones, "compromise" is a political concept premised on power relations and the convergence of strategic projects in a public sphere.

Similarly, in the phase of selective construction of cultural trauma, the Left was entangled in a symbolic antinomy as to its collective identity: by claiming the glory of Resistance, it was no longer morally defeated, while at the same time, it could claim the role of the victim of the post–civil-war and the postdictatorship polity. This antinomy has been grounded on two mutually exclusive vectors: the silencing of its strong opposition to class society (that is, the ultimate stake of the Communists in the civil war) and the affirmation of the national society they wanted to be part of. Effectively, this antinomy was premised on a particular sort of emotional reflexivity. By "emotional reflexivity," I mean a sort of emotional dynamics, a capacity, to negotiate relationships by changing the structure of feeling and, therefore, how others feel within these relationships. It is a process in which social actors have feelings about and try to understand and alter their lives in relation to others (Holmes 2008). Accordingly, defense of the Resistance was meant to destigmatize the Greek Communists and the Left in general from being labeled as traitors and national outcasts; at the same time, it was a symbolic means for transforming the trauma of humiliation they experienced after the defeat into the bestowed pride of fully fledged citizens. This destigmatizing emotional reflexivity has been carried through a legitimating discourse guided by militant testimonial zeal (Panagiotopoulos 1994) which, as a rule, framed the Greek Communists as martyrs for the homeland during the Occupation and as innocent victims of a revengeful state. It is not accidental that some of my interview subjects used the word "Golgotha" when describing their experience as victims of the war, that is, a religious metaphor through which their activities acquire a nonpolitical status.

Reflexive Construction Phase (1990–2010)

During the last twenty post–Cold War years, a number of significant and interrelated changes in all fields of social life have been taking place in Greece, adding some new qualities to the trauma process regarding the civil war. Economically, a rapid growth in the GNP mainly concentrated in tertiary sector was achieved, backed by massive revenues from the EU funds and stock market investments directed by "casino capitalism" logic and heavy consumerism. Politically, this period is characterized by the gradual sedimentation of the party system from polarized pluralism into two-party system to the extent that the two main catch-all parties, *PASOK* and *Nea Democratia,* managed to minimize or eliminate other significant political forces; thus, in the main, the total left vote, comprising a number of parliamentary and nonparliamentary parties, barely exceeds 12 percent in any elections. In spite of the strong turnout fostered by compulsory electoral participation, a waning partisanship and disenchantment with public affairs have been systematically documented. In the realm of cultural values, a privatized atomism versus reflexive individualization antinomy can be observed, so that politically adiaphoric cohorts or instrumentally oriented publics coexist with agents of post-materialist libertarian orientations and advocates of identity politics.

Albeit differentially, this political cultural *milieu* affected the way in which the civil war has been culturally interpreted by members of the first, second, and third generation. After sixty years, due to a cohort effect and a gradual disengagement from party politics, the left-wing parties included, the civil war was seen in a more distanced way; it might be true that for apathetic youngsters (the third generation) the civil war is a thing of the past, but it can be reasonably argued that for the bearers of libertarian post-materialist values of the second generation the civil war is a present-past reality. For the carrier groups of this generation, my generation, it is not just that the war's effects are still pertinent or that the civil war injuries hibernate in collective moods in spite of the emotional inoculation of "reconciliation." Rather, at stake is a coming to terms with the recent past of the country (*Vergangenheitsbewältigung*), a disillusioned stance toward the politics of oblivion either of the 1950–1974 or the 1974–1990 period, which joins hands with similar undertakings with regard to other countries' traumatic experiences (Fleischer 2008, 196, 209, 234, and 246–247) after World War II and the Cold War. This stance is facilitated by the explosion of memory and the rise of public history *vis-á-vis* postmodern consumerist lures that subvert historical consciousness. The issue gaining currency is a quest of reflexive historicity with regards to the civil war inheritance and the demise of the hegemonic politics of oblivion. It would not be much to say therefore that the master narrative of reconciliation has lost its unquestionable grip, and new sensibilities are mediating the construction of cultural trauma in all instances referred to previously.

To start with, a great controversy has been taking place since autumn 2009 over the aesthetic value and the political cultural significance of the widely watched and strongly marketed movie of Pantelis Voulgaris *Psychi Vathia* (*Soul Deep*). According to latest figures,[10] the movie has been viewed by almost 200,000 people, quite an impressive audience for the local film industry. This is a film about the vicissitudes of two young brothers who almost incidentally get involved in the opposite camps of the 1946–1949 filial war. The last scene of the film depicts the hugging of a devastated couple immediately after the very last battle of the war; the couple is made up of one of the two brothers, soldier of the State Army, and a young girl, who fought for the Democratic Army. In 1985, Voulgaris' *Stony Years*, referred to previously, as emblematic of the (self) victimization of the Greek Left, was very favourably received; *Soul Deep* has been received in an ambivalent way in many newspaper accounts and blogs: On the one side, many applaud it as the ultimate symbol of national reconciliation; on the other, critics and viewers alike question the simplistic attribution of the causes of war to the "foreigners" and the director's reluctance to delve deeply into its stakes.

The questioning or the bypassing of reconciliation is even better depicted through the unprecedented success of the 1997 biography of Aris Velouchiotes (1905–1945), founder and leader of ELAS, by the novelist and essayist Dionysis Charitopoulos: *Aris. O archigos ton atakton* (*Aris. Leader of the Irregulars*). In Greece's small book market, this 800-page, well-written biography went through three editions (the last in 2009); it has been reviewed widely and reached 180,000 copies. Aris Velouchiotes is a mythic figure of Greece's recent history, something like the local version of Che Guevara, part and parcel of the symbolic repertoire of a left political culture. He did not accept the Varkiza Agreement, and soon after (March 1945), he founded the "new ELAS" by recruiting a handful of comrades who were against the "new occupation by the British." Totally isolated and denounced by the Communist Party, which, at that time, opted for peaceful and mass-scale political activity in the cities, he was bound to fail. In June 1945, trapped by military troops, Velouchiotes committed suicide; his head hung for public display. The paradox is that a year later, KKE itself started a civil war upon premises Velouchiotes had advocated.

For many on the Left, this thrilling personality is a symbol of a virtual revolution, a signpost of what the Left could have done in order to avoid defeat. As I understand it, the great success of the book, at least among left-leaning readers, is due not just to the storytelling of the deeds of a chosen hero; it is based on a contra-factual attitude: things could have happened otherwise; we could have won the war, had the party adopted the appropriate strategy in time. Therefore, the reception of the book is about retroactive (self) critique and reconstitution of collective memory and identity of the Left well beyond the imperative of reconciliation.[11]

An additional instance resonating a more reflexive stance toward the civil war is the "'when it started versus when it ended" controversy that is taking place among political sociologists and historians in Greece, as well as public intellectuals; it is premised on the criterion that should be used to demarcate the transition of an armed conflict within a state into a civil war (Fearon and Laitin 2003; Sambanis 2002). Thus while the mainstream position until late the 1980s was March 30, 1946 to August 29, 1949, for some, it has been more appropriate to speak of civil war when one refers to the armed confrontations between ELAS, EDES, and the Security Battalions in 1943, in spite of the fact that a large-scale military mobilization was not involved. On equal measure, the December 1944 Battle of Athens should be seen as part of the civil war. Casting the blame to the Reds, the historical narrative of the right side recounts "three rounds" in the communists' plan to siege power: 1943, 1944, and 1946–1949.

Another issue, reiterating the communist historical narrative, is whether or not the 1945–1946 right-wing violence against the defeated EAM/ELAS, which erupted after the Varkiza Agreement (see previously) signals the beginning of the civil war (Mazower 2000, 6–7 and 31–32) or whether this was a "unilateral civil war"—which was to be followed soon after by a "bilateral civil war." Nowadays, however, after the legal settlement of the issue in late 1980s, most Greeks hold the view that the civil war occurred from 1944 until 1949.

With regard to the attribution of responsibility, another illustration of the demand for an appraisal of the civil war as a respectable academic and scholarly activity is underpinned by the need to redirect attention away from the question "Whose fault was it?" toward the question "How did the civil war take place?" (Marantzidis and Antoniou 2004; Mazower 2000, 8). As carrier groups of the trauma drama, scholars not only dispute details of the civil war but also disagree as to how it should be studied. Currently, a heated debate exists between traditional historians who base their work chiefly if not exclusively on the study of archives and a group of younger and postrevisionist scholars who apply oral history, memory and local studies, and clinical approaches.[12] The thrust of the dispute concerns the appropriateness of oral and local history methods and the possible disintegration of the field through topical approaches and piecemeal studies. Be it noted that this dispute strides the fence between academic institutions and spreads over the public space through newspapers, journals and magazines, especially on the occasion of the sixtieth anniversary of the end of the war.

Currently, an unintentional consequence of the trauma process in this period is the perpetrators' trauma. Research has indicated that in certain cases and under definite circumstances, on an individual and collective level, perpetrators may undergo a traumatic experience due to the suffering they caused to others. This is certainly the case with contemporary Germany (Giesen 2004). If not entirely lacking, analogous research is extremely limited in Greece and has fallen by the wayside; therefore, what follows is highly tentative, since it rests on poor empirical evidence. It is difficult to claim and document whether single individuals or the Greek Right as a collective had any regrets or guilt until 1974 for the atrocities done against the Left. If anything, the "red terror" caused its own trauma on the Right and evoked fear, sorrow, disgust, rage, hate, and vengeance. Certainly, the anticommunist victory conferred contentment, security, and, nevertheless, a self-censored silenced joy due to the hecatombs on each side and the overwhelmed demand for "forgetting."[13]

The "nationalization" of resistance was a crucial signpost for the collective identity of the Right; its effect has been quite the opposite in relation to what it conferred to the losers of the war. I argued earlier that through the nationalization of resistance, the Greek Communists felt that they were no longer morally defeated although they remained victims. The opposite seems to be the case with members of the Right involved in the civil war: Though they are still the victors on the battlefield, they have been morally degraded. The change of the regime of signification of the civil war after 1982 gave rise to embarrassment, frustration, and anger as the Right found itself deprived of the certainties bestowed by the anticommunist discourse and *ethnikofrosini*. It is somehow a postvictory trauma as people deem retroactively that their past military deeds and subsequent political attitudes are not socially recognized if not frequently denounced: "I ask you, when the state did wrong? When it was sending out its soldiers to kill themselves or now that it does not honor them?" This is the way one of the subjects interviewed by Antoniou (2007) expresses himself in view of the redefinition of the resistance. One of my right-oriented informants expressed his regret for the "psychological domination of the Communist Party" so that "historical memory and historical facts are ignored."

It might be the case that for people like him, contrary to official historical memory, *symmoritopolemos* is still a living metaphor for the description of the civil war and that reconciliation itself is not a self-evident political reality. Yet, the Third Hellenic Republic master narrative of national reconciliation and the post–Cold War political climate created an emotive and cognitive dissonance with its own account of the civil war which made people unwilling to speak about their experiences during the occupation and the civil war; actually, it was quite hard to find informants for my own research. This reluctance does not imply historical amnesia but a reaction to the official strategy of forgetting and "reconciliation" (Antoniou 2007). It is indicative that over the last decade there have been several cases where attempts of local authorities or left-leaning associations of the civil war veterans to raise monuments for the dead soldiers or prominent figures of DSE were strongly opposed. Although we do not know the depth of this state of mind, I would like to claim that we are witnessing a case of divided memory and a virtual cultural trauma specific to the depredated right-wing conservative cohorts.

Concluding Remarks

Based on personal interest, in this chapter, I have attempted to show when and how the collective suffering of the Greek civil war was socially constructed, and thus transformed into cultural trauma. After sixty years, this war still ignites the Greek political psyche because the master narrative of national reconciliation forwarded from 1974 onward lags behind a systematic reappraisal and coming to terms with the past, which steers clear of political correctness. As a result, the issue of forgiving has not yet been seriously raised.

Forgiveness is crucial to cultural trauma theory, at least its optimistic version, because a consistent concept of trauma, as a living metaphor, refers to a dynamic process that includes both the traumatic element itself *and* the process of its healing. Forgiveness is part of the healing process, an integral element of mourning. Certainly, to forgive is not to forget, nor is it denial or disavowal. Forgiveness entails transformation of negative emotions based on strong will, a will to start anew, a gesture quite opposite to vengeance. Forgiveness is never predicted, as it comes out of free will and frees both doer and sufferer from the relentless automatism of a vicious cycle (Arendt 1958, 236–241). What is more, forgiveness can be offered unconditionally only by those (previous victims) who are able to punish perpetrators (Ricouer 2004, 470). But who exactly is the victim and who is the perpetrator in the Greek civil war? Who is supposed to forgive whom?

This question was unthinkable twenty or even ten years ago due to the unshaken hegemony of the left-minded accounts of the civil war.

Today, in a period where the cultural trauma of that war is reflexively constructed, whoever utters this question has (a) to avoid negationism and historical revisionism (which is not identical with revisionist historiography); (b) to deconstruct the commanded forgetting of the civil war and the mythology that surrounds the so-called National Resistance; (c) to promote a spirit of difficult forgiveness, as it has been outlined by Ricoeur (2004).

Difficult forgiveness goes through recollection, the effort to recall and symbolically reconstruct the past instead of reliving it in the fashion of eternal return. In psychoanalytic terms, the eternal return is a sort of acting out and corresponds to reminiscence, whereas recollection is the realization by the subject of his/her history in his/her relation to a future (Evans 1996, 162). What matters is the reconstruction of the past and the rewriting of history in a progressive way. Certainly, it will be a long process which ultimately concerns the next generation as the real participants in the civil war are passing away and strong partisanship wanes. Yet, it might be less painful, and it may leave room for a mutual request for and offering of forgiveness.

Notes

1. This is based on evidence from past research, cultural documents, and original qualitative interviews conducted by others and myself. In 2008 and 2009, I selected material from ten narrative interviews composed by eight left-minded and two right-minded informants. Thanks goes to my student Katerina Koronaki for her contribution in the collection of research material and my colleagues Chris Kyriakides and Teresa Capelos for their comments on earlier versions of this chapter.

2. On March 5, 1946, Churchill demarcated East versus West with his notorious "iron curtain" statement; the Truman Doctrine and Marshall Plan followed some months later.

3. Large parts of these geographical areas belong to the Greek territory.

4. The semantic designation of the Greek civil war should come as no surprise; in many other civil wars, one can observe the same terminological civic-lessness premised on the different dependency path of each country with respect to political modernity.

5. A similar binary remembrance was put into effect in Poland with respect to the Katyn massacre and in Mao's China with regard to the massive atrocities of the Japanese army (see Eyerman and Bartmanski's and Gao's chapters in this volume). Yet, it seems to me to be misleading to draw too sharp a line between the official/public and the collective/popular memory; in the ongoing hegemony process, bridges are built and various kinds of overlapping are formed.

6. Similarly, in the trauma drama of 1974 in Cyprus, the Turkish military aggression overshadows the memory of the Greek-Cypriot coup against the legal government of the island, which actually triggered the Turkish invasion and sparked a short but harsh filial conflict just before the invasion (see the Roudometof and Christou chapter in this volume).

7. For all commonalities between clinical and cultural traumas one might find (latency, negative affect, retroactive construction), my use of psychoanalytic concepts (e.g., defence mechanism, displacement, and projection) for the interpretation of the Greek civil war trauma drama is by no means a sort of psychological reductionism, nor is it a collapse of the macro to the micro level of analysis. For one thing, a cultural trauma is not the aggregate of individual traumata but a historically constructed social event, which provides collective hermeneutic horizons. In addition, clinical traumas are constituted and administered by the inner-psychic mechanisms of repression, denial, adjustment, and working through whereas, on the contrary, cultural traumas result from issue claimers' discursive-authoritative practices who define an event as being traumatic. Provided that for Freud, there is no clear-cut distinction between individual and social psychology, I would claim for a functional equivalence between the defense mechanisms employed in the trauma drama and the clinical trauma that make possible the mediation of unconscious processes by cultural creations and narrative practices.

8. Clearly, the civil war is not independent of the British and U.S. involvement; one can find similar stories in Palestine and Israel, India, Cyprus and so on, according to the divide and conquer politics. The point is that this involvement has been imaginarily overstated.

9. Likewise, the dominant account of the civil war in today's Finland resides in the seemingly inconceivable revolt of a part of the people "against itself" by projecting the cause of the war outside the nation. Reds were "infected" or "misled" by the Russians to betray their own fatherland (Alapuro 2002).

10. http://www.myfilm.gr/6361.html. The success of the film in generating public dialogue over the civil war can be compared to both Wajda's movie *Katyn*, which, in Poland, narrated more than anything else in the past the need for the memorization of the massacred victims, and the performance of Beckett's play *Waiting for Godot* in Sarajevo and New Orleans as a symbolic means for the construction of vicarious trauma (see Eyerman and Bartmanski's and Breese's chapters in this volume).

11. Just recently, very few intellectuals of the Left deviate from this justifying discourse by discretely referring to the civil war as a strategic political option carried out by the Greek Communist Party in the 1940s and not as a fatal tragedy of the Greek people as a whole.

12. Since 1984, seventeen conferences have been organized mainly in Greece and abroad (Dordanas and Michaelides 2007) where these issues are debated. One of the major academic drivers is The Network for the Study of the Civil Wars (http://www.elia.org.gr/civil_war_greek/index.htm), founded in 2000.

13. A note of caution is in need at this point. By breaking the common wisdom about the bearers of the trauma of the Greek civil war, I do not aim to counterbalance the suffering of the two major actors, nor do I wish to make up for each one's political responsibilities. If anything, this paper deals principally with how and not why the war was carried out, nor whose fault it was.

Works Cited

Aguilar, P. 1996. *Memoria y olvido de la Guerra Civil espanola.* Madrid: Alianza Editorial.

Alapuro, R. 2002. Coping with the Civil War of 1918 in Twenty-first Century Finland. In *Historical Injustice and Democratic Transition in Eastern Asia and Northern Europe: Ghosts at the Table of Democracy,* eds. K. Christie and R. Cribb. London: Curzon.

Alexander, J. 2004. Toward a Theory of Cultural Trauma. In *Cultural Trauma and Collective Identity,* eds. J. Alexander et al. Berkeley: University of California Press.

Antoniou, G. 2007. *The Memory and Historiography of the Greek Civil War,* Florence, Unpublished PhD Thesis.

Arendt, H. 1958. *The Human Condition.* Chicago: University of Chicago Press.

Bhabha, H. 1991. Question of Survival: Nations and Psychic States. In *Psychoanalysis and Cultural Theory,* ed. J. Donald. London: Macmillan

Charalambis, D. 1989. *Clientelism and Populism. The Extra-institutional Consensus in the Greek Political System.* Athens: Exandas Publications.

Charalambis, D., and N. Demertzis. 1993. Politics and Citizenship in Greece: Cultural and Structural Facets. *Journal of Modern Greek Studies* 11(2): 219–40.

Clogg, R.1979. *A Short History of Modern Greece.* Cambridge: Cambridge University Press.

Close, D. 1995. *The Origins of the Greek Civil War.* Longman Publishing Group.

Connerton, P. 1989. *How Societies Remember.* Cambridge: Cambridge University Press.

Demertzis, N. 1997. Greece. In *European Political Culture,* ed. R. Eatwell. London: Routledge.

———. 2006. Emotions and Populism. In *Power, Passion and Politics,* eds. S. Clarke et al. London: Palgrave.

Dordanas, S., and I. Michaelides. 2007. Critical Literature Review for the Civil War (1990–2006). In *The Greek Civil War. An Assessment,* eds. I. Mourelos and I. Michaelides. Athens: Ellinika Grammata.

Evans, D. 1996. *An Introductory Dictionary of Lacanian Psychoanalysis.* London: Routledge.

Eyerman, R. 2001. *Cultural Trauma. Slavery and the Formation of African American Idenity.* Cambridge: Cambridge University Press.

Fearon, J., and D. D. Laitin. 2003. Ethnicity, Insurgency, and Civil War. *American Political Science Review* 97(1): 75–90.

Fleischer, H. 1986. *Im Kreuzschatten der Maechte: Griechenland 1941–1944. (Okkupation—Kollaboration—Resistance).* Frankfurt/Bern/New York: Peter Lang.

———. 2008. *Wars of Memory. World War II in Public History.* Athens: Nefeli Publications.

Giesen, B. 2004. The Trauma of Perpetrators. The Holocaust as the Traumatic Reference of German National Identity. In *Cultural Trauma and Collective Identity*, eds. J. Alexander et al. Berkeley: University of California Press.

Haidia, E. 2000. The Punishment of Collaborators in Northern Greece, 1945–1946. In *After the War Was Over. Reconstructing the Family, Nation, and State in Greece, 1943–1960*, ed. M. Mazower. Princeton and Oxford: Princeton University Press.

Halbwachs, M. 1992. *On Collective Memory.* Chicago and London: The University of Chicago Press.

Holmes, M. 2008. The Emotionalization of Reflexivity. *Sociology* 43 (forthcoming).

Hondros, J. 1983. *Occupation and resistance: The Greek Agony 1941–44.* New York: Pella Publishing Company.

Iatrides, J. 2002. The International Context of the Greek Civil War. In *The Civil War. From Varkiza to Grammos. February 1945–August 1949*, eds. E. Nikolakopoulos, A. Rigos, and G. Psallidas. Athens: Themelio.

Kalyvas, S. 2000. Red Terror: Leftist Violence during the Occupation. In *After the War Was Over. Reconstructing the Family, Nation, and State in Greece, 1943–1960*, ed. M. Mazower. Princeton and Oxford: Princeton University Press.

———. 2002. Forms, Dimensions and Practices of Violence in Civil War (1943–1949): An initial approach. In *The Civil War. From Varkiza to Grammos. February 1945–August 1949*, eds. E. Nikolakopoulos, A. Rigos, and G. Psallidas. Athens: Themelio.

Kohn, H. 1961. *The Idea of Nationalism. A Study in its Origins and Background,* 2nd ed. New York: MacMillan.

Kolko, G. 1994. *Century of War. Politics, Conflict, and Society since 1914.* New York: The New Press.

Lyrintzis, C. 1984. Political Parties in Post-Junta Greece: A Case of "Bureaucratic Clientelism?" In *The New Mediterranean Democracies. Regime Transition in Spain, Greece and Portugal*, ed. G. Pridham. London: Frank Cass.

Marantzides, N. 2002. Ethnic Dimensions of the Civil War. In *The Civil War. From Varkiza to Grammos. February 1945–August 1949*, eds. E. Nikolakopoulos, A. Rigos, and G. Psallidas. Athens: Themelio.

Marantzides, N., and G. Antoniou. 2004. The Axis Occupation and Civil War: Changing Trends in Greek Historiography, 1941–2002. *Journal of Peace Research* 41(2): 223–231.

Mazower, M. 1993. *Inside Hitler's Greece.* New Haven: Yale University Press.

———. 2000. Three Forms of Political Justice: Greece, 1944–1945. In *After the War Was Over. Reconstructing the Family, Nation, and State in Greece,*

1943–1960, ed. M. Mazower. Princeton and Oxford: Princeton University Press.

Mouzelis, N. 1986. *Politics in the Semi-Periphery. Early Parliamentarism and Late Industrialism in the Balkans and Latin America.* London: MacMillan.

My Film.gr. http://www.myfilm.gr/6361.html

Mylonas, H. 2003. The Comparative Method and the Study of Civil Wars. *Science and Society* 11: 1–35.

Panagiotopoulos, P. 1994. The representation of suffering in the narration of two extreme experiences: Giorgis Pikros, *Makronissos Chronicle*, Primo Levi, *Si c'est un home. Dokimes* 2: 13–32.

Potamitis, N. Y. 2008. Antagonism and Genre. *Resistance, the Costume Romance and the Ghost of Greek Communism.* In *Discourse Theory and Cultural Analysis Media, Arts and Literature*, eds. N. Carpentier and E. Spinoy. NJ: Hampton Press.

Ricoeur, P. 2004. *Memory, History, Forgetting.* Chicago: University of Chicago Press.

Riggs, F. 1964. *Administration in Developing Countries: The Theory of Prismatic Society.* Boston: Houghton Mifflin Company.

Rousso, H. 1991. *The Vichy Syndrome. History and Memory in France since 1944.* Cambridge: Harvard University Press.

Sambanis, N. 2002. A Review of Recent Advances and Future Directions in the Literature on Civil War. *Defense and Peace Economics* 13(2): 215–243.

Scheler, M. 1961. *Ressentiment.* Glencoe: Free Press.

Smelser, N. 2004. Psychological Trauma and Cultural Trauma. In *Cultural Trauma and Collective Identity*, J. Alexander et al. Berkeley: University of California Press.

Sugar, P. 1969. External and Domestic Roots of Eastern European Nationalism. In *Nationalism in Eastern Europe*, eds. P. Sugar and I. Lederer. Seattle: University of Washington Press.

Tsoukalas, C. 1969. *The Greek Tragedy.* London: Hamondsworth, Penguin.

Voglis, P. 2000. Between Negation and Self-Negation: Political Prisoners in Greece, 1945–1950. In *After the War Was Over. Reconstructing the Family, Nation, and State in Greece, 1943–1960*, ed. M. Mazower. Princeton and Oxford: Princeton University Press.

———. 2002. *Becoming a Subject. Political Prisoners during the Greek Civil War.* Florence: European University Institute.

———. 2008. Memories of the 1940s as a topic of historical analysis: methodological proposals. In *Memories and Forgetting of the Greek Civil War*, eds. P. B. Bouschoten et al. Salonica: Epikentron.

Volkan, V. 2001. Transgenerational Transmissions and Chosen Traumas: An Aspect of Large-Group Identity. *Group Analysis* 34(1): 79–97.

———. 2005. Large-Group Identity and Chosen Trauma. In *Psychoanalysis Downunder* 6 (online journal).

7

1974 and Greek Cypriot Identity

The Division of Cyprus as Cultural Trauma

Victor Roudometof and Miranda Christou

The interdisciplinary surge of interest in memory studies has been fueled both by events that have generated a "commemorative fever" in the 1980s and 1990s and by the booming of cultural artifacts (film, photography, Internet media, artificial memory storage) that facilitate the collective processes of bringing the past into the present (Misztal 2003). While, in the past, nation-states sought to monumentalize national history, today, we witness a fascination with the processes of remembering and forgetting. The utopian visions of the future dominant in the first half of the twentieth century have been replaced by the appeal of the past and a "hypertrophy of memory" (Huyssen 2003). Cultural trauma theory provides one of the most important sociological perspectives that help us capture this trend and analyze its repercussions for social life (for an overview, see Roudometof 2007).

In this chapter, we explain how "1974" became a cultural trauma for Greek Cypriots through its commemoration, institutionalization, and routinization. We approach cultural trauma not as a social process that leads to its universal acceptance, such as the Holocaust, but rather as a *master narrative* that helps the people make sense of their past experiences and shapes their current identity. We argue that the 1974 cultural trauma commemorated in the suffering caused by the island's forced division has left indelible marks on the Greek Cypriot identity, but at the same time, it has become the only lens through which Greek Cypriots refract their current concerns and future aspirations. An additional contribution to cultural trauma theory is to show how "1974" is reproduced, evoked, represented in everyday rituals, in practices unrelated and seemingly far removed from politics. In so doing, we document instances where trauma is experienced at the very level of the mundane, where cultural trauma theory's applicability has been questioned (see Spillman 2005).

In the chapter's first section, we offer a brief historical sketch of the events of the summer of 1974, and we contrast the Greek Cypriots' master narrative to the Turkish-Cypriot counter-narrative of the events. Next, we expand our analysis into the Greek Cypriot construction of "1974" as a cultural trauma and focus in particular upon its routinization. Finally, we examine the problematic nature of the trauma's transmission and reproduction in the post-1974 generations, who depend on collective memory alone for their reconstruction of the trauma. We conclude with a brief consideration of the possibility of emergence of a post-traumatic narrative.

1974: The Event and Its Narratives

The Republic of Cyprus emerged in 1960 after several years of armed struggle waged by Greek Cypriots (who made up 74 percent of the island's population) with the expressed goal of achieving the island's union with Greece. The Turkish Cypriot minority (18 percent of the island's population) objected persistently to this goal. The Republic of Cyprus was the result of a compromise worked out by United Kingdom (the colonial power controlling Cyprus between 1878 and 1959) and the motherlands of the two ethnic groups, Greece and Turkey respectively. Turkey, Greece, and the United Kingdom were made guarantor powers of the new Republic. In post-1960 Cyprus, both sides soon came to view the settlement as unworkable (Xydis 1973). On the one hand, Greek

Cypriots remained largely attached to the ideal of union with Greece. On the other hand, Turkish Cypriots were pleased that Cyprus had not been annexed to Greece but continued to arm themselves to safeguard the Republic's constitutional provisions (Attalides 1979).

In 1963 intercommunal conflict erupted following Greek Cypriot President Makarios' failed attempt to gain Turkish Cypriot agreement on constitutional amendments. The United Nations peacekeeping forces came to the island for the first time and the Turkish Cypriot community, including all members of the parliament, withdrew from the government and congregated in army-protected enclaves. While Turkish Cypriots felt threatened by pro-union Greek rhetoric, Greek Cypriots believed that the constitution was allowing the Turkish Cypriot minority to veto any decision taken by the majority. The two communities embarked on a track of conflict resolution talks in 1968 for the purposes of revising the constitution. However, the Greek Cypriot community split between those who supported President Makarios in his new political position that entailed abandoning union with Greece and those nationalists who formed an underground paramilitary organization claiming to still fight for union with Greece. In the meantime, Turkish Cypriots appeared to have given up on the idea of an independent Cyprus and presented proposals for the island's partition [*taksim*] between the two sides (Attalides 1979, 85).

On July 15, 1974, the paramilitary nationalists with the full support of Greece's military dictatorship (1967–1974) and the Cyprus-based Greek armed regiment overthrew President Makarios. Makarios managed to escape and eventually returned to power. But Turkey used the coup to claim that the rights of the Turkish Cypriots were no longer protected and that as a guarantor country it was obligated to intervene. On two successive rounds of military action (the first commencing on July 20 and the second on August 15, 1974) Turkish armed forces invaded Cyprus, eventually occupying 38 percent of the island. Unable to assist the Greek Cypriots, the Greek military dictatorship (1967–74) collapsed, paving the way for the return of democracy in Greece. The powerful and consequential repercussions of the events of the summer of 1974 for Greece are discussed in greater length in Chapter 6 of this book, by N. Demertzis.

For our purposes, we will focus on Cyprus: The invasion displaced around 180,000 Greek Cypriots toward the southern part of the island. It also caused hundreds of deaths and 1,619 missing persons.[1] Turkish Cypriots moved from the south to the north of the island, and thus they were also internally displaced (and had their own list of missing persons).

Two ethnically homogeneous regions (the north and the south) emerged as result of the invasion and the population movements. The Greek-Cypriot controlled southern part of the island maintained the title of the Republic of Cyprus and remains to this day the only internationally recognized government on the island. The Turkish-controlled northern part of the island declared itself as the Turkish Republic of Northern Cyprus (TRNC) in 1983. It was officially recognized only from Turkey, and to this day, it remains largely dependent on it.

In 2004, the Republic of Cyprus joined the European Union (EU) but the *acquis communautaire* (i.e., EU laws and regulations) has been suspended for the northern "occupied areas" (or *katehomena,* as they are referred to by Greek Cypriots). A few days prior to EU accession (May 1, 2004) the UN-sponsored Annan Plan (named after the U.N. Secretary General Kofi Annan) proposed a resolution to the "Cyprus issue" through the formation of a federal republic that would unify the island after it had been *de facto* divided in 1974 by the Turkish invasion. The Annan Plan was voted favorably by Turkish Cypriots but rejected by Greek Cypriots in a referendum held simultaneously on both sides of the divided island. Talks for a solution to the Cyprus issue are continuing until today.[2]

To understand the Greek Cypriot cultural trauma construction, "1974" must be analyzed as a "horrendous event" (Alexander 2004) that stands as a rupture in time. Demetris Christofias, President of the Republic of Cyprus expressed this notion in a talk on February 9, 2009, as follows:

> No one could have ever conceived that the treacherous coup and the Turkish invasion that followed it in 1974 would overturn the smooth course of time; these age-old habits and folkloric traditions. Along a line of other tragic consequences in our lives and the development of our land and its people, the blow to our mores, customs and the traditions of our land was devastating.[3]

As a message repeated in almost every official talk, the President's words are not exceptional even as they assert the exceptionality of a profoundly traumatic event. They illustrate the trauma's unpredictable character as well as the inability to view the event as part of the ordinary course of time: in the dominant Greek Cypriot commemorations of 1974, events are presented as a shock, as something that could not have been predicted or contained. Thus, the brutality of *uprootedness* is established in its departure from the normal course of history, regardless of the political events that could have served as a warning. For Greek Cypriots, then, the experience of uprootedness and the vision of a mythical day of return are the two major characteristics of the "1974" cultural trauma.

The metaphor of uprootedness is pervasive in the peoples' narratives of loss, denoting both the literal supplantation of a largely rural and agrarian population, as well as the centrality of the land in configuring identity (Loizos 1981). As Bryant (2002) has argued, kinship with the land partakes of religious imagery in Cyprus and it represents another element of the metaphorical familial connections of nationalism that naturalize the relationship between the people and the nation. However, 1974 did not simply deprive people from homes, fields, and orange groves; it also unsettled deep-seated cultural constructions of time and continuity that are uniquely exemplified in the agrarian rhythms of the land. This rupture in time, therefore, was both historical and cultural, with the use of chronology advancing the traumatic event into a symbol while signifying its magnitude in relation to the post-1974 epoch. Although we realize that 1974 does not carry the same international cultural capital as 9/11, our purposeful use of it in the title of this chapter echoes its cultural significance in constructing a horrendous event that was beyond comparison with any other disastrous event in the island's history.

Greek Cypriot narratives foster a nostalgic view toward the premodern pre-1974 status quo that leads to a nearly messianic expectation of restoring the lost grace of that era as part of the future. The longing for the day of return functions as a response to the suffering caused by the sudden uprooting and maintains a positive vision for the future. Despite tangible signs of adaptation in their new social and economic surroundings, aided not only by various social provisions such as housing and health care but also by a largely supportive population of coethnics in the south, Greek Cypriot internally displaced people have always maintained the hope that one day they will be allowed to return just as they were unexpectedly forced to leave (Loizos and Constantinou 2007). Even after decades of "protracted exile," this deep belief in the "myth of return" (Zetter 1999) is guided by a sense of inconceivable injustice perpetrated upon them and a metaphysical faith in divine justice.

Furthermore, this myth of return is galvanized by the idealization of the pre-1974 period as the paradise of simple and blissful life and, to a large extent, is articulated as a religious "fall from Eden" (Zetter 1994 and 1999; Dikomitis 2004; Loizos 1981). Greek Cypriots describe the occupied areas as the most beautiful, scenic, and picturesque part of the island. Just like it is inappropriate to speak ill of the dead, Greek Cypriots refrain from saying anything negative about the areas under occupation or even remembering negative occasions in those areas; except, of course, from the events of 1974. Nothing compares to an individual's occupied home: Everything before 1974 was good; everything after is bad (Loizos and Constantinou 2007). This has burdened the idea of return with unrealistic expectations. As Zetter (1999, 6) has pointed out, "What is mythologized, is what has been left behind and what, it is hoped, return will accomplish—the belief that 'home', both as a material and symbolic entity, can be restored as it was before exile."

The mythological status of a day of return has also contributed to the elevation of those "left behind" (that is, those who did not leave their houses to move to the southern part of the island) into a special symbolic status. These are referred to as "enclaved" (*englovismenoi*) Greek Cypriots who have become emblems of the resistance against uprooting. Their everyday struggle is commended and commemorated officially by the state and unofficially in the media and other sites of cultural production. Appealing to the European Court of Human Rights, the Republic of Cyprus government achieved a vote which condemned Turkey for 14 violations of the European Convention of Human rights, seven of which refer to the living conditions of the "enclaved" Greek Cypriots (*Cyprus Versus Turkey*, application no. 25781/94, May 10, 2001).

The preceding brief sketch of the Greek Cypriots' *master narrative* of cultural trauma is contested. In fact, it would be difficult to analyze Greek Cypriots' 1974 cultural trauma without raising the question of how the same events are differentially interpreted by the Turkish Cypriots. Our approach to "1974" acknowledges the contested nature of the interpretation of the events. We, therefore, should juxtapose the preceding master narrative to the Turkish Cypriot *counter-narrative*. In the Turkish Cypriot counter-narrative, the 1963–1964 intercommunal fights played a pivotal role in the community's withdrawal from participation into the institutions of the Republic of Cyprus. Life in the enclaves between 1963 and 1974 was marked by isolation and fear, and the events of 1974 are represented as a "Peaceful Operation" that delivered Turkish Cypriots from living in a constant state of fear. Thus, despite the fact that there are Turkish Cypriot internally displaced people and missing persons, "1974" has not been constructed as a cultural trauma for them (Papadakis 1998, 2003; Bryant 2008). Turkish Cypriots' history narratives emphasize the Turkish character of the island and almost ignore the existence of the southern part (see Killoran 2000; Canefe 2002; Scott 2002). For Turkish Cypriots, the events of 1974 were a mere extension of the *gradual* nature of intercommunal separation that has finally ended in the partition of the island.

In contrast, this is decoded as an abrupt and sudden shock for Greek Cypriots. For them, becoming internally displaced persons is viewed as tantamount to turning into "refugees" in their own country. Technically though, according to the 1951 Geneva Convention and the 1967 Protocol, those not forced to leave their country are internally displaced people and not refugees. Still, the United Nations High Commission on Refugees (UNHCR) has described the Greek Cypriots' condition as a "refugee-like" situation (see Zetter 1994) while the term "refugee" (*prosfyges*), along with its connotations of social status and identity, is uniformly used in Greek Cypriot discourse—and it will be used from this point on in this chapter, too. This experience has become a defining moment of trauma, not only for the generation that lived through it but, as we will show in this chapter's second and third sections, also for those born around or after 1974.

The preceding should make it clear that attempting to lay out the facts calls attention to the different interpretations of history. The politics of recognition between the two sides are played out both at the international and interpersonal levels. Turkey and the TRNC do not recognize the Republic of Cyprus even though Turkey is under pressure to do so because of ongoing EU accession talks. In turn, the Republic of Cyprus government refers to the TRNC as a pseudo-government. Peace talks are often blocked over the criteria of legitimate Cypriot citizenship especially in light of the post-1974 demographic changes. Personal encounters between Greek Cypriots and Turkish Cypriots are often trapped in miscommunication when the latter seem to treat the issue of becoming a refugee in a detached way whereas for Greek Cypriots it continues to be a traumatic experience (Anastasiou 2002). This is a major point of divergence between Greek Cypriot and Turkish Cypriot readings of the past: while for Turkish Cypriot readings history reached a turning point in 1974, for Greek Cypriot readings, history remains to achieve its closure in the future as part of a final settlement of the Cyprus issue (Bryant 2008).

To understand *why* 1974 has been encoded as such a pervasive cultural trauma for Greek Cypriots it is necessary to refer to the radical social, political, and economic transformations of the second half of the twentieth century. Following transition from British colonial status to the 1960 founding of the Republic of Cyprus, the island's economy functioned, for the first time, under the status of an independent state and slowly began to expand its agricultural and tourism sectors. The 1963–1974 interethnic conflicts and the Turkish Cypriots' withdrawal from the government fostered uncertainty but also increased the socio-economic gap between the two groups, with Greek Cypriots advancing more than Turkish Cypriots (Kedourie 2005). The major and abrupt setback was the 1974 events that brought all major functions of the economy to a halt. Nicosia's airport, the only airport on the island at the time, was caught in the buffer zone between the two sides, while a third of the population lost its entire livelihood means and the tourist industry's major hubs came under Turkish military occupation. For Greek Cypriots, a future of dark economic times was forestalled. Still, thanks to a steady stream of foreign aid, the economy in the south recovered at an unprecedented rate during the 1980s—a development that has been dubbed "the Cyprus Miracle" (Christodoulou 1992). But this was not the fate of the northern part of the island inhabited by Turkish Cypriots. The lack of an internationally recognized status caused the economy to suffer and slow down. For Greek Cypriots, however, no economic miracle can undo the pain caused by 1974: the pre-1974 reality has thus been romanticized as a peaceful period nostalgically reminiscent as a time of tradition. Whatever followed is seen as marred by the invasion and by the evils of progress and modernization that came with economic prosperity.

Into the Mundane: Everyday Rituals of "1974"

Cultural traumas are solidified through commemorative practices that transform the event into personal and collective memory. In this section, we aim to show how this trauma is experienced through the discursive, representational, and institutional practices that established the commemoration of those events not simply as an *annual ritual* but as *an everyday routine* that ritualizes the very act of remembering the trauma. In a multitude of sites that range from official ones, such as the educational system or state legislation, to unofficial ones, such as refugee associations and kinship groups, the trauma of 1974 has been constructed not as a historical event but as a present-day trauma that derives its urgency from an unresolved political problem. The invocation of a day of return is often made in the context of weekly rituals seemingly unrelated to politics. For example, the Rotary Club of Nicosia/Salamis, one of the Rotary clubs of the island founded by internally displaced professionals from the city of Famagusta (currently in the occupied part), has enshrined the longing for a day of return in the prayer that precedes each club meeting:

Oh God, our Lord,

We pray you bless this meeting and strengthen us in our deeds of love and benevolence. Also, our Lord, we ask you to deliver speedily our beloved country Cyprus from the sufferings of foreign aggression and grant that its indigenous population live in peace and security, praising thy holy name.[4]

In terms of social structures reproducing traumatic memory, the Greek Cypriot educational system has significantly contributed to the ritualization and routinization of "1974" through the cross-curricular goal of the "I don't forget" (*Den Ksechno*) objective. The slogan "I don't forget" was originally created by writer and advertising director Nikos Dimou, on the very day of the Turkish military intervention in 1974. Succinct and solemn, and accompanied by a visual image of a bleeding island (see http://home.comcast.net/~cpoyiadji/images/DenXehno. gif), it became the symbol of the invasion trauma (more at http://www. ndimou.gr/kypros_gr.asp). It has been since duplicated in numerous official and unofficial sites both in Greece and the Republic of Cyprus as a visual representation of commemoration and resistance, and it is by far the most successful visual image that has enshrined the notion of "1974" as a trauma at the level of popular culture.

The presence of the "I don't forget" logo in schools complements a cross-course educational goal of transferring the traumatic memory of 1974 to the new generation. Whereas there is no particular course devoted to the 1974 events, the whole curriculum, from kindergarten to the last year of Lyceum (ages 4–17) is infused with references to the problem of occupation. A familiar ritual in Greek Cypriot schools every September is the decoration of classrooms with landscape pictures of the northern "occupied areas" of the island and the distribution of student workbooks that feature these locations on the cover. The phrase "I don't forget and I struggle" is inscribed prominently on classroom boards as teachers hang the pictures on the walls and identify on the Cyprus map the location of northern occupied villages and cities. The principals' welcoming remarks and the minister's address to all students that is read on the first school assembly invariably include references to the problem of occupation in Cyprus and the desire to return to these areas and reunify the island. For example, in 2006 the minister wrote, "In these difficult conditions of the twenty-first century world, our homeland is waging its own struggle to achieve, through peaceful means, the liberation of our occupied areas that have been under the foot of the Turkish Attila (Turkish army) for the past 32 years."[5] In 2008, the minister's address included similar remarks,

"Unfortunately, this new school year finds Cyprus divided by occupation. I hope that this will be the last year."[6]

Educators seize every opportunity to bring up references to the problem of occupation, whether talking about Arbor Week—with references made to the natural resources of the occupied part—or Easter Week—whereby the occupation of Cyprus is compared to Christ's persecution and crucifixion. Every new school year, the "I don't forget" objective is a primary educational objective, and it saturates all aspects of the curriculum by functioning not as a distant historical event but as a current cultural issue that has touched the lives of all Greek Cypriots. Essay competitions and art exhibits regularly call students to narrate and illustrate the suffering of 1974: Students write about the beauty of the occupied villages and the pain and longing of refugees; they draw picturesque landscapes of the areas they have not visited and portray the suffering of the mothers of the missing persons.

The focus of this curricular goal is decidedly emotional rather than anything related to the specific events preceding or following the 1974 Turkish invasion. In fact, teachers avoid any references to episodes around the Turkish invasion that may taint this monochromatic view of history and they steer clear of any references to "dangerous memories" that may challenge the view that Greek Cypriots were the absolute victims of the island's recent history (Christou 2007). School fieldwork studies have documented the nature of the "I don't forget" curriculum that narrates suffering only from a Greek Cypriot perspective and serves to maintain stark contrasts between "Us" and "Others" (Spyrou 2001 and 2006; Philippou 2005; and Christou 2006). This construction of the absolute evil and the absolute victim is a necessary step in the assembly of a trauma narrative that becomes an iconic event of suffering for a social group.

Thus, "1974" is educationally reenacted as a cultural trauma through narrative, aesthetic, and religious performances that routinize an exceptional event into an everyday recurrent experience for all Greek Cypriots. It could be argued that the "I don't forget" objective is a paradoxical, if not impossible, goal: it demands that new generations identify with the memory and the suffering of events not personally experienced. But it is precisely this paradox that makes "1974" an exemplary cultural trauma, because it has, to a large extent, succeeded in imparting its emotional impact to younger generations. Even though students' reactions to the "I don't forget" curriculum can range from an awareness of obligation to a critique of others' indifference toward the problem, the younger generation reflects on "1974" with a sense of sacred responsibility (Christou 2006). As Alexander (2004) argues, cultural traumas allow members of the wider public to participate in other people's pain and thus, create new avenues of social incorporation. This can also be seen in the transformation of the phrase from "I don't forget" in the 1970s and 1980s, to the most recent (1990s) "I don't forget and I struggle" or even in some cases "I know, I don't forget and I struggle"—clearly aimed at creating a more direct sense of identification with the cultural trauma.

The trauma of "1974" is evoked on all national anniversaries and not only on the July 20 commemoration day of the 1974 invasion, a day that is commemorated by Greek Cypriot authorities as a sad anniversary and by Turkish Cypriot authorities as a day of deliverance, complete with a military parade and with the participation of state dignitaries from mainland Turkey. Its presence colors anniversaries completely unrelated to the events of 1974, such as the commemoration of March 25. That day marks the anniversary of Greek independence and is promptly celebrated by Greek Cypriots—an observance that marks their symbolic inclusion into the Greek nation. March 25 is both a religious and a secular national holiday for the day is also Annunciation Day in the Greek Orthodox calendar. It was originally selected to coincide with the anniversary of the 1821 Greek revolution for its potent symbolic character: The birth of Christ is but a metaphor for the birth of modern Greece (see Roudometof 2005). What is of particular significance in the Cypriot context though and what marks off this celebration in Cyprus, as opposed to mainland Greece, is its strong connection to a day of return to the lost homelands. In March 25, 2009, for example, in a speech delivered at a church in Nicosia, the priest made explicit references to 1974: "We must endure" he said, "and keep our faith to God in order to go through these difficult times." Hope of return to "our ancestral homelands" should not be abandoned, and the faithful should hold fast to their belief that, with the help of God, this will be accomplished.[7]

The same belief was manifested in the University of Cyprus' commemorations of March 25. Typical commemorative celebrations conclude with the signing of the Cretan folk song "When will we have a clear sky" ("*Pote tha Kanei xasteria*"). The folk song has gone through a native adaptation whereby its original place names have been replaced by references to the refugees' regions—Kerynia, the mountain of Pentadaktylus, Mofru, and so on. In its reinterpretation the song goes like this:

«Πότε θα κάνει ξαστεριά,
πότε θα φλεβαρίσει,
να κατεβώ στον Όλυμπο,
στην έμορφη Κερύνεια
στη Μόρφου καί στη Μεσαριά,

σ' όλη την Καρπασία
να δω τον Πευταδάκτυλο
να μου χαμογελάει ...
Πότε θα κάνει ξαστεριά ... »

How long till clear sky
How long until February comes around
To walk down from (Mt.) Olympus
To the beautiful Kerynia
To Morfu and Mesaria
To all of Karpasia
To see Pentadaktylus
Smile to me
How long till clear sky ... [8]

Here, the trauma resurfaces again in all its potency, forcefully altering the nature of the occasion in the Cypriot context. It is worth pointing out that the invocation of a day of return in the context of unrelated commemorative rituals is typically gone unnoticed by Greek Cypriots but is immediately visible to nonnatives.

The cultural trauma of 1974 can further be identified in everyday rituals that attempt to symbolically reconstruct the lost home in the context of temporary refugee housing. When Greek Cypriot refugees fled from their homes in July and August of 1974, many believed that the military intervention would be temporary. After all, Turkey had attempted to intervene in Cyprus already in the 1960s. Most refugees had not packed any belongings, as they believed that they would return home in a matter of days. When they narrate their experiences many years and decades after the event, Greek Cypriot refugees begin their stories by emphasizing the sudden and unforeseen displacement that forced them to leave without taking anything with them; "We left with nothing, just what we were wearing" is a common opening line. The meaning of "nothing" in this phrase implies that the body is left exposed because of its dislocation from its context. According to Connerton (1989), the body is the main vehicle of habitual memory, because through ritual bodily performances, the collectively shared history is transformed into a deeply personal experience. In this way, commemorative rituals exercise a bodily discipline that re-inscribes the event through the "mnemonics of the body" (Connerton 1989, 9).

The refugees' rituals, therefore, often attempt to recontextualize the body in the foreign environment: They build an identical fireplace as the one they had "back home" or plant an orange tree in their small backyard to take care of it as they used to do before becoming refugees. The refugees reclaim their lost past through everyday routines that maintain the traditional social bonds of the pre-1974 life (Zetter 1999). These punctuate everyday conversations of Greek Cypriots, and their stories are inevitably always connected to the cultural trauma of 1974. The reminders can be as mundane as the aroma of oranges—which, refugees are quick to say that they do not taste the same as the ones they grew back home—or as generalized as the bitterness of being the world's forgotten victims of human rights violations. Through these discursive and bodily performances of recollecting and symbolically reconstituting the occupied home and land, refugees and their families routinely evoke the horrendous event of "1974" and make it part of everyday life on the island.

More importantly, however, refugees' rituals that commemorate uprootedness and long for the day of return have come to represent the core of Greek Cypriot values and traditions. For example, in a newspaper article, a Greek Cypriot refugee woman details the making of traditional sweets and the Christmas family rituals of the past. The woman and her husband reminisce the days when these customs were authentically practiced with "religious piety," when people were pure enough to appreciate their significance and poor enough to be grateful for a pair of pants and a piece of warm pastry. The opening lines set the narrative in the context of "traditional grandmothers" of Paralimni who "reminisce their childhood years and the festive days in Rizokarpaso, Varosi and Kerynia" (occupied areas), and it is a narrative of nostalgia for a pre-1974 life, rife with the virtues of tradition (Sofroniou 2008). The article ends with the following words:

> Ms Androula, on the other hand, feels that as faithfully as she tries to preserve these customs she can never be as happy as she used to be in Karpasi [occupied area]. "I believe that refugeehood has left a bitterness inside us and it is difficult for us to be joyful and carefree like the old days," says Ms Androula expressing her grievance and wishing that warmth and peace can return to people's hearts, in a Cyprus that is free and reunited.

Just like in the President's speech, the article assembles a narrative of double-coded loss where the refugees' memories of the occupied part are the memories of tradition. The 1974 events are recounted as a break from tradition, the loss of innocence and the pain of losing both a home and a heaven of pure, authentic life. In this way, the occupied areas become a time capsule that holds not only the answer to happiness but also the solution to the crisis of identity, signified by the endangered traditions.

Trauma Transmission:
Facing the Challenges of Time

As Mannheim (1952) argues, a generation is formed through the shared experience of historical and political changes. Generations adopt quite distinct interpretations of the past, developing their own sense of collective memory related to their own experiences.[9] The older generation of Greek Cypriots has been through the anticolonial struggle in the 1950s, the turbulent years after the 1960 independence and, of course, remembers the events of 1974. In contrast, the younger generation of those born around or after 1974 lacks the first-hand experience of these events as well as personal memories of life before 1974. Therefore, they depend on reconstructions of the past to make sense of their current situation.

The existence of official refugee associations and of the state-sanctioned "refugee" label is of critical importance for the reproduction of "1974" in the next generation. Following the immediate events of the summer of 1974, and when it became apparent that return would not be easily achieved, a large number of refugee associations were established in the south—generally one association for every village or city. Not only do these associations draw attention to the centrality of kinship structure and place of origin as cultural markers of membership, but they also serve the purpose of creating a geographical reference point to the lost land. Their function is to keep the dispersed population in touch through religious and national celebrations, thereby maintaining a sense of origin and preventing dissolution of the original village unit. Refugees regularly attend the weddings and funerals of covillagers wherever they may be taking place in the southern part of the island. Death notices in the newspaper, tombstones and wedding invitations always identify the family's origin in the occupied part followed by their current, "temporary" residence (Zetter 1994).

In addition, the post-1974 designation and institutionalization of the "refugee" label has created the conditions for the universalization of the refugees' loss and the possibility that all Greek Cypriots identify with the pain of *uprootedness.* That is, official legislation enacted on September 19, 1974 (Ministry Council decision 13.503)[10] specifies that a "refugee" is a person who before and up to July 1974 permanently resided in an area that is currently under Turkish occupation. The decision was amended in 1995 to include those who owned land and property in the occupied part, even if their permanent residence at the time of the invasion was in the areas that remained under the control of the Republic of Cyprus. The legislation—accompanied by the bureaucracy of refugee identification cards and related documentation—has offered to refugees specific advantages such as access to low-cost government housing estates, financial aid for building a house or purchasing an apartment, and renting allowances. Their status is inherited patrimonially—but not matrimonially—thereby reassuring the continued construction of generations of "refugees" for several decades after the event. Intermarriage further reassures that the "refugee" status is diffused throughout the Greek Cypriot community, and therefore its existence becomes part of the fabric of all Greek Cypriots—even for those who were not personally affected.

Apart from commemorations in official institutions such as education and refugee associations, the intergenerational dynamics that weave narratives of loss and suffering in the context of the family have been important sites in the construction of the "1974" cultural trauma. Second-generation refugees, that is, those born to refugee families after 1974, grew up exposed to vivid accounts of the lost land and have adopted, to a large extent, a refugee identity (Hadjiyanni 2002). These family narratives mediate symbolically between the past and the present and create meanings that connect parents and children (Hinchman and Hinchman 1997). The telling of traumatic stories is a way of structuring experience and producing meaning out of disparate or incomprehensible events (Ricoeur 1988). In this way, the production of cultural trauma entails the creation of collective memory that is located in the interrelations of groups such as the family or the social class and forms an essential aspect of social solidarity (Halbwachs 1941/1992). Children of refugee families "remember" the occupied part and identify with their parents' pain:

> I saw a dream that Cyprus was, I saw the shape of Cyprus in the form of trees. [...] And my mother told me that maybe when I was younger and I was listening about it all the time, I created a picture of it in my mind, so it wasn't a dream. But I believed that I saw it. I feel very strongly that I saw it. And my mother told me that this place was on route to Apostolos Andreas.
>
> —Nasia, 15 years old

> During the summer when I see the orange trees, I remember the oranges of Ammochostos. Or when we have the flower festival in Larnaca, I remember that we used to have the same in Ammochostos.
>
> —Maria, 16 years old

> In our family gatherings, we talk about the invasion. And I hear how
> [my father] talks about the people who are lost and the people who
> were killed and I see him cry. And that's when you think, 'Why did
> they do this to us?' And no one cares about it. [...] He talks about
> Kerynia where they sent all the soldiers and lined them up. It's difficult
> to know that you may lose your husband or your father or your child,
> your son.
>
> —Eleni, 16 years old[11]

Nasia, Maria, and Eleni have never been to Apostolos Andreas, Ammochostos (i.e., Famagusta), or Kerynia but their "memories" of the occupied areas sound as vivid as any personal account can be. In the first narrative, the dream is a surreal account of an experience that has not taken place, and it symbolizes the metaphorical dream of return even if the return will only be a first-time visit for Nasia. The younger generation of refugees has internalized these memories to the extent that the word "remember" is used in a way that collapses the limits between personal and collective memory. As these narratives saturate everyday family encounters, the younger generation is left with a heavy legacy of memory and the burden to realize the mythical return.

On the other hand, the post-1974 economic realities on the island have conditioned different kinds of expectations for the new generation of Greek Cypriots. In the past 35 years, the Greek Cypriot society has been transformed from one where a third of the population was internally displaced as a result of the 1974 invasion into a dynamic economy that joined in 2004 the E.U. This shift from tents to mansions is the source of collective Greek Cypriot pride for the hard-working ethic that paid off. Nevertheless, the new comforts have become an uncomfortable reality that contradicts the need to maintain the "fighting spirit" for a solution to the Cyprus issue (Christou 2006). The younger generation exemplifies a materialist turn that, for the older generation, is at odds with the existential need to preserve this fighting spirit:

> The new generation ... grew up with more luxuries. They didn't go
> through the experience of being a refugee. They didn't have the expe-
> rience of living in a tent and have the tent leak during the winter and
> you don't know where to sleep. We spent two months in a bus and
> we were sleeping on the seats—from my grandfather to the youngest
> child—two months! We are another generation. We went through this
> hardship. But ... these kids are used to luxury and so they get used to
> easy money. And the parents give money too easily because they were
> deprived of it growing up.[12]

The younger generation, therefore, is constructed as the promise of the nation and as a potential obstacle in maintaining the fight for return. In this sense, the cultural trauma depends on the strength of the intergenerational dynamic that sustains it. And yet, when compared to the generation that actually experienced coexistence with Turkish Cypriots, the younger Greek Cypriot generation is more inclined to show a preference for separation (for statistics, see Webster 2005 and Georgiades 2007). The same generational pattern was also observed in the 2004 Annan Plan referendum with higher rates of negative Greek Cypriot votes by those born after 1974 compared to the previous generation (Webster 2005). This was a paradox to many observers, as the evidence overturned simplistic accounts of collective conflict predicated upon personal animosity. From within the lenses of cultural trauma theory, though, the result simply registers the successful routinization and reproduction of "1974" as a cultural trauma. For the reader of the preceding pages, it should *not* come as a surprise that those who lack personal remembrance of the pre-1974 reality will be the least inclined toward inter-communal coexistence.

The normative implications generated by the routinization of the "1974" cultural trauma can also be seen in the events that challenge its educational primacy. For example, an August 2008 circular by the Ministry of Education identified the first goal of the new school year as follows: "The cultivation of a culture of peaceful coexistence, mutual respect and collaboration between Greek Cypriots and Turkish Cypriots with the goal of removing occupation and reuniting our homeland and our people."[13] For the first time since 1974, the ministry's leadership outlined the vision of an educational system that nurtures a culture of reconciliation between the two main communities on the island; a goal that should be expected, especially given the fact that reunification has been the explicit and expressed political goal of the Greek Cypriot community as well as the official position of the Republic of Cyprus. The circular however, caused heated reactions by teachers' unions that claimed that the already burdened curriculum could not support an additional goal that may be difficult to implement. The elementary school teachers' union said that schools should not be forced to visit Turkish Cypriot institutions in the north and argued—as the head of POED claimed in an interview for a Greek television channel[14]—that such actions can "confuse" eight-year-old children and hurt teachers' and parents' "sensitivities."

In an open letter to teachers, the union pointed out that, given the "realities" in Cyprus, "the goal of 'I know, I don't forget and I struggle' remains a permanent objective under emphasis, to underscore the struggle of our educational system to liberate and reunite our homeland." Irony and blatant contradictions aside, it is important to note the language of emotional appeal ("confusion" and "sensibilities") that registers a resistance to desecrate the cultural trauma by diluting its emotional strength. The preceding example exposes the manner in which the delicate generational dynamics of trauma transmission are immersed in pedagogical dilemmas.

In April 2003, the Turkish Cypriot leadership, under mounting popular pressure from the declining economic situation in the north, decided to lift the ban on movement across the Green Line. This meant that, for the first time in 29 years, Greek Cypriots and Turkish Cypriots would be able to visit the areas that were largely inaccessible to them. This almost-surprising turn of events challenged not only existing understandings of the political will of the other side but also the supposedly shared comprehension of terms such as "state" and "authority" (Demetriou 2007). Some cynical comments by Greek Cypriots in the early days contended that the Turkish Cypriot leadership's shrewd move served to politically elevate the appearance of good will for a solution to the "Cyprus issue," while creating the conditions for Greek Cypriots to swallow the reality of division and thus eliminate the problem itself. The idea was that Greek Cypriots facing their dilapidated houses or entering them as visitors of new (Turkish) owners will give up on the hope of return and reunification of the island.

Crossing the Green Line to visit the hitherto inaccessible northern part of the island was subject to a variety of interpretations. For some, outright refusal was the only dignified response because Turkish Cypriot authorities forced all those who wish to cross to display their ID papers. This turned natives into "tourists" to their own land (Dikomitis 2005). Others, though, were moved more by material considerations, opting to cross the Green Line in search of cheaper goods and services.

To these two diametrically opposed interpretations, it is necessary to add a third and perhaps more widespread interpretation of crossing. For many Greek Cypriot refugees, crossing the buffer zone became an act of pilgrimage (Dikomitis 2004 and 2005). As Dikomitis (2004) points out, the refugees literally *moved* the earth by collecting water and soil to take back with them. Their visits to the occupied areas became a ritual of visiting their house, the church, and the cemetery. They collected soil from the graves and anointed themselves with the water running at the center of the village. Parents came with children who have never seen their ancestral lands and who were told repeatedly of these lost territories. Crossing the Green Line entailed elements of sacralization of these territories, which, in turn, maintained the mythologization of the island's occupied area.

In Search of a Post-Traumatic Narrative

Our operating assumption is this chapter has been that the events of 1974 possess the potential but not the proof that their experience would be traumatizing. We argued that, unlike the Turkish Cypriot counter-narrative, in the Greek Cypriot master narrative "1974" is constructed as a horrendous event that stands outside the scope of normal time. The experience of uprootedness and the vision of a day of return are key elements in its articulation. It is further embodied in specific groups— "refugees," missing persons, and the "enclaved" of the north—that have become collective agents of the trauma process by bearing the burden of narrating the pain and by inviting the wider Greek Cypriot community to identify with them. In this chapter's second part, we sought to illuminate the routinization of the trauma that continues to punctuate everyday life in a multitude of contexts, ranging from the watering of orange trees to the use of refugee identification cards or the prayers told in Rotary Club meetings. Thus, "1974" has been constructed as part of a *master narrative* that carries important repercussions for constructing a view of history, of group conflict and of the Other that lead to the politics of mutual suspicion (Rydgren, 2007).

Cultural trauma theory offers a powerful tool that allows us to analyze the everyday routine of cultural life as illustrating both the trauma's hold upon the social imaginary as well as its taken-for-granted character. The theory, in our view, has a highly relevant public policy dimension: Political settlements pursued independently or without full consideration of the dynamics of cultural trauma run the risk of failing to take hold within the public, and therefore, their results might be short-lived. With regard to the "Cyprus issue" in particular, we dare say that its successful resolution would need to offer not only practical solutions for dealing with the island's problems of political governance but it would also need to heal the cultural trauma through the creation of a *post-traumatic narrative* that could turn suffering into hope. In this respect, we invite the reader to view the Cypriot context as illustrative of broader dynamics that exist elsewhere, such as in the case of Northern Ireland (see Dawson 2008).

We have further detected the cultural trauma's ruptures in the process of intergenerational transmission. We argued that the focus of official remembrance under the "I don't forget" slogan has contributed to an extensive absorption into the collectivity's own suffering, even to the detriment of endorsing the goal of coexistence with the Turkish Cypriots in a future reunified Cyprus. In this respect, our argument echoes the situation of Israelis after the 1970s, as presented in Chapter 5 (by Alexander and Dromi) of this book. Perhaps a major generational difference with regard to constructions of "1974" is that the second generation's emotional connection with their occupied homes is less identified with the idealization of the past and more with the idealization of a future where the restoration of the human rights of property and freedom of movement can materialize (Zetter 1999).

Last, we would like to address the issue of a post-traumatic narrative that would move Greek Cypriots beyond the collectivity's extensive absorption into their own suffering. Certainly, the opening of the Green Line (2003) and the Annan Plan referendum (2004) have been such turning points (see Vural and Peristianis 2008 for an analysis of post-2004 developments). These events have ruptured the routinization of the "1974" cultural trauma. What was previously exceptional is today normal: The exchange of stories of suffering by Greek Cypriots and Turkish Cypriots, bilingual television programs, bi-communal village gatherings, and even the possibility that students from each community would visit the other's schools. Such incidents are still defined by their liminality and often the sense that they endanger the sacralization of the "1974" cultural trauma. One could also argue that these "dangerous memories" can be pedagogically powerful in opening up possibilities for understanding the other's pain without forgoing the collective trauma (Zembylas and Beckerman 2008).

For the younger generation, the experience of the cultural trauma remains unconnected to personal memory or contact with the other. Thus, this experience fuels stereotypes and negative predispositions about the other. In this manner, the contradiction between the people's felt pain and suffering, on the one hand, and the nationalistic sentiments monopolizing and usurping this suffering, on the other hand, remains obscure (Anastasiou 2002). Furthermore, the trauma's emotional burden has raised unrealistic expectations of what would constitute an acceptable political solution. Consequently, at this point in time, the emergence of a post-traumatic narrative remains a future objective. It might not be inappropriate here to add that in the Greek Cypriot dialect the word "baby" (μωρό) is used instead of the word "child": In a cultural context still dominated by kinship structures, people remain "babies" until they have their own (babies). In turn, the ability to symbolically emancipate from the burden of upholding the collectivity's cultural heritage and its associated view of the past develops only gradually, with the passing of generations.

Notes

    1. This number was the official estimated figure for the Greek Cypriots who went missing in July and August of 1974. This estimate has been continuously revised, especially since the beginning of exhumations by the Investigative Committee for Missing Persons (established in 1981) in August 2006. For more on the politics of the recovery of missing persons in Cyprus and the controversy on determining their actual number, see Cassia 2005 and 2006.
    2. The "Cyprus issue" is a term used to describe the unresolved situation of conflict on the island since 1974. The United Nations has used the term in various resolutions adopted by the General Assembly. From the perspective of the TRNC, there is no "Cyprus issue" but only a problem of TRNC's international recognition.
    3. From a commemorative speech given by the President of the Republic of Cyprus in the Church of Ayios Charalambos in the Geri refugee housing project, located in the broader metropolitan area of Nicosia. Translation by the authors. The full text in Greek is available at the Cyprus Press and Information Office (PIO) at http://www.cyprus.gov.cy/moi/pio/pio.nsf/All/8D2BEC4C716A7A46C2257558005C485C?Opendocument. Accessed March 4, 2009.
    4. *Grace* of the Rotary Club of Nicosia Salamis, at http://rotary-cyprus.org/nic-salamis/history/grace. Accessed March 25, 2009. The city of Famagusta (Ammochostos in Greek) used to be the largest city in pre-1974 Cyprus. Since the invasion, its Greek Cypriot inhabitants were displaced mainly to Nicosia, Larnaca, and Limassol. The old part of the city was sealed off by the Turkish forces, and the city has become a ghost town.
    5. Cyprus Ministry of Education and Culture, Minister's new school year (2006–2007) welcome letter, at http://www.schools.ac.cy/dde/circular/data/Doc5039.pdf. Accessed April 10, 2009.
    6. Cyprus Ministry of Education and Culture, Minister's new school year (2008–2009) welcome letter, at http://www.schools.ac.cy/dde/circular/data/Doc7390.pdf. Accessed April 10, 2009.
    7. The quotes are based on participant observation by Victor Roudometof, one of this chapter's authors.
    8. Translation by the authors. There are numerous variants of this folk song. Within Greece, it is often related to hardcore Greek nationalist circles.
    9. The authors would like to thank R. Marada for making this point forcefully in his presentation at the first of the two conference meetings that took place in preparation for this volume.
    10. For more information, see http://www.mfa.gov.cy/mfa/mfa2006.nsf/All/5C42EAB55AEA9A5EC22571B0003E0AF5?OpenDocument. Accessed April 16, 2009.

11. Excerpts from interviews with children of refugee families (Christou 2002).

12. Excerpt from interview with a refugee mother (Christou 2002).

13. Cyprus Ministry of Education and Culture, Minister's letter for the new school year's educational goals (2008–2009), at http://www.schools.ac.cy/dde/circular/data/Doc7387.pdf. Accessed April 17, 2009.

14. The full fifteen-minute report "Cyprus History Lessons" by Sky News can be found at http://www.skai.gr/player/tv/?mmid=25439. Accessed March 29, 2009.

Works Cited

Alexander, J. C. 2004. Toward a Theory of Cultural Trauma. In *Cultural Trauma and Collective Identity*, eds. J. C. Alexander, R, Eyerman, B. Giesen, N. J. Smelser, and R. Sztompka. Berkeley: University of California Press.

Anastasiou, H. 2002. Communication across Conflict Lines: The Case of Ethnically Divided Cyprus. *Journal of Peace Research* 39(5): 581–596.

Attalides, M. 1979. *Cyprus: Nationalism and International Politics*. Edinburgh: Q Press.

Bryant, R. 2002. The Purity of Spirit and the Power of Blood: A Comparative Perspective on Nation, Kinship and Gender in Cyprus. *Journal of the Royal Anthropological Institute* 8: 509–530.

———. 2008. Writing the Catastrophe: Nostalgia and Its Histories in Cyprus. *Journal of Modern Greek Studies* 26(2): 399–422.

Canefe, N. 2002. Refugees or Enemies?: The Legacy of Population Displacements in Contemporary Turkish Cypriot Society. *South European Society and Politics* 7(3): 1–28.

Cassia, P. S. 2005. *Bodies of Evidence: Burial, Memory and the Recovery of Missing Persons in Cyprus*. New York: Berghahn Books.

———. 2006. Guarding Each Other's Dead, Mourning One's Own: The Problem of Missing Persons and Missing Pasts in Cyprus. *South European Society and Politics* 11(1): 111–128.

Christodoulou, D. 1992. *Inside the Cyprus Miracle: The Labours of an Embattled Mini-economy*. Minneapolis, MN: University of Minnesota Press (Minnesota Mediterranean and East European Monographs).

Christou, M. 2002. *Fragments of Memory, Visions of Struggle: Political Imagination in a Greek Cypriot High School*. Unpublished Doctoral Dissertation: Harvard University.

———. 2006. A Double Imagination: Memory and Education in Cyprus. *Journal of Modern Greek Studies* 24(2): 285–306.

———. 2007. The Language of Patriotism: Sacred History and Dangerous Memories. *British Journal of Sociology of Education* 28(6): 709–722.

Connerton, P. 1989. *How Societies Remember*. Cambridge: Cambridge University Press.

Cyprus Ministry of Education and Culture. 2006. Minister's welcome letter for the 2006–2007 school year, at http://www.schools.ac.cy/dde/circular/data/Doc5039.pdf. Accessed April 10, 2009.

———. 2008. Minister's letter for the new school year's educational goals (2008–2009), at http://www.schools.ac.cy/dde/circular/data/Doc7387.pdf. Accessed April 17, 2009.

———. 2008. Minister's welcome letter for the 2008-2009 school year, at http://www.schools.ac.cy/dde/circular/data/Doc7390.pdf. Accessed April 10, 2009.

Dawson, G. 2008. *Making Peace with the Past?: Memories, Trauma and the Irish Troubles.* Manchester: Manchester University Press.

Demetriou, O. 2007. To Cross or Not to Cross?: Subjectivization and the Absent State in Cyprus. *Journal of the Royal Anthropological Institute* 13: 987–1006.

Dikomitis, L. 2004. A *Moving* Field: Greek Cypriot Refugees Returning "Home." *Durham Anthropology Journal* 12(1): 7–20.

———. 2005. Three Readings of a Border: Greek Cypriots Crossing the Green Line in Cyprus, *Anthropology Today* 21(5): 7–12.

Georgiades, S. D. 2007. Public Attitudes Towards Peace: The Greek Cypriot Position. *Journal of Peace Research* 44(5): 573–586.

Hadjiyanni, T. 2002. *The Making of a Refugee: Children Adopting Refugee Identity in Cyprus.* Westport, CT: Praeger.

Halbwachs, M. 1941/1992. *On Collective Memory,* trans. Lewis A. Coser. Chicago: The University of Chicago Press.

Hinchman, L. P., and S. K. Hinchman. 1997. Introduction. In *Memory, Identity, Community: The Idea of Narrative in the Human Sciences,* eds. L. P. Hinchman and S. K. Hinchman. Albany: State University of New York Press.

Huyssen, A. 2003. *Present Pasts: Urban Palimpsests and the Politics of Memory.* California: Stanford University Press.

Kedourie, E. 2005. The Cyprus Problem and Its Solution, *Middle Eastern Studies* 41(5): 649–660.

Killoran, M. 2000. Time, Space and National Identities in Cyprus. In *Step-Mothertongue. From Nationalism to Multiculturalism: Literatures of Cyprus, Greece and Turkey,* ed. M. Yashin. London: Middlesex University Press.

Loizos, P. 1981. *The Heart Grown Bitter: A Chronicle of Cypriot War Refugees.* Cambridge: Cambridge University Press.

Loizos, P., and C. Constantinou. 2007. Hearts as Well as Minds: Wellbeing and Illness among Greek Cypriot Refugees. *Journal of Refugee Studies* 20(1): 86–107.

Mannheim, K. 1952/1928. The Problem of Generations. In *Essays on the Sociology of Knowledge,* ed. P. Kecskemeti. New York: Oxford University Press.

Misztal, B. A. 2003. *Theories of Social Remembering.* Philadelphia: Open University Press.

Papadakis, Y. 1998. Greek Cypriot Narratives of History and Collective Identity: Nationalism as a Contested Process. *American Ethnologist* 25(2): 149–165.

———. 2003. Nation, Narrative and Commemoration: Political Ritual in Divided Cyprus. *History and Anthropology* 14(3): 253–270.

Philippou, S. 2005. Constructing National and European Identities: The Case of Greek-Cypriot Children. *Educational Studies* 31(3): 293–315.

Press and Information Office. 2009. *Commemorative Speech by President Demetris Christofias,* at http://www.cyprus.gov.cy/moi/pio/pio.nsf/All/8D2BEC4C716A7A46C2257558005C485C?Opendocument. Accessed March 4, 2009.

Ricoeur, P. 1988. *Time and Narrative,* vol. 3, trans. K. Blamey and D. Pellauer. Chicago: University of Chicago Press.

Rydgren, J. 2007. The Power of the Past: A Contribution to a Cognitive Sociology of Ethnic Conflict. *Sociological Theory* (25)3: 225–244.

Rotary Club of Nicosia Salamis. 2009. *Grace,* at http://rotary-cyprus.org/nic-salamis/history/grace. Accessed March 25, 2009.

Roudometof, V. 2005. National Commemorations in the Balkans. In *National Symbols, Fractured Identities: Contesting the National Narrative,* ed. M. Geisler. Hanover: University Press of New England.

———. 2007. Collective Memory and Cultural Politics: An Introduction. *Journal of Political and Military Sociology* 35(1): 1–16.

Scott, J. 2002. Mapping the Past: Turkish Cypriot Narratives of time and space in the Canbulat Museum, Northern Cyprus. *History and Anthropology* 13(3): 217–230.

Sky News. 2009. Open Records: Cyprus History Lessons, at http://www.skai.gr/player/tv/?mmid=25439. Accessed March 29, 2009.

Sofroniou, E. 2008. Mores and Customs of Christmas and New Year: Nostalgia for Tradition. *Politis Newspaper,* December 12.

Spillman, L. 2005. Is the "Strong Program" Strong Enough? *Culture: Newsletter of the Sociology of Culture Section of the American Sociological Association* 19(2): 1, 4–6.

Spyrou, S. 2001. Those on the Other Side: Ethnic Identity and Imagination in Greek-Cypriot Children's Lives. In *Children and Anthropology: Perspectives for the 21st Century,* ed. H. Schwartzman. Westport, CT, and London: Bergin & Garvey.

———. 2006. Constructing "the Turk" as an Enemy: The Complexity of Stereotypes in Children's Everyday Worlds. *South European Society & Politics* 11(1): 95–110.

Webster, C. 2005. Division or Unification in Cyprus? The Role of Demographics, Attitudes, and Party Inclination on Greek Cypriot Preferences for a Solution to the Cyprus Problem. *Ethnopolitics* 4(3): 299–309.

Xydis, S. G. 1973. *Cyprus: Reluctant Republic.* Netherlands: Mouton & Co. N.V. Publishers.

Vural, Y., and N. Peristianis. 2008. Beyond Ethno-nationalism: Emerging Trends in Cypriot Politics after the Annan Plan. *Nations and Nationalism* 14(1): 39–60.

Zembylas, M., and Z. Beckerman. 2008. Education and the Dangerous Memories of Historical Trauma: Narratives of Pain, Narratives of Hope. *Curriculum Inquiry* 38(2): 125–154.

Zetter, R. 1994. The Greek Cypriot Refugees: Perceptions of Return under Conditions of Protracted Exile. *International Migration Review* 28: 307–322.

———. 1999. Reconceptualizing the Myth of Return: Continuity and Transition Amongst the Greek-Cypriot Refugees of 1974. *Journal of Refugee Studies* 12(1): 1–22.

PART 3

The Performance of Suffering and Healing

8

Extending Trauma Across Cultural Divides

On Kidnapping and Solidarity in Colombia

Carlo Tognato

Colombia has been plagued by one of the longest civil conflicts in the world. The two guerrilla movements that are still fighting, the Revolutionary Armed Forces of Colombia (FARC) and the National Liberation Army (ELN) have been around for almost half a century and therefore constitute two of the oldest guerrilla movements currently known worldwide. Over the past decades, different governments in Colombia have initiated peace talks with various groups of illegal combatants. Some of them have been remarkably successful, because they have led to the total demobilization of the groups involved and have managed to reincorporate their members into civilian life and democratic politics. In the case of the FARC and the ELN, however, all contacts have been unfruitful. In the course of the 1990s, the conflict between these two groups and the state became increasingly gruesome and in the aftermath of 9/11 the two guerrilla groups were reclassified by the European Union and the United States State Department as terrorist organizations.

One of the weapons such groups have used over the years in part to pressure the Colombian government and, in part, to finance their illegal operations has been the kidnapping of thousands of people. Their victims have been subjected to infrahuman conditions while in captivity, often stacked behind barbed-wire fences in the thickest corners of the Colombian jungle, in some instances tied for years to trees with chains at their necks, undernourished, with little medical assistance, and under the constant threat of execution. At the end of 2007, their suffering reached and moved international audiences as some of the kidnap victims made a ghostly appearance in a video the FARC circulated to prove their survival. Traditionally, Colombian society has not regarded kidnapping as a national trauma. Instead, different segments of society have read it differently. In the past few years, however, things have started to change.

Theorists of cultural trauma have shed light over the sociocultural processes that underpin the collectivization of traumas. Their analysis, however, has not explicitly zoomed into the cultural mechanisms trauma dramas may tap into for the purpose of extending trauma across deep cultural divides. Addressing the emergence of kidnapping as a national trauma in Colombia may contribute in this respect. More concretely, it shows that ambivalent performances that unfold along the surface of contact between different cultural structures play a crucial role in the generalization of traumas within deeply divided societies.

On the Practice of Kidnapping in Colombia

The history of kidnapping in Colombia starts in 1933 when the three-year old daughter of an industrialist was kidnapped. Thirty years later, her father would be killed during an attempt of kidnapping. In the 1960s, the major Colombia daily, *El Tiempo,* already referred to kidnapping as a growing industry (Rubio 2003). At that time, insurgent groups began to use kidnapping as a source of funding. Since then "in Colombia freedom would become a merchandize to be exchanged for money, political rent and even rubber boots or cell-phones" (*El Tiempo* 2007b).

Colombia has not been the only country in Latin America to experience such a practice. Throughout the region diplomatic personnel, foreign executives working for multinational corporations, government officials, and local industrialists have repeatedly been targeted. Argentine guerrillas, in particular, set an ominous record by extracting millionaire ransoms from multinational corporations. During the 1970s, Colombian guerrillas mainly kidnapped diplomats and corporate executives. In the 1980s, they targeted the Colombian urban bourgeoisie. And in the 1990s, mass kidnapping at road blocks further diversified the pool of victims (Rubio 2003, 13). By that time, Colombia had already become the world leader in kidnappings. Just between January 1996 and June 2008, approximately twenty four thousand people have been kidnapped. By June 2008, almost three thousand were still in the hands of their captors and almost fourteen hundred had died in captivity. Over that period, the FARC kidnapped 6,902 people, the ELN 5,422, and paramilitaries 1,187.[1]

Kidnap victims are subjected to infrahuman conditions while in captivity. Their life is under constant threat. In case of military rescue operations, their kidnappers are often instructed to execute them. Colombia President Álvaro Uribe has compared the FARC' s detention camps to the Nazis' concentration camps, and Human Rights Watch has explicitly referred to their practice of kidnapping as a patent crime against humanity (Vivanco 2002).

During 2007, the Colombian government was subjected to increasing pressure both at home and abroad to negotiate a humanitarian exchange with the FARC and the ELN. The proofs of survival of some of the kidnap victims the FARC delivered at the end of 2007 laid further pressure on the Colombian government to reach a negotiated solution to the problem. In 2007, Venezuela President Hugo Chavez was asked by his Colombian counterpart to mediate with the FARC to obtain the liberation of the kidnap victims. Chavez pushed further the internationalization of the issue by involving different foreign actors, such as former Argentina President Nestor Kirchner and film director Oliver Stone. By the end of 2007, however, Colombia President Uribe revoked his authorization to Chavez after it became manifest that the latter was pursuing the change of FARC's terrorist status into one of belligerency. On February 4, 2008, more than ten million Colombians took the streets to protest and call for the immediate release of the kidnap victims. This constituted a historical turning point in Colombian political culture, given that public protests had traditionally been regarded by most Colombians with utter suspicion. During 2008, the streets of Colombia would be occupied again and again by three additional mass protests. On July 2, 2008, the Colombian army launched Operation Checkmate. After infiltrating the FARC's lines of communication, two helicopters were dispatched to a camp where the FARC held Ingrid Betancourt, three American citizens, and eleven policemen and army soldiers. The army managed to convince the FARC that a friendly nongovernmental organization (NGO) had put the helicopters at disposal of the guerrilla for the purpose of transporting the "prisoners" to another camp. The guards were tricked into delivering them to unarmed intelligence officers that posed as NGO cooperators. The fifteen kidnap victims were then retrieved from the camp and freed without shooting one single bullet. The leading national newspaper, *El Tiempo,* celebrated the success as a greater national triumph than the historic 5:0 Colombia scored in soccer against Argentina (*El Tiempo* 2008c).

On the Cultural Construction of Kidnapping as a National Trauma

Colombians have been traditionally quite indifferent to the suffering of the kidnap victims. In a letter to his family one of the kidnapped, Coronel Mendieta, writes, "It is not physical pain that paralyzes me, or the chains around my neck that torment me, but mental agony, the evil of the evil and the indifference of the good, as if we were not worth anything, as if we did not exist" (*El Tiempo* 2008a). A journalist has once compared the indifference of Colombians to that of the Germans before the Holocaust. War, she argues, has transformed Colombians into petty monsters that can no longer draw the line between good and evil. It has converted them into confused beings that can hardly distinguish truth from lie. War has bent their capability to react and their right to feel outraged (Duzán 2008).

In Colombia, indifference has managed to trickle down to linguistic practices. At the end of the 1990s, for example, mass media started to refer to the practice of massive kidnappings at roadblocks as "miraculous catch." In a way, this made semantic sense insofar as it was as indiscriminate as fishing with a net. However, one can hardly overlook the subtle dehumanizing effect this association performed on the victims as well as the normalization of cynicism it tacitly fostered among its audiences. Similarly, the common reference in everyday talk to the practice of "express kidnapping" as "millionaire outing" (*paseo milionario*) constitutes another indirect display of indifference. After all, it deprives the victims of the very possibility of representing it as crime. And its implicit reference to the act as something ambiguously pleasurable makes it all the more troubling, as it constitutes a form of violence men most often inflict upon women.

Colombians, however, have not only been indifferent *vis à vis* the phenomenon of kidnapping. They have also been profoundly split over the attitude one should hold toward the victims, perpetrators, and bystanders. Some have adamantly claimed that nothing can justify it, that kidnappers should be condemned irrespective of their motives, and society has an obligation to unconditionally take side with the victims. Others, on the contrary, have been willing to qualify their condemnation by stressing that one should at least solidarize with all victims first, that one cannot demonize the kidnappers, and that society may well hold a neutral position over the issue. This stance has, for example, lent legitimacy to claims that the FARC carries out crimes but its members are not criminals, or that one can be "neither friend nor enemy of the FARC" (*El Tiempo* 2007e). With the progressive marginalization of Marxist-Leninist discourse within the Colombian public sphere, such positions have been increasingly but problematically couched within a liberal discourse. The claim that solidarity for the kidnap victims and condemnation of the kidnappers is possible only after securing solidarity for all victims and condemnation of all perpetrators, after all, follows the very same twisted logic of those who suggest that solidarity with Holocaust victims and condemnation of the Nazis should require first a solidarity with the victims of all genocides and the condemnation of all perpetrators. In other words, the instrumental perversion of the liberal grammar here achieves an artificial effect that it is not only illogic from a liberal standpoint but sometimes suspiciously cynical.

Such divisions have been apparent during the debate within the major Colombian opposition party—the *Polo Democratico Alternativo*—over the participation to the February 4, 2008 march against the practice of kidnapping and against the FARC, which possibly constituted the largest public protest that has ever taken place on Colombian streets.

At the end of December 2007, a Colombian 33-year-old computer science engineer, Oscar Morales, created a group on Facebook named "One Million Voices Against the FARC." He tells that the ghostly image of Ingrid Betancourt the FARC circulated that early December to prove her survival; the photos of the kidnap victims in chains; and the failed liberation of little Emmanuel, the three-year old boy who was born in captivity in a detention camp of the FARC, moved him to do something about it. Soon enough, the group on Facebook brought together thousands of people, and Oscar Morales decided to use it to call for a march against the FARC. Through Facebook, the march was scheduled for February 4, 2008, and was organized in 115 cities around the world. Many Colombian mass media, the private sector, and the government joined the initiative and supported it both in Colombia and abroad. In the end, more than ten million people marched. The FARC reacted to the initiative by stigmatizing it as a "military weapon of espionage and destabilization" and as a plot orchestrated by the Colombian government and the CIA (Semana 2008). The official newspaper of the Colombian Communist Party, for its part, sentenced that the march constituted a typical example of manipulation of the masses on the part of the capitalist mass media and of the Colombian political oligarchy (Voz 2008). An observer of the February 4 march sentenced that Colombia got to it more divided than Israel and Palestine, "Even on the most delicate, most useful and most human matters, it is impossible to agree. We are incapable of discussing with respect. There is intolerance, anger and intense pain" (Ochoa 2008a).

Now, reaching a decision on whether to participate in the march became a thorny issue for the *Polo Democrático Alternativo,* which constitutes the umbrella organization for many political groups on the left of the Colombian political spectrum. The mayor of Bogotá, a member of that party, declared he would march as a mayor and as a citizen because he believed in the mobilization. One of the leading senators of the party, Gustavo Petro, called his party to join the march but his petition was turned down by the directorate of the *Polo.* As political pressure mounted upon the party, its leaders decided that they would not march but would rather turn up in the central square of Bogotá, protest against kidnapping, and leave the square before the marchers reached it as planned. This way, they explained, public opinion would be clear that they would not support a progovernment initiative (*El Tiempo* 2008b). In an interview former Minister of Interior, Humberto de la Calle, joked that the decision of the *Polo* not to march but to concentrate instead in Bolivar Square sounded like Clinton's famous statement that he smoked marijuana but never inhaled it (Amat 2008).

Liberal opinion-makers criticized from the pages of Colombian leading newspapers and magazines the decision on the part of the *Polo* to condition its participation to the march. Some stressed that one cannot politicize barbarism and must reject it straightforwardly, irrespective of whether those who condemn it stand on the opposite side of the political spectrum (Abad Faciolince 2008). Others warned that one cannot condition one's own adhesion to a march depending on whether its organizers include the condemnation of other forms of violence one is more sensitive to (García Villegas 2008). Others more pointed their finger to the equivocal posture certain members of the *Polo* had been keeping toward the FARC and questioned whether the *Polo*'s commitment to the values that underpinned the discourse of civil society was actually genuine. This issue, in particular, had been a recurrent theme for public debate. Some had criticized the fact that the *Polo* kept neutrality toward the insurgency and enmity against the constitutional government (*El Tiempo* 2007f). Others remarked that the *Polo* never straightforwardly condemned the FARC in the same way it did with paramilitaries (Abad Faciolince 2005).

It is important to acknowledge, though, that, despite the continuing divisions within Colombian society over the issue of kidnapping, the front of indifference and of qualified solidarity with the kidnap victims has been shrinking at an accelerating pace over the past few years to the point that today kidnapping is being regarded as a national trauma at least by a large majority of the population.

The cultural construction of kidnapping as a societywide trauma has relied on an increasing emphasis in public discourse upon the human dimension of such a phenomenon, which has progressively displaced earlier representations that paid attention to the structural conditions that allowed it. Such a discursive shift—from structure to agency—has given unrestricted primacy to the victim. A leading Colombian anthropologist, Myriam Jimeno, has recently suggested that the establishment of a general narrative of victimhood through personal testimony has crucially contributed to the generalization of solidarity for the kidnap victims across Colombian society. The telling of personal stories about the cruel death of a father, the kidnapping of a young woman, the disappearance of a son, sometimes with elaborate speeches, other times through poems or improvised words, and almost always with tears, Jimeno (2009, 15–17) insists, has managed to establish an emotional community across ethnic, social, and political lines. The exponential increase over the past decade of books that lay out the personal testimony of the kidnap victims or their family members is a clear indicator of such a phenomenon. Journalists as well seem to be keenly aware of such a trend. Salud Hernández, for example, remarks in one of her op-ed pieces in *El Tiempo* that Colombia is so plagued by so many different horrors that it will not be possible to overcome them if people do not fix their gaze on the face of the victims, on their tears, and on the tortures they underwent without acknowledging that both in mass graves and in the jungle there are and have been innocent victims who suffered. It is necessary, she says, to break the indifference and stop measuring pain quantitatively.[2]

Civil associations have crucially contributed to bring about the above-mentioned discursive shift by vindicating the primacy of the victims and defending their interests within multiple institutional arenas. A look to the activities of the most distinguished carrier group on this front, *Fundación País Libre,* which in 2006 was awarded the Sakharov Prize by the European Parliament, may be particularly suggestive in this respect.

The foundation has contributed to the organization of a series of mass mobilizations since its foundation. In 1996, it led the *"Movimiento Por el país que queremos, No al secuestro,"* which organized five marches against kidnapping in different cities of Colombia and assembled more than one million people. In 1999, it created the *Movimiento Ciudadano* "NO MÁS," which launched more than twenty marches throughout the country. And since 2004, it has promoted the celebration on December 7 of a day of remembrance of the kidnap victims, "*Un clamor por la libertad de todos los secuestrados*" ("An outcry for the freedom of all kidnapped"). At the scientific level, the foundation has backed the building of statistics on kidnapping as well as the publications of academic studies on the topic. At the public policy level, it has promoted legislative bills or administrative decrees at the national or city level with the purpose of granting special protection to the kidnap victims and their families; as well as financial support, tax exemptions, or preferential access to the health and education services that are provided by the social security system. The foundation has also sued the Colombian State before the International Criminal Court for not pursuing the leaders of the illegal organizations that have systematically carried out kidnappings and disappearances, thereby becoming the first NGO to ever lay a claim before the court. Finally, it has sponsored a bill that increases prison time for kidnappers. The bill constituted the first piece of legislation to result from a civic action with more than a million signatures to back it.

The appeal to human experience as a strategy to generalize solidarity for the kidnap victims across society has clearly been effective in the Colombian case. It would constitute an analytical mistake, however, to naturalize such effect and expect that appealing to human experience automatically triggers solidarity for the victims because this would imply to expect that human experience somehow unfolds beyond culture. Surely, the visceral dimension of human experience that is not mediated by language is probably close to a universal. Victims of torture around the world, after all, share a terrible secret irrespective of their cultural backgrounds. Most of human experience, however, is mediated by language and therefore by culture. Depending on the horizon of interpretation within which it unfolds, it will take different meanings. As Hashimoto remarks in her chapter, "wars, massacres, atrocities, invasions, and other instances of mass violence can become significant referents for subsequent collective life not because of the gruesome nature of the events *per se,* but because people choose to make them especially relevant to who they are and what it means to be a member of that society" (30). Sadly enough, the Colombian case bears witness to the fact that the view of human suffering does not automatically trigger solidarity for the victims across all society. Hernández herself, for example, admits that in Colombia different measures of pain get attached to different sets of victims. It is also important to stress that this is not only the case within societies like Colombia that are fractured by deep cultural divides. Rather, it also applies to more culturally coherent societies, where the recognition of human suffering does *per se* not necessarily result into its inscription into public consciousness as a national trauma. Heins and Langenohl's chapter in this book (Chapter 1) provides a clear example in this respect.

If human experience does not automatically serve as a common ground across cultural divides, some alternative mechanism must be in place to generalize solidarity across deeply divided societies. The fact that in Colombia solidarity with the kidnap victims has undergone a process of generalization implies that such mechanisms have been eluding the theoretical lenses we have so far employed to account for trauma dramas. To shed light over their existence and their functioning, we need to zoom in. Before doing so, however, I will dwell first on one major cultural divide that fractures the Colombian public sphere.

Colombia and Its Culturally Fragmented Public Sphere

The Colombian public sphere is deeply fractured into two camps, each of which holds to a radically different cultural metric of legitimacy in social life: the liberal discourse of civil society and the discourse of the *hacienda*.

Hard-core liberals as well as most of the Left in Colombia, particularly in the urban areas, tap into the former as their metric of legitimacy. Marxist-Leninism that for a long time permeated the political discourse of the Left during the twentieth century seems to have retreated from the public sphere, and today, the internal debates within the major leftist party, the *Polo Democrático Alternativo,* follow the cultural logic of the discourse of civil society, though not all politicians within it always manage to perform it with sufficient authenticity. The president of the *Polo,* Carlos Gavíria, for example, whom many identify with the more Leftist strand within his party, is a constitutionalist scholar, former president of the Colombian Constitutional Court, a radical liberal, a vehement defender of the principle of personal autonomy of the individual and a true believer of the virtue of rational discussion among citizen (Rincón 2002). The liberal discourse of civil society exhibits the very same structural features Alexander (2006b, 53–67) attributes to the discourse of liberty and repression that permeates the civil sphere of democratic societies. More precisely, it postulates that democratic actors are active, autonomous, rational, reasonable, calm, controlled, realistic, and sane; while nondemocratic actors are passive, dependent, irrational, hysterical, excitable, passionate, unrealistic, and mad. Similarly, it expects democratic social relations to be open, trusting, critical, truthful, and straightforward; and nondemocratic ones to be secretive, suspicious, deferential, deceitful, and calculative. Finally, it takes democratic political institutions to be regulated by rules, based on law, equality, inclusiveness, impersonality, contract, and office; and nondemocratic institutions to be arbitrary, power-oriented, and characterized by hierarchy, exclusion, personalism, and ascription.[3]

In 1991, Colombia passed a new liberal constitution, and the discourse of civil society consequently gained a more central position within the national civil sphere. Despite the new emphasis on the sacredness of the individual, on human dignity, personal autonomy, rationality, and freedom, the new system of secular collective representations fell short of providing a common political vocabulary for all Colombian society (Palacio 1999; Estrada 2004; Gutiérrez 1999; Morales 1998). As Tognato and Cuellar (2009) have recently shown, this resulted into the continual presence in the everyday practice of most average Colombians of the axiomatic system that until then had oriented the conception of agency, social relations and political institutions, the discourse of the *hacienda* (i.e., large farm).

Such a discourse builds on an organic understanding of society and therefore deems desirable whatever feeds into collective harmony and condemns whatever breaches it. It consists of a system of binary oppositions that define what is legitimate in social life and what instead must be resisted. The attributes on the positive side make up the *patron/peón* code, whereas those on the negative side identify the *bandit* code.[4] The notion of patron collapses into one figure elements that are political, religious, familiar, moral, and economic. The patron is the protector, the shelter, the moral authority, the saint, the person in charge of the workers, the lord that rules over his feud, and the owner of the house where everyone else is guest. The *peón*, on the other hand, is the subordinate that submits to the superior wisdom of the patron, the docile follower, the listener, the modest that knows his own place in society and accepts his humble part in it. If the *patron* is the head of the social body, the *peón* is its hand and can claim dignity until he fulfils his own function. On the other hand, the bandit is the peon who decided to rebel against social, and therefore natural, harmony.

As far as agency is concerned, the *patron/peón* code establishes that the patron be civilized, cultivated, compassionate, orderly, respectful, and considerate, while the *peón* must match those attributes with complementary ones—modesty, docility, humbleness, good-willingness, reverence, and generosity. On the other hand, the bandit code defines those who reject the organic order of social life as barbarian, ignorant, ungrateful, disorderly, irreverent, disruptive, and calculative. As far as social relations are concerned, the *patron/peón* code grounds them upon paternalism, loyalty, and charity whereas the bandit code structures them upon individualism, treason, and selfishness. Finally, political institutions according to the *patron/peón* code will be based on tradition, authority, personalism, and order; while bandits will build up institutions that are based on anarchy, rebellion, impersonality, and chaos.[5]

The discourse of the *hacienda* spans across broad segments of Colombian society. As Cuellar (2009) shows, since the end of the nineteenth century, both conservatives and moderate liberals have tapped into it as their metric of legitimacy in social life. Today, many see Colombia's President Álvaro Uribe as the quintessential embodiment of the *patron*. As such, his popularity rates do not suffer at all whenever he openly acknowledges in a press conference that he is having opposition congressmen followed by the Presidential Secret Police because they oppose the Free Trade Agreement with the United States and lobby against it in Washington D.C. (Semana 2007a). The *patron*, after all, is culturally entitled to protect collective harmony and to intervene against those who spoil it. In a different occasion, the conservative historian Eduardo Posada Carbó stressed that the Colombian government cannot keep saying before international audiences that in Colombia there is no conflict. He recommends that the government appeal to "a different discourse, more elaborate, more pondered, and with fewer passionate rhetorical improvisations." In a way, Posada's wakeup call politely signals that the patron can surely claim epistemic authority within his *hacienda*, but anywhere else, where the principle of personal autonomy applies, observers will immediately object to it (Posada Carbó 2008).

It would be mistaken, however, to attribute the use of the discourse of the *hacienda* just to those segments of the population that identify with the political right. The organic understandings of society based on patriarchy and Catholicism that underpin the discourse of the *hacienda* are widespread in Colombia and even creep into the discourse of the leftist guerrillas. In occasion of the Conference the FARC summoned to celebrate its 43rd Anniversary, for example, the guerrilla group issued a *communiqué* that called Colombians "to struggle for a new government capable of reconciling the Colombian family" (FARC 2007).

After pinpointing the major cultural divide that fractures the Colombian public sphere into two radically different cultural camps, I will zoom into the sociocultural processes that have paved the way to the generalization of the trauma of the kidnap victims to the rest of society in an effort to pin down the specific mechanisms that have sustained the extension of trauma across cultural difference.

Ambivalent Performances and the Extension of Trauma Across Cultural Divides

In 2007, three events in particular seem to have been pivotal to awake, as an observer puts it, "a generalized feeling of indignation and rejection" of kidnapping (Pombo 2007), thereby contributing to generalize solidarity with the kidnap victims across Colombian society: Professor Moncayo's six-hundred-mile march to Bogotá to demand the liberation of his son; the image of Ingrid Betancourt in a video the FARC circulated to prove her survival; and the story of Emmanuel, a three-year old boy born in captivity from a kidnap victim and a FARC combatant.

These three cases engage into a rather complex and possibly paradoxical exercise of cultural juggling. They are both about the celebration of civil heroism and human dignity and about the vindication of traditional values. Gustavo Moncayo turns into a national symbol of civil protest, but at the same time, he manages to walk that fine line within the Christian tradition that enables the humble, the *peón*, to rise and partake into the glory of Jesus. Ingrid, on her part, becomes a living indictment against political repression and civil indifference but simultaneously her iconic appearance in the video transfigures her into a Virgin Mary, a sign of the possibility of social unity through the common experience of pain. A journalist remarks that her image in the video bears "something of the Piety of Michelangelo, aesthetically beautiful, and humanly violent and tragic" (Pombo 2007). Finally, Emmanuel rises as a symbol of the shamelessness of antidemocratic forces, which are capable of denying the most basic rights of the weakest in society, but at the same time, he also comes to play the role of Baby Jesus who will descend at Christmas on a divided Colombia and contribute to bringing it back together.

All three cases are about ambivalent performances that unfold along the fault line between the two discursive camps that make up the Colombian public sphere: the discourse of civil society and the discourse of the *hacienda*. Such cultural mechanisms seem to have played a crucial role in zipping one camp to the other, thereby allowing solidarity for the kidnap victims to stretch across them. To see how, I will here zoom into the Moncayo case.

Gustavo Moncayo is a 55-year-old high school teacher from a southern region of Colombia. His son Pablo Emilio, a corporal of the National Police, was kidnapped in December 1997 by the FARC after an attack against the police station where he was serving. In October 2006, the FARC exploded a car bomb within the parking lot of the Military University in Bogotá, and President Uribe decided to close the door to any humanitarian exchange with the guerrilla group. At that point,

Gustavo started to publicly wear chains at his wrists and neck, like the kidnap victims of the FARC, and never stopped since (Semana 2007b). In July 2007, in the aftermath of the assassination by the FARC of eleven regional congressmen in captivity, out of despair and fearing he might no longer see his son alive, he decided to leave his home together with one of his daughters and head on foot to Bogotá to protest for the release of his son. He started his march in the middle of a generalized neglect and without support of any institution—social, political, religious, or economic (*El Tiempo* 2007c). But then he managed to catch public attention. The media would accompany him along the track. People impatiently awaited his arrival. They applauded him, hugged him, touched him, took photos with him, asked for autographs, dedicated local folk songs to him, donated money, and offered food. In a society that is marked by severe socioeconomic segregation, his march moved people from all strata. In one occasion, Moncayo remembers, an armored BMW stopped; a man came out, took a photo with him, and left. Moncayo tells that the man did not dare give him a lift. He knew that Gustavo was walking for his son (Navia 2007). Toward the end of his march, his arrival was announced on the radio, and schools would stop their classes (Miño Rueda 2007b). The march lasted forty-six days. Even the FARC acknowledged that his gesture was "valiant" (*El Tiempo* 2007d). When he got to Bogotá, Moncayo met with the president and the mayor of the city. At the end of 2007, he was awarded the National Peace Prize (*El Tiempo* 2007g). Though his painful march did not manage to obtain the liberation of his son, he managed most of the time to command the attention and the solidarity of broad and diverse segments of the Colombian society.

Surely, what immediately came to mind to a broad segment of the audiences that followed Moncayo's action was its civil vocation. It made a statement about the civil value of peaceful protest. It was a declaration of belief in the capability of the individual to make a difference. It constituted a reminder about the duty citizens have to take a stance on public issues and act. It served as a promise that in a divided society, civil rituals can bring together people from all regions, all ethnicities, and all socioeconomic strata. And it became a vindication of the fact that civil society can play a role in public life, as an activist who marched along with Moncayo pointed out (*El Tiempo* 2007a). Moncayo's march, in a way, performed a similar function to being on a campaign track for a political candidate. It transformed a private citizen into a public figure by exposing him to public problems and by committing him before multiple publics. An observer remarks that "Citizen Moncayo" turned into the symbolic transfiguration of the people. He interpreted the people and rose because of the people. And he did all that by showing dignity (*El Tiempo* 2007c).

Still, to another part of Colombian society, Moncayo was not a civil hero. He was rather the *peón* who managed to walk along that fine line within the Christian tradition that allows the humble to rise and partake into the glory of Jesus. Turner (1973) would say that the life of Jesus served as the archetypical metaphor for the performance of Moncayo.

Moncayo showed from the start to be a man of faith. When he left home, his daughter warned him they had no money. He reassured her. Along the way, they would encounter good people (*El Tiempo* 2007a). Like Jesus, he started to have followers who would march with him (Miño Rueda 2007). Public opinion would soon refer to them as "the legion" or "the disciples" (Arbaláez 2007). Ingrid Betancour once said in a letter to her mother, "We live like dead" (Ochoa 2008b). To resurrect his son and all kidnap victims from their death in the jungle, Moncayo needed to carry out a ritual of collective purification by walking the same *via crucis* Jesus did in his Passion. The media actually recognized his march as such (Semana 2007b). Like Christ, he would suffer along the way. And the media dwelt on his bleeding feet (Gonzáles Posso 2007). As Moncayo entered innumerable villages along the way, people came to the street to see him. Some knelt. Others blessed him and raised their arms to the sky, "The entire world is moved" (Arbaláez 2007). Children approached him and gave him flowers (Navia 2007). Orphans and elderly alike came to him and greeted him (Miño Rueda 2007a). A woman once implored him to enter her home. Her husband had been ill for a month; she asked him to touch him and see if he could do a miracle. "Moncayo stopped and the husband was already walking toward him." He told the man to put some water on his knees and to have faith because God helps everyone. Then, he went back to the road and marched along with the multitude (Miño Rueda 2007b). The encounter with President Uribe under a tent in Bolivar Square where he finally settled at the end of his march once again evokes parts of the script of the Passion of Christ. To the President who resisted a humanitarian exchange with the FARC, Moncayo says, "You're not the owner of life" (Forero 2007). As a journalist puts it, "the President insults, and the people do not give in. The President humiliates, and the people will look down. The President invites a fight, and the people will hide" (*El Tiempo* 2007c). Moncayo turns the other cheek before a president who loses his patience and raises his voice and before the president's advisors who arrogantly accuse him of simple-mindedness. Before a president who is insensitive to human dignity, says an observer, Moncayo vindicates the reason of humanity and, by doing so, through his pain, his impotence, his own dignity, Moncayo vindicates the outraged dignity of the public (Benedetti Jimeno 2007). The media would conclude that the ritual of humiliation against Moncayo ended up showing a President who cannot accept a horizontal encounter with the people (*El Tiempo* 2007c).

One may ask at this point who is really Gustavo Moncayo? A civil hero or a traditional saint? Concluding that for some he only embodied the former, and for others, only the latter would not faithfully reflect the complexity of his performance. His performance was just merely multivocal. In other words, it did not merely mean different things to different audiences. What is special about it is that audiences within one cultural camp had to accept that there were elements about it that did not squarely fit into their own reading of it and that fitted instead into the interpretation the other camp was giving to it. In short, Moncayo was both a hero and a saint and yet did not completely fulfill each camp's expectations about either *dramatis persona*. How could a civil hero, after all, enter the home of that woman and address her sick husband that way? And how could a traditional saint that managed to rise above his social condition thanks to his humble acceptance of suffering raise his chin instead and occasionally give politically tainted speeches along the way to those who would come to meet him?

To more concretely show the oscillations observers are forced into upon making sense of Moncayo's performance, and therefore to better appreciate its ambivalence, I will here zoom into one of the many articles the major Colombian daily newspaper published about him.

The article's title, "Moncayo, from geography teacher to national idol," starts out by leaving the reader quite uncertain about the interpretative spin the piece will take. Since a traditional saint would probably shy away from an idol status, one might conjecture at this point that the article will possibly go for a civil representation of the Colombian school teacher. Here, however, comes the first unexpected swing of the script. The reader is surprisingly pushed toward a more traditional understanding of Moncayo, as the story's opening tells us about the lady who asked Moncayo to perform a miracle on her husband. Then, the script lists the long stream of humiliations Moncayo had to go through before his march as he traveled across Colombia to meet with ministers or members of the guerrilla who never received him to hear his plea, as he got so indebted that he had to beg his neighbors for financial help, as he had to put up with the gossip of his fellow villagers who insinuated that his daughters would use the money Moncayo would raise to buy new clothes, and as people in the streets of Bogotá would glance at him as he walked around in chains and think he had gone mad. Now, the representation of a vilified dignity may well fit both within a civil and a traditional framing of Moncayo's performance. So we are back to ambiguity. But suddenly again, the author bounces the reader back into the traditional cultural camp as he reports that in one occasion Moncayo told his family that he wanted to crucify himself in protest. As the reader has not even adjusted to such a horizon of meaning yet, the script swirls him back as it states that Moncayo's daughter managed to convince her father not to undergo crucifixion by reminding him that he would no longer be able to play guitar after that, an argument that would hardly discourage a real saint. As we get drawn away from sainthood, the author swings us back again to it by depicting Moncayo as a man of faith. For a moment, one has the impression that Moncayo may in the end be a saint that follows the steps of Jesus. People, the author says, start to follow him. He passes through crowds that offer him gifts. But then, the journalist says that the crowds rhythmically shout "Moncayo, our friend, the people stands with you," and once again, the impression that he might be a traditional saint dissolves. Such a chant, after all, mimics the slogans protesters shout during strikes. If Moncayo were a traditional saint, it would not make any sense to welcome him as a protester, which would instead better fit a civil representation of him. As the author reports that Moncayo has been compared with Robin Hood, the pendulum seems to swing even farther away from traditional sainthood. From that point on, the script depicts Moncayo in the act of delivering public speeches in universities and town councils and at schools before audiences of children. One might think at this point that even Jesus gave speeches on rather political stages and liked to meet with children. However, the author tells us that the speeches are about the humanitarian exchange and this cues the fact that Moncayo takes up the *dramatis persona* of the civil activist rather than the traditional saint. The fact that people wait for him for hours along the streets and seek to take photos with him or ask for autographs would seem to confirm that indeed his performance bends more resolutely toward the civil camp rather than the traditional one. But then, the pendulum swings back and the author mentions the sick elderly with their oxygen tanks and wheelchairs who try to greet Moncayo along the streets. In addition, road workers and rich people with armored cars stop to see him. This indication of unity and social harmony, we might think, may be a possible consequence of sainthood. The fact that the story lands us on the blisters of Moncayo's feet and on his physical pain cannot but increase our feeling that his persona might rather match that of a traditional saint. But the final line of the article smashes any possible clear-cut framing of Moncayo; Moncayo says, "I am neither a hero nor a saint, just a man who got tired of so many humiliations and hit the road to seek the liberation of his son and all other kidnap victims" (Miño Rueda 2007b).

Now, the first part of this line would seem to reflect the scripted humbleness of the real saint, but the second part makes a statement that draws him closer to the activist that engages in a heroic battle against injustice.

In conclusion, Moncayo's performance is not just a multivocal performance that merely means different things to different audiences. On observing it, audiences on both sides of the cultural divide that fractures the Colombian public sphere are drawn into accepting that the meaning of the performance feverishly oscillates from one camp to the other and back without ever stabilizing on one single side of the divide. In other words, each camp is drawn into recognizing that it needs elements from the other to capture the full reality of the performance. One detects here the operation of a peculiar mechanism that sustains a molecular trade of cultural elements between two camps that would otherwise conceive the possibility of exchange between them as utterly unimaginable. For this reason, we are facing here something analytically more restrictive than plain multivocality. It is multivocality with an incipient practice of mutual recognition. We are stumbling on a case of cultural ambivalence, and this is what ultimately stitches together the two cultural camps into which the Colombian public sphere is split, thereby allowing meaning to cross over from one camp to the other and making it possible for trauma, and solidarity for the kidnap victims, to extend across both camps.

It is important to stress, though, that such a cultural mechanism can only bridge the divide on a very contingent basis. Moncayo's performance, for example, was not effective at it all the way through. Two issues, in particular, seem to have been relevant in this respect. First, to start talks over a humanitarian exchange conducive to the liberation of the kidnap victims, the FARC had demanded that the government demilitarized the territory of two municipalities in a southern region of Colombia. As his march progressed, Moncayo increasingly insisted that the government should go along with such a demand. The FARC publicly saluted his insistence and observed that "as his march was continuing, the need and urgency of a humanitarian exchange advanced in the conscience of Colombians" (*El Tiempo* 2007d). In an open letter to Moncayo an opinion-maker warned him that, by invoking the humanitarian exchange under the conditions dictated by the guerrilla, he was turning into a tactical asset of the FARC, which would throw a bleak shadow onto his march. After all, that would undermine the meaning his march had acquired, which crucially depended on its being "pristine and pure, foreign to any kind of ideological taint that would profane" it (Hernández Bolivar 2007). Now, from a civil standpoint, it would be unacceptable that the march turned into something that could help the FARC. And from a more traditional point of view, it would be unacceptable that the sacred ritual of the *via crucis* be turned into a tactical weapon in the hands of "the bandits."

Also, Moncayo's performance lost further effectiveness due to the stage on which its final act unfolded. When he arrived in Bogotá, after all, Moncayo decided to plant his tent in Bolivar Square where the Colombian Congress, the town hall, the Cathedral, the Constitutional Court and, not too far away, the Presidential Palace converge. Quite curiously, such a *mis-en-scene* exposed Moncayo to a space that, symbolically speaking, had an inherent potential for contamination and this is a risk neither a saint nor a civil hero can afford to run. Their aura, after all, crucially depends on a perception of disinterestedness that will be badly spoiled by the lures of political power (Castillo Cardona 2007; Ochoa 2007c).

Conclusion

For a long time, Colombian society has not regarded kidnapping as a national trauma. Lately, however, things have started to change. Theorists of cultural trauma have so far shown that the extension of trauma is a culturally mediated accomplishment. Their analysis, however, has not explicitly tackled the specific cultural mechanisms trauma dramas may tap into for the purpose of extending trauma across deep cultural divides. They often seem to rely upon a tacit assumption that it is sufficient for such a purpose to appeal to the profoundly human character of suffering on the part of the victims, because in the end, human experience constitutes a common ground in spite of all cultural differences. Addressing the emergence of kidnapping as a national trauma in Colombia is useful, because it shows that an appeal to human suffering is *per se* not sufficient to bridge cultural divides. Instead, one further mechanism must kick in to sustain the generalization of solidarity with the victims throughout society. In particular, I have shown that ambivalent performances that unfold along the surface of contact between different cultural structures constitute an important cultural mechanism that allows the extension of trauma in deeply divided societies.

Future work will need to clarify the idea of cultural ambivalence and more neatly distinguish it from that of multivocality, ambiguity, polysemy, or penumbra of meaning (Padget and Ansell 1993; Barthes 1977; Gombrich 1971). A variety of authors who have tapped into the latter have stressed that texts, images, or performances may mean quite different things to different audiences. In this paper, I have hinted at the fact that cultural ambivalence implies much more than that and its grammar has to do with the ways different receptions across a cultural divide are tied to each other.

The extension of cultural trauma theory (Alexander et al. 2004; Alexander 2004), I propose in this paper, may also open up a number of new fronts for theoretical development.

First, ambivalent performances that unfold along the surface of contact between different cultural structures seem to call for a notion of authenticity that does not necessarily entail the fusion of the elements that make them up, as one would anticipate instead, in the light of Alexander's cultural pragmatics (Alexander 2006a). The study of ambivalent performances may therefore positively contribute to a theoretical extension of the latter.

Second, neo-Durkheimians have more often focused on the analysis of situations in which participants fight over meaning but ultimately share a common basic cultural understanding of reality. This paper seeks to show that situations with little cultural complicity among their participants are also empirically relevant and therefore deserve the attention of neo-Durkheimians as well.[6]

Finally, in his 1997 American Sociological Association presidential address Smelser (1998) called the attention of the profession on the phenomenon of ambivalence in modern social life and urged the development within sociology of a systematic line of enquiry in this sense. Since then, however, little has been done along the line Smelser advocated. In this chapter, I have tried to suggest that revamping such an intellectual project is central for neo-Durkheimians as far as their quest for theoretical extension of Durkheim's theory is concerned.

Notes

1. "Estadísticas generales de secuestro: Enero de 1996—junio del 2008" and "Comportamiento de secuestro 1996—junio 2008," Fundación País Libre, http://www.paislibre.org/index.php?option=com_content&task=blogcategory&id=28&Itemid=84.

2. I have freely translated this passage from Hernández Mora (2008).

3. See also Alexander and Smith (1993).

4. I am grateful to Carlos José Suárez for pointing me to the salience of the idea of the bandit in Colombian traditional culture during a presentation of a preliminary version of this chapter to the members of the Research Group on "Social Conflict and Violence" of the National University of Colombia in Bogotá.

5. The fact that the discourse of the *hacienda* comes quite close to the corporate code Baiocchi (2006) talks about with reference to Brazil reflects the

partial commonalities Latin American countries share in terms of their political development as well as their social and cultural history.

6. The neo-Durkheimian tradition within sociology has systematically attempted to extend Durkheim's theoretical framework to more closely account for social life in modern societies. Alexander's recent macro-sociological model of social action as performance is the latest and possibly the most advanced step neo-Durkheimians have taken in this direction. In 2006, Reed published an essay titled "Social Dramas, Shipwrecks and Cockfights: Three Types of Social Performance," where he drew a crucial analytical distinction between situations of "conflict with complicity," in which the participants share the same cultural world, and situations of "conflict without complicity," in which the members of two different cultural worlds come into contact and exchange between each other. Reed's criterion of demarcation made it easier to realize that up to that point neo-Durkheimian sociology had systematically addressed the phenomenon of "conflict with complicity" in modern social life but had almost completely disregarded the study of "conflict without complicity," thereby falling short of completely coming to terms with the question of cultural difference. Since cultural difference appears to be an endemic feature of modern complex societies, it seems reasonable to conclude that the neo-Durkheimian quest for an extension of Durkheimian theory will hardly be completed unless it directly addresses the question of cultural reenchantment across cultural divides. Bringing into the research agenda the study of cultural mechanisms that unfold across them, such as ambivalent performances, may therefore help take one first step in that direction.

Works Cited

Abad Faciolince, H. 2005. Izquierda y guerrilla. *Semana,* December 12.

———. 2008. Sobre la marcha. *Semana,* February 4.

Alexander, J. 2004. Toward a Theory of Cultural Trauma. In *Cultural trauma,* eds. J. Alexander et al. Berkeley: University of California Press.

———. 2006a. Cultural Pragmatics: Social Performance between Ritual and Strategy. In *Social Performance,* eds. J. Alexander, B. Giesen, and J. Mast. Cambridge: Cambridge University Press.

———. 2006b. *The Civil Sphere.* Oxford: Oxford University Press.

Alexander, J., and P. Smith. 1993. The Discourse of American Civil Society: A New Proposal for Cultural Studies. *Theory and Society* 22(2): 151–207.

Alexander, J., R. Eyerman, B. Giesen, and P. Sztompka, eds. 2004. *Cultural Trauma.* Berkeley: University of California Press.

Amat, Y. 2008. El País está cayendo en un peligroso ambiente de polarización. *El Tiempo,* February 3.

Arbaláez, J. 2007. Viaje a pie. *El Tiempo,* August 1.

Baiocchi, G. 2006. The Civilizing Forces of Social Movements: Corporate and Liberal Codes in Brazil's Public Sphere. *Sociological Theory* 24(4): 285–311.

Barthes, R. 1977. Rhetoric of the Image. In *Image, Music, Text*, ed. S. Heath. New York: Hill and Wang.

Benedetti Jimeno, A. 2007. Rincón Caribe al fin apareció un Moncayo. *El Tiempo*, August 6.

Castillo Cardona, C. 2007. Golpe de estado. *El Tiempo*, August 8.

Cuellar, S. 2009. *Entre la Hacienda y la sociedad civil: Lógicas culturales de la guerra en Colombia*. MA Thesis, Department of Sociology, National University of Colombia, Bogotá.

Duzán, M. J. 2008. Y los Secuestrados, ¿Qué se pudran? *El Tiempo*, March 24.

El Tiempo. 2007a. Día 8: El profesor Gustavo Moncayo llegó a Popayán en su recorrido por el acuerdo humanitario. June 25.

———. 2007b. 24.000 colombianos han sido secuestrados en la última década; 1.269 han muerto en cautiverio. June 30.

———. 2007c. El episodio de Uribe y Moncayo: Pueblo vs. Pueblo. August 13.

———. 2007d. FARC elogian a Moncayo. No responden sobre su hijo. August 14.

———. 2007e. Los partidos y sus vínculos con grupos armados. September 14.

———. 2007f. La crisis del Polo. September 16.

———. 2007g. Gustavo Moncayo, ganador del premio Nacional de Paz, dice que prefiere la libertad de su hijo. December 5.

———. 2008a. Carta del Coronel Luis Mendieta se convirtió en símbolo de la crueldad del cautiverio en la selva. January 16.

———. 2008b. Los organizadores de la marcha del 4 de febrero ratificaron que es contra las FARC. January 30.

———. 2008c. El rescate de los 15 mejor que el 5 a 0 a Argentina. July 8.

Estrada Gallego, F. 2004. *Las metáforas de una guerra perpetua. Estudios sobre pragmática del discurso en el conflicto armado colombiano*. Medellín: Editorial Universidad EAFIT.

FARC. 2007. Comunicado: 43 Aniversario de las FARC-EP. Secretariat of the Central Command of the FARC-EP, May 25, at http://www.redresistencia.org from www.farcep.org.

Forero, J. 2007. After a Long Trek across Colombia, Hostage Advocate Not Ready to Rest. *Washington Post Foreign Service*, August 24.

García Villegas, M. 2008. Marchar sin advertencias. *El Tiempo*, February 5.

Gombrich, E. 1972. *Symbolic Images: Studies in the Art of the Renaissance*. London and New York: Phaidon.

Gonzáles Posso, C. 2007. El caminante por la libertad. *El Tiempo*, August 2.

Gutiérrez de Pineda, V. 1992. *Honor, familia y sociedad en la estructura patriarcal*. Bogotá: Universidad Nacional de Colombia.

Hernández Bolivar, S. 2007. En el lugar equivocado. Al profesor Moncayo. *El Tiempo*, August 7.

Hernández Mora, S. 2008. Con licencia de juzgar. *El Tiempo*, January 20.

Jimeno, M. 2009. La "victima" y la construcción de comunidades emocionales. Mimeo, Centro de Estudios Sociales, Universidad Nacional de Colombia, Bogotá.

Miño Rueda, L. A. 2007a. Nooooooooo. *El Tiempo*, July 16.

———. 2007b. Moncayo, de maestro de geografía a ídolo nacional. *El Tiempo*, July 22.

Morales, J. 1998. Mestizaje, malicia indígena y viveza en la construcción del carácter nacional. *Revista de Estudios Sociales* 1: 39–43.

Navia, J. 2007. Moncayo paralizó todo a su paso. *El Tiempo*, August 2.

Ochoa, L. N. 2008a. No nos tiremos la marcha. *El Tiempo*, January 26.

———. 2008b. Carta a Ingrid. *El Tiempo*, April 5.

———. 2007c. La plaza de Moncayo. *El Tiempo*, August 4.

Padget, J., and C. Ansell. 1993. Robust Action and the Rise of the Medicis, 1400–1432. *American Journal of Sociology* 98(6): 1259–1319.

Palacios, M. 1999. *Agenda para la democracia y negociación con las guerrillas.* In *Los laberintos de la guerra*, ed. F. Leal Buitrago. Bogotá: Tercer Mundo Editores.

Pombo, M. 2007. Dolor de carne y hueso. *El Tiempo*, December 6.

Posada Carbó, E. 2008. El estado y la opinión mundial. *El Tiempo*, January 11.

Reed, I. 2006. Social Dramas, Shipwrecks and Cockfights: Three Types of Social Performance. In *Social performance*, eds. J. Alexander, B. Giesen, and J. Mast. Cambridge: Cambridge University Press.

Rincón, H. 2002. El oso polar. *Cambio*, March 18.

Rubio, M. 2003. *Del rapto a la pesca milagrosa: breve historia del secuestro en Colombia.* Documento Cede, No. 2003-36. Bogotá: Universidad de los Andes, CEDE.

Semana. 2007a. Grabando, grabando … May 7.

———. 2007b. La procesión de un padre. June 25.

———. 2008. La Marcha de la Rabia. February 4.

Smelser, N. 1998. The Rational and the Ambivalent in the Social Sciences. *American Sociological Review* 63(1): 1–16.

Smith, P., and J. Alexander. 2005. Introduction: the New Durkheim. In *The Cambridge Companion to Durkheim*, eds. J. Alexander and P. Smith. Cambridge: Cambridge University Press.

Tognato, C., and S. Cuellar. 2009. Understanding Political Crises across Cultural Divides: Insights from a Military "Shipwreck" in Colombia. Mimeo, Department of Sociology, National University of Colombia, Bogotá.

Turner, V. 1974. *Drama, Fields and Metaphors.* Ithaca: Cornell University Press.

Vivanco, J. Ml. 2002. Colombia: Setter to Rebel Leader Demands Release of Kidnapped Political Figures. *Human Rights Watch*, April 15.

Voz. 2008. Editorial. February 6.

9

Claiming Trauma through Social Performance

The Case of *Waiting for Godot*[1]

Elizabeth Butler Breese

In November 2007, Samuel Beckett's play *Waiting for Godot: A Tragicomedy in Two Acts* was performed in two neighborhoods in New Orleans: Gentilly and the Lower Ninth Ward. In Gentilly, a house destroyed by Hurricane Katrina served as the set; in the Lower Ninth Ward, the play was performed at an intersection of formerly busy streets. On face value, the production of a classic French Surrealist play on the streets of two neighborhoods largely destroyed by Hurricane Katrina is curious. Why did producers stage, actors perform, or audiences attend this play in such unlikely locations? What did the play mean to the audience and actors in New Orleans? And what did the production convey to audiences other than the one physically present at the performances?

By examining productions of *Waiting for Godot* in New Orleans and in Sarajevo in 1993, I demonstrate that carrier groups and social actors use art, in addition to claims to fact,[2] to construct claims to trauma. Some claims to trauma accuse. Through fact-oriented speech and action, social actors indict a party as guilty of causing suffering. Political leaders deliver speeches to assign guilt and argue for the veracity of their claims to trauma. Textbooks teach children the "truth" of past conflicts, specifying the aggressor and the victim, the trauma and the triumph (see Gao's Chapter 3 in this book). Other claims to trauma reveal. Through expressive and artistic performance, social actors represent elements of their experience and construct them as traumatic. Painting, dance, song, film, and drama do not accuse in the political or juridical realm; social actors use artistic productions to represent, to speak for, and to construct trauma.

The productions of *Waiting for Godot* in Sarajevo and New Orleans, I argue, are social performances as well as theatrical performances that construct and express trauma. Directors, producers, actors, journalists, and city residents specify elements of trauma for the local collectivity and for a wider audience through productions of this canonical play. Samuel Beckett wrote *Waiting for Godot* in the aftermath of World War II. Now a classic of the theater, *Waiting for Godot* debuted as an avant-garde piece for a Parisian audience that was cultivating an appreciation of experimental theater. Even within this avant-garde context, Beckett revolutionized theater. *Waiting for Godot* features neither plot progression nor a clear referent (Bradby 2001, 24–25); the play, many scholars and critics explain, presents the existential experience of waiting itself (see Esslin [1961] 1980). This chapter explores how *Waiting for Godot,* a play which cannot properly be said to be "about" anything, represents trauma in these two cities. Contradicting Pierre Bourdieu's understanding of both art and culture ([1979] 1984), social actors and audiences which could be considered mixed or even lowbrow appropriate this work of high art and use it to represent and construct the meanings of their experience. Specifically, social actors in these cities use Beckett's decidedly highbrow and famously "meaningless" play to represent, dramatize, define, and communicate their experiences as traumatic.

The central proposal of cultural trauma theory is that trauma does not simply *happen*; events and their aftermath must be constructed as traumatic. Social actors make and communicate claims about their trauma—"the nature of the pain, the nature of the victim, the relation of the trauma victim and the wider audience, and the attribution of responsibility" (Alexander 2004, 13–15)—through these productions of *Waiting for Godot* to audiences physically present at the performances as well as to audiences that read and hear journalists' accounts of them. The productions of *Waiting for Godot* in Sarajevo and New Orleans are social performances whose "success" is not achieved in the register of factual truth. Like Picasso's *Guernica* and other artistic constructions and claims to trauma, the success, or re-fusion, of the social performance of trauma through *Godot* is achieved in the register of expressive aptness. We must understand both fact-based and expressive claims to trauma and their different measures of success to evaluate how and why trauma processes begin or fail, continue or stall.

Waiting for Godot and Its Reception

In the first act of *Waiting for Godot,* Estragon and Vladimir meet on a road and commence waiting for Godot to arrive. The set is simple; the stage directions indicate only "A country road. A tree. Evening." Like clowns and music-hall performers, Vladimir and Estragon banter in the form of a "cross-talk act," which features interruptions, double meanings, and misunderstandings (Bradby 2001, 43). Eventually Lucky, burdened by packages and with a rope around his neck, and Pozzo, holding a whip, enter the stage. Pozzo bosses Lucky with commands such as "Up pig!" (Beckett [1954] 1982, 20). Pozzo and Lucky depict an interdependent master-slave relationship, while Vladimir and Estragon are cross-talk performers whose symbiotic relationship takes on different shades— friends, an old married couple, or two comedians—depending on the performance (Bradby 2001, 30). Toward the end of Act I, a boy comes to announce that Mr. Godot will not "come this evening but surely to-morrow" (Beckett [1954] 1982, 55).

In Act II, the set and the actors appear physically diminished; Pozzo is now blind. As the play ends, Vladimir and Estragon discuss committing suicide but decide to wait to see if Godot will come tomorrow. Typically in drama and literature, meaning is delivered via standard elements such as the topic of the piece, progression of the plot, and character development. Actions happen in sequence, building toward an end and a resolution from which meaning or a lesson may be gleaned. *Godot,* however, does not adhere to this structure. In the characters' last exchange, they decide to go, yet the stage direction reads, "They do not move" (Beckett [1954] 1982, 109). The last pairing of utterance and stage direction in the play, when the travelers decide to go yet do not move, is an example of Beckett's treatment of the themes of movement and stasis in such a way as to unsettle meaning. Dialogue and action work at cross-purposes, and the "meaning," in a standard sense, is left open. Or, perhaps, it indicates that the meaning cannot be fixed or resolved. Throughout his life, Beckett declined to illuminate the "meanings" and symbolism of *Waiting for Godot* (Schneider 1967, 55).

Beginning with the inaugural production at the Théâtre de Babylone in Paris in 1953, critics, journalists and academics expressed considerable interest and anxiety over whether *Godot* would be "understood" and received favorably by audiences and critics. In fact, before Roger Blin agreed to direct *Waiting for Godot* at the Babylone, the play was rejected by several producers in Paris who worried it was "incomprehensible, boring, too highbrow, or too deep" (Bair 1978, 397). Despite the concerns, the first production in Paris proved extremely successful, running for four hundred performances at the Babylone before transferring to another theater in Paris (Esslin [1961] 1980, 39). Despite fears—which proved to be well-founded in some cases—that early audiences would not understand or connect with the play, *Waiting for Godot* has been staged extensively throughout the world,[3] and it is widely acclaimed as one of the premier dramatic works of the twentieth century.

Although the initial anxieties that audiences would not understand or respond positively to the play subsided as it achieved the status of classic drama, those concerns were replaced by others. Critics and academics now express concern that *Waiting for Godot* has lost its "*provocative* quality" and has become a "*safe* bet" to stage (Bradby 2001, 162). However, critics, journalists, and academics have long identified performances where their anxieties about reception are much less—or even ceased to be—of concern for reasons external to the logic of the theater (see Toole 1998). When *Godot* was feared to be too dark or too highbrow, audiences understood it. And when critics and academics feared *Godot* had become a mundane classic emptied of its theatrical surprises, audiences felt a vibrant connection to the play. In the beginning of *Beckett: Waiting for Godot*, Bradby attributes the varied receptions of the play to variations in the logic of the theater, "It was understood (and misunderstood) differently in the different theatrical cultures" (2001, 2). Yet, later in the book, he joins other critics and academics in acknowledging that the unique history of performances and audience reception of *Waiting for Godot* goes beyond the logic of the theater. In "situations of political oppression" the canonical drama has "special relevance" and becomes provocative once again (2001, 162).

Susan Sontag's production of *Waiting for Godot* in Sarajevo during the siege in the summer of 1993 is one of the productions in "situations of political oppression" cited by Bradby. In "Waiting for Godot in Sarajevo," Sontag recalls speaking with a director and producer during her first visit to Sarajevo the preceding spring about coming back to the city to direct a play. When he asked which play she would direct, Sontag recalls

> And bravado, following the impulsiveness of my proposal, suggested to me in an instant what I might not have seen had I taken longer to reflect: there was one obvious play for me to direct. Beckett's play,

written over forty years ago, seems written for, and about Sarajevo. (1994, 88)

Why did Sontag, an American writer and public intellectual with countless dramas to choose from, realize "in an instant" that *Waiting for Godot* was written for and about the situation in Sarajevo? How is it that *Godot*, the famously meaningless play, could be about the violence and suffering in that city?

In certain contexts—variously labeled political oppression or atrocity—concerns that critics, academics and journalists normally have about *Godot* lose their importance.[4] Instead of worrying whether *Godot* will be understood, critics and journalists reports it has "struck an instant chord" with the audience (Bradby 2001, 102). Instead of worrying about whether it has been performed too much, it seems instantly obvious to stage it and no other play (Sontag 1994, 88). These critics identify what, in the theory of social performance and cultural pragmatics, is conceptualized as "re-fusion" (Alexander, Giesen, and Mast 2006). In complex, mass mediated society, social life has been "de-fused" (Alexander 2006, 29). Rituals, which rely on shared meanings and cultural understandings, are rare. However, social actors in our complex social world continue to communicate the meanings of their social experiences through social performance. Performative "re-fusion" is achieved when the cultural meanings constructed, represented, and conveyed by the elements of social performance—the script, the actors, the setting, and the background—are collectively shared and understood and when they are seen as authentic. The goal of cultural pragmatics is to demonstrate "how social performance, whether individual or collective, can be analogized systemically to theatrical ones" (Alexander 2006, 29). I argue that the theatrical performance of *Waiting for Godot* is a social performance in contexts of trauma. In contexts of trauma, audiences seem to understand *Godot* and its deeply provocative qualities. "Re-fusion" in these contexts transcends the logic of the theater; audiences not only "enjoy" or "appreciate" the play, but it "speaks to" and "speaks for" their social situations.

Instead of the numerous explanations for re-fusion in these contexts, I offer one: Productions of *Waiting for Godot* have achieved fusion in contexts of trauma. To label these circumstances of trauma is more than a parsimonious solution for understanding the circumstances in which *Waiting for Godot* is something other—something more—than an avant-garde play or a classic drama. Examining these productions through news accounts and artists' statements helps clarify the relationship between collective trauma, a concept describing communities affected by disasters, and cultural trauma, which argues that traumas are not born but made.

Collective trauma theorizes important elements of mood and emotion, but we must remain vigilant that it is not events which are traumatic but it is our construction of occurrences as traumatic to cultural structures and expectations that make them so. Further, looking at productions of *Waiting for Godot* in Sarajevo and New Orleans illustrates the ways in which claims to trauma may be made performatively as well as factually. Through their productions of *Waiting for Godot*, social actors define the trauma—what the trauma means to the community, who the victims are, and who the perpetrators are—using aesthetics and performative acts rather than fact-based evidence such as testimony and statistics.

Trauma Theory: Mood and Meaning

Academic and clinical work on trauma began in the realm of psychiatry; Freud is the most famous early theorist of trauma (Smelser 2004, 32). Sociologists have specified two additional types of trauma: collective (or social) trauma and cultural trauma. Kai Erikson's seminal study of Buffalo Creek, an Appalachian mining community physically destroyed by a flood of mining sludge, illustrates the central elements of collective trauma (1976). Collective trauma holds as its main tenet that "one can speak of traumatized communities as something distinct from assemblies of traumatized persons" (Erikson 1995, 185). In his *précis* on cultural trauma, Jeffrey Alexander acknowledges Erikson's contribution of conceptualizing trauma as a collective as well as individual phenomenon but criticizes Erikson for holding a "naturalistic perspective" in which trauma is treated as a quality inherent in certain events due to their sudden, devastating, violent, or shocking nature (2004, 2–4). Later in his career, Erikson seems to argue for a less-naturalistic position for collective trauma. In "Notes on Trauma and Community," an essay reflecting on decades of fieldwork and study of disasters, Erikson points out that his dictionary defines "trauma" as a "a stress or blow that may produce disordered feelings or behavior" and "the state or condition produced by such a stress or blow" (1995, 184). Erikson encourages his readers to shift their emphasis to the latter definition "because it is *how people react to them* rather than *what they are* that give events whatever traumatic quality they can be said to have" (Author's emphasis 1995, 184). Cultural trauma goes further, arguing that trauma is produced when members of collectivities successfully construct an event or a series of events as significantly and indelibly undermining part or all of their culture and system of meanings (Alexander et al. 2004, 10 and 38). It is in the process of claiming trauma that the productions of *Waiting for Godot* speak for and construct the trauma in Sarajevo and New Orleans.

In addition to denying that traumas are born fully formed and specified, we must also unsettle the idea of the "collective" in collective trauma. Collective trauma signals that a group imagined to constitute a collective suffers a trauma together. Collective trauma, however, can form or refigure the collective—its membership, bonds, mutual responsibilities, and stance toward outsiders. We should think of Erikson's "traumatized communities" as a collective that has, in a Durkheimian sense, a reality and a set of logics external to individuals. It is this Durkheimian collective which experiences social trauma. Erikson argues that "trauma damages the texture of community" (1995, 187) in two ways: by damaging social bonds and by creating a social climate of trauma. Specifying the latter sense of damage to the community, Erikson (1995) writes,

> … traumatic experiences work their way so thoroughly into the grain of the affected community that they come to supply its *prevailing mood and temper,* dominate its imagery and its sense of self, govern the way its members relate to one another. (Emphasis added, 190)

Erikson wishes to dispel a common and rather sentimentalized vision that communities experiencing trauma enjoy a "wave of good feeling" when they realize that they and their community have survived the initial disaster; he has never witnessed this sort of euphoria in any of his fieldwork nor read about it in the recent literature (1995, 189). Instead, collective trauma is characterized by a loss of community bonds, lack of trust in the future and in one's neighbors, and a collective mood of fear and depression (Erikson 1976). Although we must be clear in our understanding of the concept of collective trauma and the language we use to describe it, I contend that collective trauma remains an important sociological concept for understanding when and how communities and collectives experience events as traumatic. Collective trauma may or may not become a cultural trauma through a "trauma process" of claiming trauma through articulation, representation, construction, and counter-construction (Alexander et al. 2004, esp. 11).

Erikson's study of the Buffalo Creek disaster indicates that collective trauma is characterized by perseveration on the traumatic occurrence. In Buffalo Creek, residents lived in constant, illogical fear of another flood. Many residents reported difficulty sleeping and feeling agitated and apprehensive when it rained (Erikson 1976, 179). The occurrence is over, but the emotions stay with the individuals and shape the collective mood. Days and weeks go by, but the mood of collective trauma lingers.

When performed in these situations, *Waiting for Godot* expresses waiting, uncertainty, anguish, and fear that the people experiencing collective trauma feel acutely in their daily lives. Like Vladimir and Estragon, individuals and collectives experiencing collective trauma do not know when their situation will end. Nor, like Beckett's hobos, do they know what that end will look like in terms of the bonds of community that have been forged, challenged, and upset during the occurrence and the collective trauma.

Collective trauma is primarily an emotional state, whereas cultural trauma is an emotional and cognitive process having to do with construction and contestation of meaning. Cultural trauma entails narratives that specify the victim, perpetrator, the relationship between them, and the nature of the suffering. In addition, social actors and carrier groups publicly question and reflect on the nature of the community and its cultural underpinnings during the cultural trauma process. They ask what it means to experience suffering and uncertainty that undermine previous foundational assumptions and values. In Sarajevo, residents involved in the production of *Godot* and audience members reflect on what it means to be a European civilization experiencing savage violence through the play. Productions of *Waiting for Godot* are social performances through which the collective can represent and communicate its present state to itself. However, productions of *Waiting for Godot* do not become social performances expressing trauma on their own. Claims to trauma do not speak for themselves. There is a "need for walking and talking—and seeing and listening to the walking and talking" that theater and social performance, and theater as social performance, can provide (Alexander 2006, 33). Like theater performances, social performances require actors, audiences, scripts and settings. Social actors perform and multiple audiences—the in-person audience, journalists, and media consumers—observe and interpret the social performance of trauma via *Waiting for Godot*.

Performing Trauma for Multiple Audiences

Beckett intended *Waiting for Godot* to defy definition and fixed interpretations (Bradby 2001, 17). The play does not feature an explicit referent, and, what is more, literary scholars have argued that Beckett's *Godot*, lacking standard plot development and resolution, revolutionized the narrative logic of drama. The meaning of the play in a standard sense is left open. Depicting waiting and uncertainty without resolution, productions of *Godot* honoring Beckett's authorial intentions could express the "mood and temper" of collective trauma. However, as we will see, productions of *Waiting for Godot* in contexts of collective trauma have gone beyond mood to articulate the meaning of the situation and the identity of "the players." Against the grain of Beckett's narrative logic, audiences and producers insert meanings into the famously "meaningless" play by specifying victims, perpetrators, and the nature of their trauma. The first production of *Waiting for Godot* in Paris provides a good example. Blin, the director, depicted Pozzo as well-dressed, upper-class, and cruel, while Lucky appeared in tattered clothing and constantly trembling. Contemporary audiences experienced "extreme horror and revulsion" at the representation—through their abusive relationship and apparent class difference—of a Nazi-victim duo (Bradby 2001, 61–63). Beckett's potentially generic master-slave pair was rendered and read in Paris as a reference to the collective trauma of Parisians at the time.[5]

The central contribution of cultural trauma is the insistence that occurrences—even horrific ones—are not automatically traumatic on a social and culture level; events must become traumatic. Groups construct and represent events and their aftermath as threatening or damaging to the meaning structures which underpin, and indeed constitute, the collective. Social actors construct events as traumatic in institutions such as courts and parliaments using fact-based evidence including numbers of the dead, the cost of destruction, and victims' and witnesses' testimony (Alexander 2004, 15–20). Individuals and groups also use artistic expressions to represent and construct trauma in the social and cultural realms. The news media play a crucial role in both fact-based and expressive claims to trauma; journalists and intellectuals report and interpret the construction and contestation of trauma narratives in other institutional realms. Through their reports, journalists and writers convey trauma constructions and "expressively dramatize" traumas in the mass media (Alexander 2004, 18).

Social performance requires actors to creatively act as well as multiple audiences to interpret the performance, including the audience that is physically present to witness the act and the news media that convey, interpret, and judge constructions of trauma. Rauer identifies three layers of audiences that witness, interpret, and judge social performance in his case study of German Chancellor Willy Brandt's *Kniefall* at the monument to those who suffered and died in the Warsaw Ghetto: an in-person audience, those who produce news accounts, and the media consumers who hear or read their reports (Rauer 2006, 259–260). Rauer disaggregates the audience of social performance analytically to understand the different ways audiences contribute to the social performance or diffuse it through their actions and interpretations. Social performance requires fusion with each layer of audience to become a salient performance. However, Rauer does not discuss the ability of social actors to shape how audiences, including the news reporters, receive and perceive the social performance. In addition to using Rauer's three layers of audience to analyze the interpretations of the social performance by the various audiences of the productions of *Waiting for Godot*, I show that analytically disaggregating the layers of audience illuminates different performative strategies of the social actors who produced and directed *Waiting for Godot* in Sarajevo and New Orleans.

The first-order audience consists of the spectators who are present for the performance; they react in real time to an action happening in their physical space (Rauer 2006, 260). Journalists and critics, the second-order audience, must interpret an occurrence and convey it to a wider audience for it to achieve social and cultural importance, for an *occurrence* to become a salient social *event* (Mast 2006, 118). There is often overlap in the layers of audience (Rauer 2006, 260); some of the journalists who reported on the productions of *Waiting for Godot* in New Orleans and in Sarajevo physically attended a performance. Journalists report on the performative act, recounting what happened and by whom. They also encode the meaning of the event, interpreting the actions and declaring their consequence. Journalists and critics pronounce a performance a "success" or a "failure." A social performance is a "success" on a theoretical level when the audience, the *mise-en-scene*, script, and the actors achieve re-fusion (Alexander 2006). To achieve re-fusion, a social performance must be perceived as spontaneous rather than calculated, authentic not manufactured (Rauer 2006, 259 and 275). Journalists and critics indicate the success or failure of a performance using these criteria and by citing and interpreting the reactions of the in-person audience. When journalists convey the reactions—laughter, gasps, comments, silence, and tears—to their readers and listeners, those who are present for the action are simultaneously audience and actors in the social performance (Rauer 2006, 260).

Journalists and critics encode the meanings of the performance for the third-order audience: media consumers. The third-order audience reads reports in newspapers and blogs, hears about the performance on the radio, and sees visual representations of it on television and the Internet. An occurrence becomes an event, and action becomes social performance, in part through the sheer dissemination to a wide third-order audience. The third-order audience members "more or less depend" on the interpretations of the journalists and critics and their assessment of performative success or failure (Rauer 2006, 260). However, the third-order audience is not populated by passive consumers; although their reactions are notoriously difficult for social analysts to capture, the third-order audience will interpret the meaning of the performance and form their own opinions regarding its authenticity and significance.

In Sarajevo during the siege and in New Orleans after Hurricane Katrina, social actors—directors, producers, stage actors, and residents—appealed to all three layers of audience in their social performance of trauma through the theatrical production of Beckett's *Waiting for Godot*. In these locations, the play expresses the mood of collective trauma in Erikson's sense. However, the metaphor of waiting does not speak for itself. The social actors make claims to trauma by inserting references to the nature of the trauma, the victims, and the perpetrators into Beckett's referent-free play. These references specify and construct the trauma for the individuals who are living through the traumatic occurrence as well for the wider public from whom those claiming trauma seek recognition and solidarity.

Waiting for Godot in Sarajevo

Susan Sontag traveled to Sarajevo in 1993 to direct *Waiting for Godot* as the city's residents were being ravaged by indiscriminate violence, power outages, and widespread hunger. Sontag appealed to three layers of audience through her performative project: those who attended the performances in the Youth Theater in Sarajevo in August 1993, the journalists who wrote about the production, and the individuals who heard and read those accounts. I will discuss how Sontag and the other social actors involved in the production made claims to trauma through the play to appeal to each layer of audience and the ways in which the play achieved, or was said to achieve, performative re-fusion. Of course, there was overlap in strategies of appealing to and interpretation by the layers of audience: what the production of *Waiting for Godot* meant, or was said to mean, to the people of Sarajevo affects what it means, or what it is said to mean, to the audiences beyond the city.

How was the production of *Godot* experienced and interpreted by the people in Sarajevo? To analyze the first-order audience almost two decades later without having attended the performance, I must rely on individuals' accounts, including Sontag's essays and comments by residents of Sarajevo as they are quoted by journalists. Artistic culture, European identity, and feeling abandoned by their fellow Europeans were very much related for residents of Sarajevo in the summer of 1993. Sarajevo's residents, who had sustained a vibrant intellectual and cultural life based in European artistic traditions, were now living without electricity or proper food and in constant fear for their lives. Many of them felt that their European neighbors allowed them to suffer due to their reticence to intervene in the violence. Under ongoing attack, residents bitterly recognized that cultural solidarity with Europe did not extend to political solidarity. Boujan Zec, a Sarajevan journalist, was quoted in *The Guardian*, "Writers like Hemingway risked their lives for liberty in Spain. Now all that Europe can do is send us a few packets of aid" (Narayan 1993, 2). By participating in the production of *Godot*, the local actors, theater support staff, and first-order audience members reinforced for themselves their collective identity as civilized Europeans worthy of being saved from savage violence. The actor Velibor Topic, who played one of the Estragons, was also quoted in *The Guardian*, "There is not only fighting on the front line. We must tell the world that we are not animals. We are cultured, we have ideas and dreams" (Narayan 1993). The production of *Waiting for Godot* and the media attention it generated was a way to showcase that culture and civility persevere in Sarajevo. As Topic indicates, the production of *Waiting for Godot*, a well-known and highbrow play, articulated their collective identity as civilized Europeans to the residents of Sarajevo as well as to audiences outside the city.

The residents of Sarajevo were also widely quoted by journalists and by Sontag saying that *Waiting for Godot* made sense to perform in their historical moment because they, too, were waiting. They were waiting for in intervention by the United States, President Clinton, the United Nations, and their European neighbors. John Pomfret includes one of the actor's reflections on the figure of Godot in his article for the *Washington Post*, "You never know when something is going to come crashing down and blow your head apart ... That's my own personal Godot" (Pomfret 1993). Using the same sort of language as the academic David Bradby when he identified *Godot's* "special relevance," a British reporter writes, "The play's message has touched a chord among Sarajevans beyond the tiny theatre-going public. 'I hear Ms. Sontag is waiting for Godot—we are waiting for the Europeans and the Americans,' commented Jovan Divjak, a Bosnian army chief. 'Did Godot ever show up?'" (Tanner 1993). The residents waited for an uncertain end to the violence, and the production of *Godot* is a way to express their status to those for whom they wait.

The journalists and critics, including Sontag herself, who wrote about the production of *Godot* in Sarajevo largely focused on the desperation in Sarajevo and how apt the metaphor of waiting was for the residents' situation. Soon after returning to the United States in the fall of 1993, Sontag wrote two similar essays about her experience directing the play in the beleaguered city. Published in the *New York Review of Books* and the *Performing Arts Journal*, Sontag targeted her reflections and interpretations of the performance to an elite, intellectual, and largely American audience. In "Waiting for Godot in Sarajevo," Sontag wrote that she traveled to Sarajevo to direct a production of *Waiting for Godot* in order to "pitch in and do something" (1994, 87). Although Sontag insisted that she could not go to Sarajevo merely to act as a witness to the violence, she is that too. In her essay, she provides details about life in the city that read like an ethnographic account. Sontag describes the emotional tableau of collective trauma, stringing together observations that echo Erikson's fieldwork in Buffalo Creek:

> ... many Sarajevans are reluctant to leave their apartments except when it is absolutely necessary ... though no one is safe anywhere, they have more fear when they are in the street. And beyond fear, there is depression—most Sarajevans are very depressed—which produces lethargy, exhaustion, apathy. (1994, 90)

Further, Sontag reports that the residents are "waiting, hoping, not wanting to hope," and they are "humiliated" (1994, 91). The forces promoting what Erikson called the "prevailing mood and temper" of collective trauma were constant; the real danger had not subsided in Sarajevo. Snipers threatened to kill people on the street and in their homes. Residents lacked electricity, and waited in lines to receive daily rations of food and water from the United Nations. Sontag notes that her actors suffered from fatigue and malnutrition; one formerly overweight actress lost more than sixty pounds during the war. The newspaper accounts of the situation in Sarajevo and of the plight of the people there mention many of the same details Sontag includes in her essays.

The second-order audience, the journalists, established that *Godot* was, in fact, an apt metaphor in large part by describing the reactions of the actors and the audience in the theater. Many journalists describe what happened and interpret the mood in Youth Theater during the performances by mentioning particular details such as what materials appeared on stage, what the actors wore, and how the house was lit. I quote John Burns of the *New York Times*:

> A charged silence settled over the theater as actors and audience took a long, painful pause, digesting a message of hope deceived that is a defining passage of a new dramatic production performed here for the first time on Tuesday. To hear the silence of the packed house in the small theater in the city center was to feel the grief and disappointment that weigh on Sarajevo as it nears the end of its second summer under siege. (1993)

By declaring a match between the situation "on the ground" and the play using the stunned, silent, pensive, and emotional reaction of the in-person audience as evidence, the journalists declared *Waiting for Godot* a performative "success." The journalists indicated to their reading and listening audience that *Godot* re-fused the setting, script, audience, and actors into a shared experience of meaning. They conveyed that everyone in Sarajevo understand exactly what *Godot* meant and why it was important to perform in Sarajevo at that moment. And, importantly, during the performance of the play, performed around the world so many times before, the Sarajevan audience saw not only a classic dramatic work; they saw themselves.

To convey to their listening and reading audience how apt the metaphor was for waiting, uncertainty, and anxiety in Sarajevo, many journalists repeated variations on the statement "the metaphor of waiting for intervention was well understood" (Narayan 1993). Often, they established the resonance of *Godot* by describing that the in-person audience was riveted by the performance, collectively understanding its significance in their place and time. However, Beckett's script and the metaphor of waiting did not speak unaided for the trauma of the Sarajevans. Sontag and the actors changed significant elements of Beckett's play, including the set, the characters, and the length of the play, to signify their circumstance and to depict their trauma for the audience beyond the besieged city. Such changes would be notable in almost any dramatic performance, but insertions into the play to establish the meaning of the situation is additionally surprising in *Godot*: Beckett and his estate are (in)famously inflexible, rarely allowing productions to deviate from Beckett's authorial intentions for the staging of his plays (e.g. the *Times* 1993).[6] More importantly for this study, by specifying the nature of the suffering and the victims, the social actors insert trauma as a referent into a play that does not carry one of its own.

Instead of one pair of protagonists, Sontag staged three pairs of Vladimirs and Estragons as "three variations on the theme of the couple" with one mixed gender, one male, and one female couple. She reports she made the decision, at least in part, to "employ"—a symbolic rather than monetary concept—more actors (1994, 92). However, a journalist quotes her explaining to her actors, "Beckett was still thinking in that old way of thinking; that if these characters are to be representative then they should be men" (Eagar 1993). In addition to lightening the burden of her exhausted and malnourished actors, Sontag explains that the extra pairs of travelers have the symbolic value of representing both men and women, male and female Sarajevans, who wait for Godot alike and together. Pomfret, writing for the *Washington Post*, declares, "This troika succeeds on the stage as each pair—two women, two men, and a man and a woman—explore different parts of the waiting game as they inhabit a world garnished with ammo boxes, sandbags and a hospital bed—part of the spiritual architecture of life in Sarajevo" (Pomfret 1993). In addition to declaring the representation of all Sarajevans through the three character pairs a performative success, Pomfret also indicates that the production introduced meanings of trauma into the set of *Godot,* which is usually exceedingly sparse. David Bradby argues that the most important aspect of the setting of *Godot* is its "neutrality: it provides an empty space, neither historically conditioned nor socially appropriated" (2001, 34). However, Sontag's actors presented *Waiting for Godot* "on a stage lit by candles, and with Red Cross boxes and UN sandbags as props …" (Pomfret 1993). In one of her nods to Beckett in her essay, Sontag comments that her staging was "as minimally furnished, I thought, as Beckett himself could have desired" (1994, 96). She fails to mention the war paraphernalia invoking the Red Cross and the United Nations, material representations of trauma, decorating the stage.

Sontag only staged the first act of the play. In her essay on the production, she points out that the first act is "itself a complete play" without the repetition and the stasis of the second act (1994, 97). She reports that she decided to stage only the first half of the play because her actors and audience could not sustain the energy required for a longer performance. However, Sontag undermined her explanation of this as a logistical decision in comments to her audiences. Pomfret attended a performance in Sarajevo where Sontag announced, "Its correct title, then, is 'Waiting for Godot: Act 1.' We are all waiting for Act 2" (Pomfret 1993). Of course, Beckett's Godot never arrives. Sontag's Godot may still arrive in the Act 2 that is yet to unfold. Until he arrives—and perhaps even if he does—he is a guilty party in their trauma.

So far, it sounds very much like all the journalists agree that *Waiting for Godot* represented the situation in Sarajevo and that the residents of Sarajevo responded to this resonance and relevance. This is largely true. But that is not to say that there were no criticisms of staging *Godot* in Sarajevo. The criticisms, however, did not pertain to whether or not the claims made implicitly and explicitly through the play—that the Sarajevans suffer from deep existential uncertainty and physical decline as they wait for the United States, the United Nations, and their European neighbors to intervene in the violence. Rather, whether or not the play will be taken as a legitimate, successful social performance of trauma hinges on whether the performance was spontaneous and authentic. Specifically, Sontag's motivations to come to the beleaguered city to direct the play were at issue for the layers of audiences. The critical question is not whether the meanings encoded by the performance are correct; the critical question is whether Sontag should have directed the play.

A vehement critic, Richard Grenier, wrote that Sontag has resumed "her position as the artist-moralist of the Western world" in the "lime-light" of Sarajevo (1993). Grenier's was the most ardent formulation of what occurred in whispers in other news pieces: Did Sontag seek out this high-profile cause to boost her own career, or did she seek to bring the world's attention to the situation in Sarajevo? Is it legitimate for an intellectual from the United States to travel to a war zone to direct a play? Although these questions were certainly not uniformly answered or resolved, many reporters' accounts assure the third-order audience that Sontag's presence and her work in the embattled Sarajevo theater scene were welcome by the Sarajevans. An editor of a Sarajevo news-paper that continued to publish during the shelling, Kemal Kurspahic, commented on the status of Sontag, "She is not a war tourist ... She has really tried to come here and talk to us and understand the situation" (Narayan 1993). The same news story states, as do several other reports, that Sontag declined, out of a sense of equality and solidarity, to wear her flak jacket. Some reporters write that a flak jacket lies nearby the famous intellectual, but, like her actors, she goes without its protection. Weigh-ing in on her authenticity as an artist in Sarajevo, Sontag tells a reporter, "You have to have some reason to be here. I'm not just a voyeur. I was invited to take part in a theatre festival ..." (Narayan 1993). Journalists and critics declared Sontag's production of *Waiting for Godot* a performative success. The meanings of the play resonated with the situation and the people. Sontag's changes to Beckett's stage directions were not overdone and those embellishments did not take away from, and in fact added to, the power of the play. Sontag's position and job as director were (largely) authentic and the production's connection with the audience seemed spontaneous and strong. In short, most journalists declared *Waiting for Godot* in Sarajevo a successful social performance of trauma.

Waiting for Godot in New Orleans

Graphic and performance artist Paul Chan knew of Sontag's produc-tion of *Waiting for Godot* in Sarajevo when he brought a production of Beckett's play to New Orleans in November 2007. Chan considers his production of *Godot* "within the lineage of imagining what it means to create art in places where we ought not to have any" (Simon 2007). Like Sontag's production in Sarajevo, Chan dramatizes and communicates the situation of the people living in New Orleans after Hurricane Katrina to the city's residents and to the wider world. And like Sontag's production, Chan and the director Christopher McElroen and the stage actors added specific references to their city and their situation to Beckett's austere drama to represent and to construct what it means to live in New Orleans after Hurricane Katrina. In a sense, Chan had at his disposal Beckett's script for the play as well as a script written by Sontag's production, the production at San Quentin, in South Africa and elsewhere for how to stage *Waiting for Godot* as a metaphor for trauma. The second "script" of *Godot* as a social performance of trauma indicates what can be altered in Beckett's play to make it speak for and construct trauma. Journalists comment on this "lineage" and how Chan uses the script passed down to him from Sontag, the prison productions, and others (Simon 2007; Cotter 2007). Also like the production in Sarajevo, in addition to expressive aptness which is required for the play to express and narrate trauma, the legitimacy of artists who direct and produce the play are at issue for residents and journalists.

Supported by the New York–based public art nonprofit Creative Time, Chan's production went well beyond Beckett's script and the previous productions from this "lineage" to mount a social performance of community and trauma. To advertise the performances, Chan and his theater group posted signs including only Beckett's first stage directions, "A country road. A tree. Evening." This whispering campaign knew no boundaries of class, race, or hurricane destruction; "good" and "bad" neighborhoods alike were garnished with the signs (Cotter 2007). A journalist for the *New York Times* describes that they "added up to a visual network, art as a connective tissue for a torn-apart town" (Cotter 2007). The journalist interprets for his readers that the social bonds that were broken by the storm will be restored through art's catharsis. Before the show went up, the producer and others involved with the production hosted theater workshops and attended potluck dinners with a variety of New Orleans residents. The local coverage in the *Times-Picayune* of this multifaceted art project helped to send out a casting call for local actors to audition for the play (Cuthbert 2007a). Chan cast three actors from the Classical Theater of Harlem production of *Waiting for Godot*, including Wendell Pierce who plays Detective Moreland on the popular television series *The Wire* and is a native son of New Orleans, as well as local actors (Cuthbert 2007b). The *Times-Picayune* listed phone numbers to call for reservations for the show and issued a call for volunteers to help with various aspects of the production (Cuthbert 2007b); the local paper also advertised that at each of the free performances the audience would share a gumbo dinner before being led into the seating area by second line bands (Cuthbert 2007d). In his artist statement, Chan explains that staging the play out-of-doors in Gentilly and in the Lower Ninth Ward accompanied by a brass band "connects with the city's storied tradition of street performance, from Mardi Gras to the Second lines that leisurely snake through streets and neighborhoods" (Chan 2007). Cotter (2007) reported in the *New York Times* that thousands of people attended the shows, and an extra performance was added to accommodate audience demand. The first-order audience did not merely occupy seats in a theater. Local residents, food, and music were part of the performance in New Orleans. On the day of the first performance, the *Times-Picayune* quoted Pierce exclaiming with a laugh, "We're gonna have a lot of New Orleans in this!" (Cuthbert 2007d). The local flavor surrounding the stage performance expresses to residents and to those outside the city that New Orleans has a unique and vibrant culture that should not languish or disappear.

News accounts of the project largely focused on the parallels between the characters, setting, and plot of *Godot* and the residents and their lives in New Orleans. Holland Cotter, writing for the *New York Times,* comments on the apt pairing of the text and the landscape in Gentilly and the Lower Ninth Ward, "Under the circumstances, Beckett's words sounded less like an existentialist *cri de coeur* than like a terse topographic description" (Cotter 2007). Cotter conveys to his reader that the set of *Godot,* which seems peculiarly sparse to many audiences, is simple description of reality in New Orleans. The text and the landscape merge, but a journalist for the *Times-Picayune* writes that the resonance between the play and the situation is fully expressed only through the performance, "Many lines in the 'Godot' text take on new meaning post-Katrina, but it is not until the actors speak them at the barren intersection in the Lower 9th Ward—both blighted and beautiful—that their full immediacy and import is felt" (Cuthbert 2007d). Another journalist for the *Times-Picayune* illustrates this "immediacy and import" by quoting the woman who sat next to him at the performance in the Ninth Ward. As Estragon sat on a curb on the stage, the woman in the audience remarked, "He's sitting there like me sitting on my stoop" (MacCash 2007). Beckett's characters and the characters in the drama of Katrina wait just the same, sitting on the stoop and watching up the road for Godot to arrive.

Like the woman in the Ninth Ward who sits on her stoop, several news articles about the production of *Godot* convey that the characters in this social performance have their own experiences of waiting like Beckett's hobos, the stage characters. Mark McLaughlin, who plays Lucky, told a reporter for the *Times-Picayune,* "I see this 'Godot' every single day on my block, where a Baptist church is a clearinghouse for all kinds of people in need" (Cuthbert 2007d). An article in the *Times-Picayune* divulges that Pierce, the famous television and movie actor, is angry about his parents' experiences dealing with government bureaucracy and "politics" to get recovery money after losing their home during Katrina. The reporter writes, "They went down to the office and found themselves playing an absurdist scene right out of 'Godot'" (Cuthbert 2007d). The characters of the social performance of trauma go beyond the stage actors. Radio and newspaper journalists introduce their third-order audience to Lower Ninth Ward resident Robert Green, whose mother and granddaughter both perished in the storm. Chan gave Green a copy of *Waiting for Godot*. Although skeptical of an outsider producing a play on the streets of his neighborhood, Green eventually read the play. Immediately after, he left an emphatic message on Chan's answer machine: He had to be part of the project (Simon 2007). A writer for the *Times-Picayune* places Green in his scene on show night. Green welcomes the play's audience, but the journalist hesitates to say "to his neighborhood" because Green's neighbors are gone, and he waits for them to come back (DeBerry 2007). Green is Vladimir and Estragon, and they represent him. The stage actors bring Beckett's characters to life on stage, and they are bringing Green's story to life as well.

In Sarajevo, *Godot* was performed concurrently with the violent siege; in New Orleans, more than two years elapsed between the storm and the production of *Godot*. Through the multifaceted social performance, the *Waiting for Godot* production and project in New Orleans articulated that the people in New Orleans continue to wait for their trauma to end. One way that the production represented the residents of New Orleans as "victims" was by casting a mix of African-American and local actors. The Lower Ninth Ward and Gentilly are predominantly black neighborhoods. Flooding in the city and the miserably slow response from the state and federal governments disproportionately affected black neighborhoods and black residents. By casting Beckett's travelers to "look like" the people in New Orleans, the production represented the identity of the victims of an ongoing trauma.

Journalists conveyed to their audience that the play represents the situation of the people of the Crescent City. Like Beckett's hobos, they wait for an object of desire, which they know only in a hazy form. And through the production, the actors and audience reflect on the meaning of their situation: Who is Godot? When is relief coming? How have the storm and its aftermath changed their city, and what, if anything, remains the same? None of the local or national newspaper or television reports that I surveyed disputes that Beckett's play uniquely represents life in New Orleans. Like in Sarajevo, questions about the legitimacy of the play, and the legitimacy of the social performance carried on through and around it, focus on the producers and directors who came to New Orleans from outside the city. Can artists legitimately create a claim to someone else's trauma? We learn from the productions of *Godot* in Sarajevo and in New Orleans that they may if they properly engage the local population by hiring them as actors, costumers, and stagehands. Chan partners with various community groups; two separate articles in the *Times-Picayune* and an article in the *New York Times* list a long roster of local partners in the *Godot* project including high schools, universities, and community organizations (Cuthbert 2007a; Cuthbert 2007c; Cotter 2007). Writing for the *Times-Picayune,* MacCash and Cuthbert write that Chan made New Orleans his "temporary home" for the duration of the *Godot* project (2007). He remains an outsider, but they convey that he is not merely a tourist-artist cashing in on New Orleans's misfortunes. In fact, they go on to quote an art world insider who suggests that having big-name artists and actors can be a good thing because the "power elites" of the art world will be at New Orleans's "doorstep" thanks to Chan's project. And, indeed, national and international newspaper and radio journalists covered Chan's project and, through this coverage, conveyed the meaning of the play and the meaning of the trauma to a wide audience. David Cuthbert, who covered the production over a span of two months for the *Times-Picayune* summed up the project's success in unifying and representing the broken city and its people for his readers: "The haves and have-nots in New Orleans right now are those who have seen 'Godot' and those who haven't" (2007e).

Claims to Trauma

Journalists, critics, and academics declare that *Waiting for Godot* is a metaphor for difficult situations. The set is a metaphor for the bleakness of landscape following a disaster; the depiction of waiting is a metaphor for waiting for suffering to end. However, even the most apt metaphors do not speak for themselves. I challenge the notion that the play simply stands for the situation of trauma. Instead, I show that social actors inject the play with meanings to express their situation as a trauma. Yet, to speak too explicitly of blame and the status of victims turns metaphor into bald politics. If made explicit, claims to guilt and innocence may be accepted or rejected on factual grounds. Like so many paintings (Picasso's *Guernica* is perhaps the most famous example) and films (such as *Katyn* directed by Andrzej Wajda, discussed by Bartmanski and Eyerman in Chapter 10), and other artistic representations, *Waiting for Godot* constructs the trauma and expresses charges of guilt without making accusations in the political realm or a court of justice.

The success of *Waiting for Godot* in Sarajevo and New Orleans was not judged according to factual accuracy. Such a rubric simply would not make sense. Instead, the audiences to these productions of *Waiting for Godot* pronounced the performances a success or failure based on the performances' ability to express and depict the experiences of the residents in each city. This is not only a separate rubric from other claims to trauma; it is, of course, a different rubric of success than most theatrical performances. The acting, directing, costuming, and stage design were not based exclusively on the logic of the theater but also on the logic of social performance. Audiences expected the actors to embody Vladimir and Estragon, sure, but there was an expectation that they personify the residents of the cities as well. The script, the set, the actors, and the plot of the trauma needed to achieve re-fusion through the performance of *Godot* for the production to be a successful social performance. Even audiences that are not the highbrow consumers of avant-garde theater that Beckett had in mind appreciate *Godot* not only as a masterpiece of the theater but also as a representation of their plight. Two writers for the *Times-Picayune* state that if they were exposed to *Waiting for Godot* in another circumstance they might have thought the text too highbrow, but in New Orleans, it is perfectly suited to the situation (DeBerry 2007; Maloney 2007). The writers are not intimidated or bored by the play because it represents life in their city.

The success of the social performance also depends on the authenticity and legitimacy of the artists who conceive and promote the performance. Audiences ask what it means that *Waiting for Godot* was performed in their cities only because a famous (in the case of Sarajevo) and well-funded (in the case of New Orleans) intellectual and artist produced the play. Accordingly, audiences ask what is the status of imported intellectuals? Are they seeking attention for themselves? Are they investing in the community or just putting up a production and leaving? Sontag and Chan walk a performative tight-rope. They must be able to create art that fuses with the local audience. Yet to create a social performance making claims to trauma they must be able to reach beyond the city to journalists who will convey the construction of trauma to a national and international audience. They must be local and global, speaking to and speaking for both.

In his essay "Notes on Beauty," Peter Schjeldahl writes, "Insensibility to beauty may be an index of misery" (1998, 59). In contradiction to this assertion, actors, directors, producers, and audiences seek out and shape Beckett's *Waiting for Godot* to claim and construct trauma. Accounts of these productions indicate an astute sensitivity to and connection with this great work of theater. Social actors have shaped this artistic masterpiece to specify and communicate the circumstances and the perpetrators and victims of their trauma to themselves and to a wider audience; they have turned theater performance into social performance of trauma. Indeed, I argue that social actors make claims to trauma through beauty, through aesthetics and art works, that will not be not be judged based on factual accuracy but on the aptness of the expression of meaning.

Notes

1. The author wishes to thank Ron Eyerman, Joseph Klett, Natasha Kirsten Kraus, Shai M. Dromi, and Amy Hungerford for sharing their ideas regarding this project and for their comments on earlier drafts of this chapter. The author also wishes to thank Benjamin Alexander-Bloch for supplying articles from the *Times-Picayune.*

2. Claims to fact, of course, may correspond to something "real" and they may not. Valentin Rauer's theoretical explanation of his analysis of Willy Brandt's *Kniefall* inspires my argument regarding claims to expressive aptness through social performance (2006).

3. The first production in the United States was, in the words of the director, a "spectacular flop" (Schneider 1967, 56). Staged in Miami, the producers advertised *Waiting for Godot* as the "the laugh sensation of two continents" starring the well-known comic actors Bert Lahr and Tom Ewell (Bradby 2001, 93). The director attributes the production's failure to the audience's expectation of attending a light comedy (Schneider 1967, 56). Due to the "disastrous" run in Miami, *Godot's* first opening New York City was canceled (Bradby 2001, 93). After reorganizing the production and replacing the director and some of the actors, *Godot* opened on Broadway in April 1956 (Bradby 2001, 93). The production in Miami is the first of several examples of *Waiting for Godot* failing to some degree when it was used primarily as a star vehicle or to earn large profits for the theater and production company (see Rich 1988). Instances of failed or less successful *Godot* productions underscore the interest of productions that succeed.

4. *Waiting for Godot* has been staged in many contexts of trauma or potential trauma (Smelser 2004, 35–36). In addition to the very first performance of *Godot* at the Théâtre de Babylone shortly after World War II and the Nazi occupation of France, *Godot* has been performed in prisons in the United States and Sweden, in Haifa with references to the plight of Palestinians in Israel, and South Africa during Apartheid by a mixed-race cast (Bradby 2001).

5. Beckett was part of this "collective" in Paris after the war. When he returned to Paris after spending years in Provence waiting for the war to end, Beckett found his beloved city and his relationships with friends and colleagues irrevocably changed (Bair 1978, 373). As a text, *Waiting for Godot* was born out of Beckett's personal trauma and the mood of collective trauma in Paris following the war.

6. This news piece states that Sontag's "real accomplishment" is staging *Godot* with female actors while the Beckett estate sues other productions for the same substitution.

Works Cited

Alexander, J. C. 2004. Toward a Theory of Cultural Trauma. In *Cultural Trauma and Collective Identity*, eds. J. Alexander, R. Eyerman, B. Giesen, N. Smelser and P. Sztompka. Berkeley: University of California Press.

———. 2006. Cultural Pragmatics: Social Performance Between Ritual and Strategy. In *Social Performance: Symbolic Action, Cultural Pragmatics, and Ritual*, eds. J. Alexander, B. Giesen, and J. Mast. Cambridge: Cambridge University Press.

Alexander, J. C., R. Eyerman, B. Giesen, N. J. Smelser, and P. Sztompka. 2004. *Cultural Trauma and Collective Identity.* Berkeley: University of California Press.

Alexander, J. C., B. Giesen, and J. L. Mast, eds. 2006. *Social Performance: Symbolic Action, Cultural Pragmatics, and Ritual.* Cambridge: Cambridge University Press.

Bair, D. 1978. *Samuel Beckett.* New York: Harcourt Brace Jovanovich.

Beckett, S. 1954. *Waiting for Godot: A Tragicomedy in Two Acts.* New York: Grove Press.

Bourdieu, P. [1979] 1984. *Distinction: A Social Critique of the Judgment of Taste.* Trans. Richard Nice. Cambridge: Harvard University Press.

Bradby, D. 2001. *Beckett: Waiting for Godot.* Cambridge: Cambridge University Press.

Burns, J. F. 1993. To Sarajevo, Writer Brings Good Will and "Godot." *New York Times*, August 19.

Chan, P. 2007. Waiting for Godot in New Orleans: An Artist Statement, at http://www.creativetime.org/programs/archive/2007/chan/artist_statement.pdf. Accessed February 3, 2011.

Cotter, H. 2007. A Broken City. A Tree. Evening. *New York Times*, December 2.

Cuthbert, D. 2007a. Katrina "Godot" a Go: Wendell Pierce Set to Star in Hurricane-Themed Adaptation of Classic Play in New Orleans. *Times-Picayune*, September 15.

———. 2007b. (No Title). *Times-Picayune*, October 26.

———. 2007c. "Godot" Makes the Bean Scene. *Times-Picayune*, October 27.

———. 2007d. A Play in the Street: For New Orleanians, "Waiting for Godot" Hits the Spot. *Times-Picayune*, November 2.

———. 2007e. Audience Completes "Godot": The play is not the thing if no one is there to hear it. *Times-Picayune*, November 10.

DeBerry, J. 2007. Waiting, Wondering? We Can Relate. *Times-Picayune*, November 6.

Eagar, C. 1993. Radical-Chic Sontag Waits for Godot as Shells Shake Theatre of the Absurd. *The Observer*, July 25.

Erikson, K. T. 1976. *Everything in Its Path: Destruction of Community in the Buffalo Creek Flood.* New York: Simon and Schuster Paperbacks.

———. 1995. Notes on Trauma and Community. In *Trauma: Explorations in Memory*, ed. C. Caruth. Baltimore, MD: The Johns Hopkins University Press.

Esslin, M. 1980 [1961]. *The Theatre of the Absurd,* 3rd ed. Middlesex, UK: Penguin Books, Ltd.

Grenier, R. 1993. Sarajevo and Susan's Sweet Sensibilities. *Washington Times,* August 30.

Maloney, A. 2007. Wait with Me: N.O. May be the Richest Ravaged City in the World. *Times-Picayune,* November 9.

Mast, J. 2006. The Cultural Pragmatics of Event-ness: the Clinton/Lewinsky Affair. In *Social Performance: Symbolic Action, Cultural Pragmatics, and Ritual,* eds. J. Alexander, B. Giesen, and J. Mast. Cambridge: Cambridge University Press.

MacCash, D. 2007. Worth the Wait: Standing-Room Crowds Create Havoc, but "Godot"-Goers go with the Flow. *Times-Picayune,* November 6.

MacCash, D., and D. Cuthbert. 2007. Artist Paul Chan Brings his "Godot" to a Waiting City. *Times-Picayune,* November 2.

Narayan, N. 1993. A Candle in the Dark. *The Guardian,* August 20.

Pomfret, J. 1993. "Godot" Amid the Gunfire; In Bosnia, Sontag's Take on Beckett. *Washington Post,* August 19.

Rauer, V. 2006. Symbols in Action: Willy Brandt's Kneefall at the Warsaw Memorial. In *Social Performance: Symbolic Action, Cultural Pragmatics, and Ritual,* eds. J. Alexander, B. Giesen, and J. Mast. Cambridge: Cambridge University Press.

Rich, F. 1988. Stage View: Cutting to the Heart of the Way We Live Now. *New York Times,* December 25.

Schjeldahl, P. 1998. Notes on Beauty. In *Uncontrollable Beauty: Toward a New Aesthetics,* eds. B. Beckley and D. Shapiro. New York: Allworth Press.

Schneider, A. 1967. Waiting for Beckett: A Personal Chronicle. In *Casebook on Waiting for Godot: The Impact of Beckett's Modern Classic: Reviews, Reflections and Interpretations,* ed. R. Cohn. New York: Grove Press.

Simon, S. 2007. Still Waiting on Repairs, New Orleans Hosts "Godot." Weekend Edition Saturday, National Public Radio, November 3.

Sontag, S. 1993. Godot Comes to Sarajevo. *New York Review of Books* 40: 17, at http://www.nybooks.com/articles/2433. Accessed December 14, 2009.

———. 1994. Waiting for Godot in Sarajevo. *Performing Arts Journal* 16(2): 87–106.

Smelser, Neil. 2004. Psychological Trauma and Cultural Trauma. In *Cultural Trauma and Collective Identity,* eds. J. Alexander, R. Eyerman, B. Giesen, N. Smelser, and P. Sztompka. Berkeley: University of California Press

Tanner, M. 1993. A Long Wait for Godot. *The Independent,* August 2.

(No Author). 1993. Waiting for Godette. *The Times,* September 1.

Toole, D. 1998. *Waiting for Godot in Sarajevo: Theological Reflections on Nihilism, Tragedy, and Apocalypse.* Boulder, CO: Westview Press.

10

The Worst Was the Silence

The Unfinished Drama of the Katyn Massacre

Dominik Bartmanski and Ron Eyerman

> *The worst was the silence, the prohibition against speaking openly of their death, of a dignified burial, for half a century. It was forbidden even to visit the places of execution. My younger sister, Zosia, always envied those friends of hers whose parents had died in Auschwitz. They at least could go to the grave sites, and didn't have to hide the truth...*
> —Stanislawa Dec, (quoted in Kaczorowska 2006, 150)

On April 7, 2010, Russian Prime Minister Vladimir Putin made an unprecedented symbolic gesture. He placed a wreath at a burial site near the Russian village of Katyn in a ceremony to commemorate the seventieth anniversary of the massacre of Polish military officers and elite civilians in the early stages of World War II. In his speech, Putin paid tribute to "Soviet citizens, burnt in the fire of Stalinist repression of the 1930s; Polish officers, shot on secret orders; soldiers of the Red Army, executed by the Nazis" (*New York Times* April 8, 2010, A16). The story of responsibility for this mass murder of Poles is one of dispute, suppression, "the great efforts of obfuscation of Soviet propaganda" (Snyder 2007) and protracted marginalization. Therefore Putin's words came as an unexpected but promising sign of much-needed change. Three days later, on April 10, an airplane carrying Polish President Lech Kaczyński, high-ranking Polish officials, and the heads of the Polish military crashed nearby while on their way to a similar ceremony. All 96 people on board the plane were killed. Upon hearing of these deaths, former Polish president and leader of Solidarity, Lech Wałesa said, "This is the second disaster after Katyn … They [the Russians] wanted to cut off our head there, and here the flower of our nation has also perished" (Wałesa 2010). Shortly afterward, Wiktor Osiatyński, a Polish professor of law, provided a general context for understanding this and many similar responses to the catastrophe when he wrote in the *New York Times*, "By the time Mr. Kaczyński took office, Katyn had gone from a secretly remembered event to a symbol of Polish heroism and independence" (Osiatyński 2010). This chapter unpacks the mechanisms and meanings of this remarkable transformation.

In what came to be called the Katyn Massacre, the precipitating occurrence was the mass murder of over 14,500 Polish military officers and over 7,000 other Polish citizens rounded up by the Soviet army and executed by the NKVD in April 1940 following the Soviet invasion of eastern Poland on September 17, 1939. When some of the corpses were first discovered in spring 1943, the Soviets claimed the Germans were the perpetrators. The directly affected groups were the Polish military, at that time under attack not only from the west by the German army but also from the east by the Soviets, and the families and friends of those killed. However, neither the army nor the relatives of the murdered soldiers knew the precise circumstances of what happened. This was partly due to the fact that Poland and the Soviet Union were not officially at war and that the relations between their armies were not clearly defined or understood. It took years to establish the historical facts and to narrate them in a coherent and meaningful way. Another reason was the concerted attempts made by the wartime governments in the United States and Great Britain to silence any public discussion in the fear of alienating their Soviet ally, as well as the systematic attempts by the latter to cover up the facts. There was also the knowledge that many atrocities had been committed by the Germans, so that the claim of German responsibility by the Soviet government did not appear outlandish. Any attempt on the part of Poles to raise the issue of possible Soviet guilt was treated as pro-German treason: During the war it formed a pretext for

Stalin to break off diplomatic ties with the Polish government-in-exile, and after the war an anti-Soviet, counter-revolutionary caveat would be added. As time progressed, the directly affected collectivities expanded from the military and relatives to include the Polish nation as such. Once construed as trauma, Katyn became an important symbol in the struggle for independence from Soviet domination. It was this potential as anti-Soviet propaganda that in large part motivated a renewed official interest in the United States and Great Britain during the Cold War. For those affected family members, however, the murders always remained an issue.

Because of all this contestation, as well as the horrendous context of mass murder in which it occurred, this particular war crime could emerge as cultural trauma capable of deeply affecting whole collectivities only insofar as the claims to truth could be firmly established and the symbolic attribution of suffering and guilt effectively enacted in the form of a story couched in generalizable moral terms. With other incidents of mass killing why was it that Katyn emerged with such symbolic force? The present project aims at exploring the social conditions under which these claims were made, as well as the cultural trajectory of the trauma narrative that followed the incident. We will investigate *how* the war crime of Katyn entered Polish collective identity, *when* it unfolded, and *what* were the results of the transformation of that crime into a major cultural crisis that to this day overshadows Polish-Russian political relations.

While looking at the historical facts, we realize that there are several important social processes at stake. From the very beginning, the construction of the trauma narrative of the victims was accompanied by what we may call a counter-trauma narrative by the perpetrators who sought to set forth an incorrect attribution of responsibility for the war crime and to actively conceal its circumstances. We recognize that the unequal distribution of political and military power during World War II, not only between Poles, Germans, and Russians but also between Poles and their Western allies, played an important role in conditioning the context of the whole story. In fact, we claim that a distinctive characteristic of traumatic narratives is an asymmetrical relation between perpetrator and victim and that this, in part, is what makes cultural trauma. Another complicating factor is that the incorrect attribution of German guilt made by the Soviets carried a degree of plausibility, at least during the war and for those outside Poland. Finally, even after the war there existed groups in Soviet-occupied Poland, ethnic Poles among them, who resisted the generalizing efforts on the part of the victims, as they considered such efforts reactionary nationalism.[1] We deal with a situation that might be described as the emergence of a dialectic between a trauma narrative of relatively weak victims based on strong premises and the counter-trauma discourse of relatively strong suspects based on weak premises. While this power distribution matters, it is necessary to explore the cultural and social conditions under which the correct attribution of responsibility for the massacre was prevented, the controversy sustained, and an eventual resolution made possible.

We recognize that it was not only the sheer power of political and military control but also the intellectual attachments and emotional dispositions of various social groups on all sides that played a significant role in framing and handling the issue. These attachments, a set of time– and place–specific cultural codes and attitudes, shaped the ways in which the incident was approached during the war and subsequently thereafter. These embedded cultural codes initially obscured and suppressed the tragedy of Katyn. From the perspective of cultural sociological theory, the very fact of the memory of painful experience being suppressed, not only the murders themselves, contributed to the emergence of collective anxiety and enabled victims to construct yet another dimension of their collective injury.

The memory carried by the families of the victims was suppressed through the political control the Soviet Union effectively exerted in Poland between 1945 and 1989. As a result, discussion could not be introduced into the domestic public sphere, the locus of crucial engagements with the incident. However, public discussion was possible at least to a certain extent within the Polish diaspora, especially in France, England, and the United States. The publicized trauma narrative of Polish emigrants and exiles was fueled by their own private memories and the pain of the relatives of those killed who remained in Poland. However, as long as the Cold War status quo maintained the political and cultural structures that initially sought to repress the discourse of Katyn, there could be no collectively felt trauma, since public discourse was impossible. The potential symbolic power associated with private suffering can only be fully actualized in the broad public sphere. Cultural trauma became possible only when the directly affected individuals and communities were able to express themselves, verbally and visually, in a sustained way and project their personal tragedies onto the larger moral screen of the nation. In this sense, the story of Katyn as cultural trauma is different from others discussed in this volume. It is a story of the power of political authority to suppress and that of carrier groups to resist and of a wound that would not heal.

We distinguish three crucial carrier groups, survivors, relatives, and intellectuals/politicians that were crucial in this process of creating and sustaining the trauma narrative. These groups maintained their own organizations but attempted to use the public institutions of their host countries as well. Some of them delivered extraordinary testimony replete with thick descriptions that almost single-handedly established Katyn as a collective tragedy because they endowed the incident with great moral significance and historical authenticity, for example, Józef Czapski's *Inhuman Land* published in England in 1951. However, it was only under the changing political and cultural conditions following the Autumn of Nations of 1989 and the rise to power of Mikhail Gorbachev in the Soviet Union that this traumatic memory could truly become a powerful public phenomenon, a grand trauma drama. For the first time in the postwar period, it became possible for public representations to widely surface and for an international discourse to emerge. In short, the incident at Katyn underwent a metamorphosis from a military and political conflict and tragedy known by few to a class and ethnic cleansing discussed by many. In the process, the Katyn Massacre became completely transformed from war crime to cultural crisis in which the foundations of collective identity were brought into play, what we call a cultural trauma.

The most recent visualization of Katyn (2007) by the well-known film director Andrzej Wajda and the whole gamut (and lack) of response to his film, have themselves created a cultural story whose complexity reflects that of the actual trauma construction. As we will discuss, there are at once compelling personal, national, international, moral, and intellectual aspects to this film and its reception that help illuminate the cultural trauma process. Since this response was brought to public light by a single event of artistic intervention, an analysis can contribute to the understanding of the wider process of trauma construction by adding a performative analysis to the more traditional historical presentation of the story at hand. Such extraordinary individuals as Czapski and Wajda, both at once visual artists and intellectuals, were very much aware that even tragic events require powerful representation if collective memory is to be firmly entrenched. This is the case not only for those who directly identify themselves with those murdered and their families because of national and civic ties but also for those who empathize with the victims because of more general moral ties. Wajda (2008) emphasized the importance of "*showing* Katyn to the world" and anticipated a moral and cultural shock in response to the film. Thus we have to recognize an iconic aspect of trauma construction as well as the more discursive aspects. In the introduction to *Inhuman Land* (in the 1984 edition), Józef Czapski mentions that his greatest reward was that so many years after the incident, people still wanted to hear his Katyn story. His mission, he thought, had therewith been completed. From the very beginning, however, Czapski was convinced there was a profound paradox involved in this willingness to remember such tragedy: "it would be impossible to live, impossible to smile, if one always remembered things and never erased any memories" (Czapski 2001, 96). Yet because of the official denial, such remembering was in this case commanded. The reception to the artistic representations of Czapski and Wajda and their own attitudes toward them should be culturally unpacked, for they contain a possible key to understanding what it really means that social actions become cultural events through the process of symbolic construction, not simply through their own force. This perhaps is one of the central insights that this Katyn case study can provide sociological theory.

A Timeline of the Occurrences

In August 23, 1939, the governments of Germany and the Soviet Union signed a nonaggression agreement, popularly known as the Molotov-Ribbentrop Pact. This agreement essentially eliminated Poland from the map, since it divided its territories between Germany and the Soviet Union. The document also contained a secret agreement that legitimated the elimination of Poland's intelligentsia, presumably because it would make the occupation of the territories that much easier and longstanding. In early spring of the following year, approximately 14,500 Polish citizens (the issue of whether or not they were prisoners of war is a legal issue, as no formal declaration of war against the Soviet Union was made), primarily reserve and regular military officers but also members of the police corps, were murdered in several killing grounds on the eastern front.[2] These individuals were generally recognized as the cream of Polish society.[3] The killings were carried out with German-made revolvers by the Soviet secret police (NKVD); the victims being executed individually with a single shot to the back of the head and their bodies then buried in stacked layers of tightly-packed mass graves.[4] The style of execution was well known and associated with the Soviet secret police. The prisoners, mostly men but including at least one female officer, had been held in three separate camps and killed within a period of a few weeks. Many prominent Polish Jews were included amongst the victims, about 5 percent of the inmates of one of the three camps (Kozelsk) were Jews according to one account, among them the chief rabbi of the Polish army (Paul 1991, 70).[5] There were also Muslims among the dead, and the monument that has been erected in the memory of the Katyn Massacre contains four different religious symbols.[6] The extent and impact of these murders only slowly emerged after the betrayal of the nonaggression pact and the German invasion of the Soviet Union in June 1941.

On April 13, 1943, in a broadcast carried by all German controlled radio stations, including those in occupied Poland, Radio Berlin announced that "the local population indicated a Soviet execution site at Kosogory ... about 3,000 bodies ... had already been uncovered in a huge pit ..." and that these were the bodies of "thousands of officers of the former Polish army, interned in the U.S.S.R. in 1939 and bestially murdered by the Bolsheviks" (Paul 1991, 128, 210). Four days later, the Polish government in exile requested that the International Red Cross (IRC) investigate this claim. Coming as it did in the wake of the defeat at Stalingrad, the discovery of the bodies at Katyn, which the German command mistakenly thought represented all the murdered Polish officers, presented a significant opportunity in the propaganda war. "Goebbels now saw an opportunity to divide the Allies. He wrote in his diary that as soon as he heard of this statement, he secured Hitler's sanction for the German Red Cross to ask the IRC for an investigation of the Katyn graves" (Cienciala et al. 2007, 218).[7] This ensured that any investigation of the graves at Katyn would necessarily be couched within the wider political conflicts and intrigues of the war.

Following a German request, an international commission of forensic experts was deployed to the Katyn forest to exhume the bodies. This occurred between April 28 and 30, 1943. The commission produced a 350-page report identifying the bodies and establishing the cause and approximate time of death. The Polish Red Cross, which at first refused to participate for fear of supporting German propaganda (and indeed the Germans thought Polish representation necessary to making their case believable), was represented at the site by a group of forensic specialists and other technicians, including some who were active in the Polish underground. The advancing Russian army and the lack of further discoveries caused the Germans to suspend operations, and by June 1943, the Polish representatives returned with their information to occupied Poland.[8] Their personal testimony strongly suggested Soviet guilt, but the use of German pistols and the difficulty in establishing the exact date of the executions, along with the clear propaganda motivations of the Germans, allowed doubts to continue, at least among those so predisposed. In addition to the periodical radio pronouncements (in Kracow and other major occupied cities the names of the dead were solemnly and repeatedly announced over loud speakers), lists of the dead were published in German language newspapers throughout occupied Poland. However, the question of who carried out the killings was publicly disputed, with the Germans accusing the Soviets and vice versa. Two days after the Berlin announcement (April 15, 1943), Moscow fired back with this statement: "In launching this monstrous invention the German-Fascist scoundrels did not hesitate at the most unscrupulous and base lies, in their attempts to cover up crimes which, as has now become evident, were perpetrated by themselves" (cited by Paul 1991, 211). Stalin took the cooperation between the Polish Red Cross and German authorities as a pretext to break off relations with the London-based Polish government, referring to them as "Hitler's Polish collaborators." This became one of the interpretative frames that would define any attempts by Poles to dispute the Soviet claims of German guilt, at least until the end of the war.

The long list of German atrocities and the fact that the material evidence in the case, the inability or unwillingness to set the exact date of execution and the origin of the weapons used, contributed to the uncertainly of the perpetrator. Who the victims were was, of course, clear. What they represented, and to whom, was also relatively clear. For the Germans the dead represented proof of Soviet ruthlessness, something to counterbalance their own image in the eyes of the world. The discovery of the bodies also helped alleviate some of the sting of their failing military strategy, at least at the level of political propaganda. For the Soviets, the dead bodies were useful as yet another signifier of German barbarism, an aid in their own propaganda efforts to convince Poles and the rest of the world of their good intentions that they were protecting and liberating rather than occupying their country. Their attribution of German responsibility was made all the more believable by Allied propaganda and by the ruthlessness of the German forces in Eastern Europe. For the Poles, the dead represented yet another example of their victimization, part of a long history of being caught between powerful and aggressive neighbors. It also meant a blow not only of their military but to their desire for sovereignty. There may have been some Poles who saw Katyn as a tragedy yet did not share these national aspirations to the same extent and viewed the massacre in military terms only. If they did exist, one can speculate that these would be members of the Soviet-sponsored Polish army and of the communist wing of the underground in occupied Poland. While they make no mention of Katyn, of course, some of Wajda's earlier films explore this tension within the Polish resistance. There were also ethnic minorities within the shifting Polish borders for whom the uncovered graves might have meant something different.

Katyn and the cry for vengeance became a strong motivating agent in both forces of the Polish military fighting in the war. The Soviets would name a tank the "Avenger" with this in mind. It was also a strong motivating force in the Polish resistance and in what was called the Home Army, the force behind the tragic Warsaw Uprising in 1944. The Soviets viewed the Home Army through the same lens it viewed the London government-in-exile, as Polish nationalists who were a threat to Soviet aims in the region, and they did all they could to discredit and destroy both.

At the Nuremberg tribunals in 1946, the prosecution of the perpetrators of the Katyn Massacre fell under Soviet jurisdiction as it occurred in their allotted zone. The indictment read, "In September 1941 11,000 Polish officers, prisoners of war, were killed in the Katyn woods near Smolensk." While it did not name the Germans as perpetrators, it was clear from the dating of the event where the blame lay, as the region was at that point under German occupation. The case presented was based on the findings of the earlier Soviet report (Paul 1991, 335). German lawyers put up a strong defense and there was much suspicion of Soviet guilt. In the end, the Soviets formally withdrew their claims, and the case was omitted from the final verdicts announced in late September 1946. Besides the general ambiguity amongst the Allies, another reason given was that the tribunal was concerned only with German war crimes. Great Britain and the United States were reluctant at that point to confront their Soviet allies on this matter and sought to bury the issue. The Polish government-in-exile had expected this and sought, unsuccessfully, to have the issue of Katyn excluded entirely from consideration at Nuremburg. It is now assumed that the Russians decided in the end not to press the issue because their case was so clearly weak and the possibility of exposure strong. One can speculate that had the Katyn Massacre been fairly and completely treated at Nuremberg, there might never have evolved the cultural trauma that came later. The killings would have been treated as a war crime among many and the issue resolved with the attribution of guilt and the allocation of punishment. A memorial would perhaps have been constructed and Polish families given a site to grieve and remember their lost loved ones. The politics of war and peace made that impossible however.

With the continued Soviet presence, any discussion of Katyn was strictly forbidden in postwar Poland. For an account of what happened, Poles were directed to the official account of the war given in the *Great Soviet Encyclopedia*. As something publicly forbidden, reference to Katyn was kept within the bounds of the private sphere, while in the underground of public memory, it became a symbol of Soviet oppression. For those Poles who actively participated in and supported the Communist government, any reference to Katyn was interpreted as nationalistic propaganda and thus as reactionary, whoever was deemed the perpetrator. For them, the issue was best resolved as yet another tragic event of war, a war which had in the end led to a revolutionary change in direction.

If public discussion was forbidden in Poland, this was not the case for *émigré* Polish communities in the West. During the Cold War and under pressure from Polish Americans, most notably the Polish American Congress (PAC), established in 1944, a congressional committee, the American Committee for the Investigation of the Katyn Massacre or the Lane Committee was established. In 1951 the House of Representatives established a select committee to investigate "the facts, evidence and circumstances of the Katyn forest massacre" (Sanford 2005, 142). Some of the witnesses called to testify wore hoods to avoid identification, fearing for their relatives in Poland. Hearings were held throughout 1952, in the highly politicized atmosphere of the Cold War. In its final report published in December 1952, the committee named the Soviets as the responsible agent and recommended referral to the United Nations and the International Court of Justice. It also called for the establishment of an international commission to investigate Katyn and other crimes against humanity perpetrated by the Soviet Union. The USSR was denounced for "one of the most barbarous crimes against humanity" (Sanford 2005, 144). In 1965, a postage stamp was issued in the United States commemorating Katyn, sponsored by Congressman Edward Derwinski of Illinois from Chicago, a city with a large Polish-American population.[9] A campaign to establish a Katyn monument in Great Britain, strongly supported by the American-based Polonia, an association of Polish Americans, was begun. Books began to appear on the topic in Great Britain, and in 1971, the BBC broadcast a program, which raised the issue of Soviet responsibility. In 1972, the British *Daily Telegraph* printed the headline "Russian guilt for Katyn Reaffirmed" (Sanford 2005, 180). Finally, in 1976, a memorial monument was erected in London but without any mention of the perpetrators.

Knowledge, Remembrance and Meanings of Katyn Massacre in Poland, 1943–2008

The sixty-five years of the Katyn trauma drama in Poland have constituted a narrative of protracted civil struggle for historical transparency and moral repair. To state briefly the difference between the postwar situation of the Polish diaspora in Western Europe and the United States and in-country citizens, one could say that whereas the story of Katyn was an inconvenient truth in public discourse in the West, it remained a rather cumbersome official lie and a publicly suppressed issue in Eastern Europe until 1989. In fact, it continued to be a political taboo in the official discourse of Russia afterward too, a circumstance that sheds additional light to the conditions of Soviet occupation in the region and its cultural legacy.

The time between the first public information about the existence of mass graves in the Katyn Forest in April 1943 and the first official celebration of the Katyn Remembrance Day on April 13, 2008 was a period during which this issue gradually became a key signifier of Polish victimhood, especially with reference to the Soviet Union. Much of this time was consumed by civil perseverance and moral dedication to an issue that was silenced and consigned to oblivion by the highest echelons of authority. To many, the issue seemed almost lost; to others, it remained vague or virtually unknown.

For those Poles who knew the facts established in 1943 and remembered thereafter, this was a dramatic period not only because of the emotional character of the knowledge they possessed but also due to the fact that before 1989, (1) this knowledge had been suppressed for decades; (2) its bearers were systematically persecuted, threatened, or socially marginalized; (3) a false account of the incident was disseminated from the outset of People's Republic of Poland; and (4) the issue was ignored altogether from the 1960s on in the official media.

Beyond this, there were an even greater number of individuals for whom the drama consisted in an anguish of uncertainty intertwined with the premonition that the Katyn killings were not an isolated case. As time elapsed, the worst-case scenario was finally confirmed. Prior to that confirmation, however, Katyn symbolized in an incrementally increasing number of circles the array of physical and psychological damage historically inflicted upon the Polish people. It signified at once the extermination of Polish prisoners of war in the Soviet Union, a long-lasting uncertainty and confusion concerning the facts, the brutally enforced silence, the gaping lack of information about those "lost in the east," and official hypocrisy, obfuscation, and deception. The specificity of Katyn consists then not simply in the systematic nature of the atrocities committed and of the groups targeted but also in the fact that the mass killings were cynically appropriated and used by Nazi German and Soviet governments for their own political purposes, initially with the more than tacit support by other governments.

Knowledge of the murders was scattered, incomplete, and overshadowed by the perpetrators' counter-narrative. Since memory and recall are indispensable for the experience of trauma, and since recall does not exist without a cognitive referent, the conditions for the emergence of cultural trauma might seem very unfavorable. Indeed, the Soviet political realism of the time conditioned an overwhelming corruption of reality, a paradigmatically Orwellian situation in which control of the present depended upon strict control of the past. The latter meant the destruction and falsification of any contrary evidence, the psychological and physical torture of inconvenient witnesses, and above all the blurring of key social meanings and the degrading of individual life. In this process, language itself was permeated by sayings such as an ambiguous Russian phrase "to lie like an eyewitness" (Nim 2008, 22).

All this ensured a situation of perennial fear and disorientation. However, this particular circumstance appears to have multiplied and congealed the emotional trauma felt in thousands of Polish households. Katyn began to emerge not only as a tragedy of individual grief but also a trauma narrative of scant, robbed, and persecuted collective memory. This concerned and encapsulated not only what was coded as extraordinary injury but also the necessity of dealing with silence, uncertainty, and falsehood in the course of ordinary daily life.

Actual memory of the occurrence was relatively scarce for the simple reason that only approximately 394 out of the thousands captured left the detention camps alive, spared by NKVD and initially grouped in a separate camp. As one of the survivors noted, the aforementioned Józef Czapski (2001, 71), the prisoners had not even considered the possibility of mass extermination. The very few who survived and could be regarded as witnesses at first did not realize what exactly was going on in fall of 1939 and spring of 1940. For many Polish citizens, the first weeks of terror and havoc caused by the joint invasion of Poland meant a brutal confrontation with the informational chaos and political arbitrariness of an invading power. For this reason, it seems more adequate to speak here of the tedious processes of ascertaining and verifying knowledge, about channels and frameworks of communicating and disseminating it, and finally about acts of commemoration, artistic representation, and responses to them.

A key sociological issue concerns how witness-based remembering is conveyed and translated to the collective level and subsequently transformed into sustained social remembrance. In addressing this, we would emphasize the role of discursive frames and visual representations predicated on specific cultural binaries that, in turn, are intertwined with emotional attachments. First of all, there is the dichotomy of truth and lie employed in all the narratives surrounding this case. This fundamental binary is often accompanied by other oppositions such as the innocence and guilt, decency and perfidy, openness and secrecy. Second, in addition to the fundamental division of the public and the private one can speak of the dichotomy of the official and the underground; the state and civil society. These binaries are not, of course, fast and fixed, but it is important to recognize that under the Communist regime they often overlapped. The transmission of private narratives into public discourse was severely restricted and, in the case of Katyn, mostly impossible during the closing years of World War II and immediately thereafter, until the so-called political thaw of 1956, when one can notice a narrative shift from the claims of German guilt to a muffled silence on the part of the authorities. Public discussion continued to be seriously hampered until the collapse of 1989. However, private discussion and familial transmissions of memory could never be completely muffled, and these eventually carved out a significant social niche whose meanings and cultural relevance began to be publicly felt. As we shall later demonstrate, this particular tension between state order and social order can easily be reinscribed within the mythical tragedy of Sophocles's play *Antigone,* which as Breese demonstrates (Chapter 9 in this book) with reference to Becket's *Godot,* helped articulate the feelings held by many Poles when performed in the immediate postwar and then reframed in Wajda's *Katyn.*

On top of this, we deal with yet another binary, namely that between what can and cannot be spoken, what can (and should) be told and discussed, and what constitutes the unspeakable. On the one hand, speech and text are connected to an anthropological imperative to express oneself to witness and testify (Suleiman 2006). As the Lithuanian author Tomas Venclova writes, "speaking and writing means overcoming and transcending" (1999, 129). Some, of course, might disagree or at least point to a danger, as Adorno seemed to do with his famous remark about the possibility of poetry after Auschwitz. Certainly, speaking and writing about the forbidden truth of Katyn, whether in private or in public, was one of the few forms of overcoming and transcending the Communist regime that suppressed it. The construction of cultural trauma involves a specific distribution of the sacred and profane and an understanding of the symbolic borders of its representation and reception. According to Izabella Sariusz-Skapska "to not cross the border between testimony and the silence of things that are ineffable is a condition of reliability of representation" (2002, 22). The "ineffable" is here understood as something that cannot be fully communicated, not only because of the limitations of the language employed by storytellers but also because of the impossibility of full entrance into the narrative on the part of recipients. Moreover, there are borders to what should be communicated, in that the risk associated with crossing such borders can mean either the banalization of the victims' suffering or the fascination with the profane and evil, a point made by Adorno in the reference above. Therefore, while researching forms of knowledge, remembrance and post-memory, one faces the double problem: (1) the politically molded possibility to represent and (2) the culturally molded ability to speak out and be heard in a particular social context.

If we take into account the politically shaped possibility of public expression, we can distinguish at least three general periods within the temporal brackets we've already established in demarcating the processes of collective trauma construction. This begins with the obtaining and transmitting of knowledge of the incident. It includes the remembrance enacted and the transformation of a tragic occurrence into a significant event, intellectually and artistically represented under various social conditions in the following, heuristically delimited political eras: 1943–1956, 1956–1989, and 1989–2010. With reference to the second criterion of the culturally shaped ability to communicate, a specific periodization is much harder to establish. Such a process is always affected by political conditions but is also responsive to various other circumstances that have their own, often nonlinear, logic of temporal change. However, one can distinguish one particular circumstance that crucially affected the emergence and maintenance of cultural trauma with reference to Katyn: the lack of symbolic closure in the trauma drama. A recurrent string of metaphors that are intuitively crucial in this respect are injury, wound, and scar. A cultural trauma emerges with recognition, symbolic elaboration, and meaningful representation of social wounds that are felt to remain open. It continues to exist as a cultural process that tends, as it were, to turn wound into scar, something healed but still present as meaningful referent. Symbolic closure is vital at this point; the lack thereof keeps the wound open and fosters anxiety derived from deprivation of coherence in a narrative marked by tragic occurrence.

The specific carrier groups with firsthand knowledge of the mass killings and those who harbored the most emotionally charged memory of the massacre, such as the families of the murdered, were either hunted or closely watched by the authorities. Polish forensic specialists and other experts who visited Katyn in 1943 were defined as one of the most significant among these carrier groups. Though the few surviving eyewitnesses either fled the country or been imprisoned, some did manage to pass on their knowledge to specialists and lay people and, in this way, contribute to the more general framing of the incident. But it was the personal trauma of the families, especially of the wives, mothers, and children of those killed that supplied the critical mass of highly emotionally charged tragic narratives (see, for example, those collected in Kaczorowska 2003 in Polish and 2006 in English). Their situation became particularly dramatic as any inquiries concerning the fate of "the lost in the east" and the public sharing of knowledge and opinion about Katyn began to be prohibited and persecuted. Yet thousands of women waiting in vain for their husbands, brothers, and sons were one of the key elements that imperceptibly undermined the official discourses.

Their forced silence in the first decade following the war compounded the sense of helplessness and initially confined their suffering to the private sphere. The dissemination of "false information about the Katyn crime" was punishable by a two-year sentence of forced labor. Acts of invigilation targeting the families took place and those caught spreading "false knowledge" could even be accused of espionage (Oseka 2007, 7). If one was identified as a child of those "lost in the east," the entrance to higher education and other institutions and occupations could be seriously hampered or made impossible (Kaczorowska 2006). Once drafted into the Polish army, the sons of those murdered could be directed to work in mines and other industrial locations controlled by Communists (Skąpski 2009, Bartmanski interview).

Under such strenuous political and social conditions, the family members of the murdered officers were important carriers of remembrance, not only because of the knowledge some possessed but most importantly because of their emotional attachment to the wider case. The atmosphere of fear engendered by the strict official control of the Katyn narrative fostered general suspicion toward the government and its official propaganda. As members of elite families, many came to feel responsible for saving the traces of what was for them a true Polish heritage, the vestiges of their life-world that now was to be systematically erased. That feeling was buttressed by the fact that many in this category belonged to the first generation raised and educated in the independent Poland created in 1918, after 123 years of political nonexistence (Ksiazek-Czerminska 1999, 7). For some, the imposition of a Communist regime might have appeared as a continuation of previous Russian domination under a different banner. The disappearance of their relatives and their inexpressible fate was thus intimately linked to the Soviet occupation of Poland, and within that, the binary of truth and lie was mapped onto the division of state and society. Although not quite underground heroes, the relatives of the murdered formed one of the key mechanisms of transmission of remembrance into the public sphere. In the first period this was completely "privatized" and restricted to the occasional distribution of leaflets and individual acts of sabotaging official propaganda. As their official and personal abandonment persisted, their fate eventually became emblematic.

In short, the first period of the emergence of the trauma narrative was marked by shock, confusion, and symbolic struggle concerning the deaths and the surrounding circumstances. The key narratives were created in this period, and the clash between a victim discourse, the related counter-discourses, and the attempts at covering up the story, all shaped their reception. Already in the 1940s, the name "Katyn" was being openly mentioned in Poland along with the symbols of German genocide—Auschwitz and Majdanek (Oseka 2007, 7). The official discourse blaming the Germans subsided in the wake of Stalin's death in 1953 but continued to be one of the key elements legitimating Poland's Communist government, and there were certainly Poles who actively supported the regime and its claims about the fate of those killed at Katyn. It was only in 1956 that the political climate was changed unequivocally, and many of Stalin's crimes were revealed by the Soviet government itself. This provided a new context for the evaluation of what was now commonly known as the Katyn Massacre. However, official propaganda did not cease to employ the standard Soviet version for its own purposes of political and cultural control. Throughout the 1950s, "Katyn" had its own entry in official encyclopedias, where it was described as a geographical location in Russia and identified as the site of a massacre of Polish citizens by the German military after the territory had been seized in 1941 (e.g., Suchodolski 1959, 407).

The next twenty-five years saw an official silence on the issue from Poland's Communist authorities. The encyclopedia published by Polish Scientific Publishers (PWN) in 1965 makes no mention of Katyn. This situation did not change in subsequent decades. It is hard today to judge what the exact motivation was behind the change of strategy in approaching Katyn. Yet, it is not the shift itself or the political intricacies that are of the greatest significance but rather its cultural consequences. In the eyes of the vast majority of those who remembered the deaths symbolized by Katyn or found out about the massacre in the wake of the thaw of 1956, the introduction of total censorship on the issue had one fundamental meaning, namely that it was an indirect, and probably unwitting, acknowledgment of Soviet responsibility (Oseka 2007, 7).

From this moment on, a series of persistent iconic and discursive actions took place. The official silence was countered by repeated unauthorized civil undertakings. The symbolic opening of publicly enacted resistance in this period was marked by the inception of the so-called "Katyn Valley" in the main Warsaw cemetery on All Saints' Day in 1959. A commemoration site for the Katyn victims was created on a location where unidentified persons placed a cross and plaque, which was openly called "the symbolic grave of the Polish officers murdered at Katyn." Perpetrators were not explicitly named but the plaque stated that the officers "perished on foreign soil at the hands of a cruel enemy" and that "they deserve memory and honor." The traditional candles were laid all around in spontaneous acts of recognition. The site was destroyed by the state militia after only one day in existence. It was then officially announced that "order was reintroduced to the cemetery" (Sawicki 2007, 18). Though "state order" was promptly reinstated, this public manifestation revealed the existence of an underground order, which had symbolically destabilized it. This brief but visible cry for recognition triggered a sense of moral empowerment, first in Warsaw and later in other cities. The "Katyn Valley" became a bottom-up commemorative site in the years that followed. This cry for recognition was a signifier of a secretly lived trauma expressing a deeply suppressed "we," and the response of the authorities clearly showed that they too cared very much about the incident. The government treated the situation seriously, initiating an official investigation and launching a secret police operation that consisted in systematic intelligence efforts to find out who lay behind the "cemetery event." The results, however, were poor and what might be called resistance performances continued to be enacted at this site until the collapse of the regime in 1989. These performances occurred not only on November 1 but also on other symbolic occasions such as April 13 and September 17. The apogee of this string of actions was reached in the heyday of the Solidarity struggle in 1981 when a four-meter-high monument weighing eight tons was put on this site in the Katyn Valley. Like all previous material symbols of resistance erected on that place, it was promptly removed by the authorities. It was however much discussed in private circles where it was interpreted as yet another demonstration of civil disobedience and political criticism. In effect, the fame of the Katyn Valley had been discursively and iconically cemented, at least in the capital city and with those connected to the incident (Sawicki 2007, 19). In the end, the story of these cemetery performances indicate that the dedication with which the authorities sought to erase the remembrance of Katyn was directly proportional to the cultural potential of this memory as a general signifier of the Soviet-related Polish sufferings and, ultimately, the extent of the moral debacle of the Polish Communist regime.

A quarter of a century after Katyn Valley was created as a symbolic space of anticommunist contestation, there appeared in Poland the first school textbook that described the Katyn Massacre vaguely enough to create precedence in the official discourse. The civil success of Solidarity was preceded by the election of a Pole, Karol Wojtyła, as Pope John Paul II in 1978, effecting a wave of unauthorized discourse about Katyn. No one seemed to be afraid anymore of talking about Soviet responsibility in the Solidarity-inspired time of an unprecedented "festival of freedom" (Materski 2008, 122). Underground materials were circulated around the country, and meetings organized by the Church played an important role in the life of city intelligentsia, the group now most directly attached to the story of Katyn. By then, the Iron Curtain was already porous enough to let in information from the outside. This created a "strange situation" in which the official censorship itself began to be unsure about what exactly was allowed to be published (Abarinow 2007, 11). As a result, there was a plethora of illegal publications created or smuggled into the country from Western Europe and the probability of encountering information about Katyn increased. The grand international myth of Solidarity was emerging, even if the movement itself was temporarily muffled by the martial law introduced by the communist government in 1981.

Though still relatively arcane, the truth about Katyn became an undeniable fact of life for many representatives of the Polish intelligentsia, a commonly recognizable cachet of increasingly self-confident societal "us" against the discredited governmental "them." Incrementally growing social pressure effected further alteration of the ruling party's stance and in closing years of the 1980s, the Katyn Massacre was sporadically thematized in official media and political institutions. This was also the time when the first large-scale sociological research on Polish collective memory was conducted. Two things about these studies are striking: (1) 23 percent of those surveyed declared that they talked about history "often" and 54 percent "sometimes;" (2) less than 3 percent declared that they talked with others about such things as Katyn or the Ribbentrop-Molotow Pact, and barely 5 percent discussed the Stalinist period in Poland or the Martial Law (Szacka 2007, 3). The overall cultural impact of Solidarity and the anticipatory climate of 1980s were obvious, but the research revealed the scale of damage caused to Polish collective memory by official propaganda. A clear discrepancy between a heightened general historical interest and specific discursive commitments indicated the cultural legacy of four decades of autocratic rule. Even if, as a later study showed, 40 percent found out about Katyn during the Communist period, that awareness was one among many other tragic incidents, which seemed to indicate that as trauma Katyn was still apparently confined only to those directly connected to its occurrence. The excitement and then euphoria associated with the end of communism appeared to be one of the exhausted, as far as collective identity was concerned. However, in view of those who cultivated a still circumscribed but now stronger commitment to the issue, the end of the 1980s meant a renewed hope. The demand for proper recognition of Katyn, however slim, seemed unquenchable.

In the newly forged climate of broader political change in Eastern Europe, a series of new discourses concerning Katyn had made an ineradicable impact on the Polish intelligentsia. Thus it came as a profound disappointment when, on July 14, 1988, Mikhail Gorbatchev announced at the official meeting with the representatives of Polish intellectuals at Warsaw's Royal Castle that "there exists no secret documentation which would shed a new light on the Katyn crime" (Materski 2008, 124). For a truly radical change in the official presentation of events, Polish citizens had to wait until the revolution of 1989, and specifically until April 13, 1990, when the official news agency of the Soviet Union (TASS) finally acknowledged, even if under somewhat inadvertent circumstances, Soviet responsibility for the massacres at Katyn, as well as the existence of other extermination sites at Mednoe and Kharkov.[10] This occurred exactly one-half century after the world first heard the terrible news about Katyn.

Changes in Moscow at the outset of the 1990s seemed to create sufficient symbolic space for a relatively open, long-term dialogue with by then completely altered Warsaw. The eventual release of the relevant Soviet archives was promised and reconciliation appeared possible. A full disclosure of knowledge and responsibility would mean a clear symbolic closure. This potential, however, was never fulfilled in the manner suggested by the collapse of communism in Eastern Europe. In Polish society itself, however, a qualitatively unprecedented era of the Katyn trauma drama began. Wajda has said that this was the time when his cinematographic intervention into the Katyn trauma story should have taken place (Wajda 2007, 5).

The Round Table Talks in the spring of 1989 made possible the first partially democratic elections in Eastern Europe. Lech Walesa became president in 1990 and the Polish Communist Party was officially dissolved. The opening of the last decade of the twentieth century constituted a point of no return in the unfolding Katyn trauma narrative. However painful, new concrete prospects of unfettered inquiry and commemorative catharsis were opened. Still, it took another decade to realize a partial symbolic closure and then nearly another to launch the fully fledged process of official ritualization inside the country. Despite what might be interpreted as a significant delay in the official commemoration of Katyn, the event did emerge as a key signifier of World War II tragedy and of Polish trauma stemming from the Soviet occupation. This metamorphosis of formerly subterranean and private tragedy into a central traumatic narrative of the country's history is remarkable. The finally liberated country caused many tragic but previously stifled Polish memories to surface. As Michael Kimmelman wrote in the *New York Times,* "Poles have especially good reason to see themselves as long oppressed, having been fought over and occupied for much of the last century by vicious regimes" (2009, 6). How then has it been possible that this particular incident and its ordeal became a distinctive trauma narrative?

After 1989, the most apparent change was the sudden public visibility of Katyn. Books, articles, documentaries, discussions, and monuments of various kinds filled the media and public sphere in general.[11]

The classic accounts of the incident and its circumstances finally found their way into bookstores and libraries. Among these were Czapski's diaries and *Without a Last Chapter* by Władysław Anders along with novels such as *The Silent, the Invincible* by Włodzimierz Odojewski and *Katyn: Post mortem* by Andrzej Mularczyk. The latter would become the narrative base for Wajda's film, which was originally conceived with that very title. Perhaps most significant of all was the emergence of a new civic association, the Katyn Families Association, with affiliation abroad as well as in Poland. Through it, the few relatives of the victims who remained alive could finally speak out and express their anguish in an organized, public fashion. It was this nongovernmental and explicitly apolitical organization that created a symbolic forum and established itself as a key carrier of remembrance and an indelible sign of an unhealed Polish war wound. It became voice for the articulation of a half-century-long persecuted memory.

The priority of the Association's public mission was to establish officially sanctioned symbolic cemeteries at the three massacre sites revealed by Gorbatchev. Finding the other sites where over seven thousand other bodies lie hidden was also deemed crucial. The first goal, understood as the symbolic act of dignified commemoration and of "emphasizing the drama," had been realized, while a second still remained. For this reason, symbolic closure was felt only as partial. However, the official opening of the Katyn cemetery on July 28, 2000 meant a watershed in the issue and could potentially function as a form of symbolic closure. For the families of the victims it definitely had this effect and could possibly work in similar way for the whole of Polish society. This was because over the years Katyn had become an effective synonym for all the Soviet atrocities suffered by Polish citizens during World War II (Skąpski 2009; Bartmanski interview).[12] In the immediate aftermath of the catastrophe of April 10, 2010, another kind of national "catharsis" seemed possible. The outpouring of grief following the death of the Polish president and 95 of the nation's elite, including Andrzej Skąpski who was to make a speech at the ceremony on behalf of the Katyn families, released great emotion. This trope of catharsis was indeed used in national and international discourses (Iwinski 2010; Zaremba 2010). Whatever was achieved quickly gave way to yet another protracted drama of suspicion and accusation. Public discourse turned very divisive and involved a re-politization of the symbol of Katyn, causing relatives of the fallen who are members of the Association to speak out against the "appropriation of the trauma of Katyn for political and personal ambitions" (*Gazeta Wyborcza* 2010).

As the Polish Parliament unanimously declared the April 13 the National Remembrance Day for the Katyn Victims in 2007, with the first official commemoration the following year, the Katyn trauma was at once reopened and closed. On the one hand, it contributed to the emergence and maintenance of cultural trauma. On the other hand, there was the recognition, especially among Association leaders, that even the most tragic events require self-reflective representation and specific narratives that connect them with more global human aspects of life. And finally, there was the more general understanding in Polish society that even such deeply tragic events need to be, at least partially, laid to rest.

Beside the efforts to officially commemorate the massacres, more personal stories and accounts of the children of the silenced have emerged in the country. These kinds of testimonies that Geoffrey Hartman (Hartman 2009) refers to as "little narratives" appear to stem from the conviction that in the absence of important authentic documentation, only literature and private memoirs can fill the lacunae of knowledge, recognition, and empathy.[13] Through these narratives, many published for the first time by the Katyn Families Association, and other representations based on them, the victims of Katyn were reintroduced to the public sphere as prisoners of an undeclared war, killed without trial or funeral, whose names had been consigned to anonymity. They also showed what this meant and continues to mean to those connected to the victims. For them, the feeling remains that the crime was left, and still remains, without punishment, followed by lie and indifference, instead of recognition and compensation. This feeling is not, in fact, confined to the families alone; it is a historical reality. An authoritative monograph in English on the issue published only in 2007 is symptomatically titled *Katyn. A Crime Without Punishment,* and the book opens with the statement that its subject matter is "one of the most heinous yet least known of the Stalinist crimes" (Cienciala et al. 2007, 1). The statement captures the gist of the issue emphasizing not only tragedy caused by physical but also systematic symbolic violence and continued problems with further investigation. Moreover, because the victims appeared to have been chosen by the perpetrators according to specific military and social criteria, and because they were denied what constitutes human symbolic conduct in boundary situations, they could be perceived as emblematic victims of communist control and their families as Antigonic figures that may potentially allegorize Poland's lot in and after World War II. Even though the relevant novels, memoirs and diaries remain low-impact media, the murdered members of prewar Poland's elite were finally publicly represented in their own country as regular family members, not simply soldiers. They were rescued from anonymity through narrative frames that connected them to their daily life-world destroyed by the grand conflagration of

World War II. They also indicated that the victims were viewed both by the families and the perpetrators as one of the carriers of Poland's political and cultural independence.

All these symbolic components and anthropological imperatives have been artistically condensed in Wajda's film *Katyn* (2007), to date the most internationally visible artistic statement about the incident. The film explicitly thematizes the Antigonic element. It depicts the incident itself realistically, even if at times too theatrically, and links it to the contemporaneous crimes of Nazi Germany. Most importantly, however, it focuses primarily on what the massacre meant to families, particularly to wives and sisters of the victims. In the first set of memoirs published under the title "Written with Love," one finds reference to the "terrible silence" that shrouded longing and despair (Bakowska 2000, 9). Wajda, whose father was among those murdered in Kharkov, visualizes this aspect and reveals through it the cold-blooded destruction of a particular life-world. By shifting the attention from the soldiers themselves to those who loved them and whose loss was publicly unrecognized, he makes the extension of sentiments and identification possible, and thereby reveals the existential depth of the Katyn trauma. Staging the women as Antigones can be seen an instantiation of intertextuality that renders the story potentially generalizable.[14]

The film has received international recognition and was received as a shocking story, from Berlin to Los Angeles. However, the difficulties with global distribution of the film,[15] the reluctance of certain audiences to be confronted with it,[16] and what some viewed as a problem of an occasionally "too arcane" contextualization of the film (Applebaum 2008) have decreased its anticipated, immediate international impact. The director was apparently aware of the predicament created by *Katyn's* obscure historical references, something which may make parts of the film politically illegible (Wajda 2009, 16), but as a part of the legacy of great silence concerning various aspects of Soviet history this very predicament renders the movie a kind of invitation to unpack East European mysteries. This problem was reversed with Polish audiences. The Katyn trauma narrative appeared so symbolically and politically charged that the film has been susceptible to political instrumentalization, not unlike the official remembrance of the massacre mentioned previously. Referring to this danger, Wajda has stated that he is more afraid of the film's allies than its enemies (Wajda 2007, 5) and his effort to avoid political traps was noticed and lauded in the country (Sobolewski 2007).

Regardless of the specific problems of immediate reception, the widespread visibility of a film by the country's most famous director created a significant intervention that may serve as a pattern to follow, as Wajda himself suggested in one of the interviews. The critic cited previously opened his evaluation of the movie by emphasizing that "this cinematographic image of Katyn will enter the collective imagination in Poland" (Sobolewski 2007). As such, it has made any lack of knowledge of the incident at least much more shameful than before, if not impossible. Certainly few in Poland could fail to notice the film upon its release in the fall of 2007. Before the first screening, 95 percent of Poles surveyed declared they knew the name "Katyn," yet as many as 40 percent claimed not to know who exactly was to be blamed for the deaths and as many as 10 percent believed that the perpetrators were the Germans (Gazeta Wyborcza 2007).[17]

Upon its release in September 2007, the film was viewed by 1,021,881 persons in Poland during the first two weeks, 265,000 of which viewed it in the first weekend of its screening (Wprost 2009). By October 20, 2007, the number had already reached two million (Wirtualna Polska 2009). By the end of 2008, the number of viewers reached 2.7 million (Money. pl 2009). Such attendance could not fail to alter the survey figures mentioned before. Above all, the film represented and recalled Katyn as a grand symbol of individual despondency *vis-à-vis* totalitarian power and reinscribed this recollection within a personally and concretely grounded narrative. Due to such construction, the film vividly depicts a group experience and, thanks to this portrayal, makes decisive strides toward confirming a collective nature of the event, and hence Poland as a cultural community with particular history. To paraphrase the words of Tomas Venclova, Wajda's film is one of the more important representations that have attached anew the meaning of human suffering to the sign of Katyn and aided in overcoming the victims' silence (1999, 133).

Conclusion

The theory of cultural trauma points in several fruitful directions. It can refer to a "tear in the social fabric" as well as to a narrative structure and public discourse which emerges in response. In this essay, we have traced the history of Katyn as trauma narrative, the attempts by various actors and carrier groups, to bring to light and establish the mass murder of members of Poland's elite as a cultural trauma affecting a wider collective than the individual victims and their families. In an insightful discussion of the difference between psychological and cultural trauma, Neil Smelser (2004) finds one essential difference in the fact that cultural traumas are made not born. He goes on to define a cultural trauma as "an invasive and overwhelming event that is believed to undermine or overwhelm one or several essential ingredients of a culture or the culture as a whole" (Smelser in Alexander et al. 2004, 38). What we have traced in this essay are the attempts by individuals and then groups to firmly establish Katyn as such an event. One may metaphorically understand this process as opening a very heavy door to a big dark room—though quickly overwhelmed, we come to see and fully understand all there is inside only gradually, never instantly.

As we have seen, the case of cultural trauma of Katyn starts with the fundamental problem of the knowledge of facts, something usually taken for granted in trauma discourses. The very awareness of occurrences was for a long time partial and what was known was either suppressed or framed in a way that made the story controversial. The specificity of the case forces us to ask new general questions about the relation between such categories as knowledge, awareness, memory, commemoration, representation, and mass media. The sociological definitions of these terms are often taken for granted and their epistemological status hardly explored. One of the values of this study is that it may contribute to a better understanding of what we really mean when we employ these concepts in sociological practice and how complex that task of reconstruction really is.

Beyond power/knowledge there seems to exist the complex notion of memory/knowledge. Both definitional elements of the latter are mutually constitutive and fundamental. Yet, they are also largely passive phenomena. Memorizing something constitutes a necessary but not a sufficient condition of using it, that is, making it consequential for one's biography and the environment. There is, of course, no memory without knowledge; memory needs its objects (thus one can speak of memorialization as sites of memory as well as of commemoration and the accompanying ritual practices). At the same time, we cannot really know anything if we do not have memory. In actual practice, these categories largely overlap and thus exist as culturally shaped networks of meanings, not isolated cognitive entities.

Therefore the issue of cultural trauma is less a matter of traditionally conceived memory and more a matter of what structures memory and then what and how "activates" it. The memory/knowledge compound requires symbolically unpacking and articulation through social performances in order to be turned into active remembrance and acts of empathy. Memory/knowledge appears often as something essentially "dormant." To be become "active" and thus culturally consequential, it requires emotional commitments of various groups, ritualization of its core messages, and recurrent presence in different public media, especially visual ones. Above all, it needs to be experienced affectively and represented artistically within channels of broadly conceived popular culture if it is to matter for modern collective sense of belonging and continuity, identification and empathy.

We have also suggested that the denial of representation and lack of symbolic closure only deepens cultural trauma. The Soviet-imposed communist regime of Poland sought to silence the relatives and children and thus erase the traces of the past because it knew that as long as the memory of crimes symbolized by Katyn lived on, its legitimacy remained tenuous. Similar mechanisms of domination took place later elsewhere, for example in Pol Pot's Cambodia, where, as Ben Kiernan observes, "the Khmer Rouge hoped to use children as the basis of a new society without memory" (Kiernan 1997, xvii).

As for symbolic closure, we have tried to show that "the very fact that the story of Katyn was suppressed only made the mystique stronger" (Osiatynski 2010), thus making the imposed silence the story's "worst" aspect. Symbolic closure is also necessary for launching the processes of reconciliation. Here we can distinguish specific aspects: overcoming anonymity and disclosing all information; overcoming the silence of the victimized; the open acknowledgment of guilt by the perpetrators; the establishment of ritualized commemoration; establishing a reconciliation dialogue between representatives of perpetrators and victims. These elements of civil repair between Poland and Russia have only slowly and imperfectly been established since 1989. The remarkable immediate response on all sides to the plane crash on April 10, 2010 suggested that the case could finally cross the positive point of no return, making the requirements of full reconciliation more clear. Referring to the unprecedented openness of Vladimir Putin and the Russian authorities Polish Minister of Foreign Affairs Radosław Sikorski said, "I believe that Putin's reaction stems from the fact that he understood what Soviet Russia did to Poland, felt our pain, when another tragedy took place in Katyn" (Sikorski 2010). These words touched upon one of the social dynamics we have discussed in this article, namely that in order for cultural trauma to emerge a confluence of contingent and symbolic elements that construct a clear and accessible context for empathy and understanding is needed. If this condition is fulfilled, even unlikely identifications are possible and even the most oppressive silence can be overcome. Artistic representations like Wajda's *Katyn* are poignant stories that may function as "intellectual shock" (Hartman 2009). They condense many meanings of human tragedy under a single name. Katyn has become such a name.

Notes

1. This would include Lithuanians and Ukrainians, for example (Snyder 2002), as well as those Poles who fought in the Soviet army and those Polish Communists who remained true to communist ideology.

2. There were also about 7,000 civilians killed at other unknown locations. According to Paul (1991, 105), "for unknown reasons, the NKVD decided to spare 448 men from a total of 14,500 ... of those spared, 245 came from Kozelsk, 79 from Starobelsk, and 124 from Ostashkov." See Cienciala, et al. (2007) for the definitive numbers.

3. According to Paul (1991, 65) "the German and Soviet governments collaborated closely in their efforts to eliminate the Polish intelligentsia." He and others suggest that the two governments may also have colluded in the Katyn Massacre, making later claims and counter-claims of guilt and responsibility even more complicated.

4. Only one eyewitness lived to describe the moment and method of execution, Stanislaw Swianiewicz, now a professor of economics and author of *In the Shadow of Katyn* (Wcieniu Katynia) in 1976.

5. Saloman Slowes who survived and in 1992 published an account of his experiences discusses the fate of many Jews in the camp.

6. One survivor, Father Zdzislaw Peszkowski, recounts, "At Kozelsk, I discovered Poland." Allen Paul, who interviewed Peszkowski in 1989, explains, "What he meant was that, at Kozelsk, he met the best that Poland could offer. At 21, he had been thrown together with men from all parts of the country, a cross-section of the nation's professional elite" (Paul 1991, 70–71). Peszkowski was not a priest at the time, but after receiving a PhD in Polish literature from Oxford after the war, he was ordained in the United States in 1954.

7. Paul puts it this way, "The Germans recognized from the outset that their discovery presented a golden opportunity to split the Western Allies. They were keenly aware of the serious rift between the Soviets and the Polish government-in-exile over disputed territory in the western Ukraine and western Byelorussia. The Germans knew also that more than ten thousand Polish officers captured by the Soviets in 1939 were still missing when General Anders and his army-in-exile left the U.S.S.R. in 1942" (1991, 207).

8. The advancing Red Army also was the precipitating cause of a very dramatic attempt to preserve some of the incriminating documents that would help establish Soviet guilt. The documents found on the bodies of the victims at Katyn, such as newspaper clippings and other dated material which would have importance in establishing the date of the executions were hurriedly collected by the Germans and shipped to occupied Poland for safe-keeping for fear of falling in the hands of the NKVD which was keenly aware of both their existence and importance. These documents were later packed into fourteen shipping crates as the Russian army approached Krakow, where they were kept and sent to Germany. Further advances by the Soviet army and the pursuit of the NKVD pushed the documents farther and farther westward, until they ended up in the private home of the elderly father of Dr. Werner Beck, one of the forensic experts enlisted

by the Germans to carry out the exhumations at Katyn. Beck had himself seen to it that the documents arrived there, all the while with the Soviets in hot pursuit. The crates we finally burned on at his request, before they could fall into Soviet hands. All this came to light during the American House hearings in 1952, before which Beck testified (see Paul 1991, 269ff, for the full account).

9. Poland now issues a commemorative stamp for each ten-year anniversary. The first one issued to mark the 50th anniversary in 1990 shows a simple cross, while the 60th anniversary was marked with a more elaborate picture of a Catholic priest and a commemorative cross.

10. As a matter of fact, Soviet government led by Gorbatchev had appeared to be forced to admit its guilt officially after a few Russian historians, such as Natalia Lebedeva, obtained a rather unwittingly issued permission to examine NKVD archives that indirectly proved Soviet responsibility (Materski 2008, 125–126). The text of the TASS announcement itself was cautious but powerful enough and launched an avalanche of irreversible changes to the issue.

11. By 2010, there were so many commemoration sites that when another was proposed the head of the Katyn Families Association, Andrzej Shapski, was ready to say "that's enough" and that the money collected for this monument could be put to better social use (January 30, 2010, www.gazeta.pl).

12. Two other official cemeteries were opened in the same year in Kharkov in Ukraine and Mednoe in Russia.

13. To this day the Russian government has not delivered to the Polish side 21,857 personal NKVD folders of the killed. It claims that they had been destroyed. However, there is no confirmation that they were indeed burned (Materski 2008, 131).

14. In an interview Wajda explains that he had to choose between making a film about his father, the murdered officer, or his mother, the distraught and waiting relative. This he says is why the film took so long to make. In the end, he has tried to combine both stories (special features on the DVD). The character of the movie as an "Antigonic gesture," however, was obvious to the Polish critics (see Sobolewski 2007).

15. The director complained especially about the problems caused largely by the indolence of Polish National TV, responsible for the movie as a commercial product. Wajda described it as "murdering of the film" (Wajda 2009, 16).

16. *Katyn* has so far been largely omitted as an "inconvenient" picture; for example, in Italy, the fact that may be linked to the influence of Italian leftist circles (GW, April 23, 2009). Even one of the biggest cinema networks in the country that belongs to the family of Silvio Berlusconi launched only a DVD distribution of the movie. Whereas this may have come as an unexpected disappointment for some, it has not been surprising that the Russian distribution of the movie is almost nonexistent.

17. There is here, of course, a methodological problem at stake, namely how can researchers be sure that the statement "Yes, I have heard about Katyn" is not distorted by a more general framework that stigmatizes ignorance. It would perhaps be better to possess in this respect studies that elicit pertinent knowledge

or lack thereof indirectly. Still, even if the figure of 95 percent regarding those who declared they knew of Katyn were exaggerated, it is not unrealistic to assume that the vast majority of society indeed have heard about it by 2007 and thus could identify and respond to the issue. It is also interesting that the legacy of the communist propaganda is still visible. Even in the European countries not exposed to it in history associating Katyn with Nazi German apparently exists, for example, in Sweden where the daily Dagens *Nyheter* confused historical facts in this way while introducing Wajda's movie. See http://wiadomosci.onet .pl/1698369,12,item.html.

Works Cited

Abarinow, W. 2007. *Oprawcy z Katynia (The Perpetrators of Katyn)*. Krakow: Znak.

Applebaum, A. 2008. A Movie That Matters. *New York Review of Books*, vol. 55, no. 2, February 14.

Cienciala, A. M., N. Lebedeva, and W. Materski. 2007. *Katyn. A Crime Without Punishment*. New Haven and London: Yale University Press.

Czapski, J. 2001. *Na nieludzkiej ziemi (Inhuman Land)*. Krakow: Znak.

Gross, J. T., and I. Gross. 1981. *War Through Children's Eyes: The Soviet Occupation of Poland and Deportations, 1939–1941*. California: Stanford University Press.

Hartman, G. 2009. Introduction. In *Remembering Holocaust*, ed. J. Alexander. Oxford: Oxford University Press.

Iwinski, T. 2010. http://www.tokfm.pl/Tokfm/1,103454,7761693,Tadeusz_ Iwinski__Wierze__ze_to_bedzie_trwale_katharsis.html. Accessed April 12, 2010.

Janion, M. 2009. *Opowiadać o ludzkim cierpieniu – z profesor Marią Janion rozmawia Andrzej Franaszek (Talking about human suffering—interview with Maria Janion)*. Tygodnik Powszechny, at http://tygodnik2003-2007 .onet.pl/0,1390123,druk.html. Accessed August 25, 2009.

Kaczorowska, T. 2006. *Children of the Katyn Massacre*. Jefferson, NC: McFarland.

Kiernan, B. 1997. Introduction. In *Children of Cambodia's Killing Fields. Memoirs by Survivors*, D. Pran. New Haven and London: Yale University Press.

Kimmelman, M. 2009. Poland's Complicated Past Sparks Soul-Searching. *New York Times*, April 20.

Kościński, P. and T. Serwetnyk. 2008. Polacy gotowi wybaczyć Rosji Katyń (Poles are ready to forgive Russia the Katyn Massacre). *Rzeczpospolita*, February 8.

Ksiazek-Czerminska, M. 1999. Wstęp (Introduction). In *Pisane miłością – losy wdów katyńskich (Written with Love – Lives of the Katyn Widows)*. Gdynia: Stowarzyszenie Rodzina Katynska.

Materski, W. 2008. *Katyń, nasz ból powszedni (Katyn, our daily pain)*. Warszawa: Rytm.

Nim, N. 2008. Dziękujemy Wajdzie za Katyn (We thank Wajda for "Katyn"). *Gazeta Wyborcza*, March, 20.

Orla-Bukowska, A. 2006. New Threads in an Old Loom: National Memory and Social Identity in Postwar and Post-Communist Poland. In *The Politics of Memory in Postwar Europe*, eds. R. Lebow, W. Kansteiner, and C. Fogu. Durham: Duke University Press.

Osęka, P. 2007. Kłamstwo specjalnego znaczenia (A special lie). *Gazeta Wyborcza*, September 15–16.

Osiatynski, W. 2010. Polish Heroes, Polish Victims, at http://www.nytimes.com/2010/04/16/opinion/16osiatynski.html?emc=eta. Accessed April 16, 2010.

Paul, A.1991. *Katyn*. New York: Scribner's.

Sanford, G. 2005. *Katyn and the Soviet Massacre of 1940: Truth, Justice and Memory*. London: Routledge.

Sariusz-Skąpska, I. 2002. *Polscy świadkowie GUŁagu (Polish witnesses to Gulag)*. Krakow: Universitas.

Sawicki, J. 2007. Zanim powstala Dolinka Katyńska. Pamięć o Katyniu w pierwszych dekadach istnienia PRL (Before the Katyn Valley Was Created. The Memory of Katyn in the First Decades of the People's Republic of Poland). *Tygodnik Powszechny*, September 23.

Sikorski, R. 2010. http://www.tokfm.pl/Tokfm/1,103087,7761052,Sikorski_dzwonil_do_Jaroslawa_Kaczynskiego__Mam_straszna.html. Accessed April 12, 2010.

Slowes, S. 1992. *The Road to Katyn*. Oxford: Blackwell.

Snyder, T. 2002. Memory of sovereignty and sovereignty over memory. In *Memory & Power in Postwar Europe*, ed. John-Werner Muller. Cambridge: Cambridge University Press.

Sobolewski, T. 2007. Gest Antygony (Antigone's Gesture). *Gazeta Wyborcza*, September 17, at http://film.gazeta.pl/film/1,22535,4497644.html.

Szacka, B. 2007. Tylko elita pamięta? (Does only the social elite remember?). *Gazeta Wyborcza*, September 15–16.

Szumer, M. 2007. Obchody przesunięte (Commemoration postponed). *Metro*, n. 1184, October 5.

Venclova, T. 1999. *Forms of Hope. Essays*. Riverdale-on-Hudson, NY: The Sheep Meadow Press.

Wajda, A. 2007. Przeszłość nieopowiedziana – z Andrzejem Wajda rozmawiają Joanna Olczak-Ronikier i Tomasz Fiałkowski (An Untold Past—An Interview with Andrzej Wajda). *Tygodnik Powszechny*, September 23.

———. 2008. Pokazałem światu Katyń (I have showed Katyn to the world). *Gazeta Wyborcza*, February 26.

———. 2009. TVP blokuje "Katyń" (Polish TV blocks "Katyn"). *Gazeta Wyborcza*, January 2.

Wałesa, L. 2010. www.nytimes.com/2010/04/11. Accessed April 11, 2010.

Zaremba, M. 2010. Kulturkronikan (Culture Chronicle). *Dagens Nyheter,* April 13.

Zawodny, J. K. 1962. *Death in the Forest.* Notre Dame: Notre Dame University Press.

Zaslavsky, V. 2008. *Class Cleansing: The Massacre at Katyn.* New York: Telos Press.

11

Unassimilable Otherness

The Reworking of Traumas by Refugees in Contemporary South Africa

Ari Sitas

> Brothers and sisters ... of Africa ... African brothers and sisters ...
> how long ... well, can you hear me? How long must we suffer this...?
> (inaudible) ... killing and mayhem".
> —Alain (Refugee, DRC), speaking at the 2004 meeting
> of the Refugee Forum, Durban

> We are very good at writing position papers. If you read them, you
> will say, "this is what Zimbabwe is looking for." But there is no one
> to implement it. They are busy writing position papers.
> —Mujodzi Mutandiri, quoted in *Mail and Guardian*,
> February 19–25, 2010

In a piece titled "Freedom Fighters of the Diaspora," the press in South
Africa was beginning to capture what has been happening at a subterranean level in Johannesburg, Durban, Cape Town and increasingly, Eastern

Cape towns among refugees from the rest of the continent. Although the article focused on a number of remarkable Zimbabweans, the same themes could have been explored for Congolese, Eritreans, Ethiopians, Rwandese, Burundians, Somalis, Sudanese, and a growing number of West African refugees.

Since 1994, a stream of refugees has arrived in South Africa from a number of conflict zones on the African continent. They had all fled from frightening scenes of violence and war in their countries. This paper is a tentative first step in reflecting on how this post-1990s generational cohort of 30- and 40-year-olds of a peculiar third African Diaspora is constructing and reorganizing an African tragedy and an African trauma. Like prior generations from the continent who discovered each other in Europe or the Americas, it constructs a shared experience of Africa and Africans where the national and ethnic details are bracketed away.

There is a persistent feeling articulated by collectivities in Africa that they "have been subjected to a horrendous event that leaves 'indelible' marks on their group consciousness, marking their memories forever and changing their future identity in fundamental and irrevocable ways" (Alexander et al. 2004, 1). All movements on the continent—national or ethnic—have been involved in powerful constructions of "cultural traumata." The key difference lies in the constructions' fate: Unlike the trauma of the Holocaust, for example, very few of the narratives have emerged as moral universals and most narratives resonate within African communities but rarely beyond them.

The vintage formulation has Africa (especially sub-Saharan Africa) as a continent of humanism, sociality, and equality before the European pillage with the key trauma constructed around slavery, racism, and, after the late nineteenth-century imperial scramble for its resources, colonialism. For reasons that will become obvious as the paper unfolds, it is a disturbing construction because it asserts an "unassimilable otherness" from the rest of the world.

The contribution here is, therefore, a first attempt in the direction of understanding the symbolic figuration—a figuration that is increasingly defining the perception of current realities and of specific being-in-the world, a *Dasein* in Heideggerian parlance—of this trauma construction.

The paper relies heavily on narrative accounts elicited from 17 refugees; to that were added two focus-group discussions organized by SANKOFA in Durban and records and observations of *how* their plight was articulated at public events and gatherings under the auspices of the provincial African Renaissance Initiative.[1] Finally, the above was supplemented by a careful reading of ten "position papers" circulated by them in their countries through their networks. Unfortunately, only eight of the participants could be reached after the 2008 xenocidal attacks carried out by South Africans against their communities. This explosion of violence against other African foreigners that displaced close to a million people has sharpened their sense of vulnerability.

Respondents and participants in the Renaissance initiative came from the following countries: Democratic Republic of the Congo (3), Rwanda (3), Burundi (1), Somalia (2), Ethiopia (2), Eritrea (1), Zimbabwe (3), Nigeria (2), and Madagascar (1). For the purposes of this account, I will generalize their areas into larger units to avoid easy identification of voice. Thus, instead of referring to countries, I will speak about Great Lakes, Horn of Africa, SADC, and West Africa. Although the overall trajectory of conflict has been on the decrease since the formation of the African Union, conflagrations in Kenya, Nigeria, Zimbabwe, and the Ethiopian invasion of Somalia keep waves and waves of people on the move. Most certainly Burundi and Rwanda seem to have moved on from strife. The Congo, save the Eastern parts, seems to be stabilizing. And, despite war in much of the Horn of Africa and the fact that daily conversations hint that war is imminent once again (*Giorgis*, Horn of Africa), these countries have experienced some stability after their disastrous battles. Furthermore, Zimbabwe has a rocky settlement, and Nigeria seemed to have weathered the social explosion of violence between Muslims and Christians in the north (UNCR 2008 and 2009).

The refugees' arrival to South Africa straddled a ten-year period: It started in 1994 with the first Great Lakes refugee and ended with a West African refugee who arrived in 2005. Nine of the respondents came to South Africa during the 1990s, eleven in the 2000s. All of them are men. Since their arrival, twelve of them have been joined by their wives and kin. Eight have remained alone but have facilitated the passage of a number of relatives to South Africa and from South Africa to other destinations. For example, most of Pierre II's family (from SADC) is spread between Reunion Islands, Mauritius, South Africa, Canada, and Australia.

The Lake District refugees arrived from one of the bloodiest wars in the post-1970s period anywhere in the world: the second Congo War of 1998–2003. The estimate of lives lost is 3.8 to 13 million, and this figure includes combatants and noncombatants alike (Amnesty International 2004, UNCHR 2005/6). But the Congo War must be seen within the context of a broader Great Lakes Crisis in the 1970s, which includes the enormous tragedy of the Rwandan genocide in which anything from 1 to 4 million Tutsis died. Despite the overthrow of the Interhamwe power bloc among the Hutu and the return of some stability refugees kept on arriving in South Africa well into the 2000s (Mamdani 2002; Mann 2005).

Farther north, the turbulence on the Horn of Africa was deeply linked with the Ethiopian Revolution, the rule of the Derg and Mengisthu that cost 150,000 to 500,000 lives and is equally responsible for mass migrations, according to the respondent Assefa, from the Horn of Africa. Once the state collapsed into a number of feuding territorial warlords, thousands of Somalis joined their fleeing neighbors.

Since 1994, South Africa had become one of the key destinations for such refugees. These Diasporic communities and their intellectuals who were attuned to and defined change processes in their societies insisted on South Africa as a desired destination due to prior constructions. The ability of a society to avoid a bloodbath and move toward a negotiated revolution that prioritized human and social rights resonated within their communities.

It is estimated that refugees from the Horn of Africa and Lake District make up a sizeable proportion of the 5 million people who have crossed into South Africa. Most of them are illegal economic migrants and, in turn, have come to constitute about a tenth of the country's population. They have all subsisted on the margins of economic activity in the urban areas and still survive within networks of a broader community of economic refugees from their countries of origin. What they had not imagined, however, was how harsh the reality of a free South Africa—the South Africa of Mandela's land—would be (Adam and Moodley 2005; Boraine 2006).

Diasporic Public Intellectuals in Africa and Trauma Narrations

As a number of studies have shown, the process of gaining a refugee status in South Africa is cumbersome, hostile, bruising, and takes anything up to two years to be completed (Michael 2004; Gordon 2007; and Banoo 2008). Over and above working within their communities for cash, using their educational qualifications as a platform to enhance their future life-chances was key to their survival strategies in South Africa. They did both while waiting for their refugee status to be verified.

The difference between the cohort under discussion and the vast majority earning their keep in the unregulated side of the economy is that they possess some educational capital which had been interrupted by the violence. For example, seven had an incomplete undergraduate education, five had a basic undergraduate degree, and eight an interrupted post-graduate one. Those who had to flee quickly spent a lot of time try-ing to retrieve relevant documents in order to verify their educational achievements, using labyrinthine connections to their homeland. And in the case of the Great Lakes refugees, part of their plight was getting local education authorities to make sense of educational systems they knew nothing about. Most of them were admitted into the first years of tertiary education because, no matter what their prior qualifications were, their proficiency in English was poor.

Their commitment to educational advance harbored a dual jus-tification: the obvious one was about a better positioning in the labor market. The other led straight into the theme of this paper—that they saw themselves as new African *public* intellectuals. They were spokesmen for their national case-study in South Africa, connected to processes of change in their countries, and committed to Pan-African solutions. They were keen participants in the initiatives that Thabo Mbeki started through the African Renaissance Initiative and by Minister and later Premier Sbu Ndebele in KwaZulu-Natal, the African Renaissance Development Trust (Focus Group 1, June 2002). No matter what the detail, in terms of the cultural trauma theory they were and they saw themselves as carrier groups defining and constructing a new version of an African trauma.

To speak of "carriers" on the African continent is to speak of a cadre of educated intellectuals. Scholarship has traced the ways in which the early exponents of colonial nationalisms set about mobiliz-ing people, defining the colonial dramas and traumas and constructing national anticolonial identities (Langley 2000). These, "lonely bilingual intelligentsias," in the words of Benedict Anderson (1991), unattached to "sturdy local bourgeoisies" because they were negligible in colonial society, created the first waves of continentwide and colonial-societywide figurations.

Two generations back during colonialism proper, that is, after the scramble for Africa was completed and the Berlin conference defined the borders and parameters of European colonies, it was Diasporic students, post-graduates and *émigrés* in London, Paris, and Lisbon who defined the ideas of African Nationalism and Pan-Africanism with the core elements of its trauma woven around slavery and colonialism.

The mandatory migrations to colonial capitals that this involved became the platform for a cohort of social thinkers who devoted them-selves to struggles for independence, self-determination, and African unity. There was no accident in the fact that Kwame Nkrumah and Julius Nyerere, Eduardo Mondlane, and Amilcar Cabral, Leopold Sedar

Senghor, Aime Cesaire, and Zik Azikiwe were social thinkers, utopians, and political leaders during and after their intellectual sojourns to the West. They spoke the colonizer's language, studied in it, and, as leading political figures, mobilized national sentiment through their vernacular languages. Although the patterns of nationhood and trauma varied between Paris, London, and Lisbon (and for those advanced through the American church networks different as well) the key ideomorphic elements of a common experience were there (Davidson 1972, 1973, 1976, and 1981; Langley 1979; Gilroy 1992; and Young 2001).

The poetry of Negritude was a defining influence for all. Its powerful construction of slavery as an African holocaust and of a hell on earth, deeply enhanced by the writings of Diasporic intellectuals in the United States and the Caribbean, became the dominant trope for that generation and for the generations that were to follow. Cesaire's (1969) *Return to My Native Land* on the eve of World War II and later his *Discourse on Colonialism* became its axiomatic texts.

His words, articulating colonialism as a barbarism prefiguring Nazism, still resonate with the current generation: "barbarism, but the supreme barbarism, the crowning barbarism that sums up all the daily barbarisms, that it is Nazism, yes, but that before they [Europeans] were its victims, they were its accomplices; that they tolerated that Nazism before it was inflicted on them, that they absolved it, shut their eyes to it, legitimized it, because, until then, it had been applied only to non-European peoples; that they have cultivated that Nazism, that they are responsible for it ...'"(1979, 174). For the poet of Negritude, the trauma was unfathomable: "millions of men torn from their gods, their land, their habits, their life—from life, from the dance, from wisdom" (1979, 178).

Cesaire (1969 and 1990) was to embrace whatever colonists ascribed as backwardness and provocatively invert it. Julius Nyerere (Pratt 1976) was to sit down and draft a pacific, harmonious, and socialistic precolonial past and so it went—a community of intellectuals/carriers crafting a major idea of Africanity and its traumas. "It is there" argued Jean-Claude (of the Great Lakes District), "in the writings of Nyerere and Nkrumah and it is the impulse of the poetry of Cesaire ... that we find a voice."

The feeling of nationhood or ethnicity, the commonality of national sentiments among people was experienced (to echo Benedict Anderson 1991, 23ff) as a "deep horizontal, comradeship," in Africa and a comradeship in victimhood, of world racism, slavery, and colonialism.

The power of this imaginative construction was clear: Despite status distinctions, stratification, and downright exploitation that might have prevailed in a society, people experienced and articulated sentiments, beliefs, and acted in ways that reflected such comradeships. These dilemmas and imaginings form the substance of a recent book edited by Mkandhawire (2007) called *African intellectuals: rethinking politics, language, gender,* which captures such contours of feeling and resistance.

The second generation was, by contrast, a product of postcolonial national education systems and of the Cold War. A key feature of this period was also a shift in foreign destinations away from the old colonial powers and included migrations to the Soviet Union, China, or Cuba. Furthermore, during and after the Cold War, the main destination shifted toward the United States and decisively since 1994 to South Africa. The current generation sees itself as different from prior generations of carrier groups, because theirs is an attempt to save Africa (and by implication their countries) from a postcolonial crisis where the state has failed its "mandate" and "its people" (Jean Claude, Alain, Hercule, Johnas, Tito, and Mario interviews).

Thus, as I have argued elsewhere (in *The Ethic of Reconciliation* 2008, 25), "The first generation (of intellectuals) after the Second World War still believed in the 'goodness' of the nation while the second … (Cesaire and his contemporaries) believed in sacrifice and altruism, the necessary qualities for creating a future for the unborn. The state was the nation's avant-garde and the concentrate of force necessary for development. The cracks begun in earnest during the turbulent 1970s—the state was seen to be failing the nation. The new generation…. And when 'saving the nation' produced new elites and worsening forms of governance, the priority emerged to save its subjects—real, concrete and visceral subjects in the 'here' and 'now.'"

The Public and Oral Articulation of Trauma Narratives

There is no space here to provide a thick description of the gatherings within the African Renaissance initiative in South Africa and the power of orality and orature in public constructions of identity and identification. The "orature" of such events, the forms of poetry, rhetoric, and interaction have been discussed often by social scientists and have formed a backdrop for studies of social mobilization (Sitas 1980; Gunner 1989).

The initiative was set in motion by Thabo Mbeki when he was a deputy president in the Mandela administration and was propagated by cohorts around his leadership in the African National Congress and key leaders in the state administration. It was seen as a way of creating moral and social solidarity in the country but also as a platform for the transformation of the Organization of the African Union and the solidarity necessary to create a development agenda for the whole continent. It was therefore associated with his statecraft on the continent and as a key lever for helping decolonize South Africa.

Although state-led at first, the initiative took two dramatic turns: in the civil war–torn province of KwaZulu-Natal, it was seriously taken on by the incumbent leadership of the African National Congress to move the province beyond conflict, so it shifted the emphasis from state to civil society and made it a joint project with its erstwhile "enemies"— the leadership of the Zulu-centric Inkatha Freedom Party. The shift to civil society energies brought into prominence cultural movements like SANKOFA (taken from the mythical Ghanaian bird that flew back in time to heal the future), which organized many of its public events and performances.

Its emphasis on an *African* Renaissance was appealing to a growing body of foreign African academics and before long, to *émigré* and refugee intellectuals, who saw this as a wonderful way of revitalising currents in their own societies. The movement was particularly active in the KwaZulu-Natal province and meetings of between 100 and 1,000 people occurred weekly or biweekly between 1999 and 2003; the meetings culminated in bigger public events every March. They involved the participation of strong delegations from Atlanta in the United States coordinated by the National Association for the Advancement of Colored People (NAACP) and delegations from Africa, including mayors of major cities, activists in social and cultural movements, and intellectuals. For the leadership of the initiative and the leaders of SANKOFA, refugee participation was part and parcel of developing an awareness of a broader African plight. The initiative lost its momentum because of the increasing disquiet around the Mbeki administration's socioeconomic policies and the identification of key leaders in the movement with these policies.

All observations in the paper therefore, especially of the gatherings and events, are taken from this context. They all involved three cycles of performance and each one of such a cycle was composed of numerous parts. Indeed, very little of the constructions of horizontal comradeships can be understood if we remain with a scripted-text perspective of nationhood or pan-Africanism.

In the gatherings that involved the refugees in question, the speaker at the microphone would invariably start with establishing a commonality—"the brothers and sisters of Africa" discourse this paper started with. It was a call to shift out of ethnic or national traps and accept a broader identity, an identity that is assumed to be organic and immediately understood. The voice of our Rwandan, Congolese, or Ethiopian speaker was uncommon—in English but an English without the local inflections. Although 90 percent of the gathering was of Zulu descent, the language of the microphone was English, and on two of the occasions I attended, translations into isiZulu happened as an afterthought.

The commonality of the appeal was immediately backed up with an acknowledgment of the host country: the expressions of "Mandela's land," "this beautiful country," "this free part of Africa," or "this southern part of Africa," and here, variety and difference were "familiarized"—the narrative was expressed as if one was visiting a homestead, praising the host and invoking not only the generosity but also the importance of being hosted by these hosts. Of course, such expressions were common before the xenophobic turn of affairs alluded to.

Third, the speaker moved toward endearment by stating that "in my culture, we would say this in greeting" followed by a greeting in his or her vernacular, and then this very idiomatic statement would be translated by the speaker. It further reinforced the trope that beside the difference between "their" cultures, there was oneness. At this stage, on two occasions, the formal translator on the platform would retort by giving an example from the local culture; this received always murmur and applause.

The three "moves" would constitute the first cycle of signification. The second would involve the deepening of the bond that bound speakers from afar with the locals. This bond was about suffering, a broad undefined suffering always addressing the audience with a reminder that they too did know suffering. Translated into isiZulu would be *isikhala*—a polysemic word that borders almost on the Marxian concept of alienation, of homelessness, pain, and suffering.

The acknowledgment of suffering then slid invariably toward the White Man as a perpetrator in the imaginary—nothing specific—"he" as a transhistorical entity, a Manichean counterpoint. Nothing about the *Interhamwe* on Rwandan lips, of Mobutu or the various factions of the Congo, of the Derg or the Amharas, or of the warlords was ever mentioned—only a broad context of the White origins of a suffering.

Speeches then reached out to the transatlantic experience of slavery and into the forms of forced/corvee labor on the continent of mines and plantations—it was about the suffering of servitude and about real and metaphorical bondage. This completed the second cycle of the performative encounter.

The third cycle got down to graphic detail; it was an invocation of the violence they had come from and the horror that the metaphoric neighbor was the perpetrator, which in many cases was true, as in the Rwandan and Congolese conflagrations. It was not a personal experience or testament though; I never heard of what happened to the individual speaking as such from the stage, and I only came to hear about personally endured atrocities during one-on-one conversations. I might have expected that Hutu, Ethiopians, and Somalis would have different approaches to such gatherings, but they did not; the three performative cycles were similar no matter who spoke or invoked the past.

In the end, the performance listed general details—the kind of misdeeds, rapes, hackings, stabbings, burnings, shootings, bombs that happened. It was the killer neighbor that was invoked but with a question left hanging: who put the knife in his or her hand? The public gatherings of the African Renaissance movements where all the above were exercised did not provide an answer. What followed usually (at least in the gatherings I witnessed) were appeals to the ancestors, attempts to appease their confusion and the embellishment of the situation through biblical, Islamic or ancestral forms of symbolism. Whether Israelite or martyr, the subject of violence was standing in front of the gathering asking Africa to return, resurrect, and be reborn (renaissance).

The Texting of the Trauma Message

Written position papers on the "situation" in their countries addressed to their compatriots were nuanced in different ways. Like in the oral contexts of communication, they invariably started with the establishment of a "we," but the "we" was of concerned African intellectuals from, let us say, Nigeria, Chad, or Zimbabwe. The "we" was concerned about an X, and this X was a local, regional, or national issue. "We are concerned," for example, "about the continuous violence in Kimvu" or the "escalation of violence in Southern Sudan" or the "postelection violence in Kenya" or "the harassment of the opposition in Zimbabwe" (Anonymous Papers 1 [2006], 2 [2008], and 7 [2009]).

The sense of a broader silent and silenced community was palpable. "We feel compelled to break our silence... We cannot remain silent... We understand why people have been cowered ... Speaking out has become a necessity ... I know our words will not reach deaf ears" (Anonymous Papers 2 [2008], 3 [2008], 6 [2009], 8 [2009], and 10 [2009]).

Save in three cases (Anonymous Papers 1 [2006], 7 [2009], and 8 [2009]) where a long local history was rehearsed, the rest of the narrative in the texts leaped immediately to a generality of a common *African* experience—ever-exploited and used by all and sundry including "contemporary corrupted elites including the servants of Western Masters, the Kleptocrats, and the ethnic chauvinists" (Mario, Interview).

This was contrasted to a wonderful past. Jean-Claude from the Lakes District punctuated the feeling, "even if we had kings—and we did have ... the baKongo were a wonderful kingdom and so were the Lua and the Lunda ... the chiefs and kings were close to their people ... The slave trade destroyed them all." The continent's modernity carries a trauma with it since the sixteenth century, and since then, there has been the degradation and violence of the "fall" from that humane and most social past. Although this is accurate for many precolonial polities, there is no escape from the historical fact that many were rather powerfully hierarchical. Then what became part of a contrast that juxtaposed the organic, endogenous, and authentic against the inorganic, exogenous, and foreign. Yet most of the historical nuance was about the Cold War to make a point of how, once more, the continent's leaders were manipulated to serve other masters who fought out their proxy adventures on "African soil." This made sure the continuation of "remote-control colonialism" as "neocolonialism," which spawned tribalism and ethnic strife. In short, most forms of disunity were read off a master-narrative of division and divide and rule emanating from the West and from the Soviets.

Then, what emerges in the scripted papers is the moment of defiance. They are an invocation to reject categorically, to stand up once again proud, to assert, to decry, and to challenge the unacceptable, the oppressive, and the unimaginably arrogant derogation. This went hand in hand with the metaphors of slavery: to unshackle, to smash the chains of servitude, to lift the heads up from servile postures. And in the name of the poor and voiceless, the absolute majority and a democratic impulse the demand to say a historic "no."

There were, therefore, distinct tropes in the construction process that needed to be explored further. The differences between the "affective" style of the oral forms of communication in large gatherings and the "declaratory" style of the pamphlet are distinct. Yet they embellish in different ways a core trauma: the mark of being an African and black in a hostile world.

What these public interactions in both oral and written form highlighted were patterns of performance, yet the key question remained: who did the performance address?

Imagined and Real Publics for the Old and New Narrations

In the performances studies here, there were always real and imagined audiences, and any affective or declaratory utterance embodied a utopian hope for a hearing and a solidarity that ought to follow such a hearing. Addressed were one's "own people," "other suffering people," and usually a broader liberal or tolerant world (Focus Group 1 2001) or other imagined and ideologically linked cohorts (Focus Group 2 2001). In short, any utterance or enunciation presupposed an attempted communication to *heteronomous* publics. Who were the members of such publics that were imagined or known to be available?

The first generation of intellectuals from Africa appealed to publics in Europe on the moral grounds of self-determination. Here, they had more responses from a liberal and humanitarian clergy and from students and radical intellectuals like Jean Paul Sartre than from political liberals who believed that colonial administration, stripped of its oppressive features, was about progress and development and was a lever that would lift people out of backwardness.

In the Soviet world was a yet more ready audience. Self-determination and the right of subjects to constitute native republics was part of the core Comintern position on the colonial question; it was a core part too of the Stalin legacy on the "national question." The horrors expressed *vis-à-vis* slavery and colonialism fit well with the direst narratives about imperialism and the savagery of capital and capitalism.

A third public was being constituted as more and more third-world countries gained independence: China and India by the late 1940s strode toward independence and revolution, respectively. Others were to follow suit and, to use shorthand, in the ensuing decade, a nonaligned Bandung public was becoming available to such discourses.

As mentioned previously, the second generation was trapped in the snares of the Cold War. At the continental level, support for struggles against Apartheid South Africa and the Portuguese colonies of Angola and Mozambique provided grounds for a unified effort, but the pan-African idea was scuttled. The heteronomous publics of the previous generation started becoming Cold War fortresses.

Intellectuals in Africa appealed instead to the post-1968 generation's sensibilities in Europe and the United States. But it did matter with whom one sided in the Cold War; this was even true of life and audiences in the more liberal and tolerant cities of the world like London and Paris, where many of the African intellectuals had gone as the continent was overrun by militarists and by rapacious power elites.

The refugees under discussion are an important group within the "third generation" of intellectuals. The past traumas were woven by them with the forms of violence they had just escaped. The recent and (mostly) unprocessed experiences that had caused their flight were unspeakable and unwriteable. Memory—including stories of being recruited to fight in grassroots militia and killing or having their kin killed—brought with it forms of disturbance and often somatic distress. The intensities of oral mobilizations in villages, executions, rape, looting, fear, remorse about beliefs in evil others, anger at the banditry of operations, lives in refugee camps, and voodoo-linked experiences were processed through cultural formations, through grief rituals and through a politics of avoidance. They also crafted a metanarrative of suffering against what they believed were corrupt regimes. If there were serious limits to the audiences that the first two generations could reach, the third generation has not been trying to have an audience at all beyond the continent—its trauma weaving is for an imagined "own" people. Here, then, is the difference from prior generations: the cultural and civilisational turn that Samuel Huntington has written about in his Clash of Civilisations finds a serious echo in the narratives of the current generation of African refugees and migrants. They, too, argue that the universalism of the West's norms was a ruse for further domination, and therefore, such norms should be made parochial and idiomatic. They assert that they belong to a different cultural formation. Africans must modernize without Westernizing; there is no cosmopolitanism but West-politanism and Afropolitanism.

Secondly, exilic migrants in the West are adding to the weaving of a different experience of Africanity as they speak of a cultural and "unassimilable otherness." This is particularly powerful in the creative work of performers and writers who are of African descent but who are citizens of European states. "As long as they think they can push you/Around with unwritten laws/About which country you should live in/You are not safe" intones Lemn Sissay, who is of Ethiopian descent (2008). Any careful scrutiny of Lemn Sissay's performance poetry brings home his point: "Let the aged Ethiopian man in the grey block of flats/Peer through his window and see Addis before him/So his thrilled outstretched arms become frames/For his dreams." Examining the poetry of young Wari (of Somali descent) or of Dorothea Smartt (of Caribbean descent) points to a similar structure of feeling: it articulates a powerful aesthetic of distantiation: "Who will heal and elevate to light/the souls of your ancestors if you refuse to remember?" (Smartt 2008) In all their works, lyricism turns into discord when England is described: "Englan' as a Bitch" as well as Babylon and as Purgatory. Paul Gilroy's "slave sublime" in Diasporic communities has been turned further away from the original impulse into a "disaffective" trope discouraging appeals to solidarity.

In short, the cultural formations of black residents in the West's metropolises suggest a distancing from the West's concerns and a turning to each other to endorse or appreciate the distance.

South Africa's Location

The transition to a national democracy in South Africa demonstrated that despite clashing nationalisms and differential and irreconcilable traumas, it was possible to find a third-space abstracted from historicity to facilitate change. Arguing that the past was regrettable and apartheid an ecumenical sin, South African power elites and political movements agreed to move on. Most of the respondents noted how touched or moved they were about such a possibility. The performative process of creating a "forgiving" and transcendent nation was enticingly appealing to most, especially for those refugees who had come from devastating conflicts, including Hercule and Maurice (from Great Lakes). As Hercule suggested, if only their own societies could reach a consensus that the past was regrettable, life would move on (for an account of reconciliation, see also Villa-Vicencio and Verwoerd 2005).

On the pragmatic level, economic opportunities to supplement incomes were also a significant pull factor for migration to South Africa (*Maurice*, Great Lakes, *Aziz*, Horn of Africa, interviews). One in every four people in the country until 2008 was a foreign migrant, and these migrants engaging themselves actively in the nooks and crannies of the South African economy and boosting the dynamism of its informal trade, and each one of the intellectual refugees had to be involved in "home" communities to finance their studies, accommodation, and activities (according to Mario from Horn of Africa). Whereas opportunities to eke out an existence were abundant, solidarity was not.

At first, the migrants were alarmed by the degree of xenophobia shown by locals and the lack of solidarity and compassion. What devastated their existential and ontological assumptions was how xenophobia turned to *xenocide* in 2008. The shock of the South African xenocidal attacks in Gauteng and Cape Town and the threat of them in Durban created a new crisis. Some expressed anger at South Africa's role toward Zimbabwe (here, there was direct division between ZANU-PF supporters and opposition intellectuals, but the former can hardly be called refugees) and about Sudan/Darfur. But the attack on any other foreigners from Africa, involving refugees and immigrants from thirteen countries, destroyed in their minds the power of the South African "model" (according to Alain from Great Lakes). But these attacks did not alter much of the ongoing process of weaving, displaying, and narrating the trauma.

The tensions and nuances in this process of construction and reconstruction are many, and they would need more qualitative research over a longer period of time. The key point is that the refugees' self-ascribed authority to *articulate* the trauma and the modality of its articulation is—whether oral, written, or retold to a keen listener—a shifting and sometimes incoherent discourse. As a discourse, it is made up of discursive contours that are constantly brought together to define the location of an African trope. In the next few pages, I will analyze seven such contours.

I am suggesting that most tropes or narrations of a trauma tend to bring together a number of discursive units: They define a "we," the subjects of the trauma. They define the "they" of the "blame," point to the continuance of the "blame stressors," and point to the social condition this generates. Further, they distinguish their voice from what went before, and they point to the political sociopolitical implications of all the above, and in this case, given Africa's unique multiethnicity and diversity, it has to point to how unity is plausible in diversity.

The Discursive Contours of the Trauma Narrations

Seven contours need to be traced if the contemporary definition of Africa's trauma can be put in some sharp relief. I will take each one of them in turn. These contours and their commonalities are present in the oral performances and written texts outlined above and in the cultural formations of Africans in this new Diaspora.

First, there is a social being, which is African that is deeply marked by the trauma of racism and slavery; it shapes both its possible solidarities and patterns of life. The color line is defined by historical wounds on whose base colonialism erected a racial superstructure. The first modality, therefore, is about the existence of a different African ontology that is uniquely different from the rest—our understanding of being, beings, and social beings is distinct and that defines both an African cosmology, community, and, simultaneously, an alterity.

In some of its more essentialist manifestations, there is a serious tension with Islam and Christianity. The Senegalese filmmaker Sembene Ousmane, for instance, has consistently painted Islam as an alien colonizer and the poet Mazisi Kunene (1982) has never tired of attacking the role of Christian missionaries. Whereas the previous generation sought out an ecumenical conception of an equal world, in the current reconstruction Africans are articulated as bearers of a core difference: Africans are coded as part of an "unassimilable alterity." Whatever Europeans claim, the argument goes, is also idiomatic and not universal.

The second contour is about "the corrupted." The interviewees agree that the agencies of violence and of conflict are African and African-led. But the cohorts, power-elites, rulers who come to benefit from it are seen as "corrupt" or better, "the corrupted." The inflection is important, as corrupt is not so much a personal attribute as the result of pressure from external forces. In this way, the problem of corruption is not owned, but instead fingers are pointed at inflictors of the problem—not corrupt, but corrupted. It refuses to own "the" problem. "They" have been victims of external forces and/or internal servants of external forces and have been corrupted by Western interests and by, to use Bayart's expression, the "politics of the belly" (1993). Although culpable, "monstrous" and "obscene" in the words of Acille Mbembe, they have been *made* culpable by resource bandits, by the Cold War and by polarizations between "Christianity and Islam … and Western multinationals" (2002). Pierre II (SADC) blames all the misfortunes of the recent troubles of his island country to such corruptions. The World Bank also appears as an extension of all of the above evils and, most importantly, South African power elites are seen to have been totally absorbed in such corruptible snares. The new elites and the forces that control them are part of the new scramble for Africa's resources.

Jean Claude is particularly upset about the conflagration in the Congo. Whereas in the past, "Lumumba's mistake was to underestimate the French, the Belgians and the Americans … siding with Russia in the Cold War was a mistake …" (Jean Claude interview). As a mistake it plunged the country into a failed uprising, a guerilla war, and a devastation meted by mercenaries. And, "resource banditry: Katanga, whoever controls Katanga gets the loot … you see African faces with guns but where does the loot go? Where do you think it goes?" (Jean Claude interview).

Tefera agrees about the Cold War: "the misery of the Cold War—are you with the Russians or the Americans … and then, who funded the guerillas? The Tigrayans? The Eritreans?"

The third aspect is the awareness through their networks of the growth of neoracism in Europe and in the old Soviet world and the tightening of immigration in the North Americas and Europe. "As good pastoralists" Aziz states, "we know that Europe is a better grazing ground once you are in, but it is difficult to get in … Our brothers there they are doubly oppressed—for being black and for being Muslim" (Aziz interview). He goes on to assert, "African immigrants in the USA are the most educated and highly skilled professionals you will ever find … the African Americans are really suffering, there …"

Tito concludes, "everywhere, black is discriminated, suspected, pushed around—you see the national teams of France and England and you would think that most probably that Queen Elizabeth was black." Discrimination in Europe and race-based attacks have been on the

increase, and that is why the EU has created the Racism and Xenophobia (RAXEN) Observatory to monitor this escalation (Charakis Kristis
ed. 2004). The cohort informing this study understood all that. What
troubled them was South Africans' vicious response to their presence.
There is a strongly shared belief that the West and whites in general are
in the main "unreconstructed racists." Despite attempts to dismantle the
last vestiges of institutional racism, racism and xenophobia are on the
increase in all major cities in Europe and, it has "infected even South
African blacks who see other Africans as inferior and exploitable crea-
tures," says Aziz (from Horn of Africa). For the Great Lakes people in
this study, "South African mentalities" have been irreparably damaged
by Apartheid. The only thing that procures safety for refugees are bribes
and allegiance to "important protectors." There is a growing consensus
that the attacks on other Africans were not about any "phobia" but about
feelings of superiority.

Fourth, their contemporary existence is defined by their exilic and
peripatetic existence. They expressed being at home anywhere and no-
where in the world and strategically, instrumentally, and substantively
they are citizens of convenience. And this wandering is part and parcel of
their self-understanding. It is not that the respondents here had travelled
intensely but that they were connected to people who have spread out in
far-flung ways. Their strategic and heuristic use of local space brought
and brings ire among locals who feel that they do not have a sense of
belonging and commitment to local priorities.

Also, as they emphasized, one could disappear in Paris, for example,
within a large enclave of African-ness, which had limited interaction
with locals. Similarly, one could be invisible in Johannesburg and stay
in touch with the fastest growing cities in the world—Lagos, Kinhasa,
Addis Ababa and their networks of opportunity and mobility. Clearly,
their idea of struggle has shifted away from a peasant base or dreams of
a peasant revolution. All this adds up to a different structure of feeling
from the generations that preceded them. "My cousins are in Valoon and
I have a sister in Bordeaux ... South Africa was good for a while but no
... I think the best place is in Louvain—there people are less racistic [sic]
..." said Jean Claude (from Great Lakes).

What kept them in touch are cell phones with roaming access, cheap
Bangladeshi call shops, and Internet cafes organized by other Diasporic
Africans. Most of their country migrants are linked to entrepreneurs
who make cheap telephone and Internet time available and, most importantly, to freight and money-moving agencies. As citizens of the world,
they imagine home could be anywhere, "Oh we are in California ... in
New York and quite a few in Italy. Dubai and the Gulf too is becoming

an attractive destination ... South Africa is either a first step or a final destination. You can choose ..." says Tefera (from Horn of Africa).

Fifth, despite the fact that they borrowed much from the old, such as their understanding of the trauma of racism, slavery, and colonialism, they were circumspect about violence. They had seen too much of it. The generation celebrates Fanon (1967) of the *Black Skins, White Masks* variety but it does not have the stomach for the violence implied in the *Wretched of the Earth* (1966) (Gibson 1993). All the Zimbabweans I interviewed were re-reading the anarchic energy of Dumbudezo Marechera (1988) endorsing his rejection of all postcolonial elites and regimes of power.

The esteem that older guerilla struggles garnered or the admiration of strong military officers that could rise above the corruption and divisions in the nation-state were carefully pushed aside—the Great Lakes disaster, the wars that ensued after Frelimo and MPLA took power, the violence of the Ethiopian revolution and its overthrow, and their fighting over lost and desperate causes made them more committed to nonviolent outcomes. "For some of us, the thought that a total war or a total insurrection would right the wrongs and fix the past is not acceptable anymore," said Tefera (Horn of Africa). Similarly, "there are strong currents that are arguing for raising money and buying 'equipment' but it is an idle threat," according to Jean Claude (Great Lakes).

Sixth, there was an acceptance of a democratic imaginary. The old idea of an anti-imperialist imaginary stopped at self-determination, but its content was rarely democratic. To repeat what has been argued previously, the old traumas of the prior generation hinged on a metanarrative of slavery and colonialism that was constructed as a common experience of what Paul Gilroy had (following du Bois) termed a double-consciousness. This was the terrain of *émigré* intellectuals of the second African Diaspora who wove a powerful discourse of a continental trauma. Formulated in the capitals of the colonial world by *émigré* intellectuals who were meeting each other for the first time, it prohibited assimilation to the norms of the colonizer and demanded self-determination. As Tefera notes in this self-determination imaginary, "Ethiopia has always been the beacon of self-determination for colonized Africans."

Yet self-determination did not necessarily mean democracy. In this cohort, there was a commitment to a democratic imaginary necessary to put an end to the corrupted elites of postcolonial society. This they distinguished from the West's human rights approaches, which they considered self-serving and a way of Westernizing non-Western societies. They pointed to historical precedent: it was racism and colonialism that denied African people their democratic rights, for example, the Black Codes, Lugardian forms of indirect rule, segregation, and Apartheid. As Maurice (of Great Lakes) said, "The West has always denied Africans equal rights."

Finally, multiethnicity, they argued, has to be saved from its political exploitation, and societies ravaged through ethnic cleansing and violence must be reconstructed through reconciliation processes. It is heartening to read in Michael Mann's work that "unlike Europe, there has been no long-term trend toward an ethnically cleansed African continent" (2005, 262). The sheer multiethnicity of the continent has always provided checks and balances in the construction of larger polities. Yet, war, violence, displacement, and flight have been a defining feature of sociopolitical life devastating large tracts of the Continent. The number of refugees and displaced people far outnumber other parts of the world as a proportion of the population. Yet, the modulation has less to do with this violence than with the nature, intensity, and meaning-making processes. The consensus among informants was that multiethnicity is no problem *per se*; it is its political exploitation that should be avoided.

Here, Assefa differed with Aziz on their interpretations, "It is their (ethnic differences) careful usage that is important, like in Ethiopia where ethnic elections combine with cross-ethnic party existence." Aziz disagreed, saying "it will start again ... the minute you give ethnicity a political canton you might as well break up your country ... It will not avoid the bloodshed later ... How long are we to blame colonialism for the impossibility of forming strong nations?" He adds that "the arbitrary borders were drawn a hundred years ago, how long do we have to perpetuate the vulnerability?" His conclusion is clear: "like the umma of Islam, Africanity should bind all."

These discursive units and contours are constitutive of the trauma trope as it unfolds in and about Africa. Such "contours" become mutually reinforcing as they afford both generalization and particularity: All little corruptions can be subsumed under the general one. The general one can wear a black mask but it is essentially white. Both perpetrators and victims can be victims; all elites can be criticized as well as absolved of the "key crime"; and economic survival in the "cruel new global world" (Tefera interview) can be seen as resilience and pluck.

All trauma narratives have to absorb and situate concrete experience, and they do so by imaginatively creating primary (archetypal) and paradigmatic codes.

The task here is not to raise moral or philosophical problems but rather to understand the emotional geography of a sustained cultural trauma which remains, among African intellectuals, a subaltern discourse in and of the world. Like any discursive formation it has its own erasures: externalizing culpability, proscribing universalism, dissolving difference into a similitude. Whether it leads to a more profound humanism or not, is a matter of conjecture or political engagement.

A Tentative Conclusion

The refugees who have articulated the previous statements are only a small part of migrating humanity in Africa, yet their voices have been amplified in the last few years as xenocidal attacks in South Africa targeted all foreigners. By implication, these attacks targeted people who did not come from such conditions of existential strife. One of the participants, Adebayo, graphically described their plight as being on "the famished road" referring to a powerful novel of the same name by the Nigerian author Ben Okri (1991). More appropriate to their plight would be the African traveler of Okri (1995), who in seeking self-identity in Africa knows that, to get there, one has to cross a bridge over an abyss. The only way to do so is by holding the bridge up. No prior or contemporary others would or could do it for him or her.

The narratives of slavery, racism, colonialism, and now of postcolonial violence by the "corrupted" is not trying to reach all audiences. The refugees all knew that their plight would be heard by a small range of people. Most certainly for the moment, a Nelson Mandela–like universalism is not part of their vision. They understand the meaning of a people being identified as an existential deviant and then dealt with in a horrific manner. Most of them are aware of the Holocaust itself as a traumatic event, and while it echoes strongly with them, I want to suggest it shrinks somewhat in significance because of three important factors: naturalization, nativization, and the spread of Islamic ideas.

It is natural that perpetrators of a system like slavery would—with its racism, its camps dotting the African coastline ("slave factories" as they were known), its Guinea-holds (slave ships), and its forms of exterminism—import such a system into Europe in times of crisis. In the words of Fanon and Cesaire, the Holocaust was an internalization of slave and colonial-based holocausts. Second, three of the respondents pointed to Mahmood Mamdani's work as a recent exposition of the origins of scientific and Nazi racism in Namibia. The naturalization therefore leads to nativization and the experience of Africans was considered worse than the experience of the Jews: "Nobody invoked the Human Rights

Declaration (the U.N. declaration of 1949) to overthrow or implement a regime change in the USA in the 1950s and 1960s on the basis of Black or Negro rights," said Amos (from SADC). Third, the spread of Islamic ideas in West and East Africa brings the plight of the Palestinians as the victims of Israeli "suprematism" supported by "white regimes" in the West (Aziz interview).

The main point I want to make is that this cohort asserted and accepted an "unassimilable otherness" from the rest of the world. They were not puzzled anymore about the lack of empathy for Africa's traumas, but they have made "the" distance part of their defining ideas.

There are three points to conclude with: first, it is important to understand a relevant but more private and existential process occurring alongside all of the previously stated. Underneath the public construction, there is a more visceral process underway where the refugees' own irreducible traumas are being played out within smaller communities of care, and where grief processes are trying to recenter such traumatized individuals toward effective forms of social competence. The Adebayos, Azizes, and Teferas of this narrative are reconstructing livelihood strategies, gender relations, transnational forms of communication, and coexisting and new defensive combinations and norms. The moral calculus to be found in the distance between a public trauma and the private working-through of the horror of the actual event is of vital and continuing scholarly relevance.

Second, the political importance of understanding this cohort is undoubted. This necessity to create a genuine international discussion is not just a scholarly undertaking but a commitment to help in the political process that has been nudging the continent toward pacific solutions to seemingly intractable polarizations. The emergence of the African Union (with a stronger normative mandate than the Organization of African Unity, seeking to emulate the success of the European Union in creating a pacific Europe) is seeking ways to move power blocs beyond the contours of their existing cultural traumas. A theory of cultural trauma is timely to modify the construction's impact and to work with dispositions toward reconciliation across historic fault lines.

Finally, Africa's experience of violent change and transformation and the subsequent public construction of traumata demand deeper levels of understanding. What is provided here is a first tentative interpretation of a process. It would be vital to continue listening to the inflections of the oral world of such public constructions and try and see whether the *three* cycles of such performative constructions are generalizable as collective forms of symbolic figuration. For example, will people who control the foreground—the microphone or the loudhailer—go through a discursive construction that starts with the establishment of a commonality ("the brothers and sisters of Africa"), asks for a shift out of the "particular" (ethnic or national traps), and accepts a broader identity that is assumed to be organic and immediately understood? Would the second cycle always involve the weaving of a broad undefined suffering shared by all? And, would they always finger the White Man as the Manichean Beelzebub, the servitude inducer? In the third cycle, will all the horrific experience of the present and its details flow straight out of the last two? Is this the trope of the visceral and oral construction of a public trauma?

Interviewees

Great Lakes Region: Jean Claude, Pierre, Alain, Maurice, Hercule, Brother, and Maurice
West Africa: Adebayo and Johnas
SADC: Moses, Emmanuel, Tito, and Pierre II
Horn of Africa: Tefera, Assefa, Giorgis, Mark, Aziz, Mario

Note

1. The initiative was really underway between 1999 and 2005; the original refugee forums were initiated by the social justice wings of church congregations in the province. The first links with SANKOFA, the nonprofit Organisation of the African Renaissance Initiative headed by Professor Pitika Ntuli, which involved often the Zambian-born historian Yonah Seleti and myself, were established in 2001. The broader African Renaissance Development Trust headed by Sibusiso Ndebele (the minister of transport at first and later premier of the province). I served as a trustee until 2004. The interviews were conducted between 2001 and 2005 as an attempt to provide the contours of the new cultural formation for further discussion. Deepest gratitude to Astrid Von Kotze, who spent hours listening to and helping shape the coherence of this text and to Jeffrey Alexander for critical commentary.

The interviewees are listed at the end of the chapter, according to their region of origin (see the Interviewees section).

Works Cited

Adam, H., and M. Kogila. 2005. *Seeking Mandela: Peacemaking between Israelis and Palestinians (Politics, History, and Social Change).* New York: Temple University Press.

Alexander, J., R. Eyerman, N. J. Spencer, and P. Sztompka. 2004. *Cultural Trauma.* Berkeley: University of California Press.

Amnesty International, Annual Report. 2004/2005. *Democratic Republic of the Congo.*

Anderson, B. 1991. *Imagined Communities.* London: Verso.

Anonymous Paper 1. 2006. *On the Challenges of the DRC.*

Anonymous Paper 2. 2008. *On the Violence in Southern Sudan.*

Anonymous Paper 3. 2008. *On the Rising Tensions on the Horn of Africa-Invasion of Somalia.*

Anonymous Paper 4. 2008. *On the Continuing Strife in Chad.*

Anonymous Paper 5. 2009. *On the End of the One-party State in Africa.*

Anonymous Paper 6. 2009. *On Repression in Zimbabwe.*

Anonymous Paper 7. 2009. *On the Violence in Zimbabwe and Kenya.*

Anonymous Paper 8. 2009. *On the Delta Troubles in Nigeria.*

Anonymous Paper 9. 2009. *On the Eastern Congo.*

Anonymous Paper 10. 2009. *On the Violence against other Africans in South Africa.*

Banoo, S. 2008. Failure to Protect Refugees in South Africa. MA Thesis, Global Studies Programme, Albert-Ludvigs University, Freiburg.

Bayart, J. 1993. *The State of Africa: the Politics of the Belly.* London: Longmans.

Boraine, A. 2006. The Price of Peace. In *Retribution and Reparation in the Transition to Democracy,* ed. J. Elster. New York: Columbia University Press.

Cesaire, A. 1969. *Return to My Native Land.* Harmondsworth, UK: Penguin.

———, ed. 1992. *Discourse on Colonialism.* New York: Monthly Review Press.

Charakis K., ed. 2004. *Racist and Anti-Social Tendencies in Cypriot Youth.* Athens: Sakkoulas Press.

Cranford P. 1976. *The Critical Phase in Tanzania, 1945–1968: Nyerere and the Emergence of a Socialist Strategy.* Cambridge: Cambridge University Press.

Davidson, B. 1972. *In the Eye of the Storm: Angola's People.* Harmondsworth, UK: Penguin.

———. 1973. *Black Star: a view of the life and Times of Kwame Nkrumah.* Harmondsworth, UK: Penguin.

———. 1976. *Southern Africa: the New Politics of Revolution.* Harmondsworth, UK: Penguin.

———. 1981a. *The People's Cause: a History of Guerillas in Africa.* London: Longmans.

———. 1981b. *No Fist is Big Enough to Hide the Sky: the Liberation of Guinea and Cape Verde.* London: Zed Press.

Eyerman, R. 2001. *Cultural Trauma: Slavery and the Formation of African American Identity.* Cambridge: Cambridge University Press.

Fanon, F. 1966. *The Wretched of the Earth.* London: Grove Press.

———. 1967. *Black Skins, White Masks.* London: Grove Press.

First, R. 1970. *The Barrel of a Gun: Political Power in Africa and the Coup d'etat.* London: Allen Lane.

Fukuyama, F. 1992. *The End of History and the Last Man*. London: Penguin.

Gibson, N. C. 2003. *Fanon: the Postcolonial Imagination*. Cambridge: Polity Press.

Gilroy, P. 1992. *The Black Atlantic: Modernity and Double Consciousness*. London: Verso.

Gordon, S. 2007. Trade Union Responses to Alien Workers in South Africa, MA Thesis, Global Studies Programme, Albert-Ludwigs University, Freiburg.

Guevara, C. 2001. *The African Dream: The Diaries of the Revolutionary War in the Congo*. London: Grove Press.

Gunner, E., ed. 1999. *Politics and Performance*. Johannesburg: University of the Witwatersrand Press.

Huntington, S. P. 1989. *The Clash of Civilizations and the Remaking of the World Order*. New York: Simon & Schuster.

Kunene, M. 1978. *Ancestors and the Sacred Mountain*. London: Heinemann.

Langley, A. J., ed. 1979. *Ideologies of Liberation in Black Africa: 1856–1970*. London: Rex Collins.

Mamdani, M. 2002. *When Victims Become Killers: Colonialism, Nativism and the Genocide in Rwanda*. Princeton: Princeton University Press.

Mann, M. 2005. *The Dark Side of Democracy*. Cambridge: Cambridge University Press.

Marechera, D. 1984. *Mindblast or the Perfect Buddy*. London: Heinemann.

Mbembe, A. 2001. *The Postcolony*. Berkeley: University of California Press.

Michael, A. 2004. The Commissioner for Refugees: A Regime Theoretical Analysis of Global and Local Impact, MA Thesis, Global Studies Programme, Albert-Ludwigs University, Freiburg.

Mkandawire, T. 2005. *African Intellectuals: Rethinking Politics, Language and Gender*. London: Zed Books.

Okri, B. 1991. *The Famished Road*. London: Jonathan Cape.

———. 1995. *Astonishing the Gods*. London: Phoenix House.

Ong, W. 1982. *Orality and Literacy: the Technologizing of the World*. London: Routledge.

Sissay, L. 2008. *Something Dark*. London: Oberon.

Sitas, A. 1980. Traditions of Poetry in Natal, *Journal of Southern African Studies* 16(2) 307–326.

———. 2008. *The Ethic of Reconciliation*. Durban: Madiba Press.

———. 2010. *The Mandela Decade, 1990–2000: Essays in Labour, Politics and Society*. Pretoria: University of South Africa Press.

Smartt, D. 2008. *Ship Shape*. London: Caribbean Voices.

United Nations Committee on Human Rights. 2005–2006. Reports.

United Nations Committee on Refugees. 2008–2009. Annual Reports.

Vail, L., ed. 1989. *The Creation of Tribalism in Southern Africa*. Berkeley: University of California Press.

Vansina, J. 1965. *Oral Tradition. A Study in Historical Methodology*, trans. H. M. Wright. London: Routledge & Kegan Paul.

Villa-Vicencio, C., and V. William. 2005. *Looking Back, Reaching Forward: Reflections on the Truth and Reconciliation Commission of South Africa.* London: Zed Books.

Young R. J. 2001. *Postcolonialism: An Historical Introduction.* Oxford: Blackwell.

About the Contributors

Jeffrey Alexander is the Lillian Chavenson Saden Professor of Sociology and co-director of the Center for Cultural Sociology at Yale University. He works in the areas of theory, culture and politics, developing a meaning-centered approach to the tensions and possibilities of modern social life. His recent publications include *Remembering the Holocaust: A Debate* (Oxford University Press 2009) and *The Performance of Politics: Obama's Victory and the Democratic Struggle for Power* (Oxford University Press 2010). His collection *Performance and Power* is forthcoming.

Elizabeth Butler Breese is a PhD candidate at the Department of Sociology at Yale University and a junior fellow at the Center for Cultural Sociology. Her recent publications include "Meaning, Celebrity, and the Underage Pregnancy of Jamie Lynn Spears" (*Cultural Sociology* 2010) and "Reports from 'Backstage' in Entertainment News" (*Society* 2010). Her dissertation is a cultural sociological study of the news and journalism in the United States.

Dominik Bartmanski is a PhD candidate at the Department of Sociology at Yale University and a junior fellow at the Center for Cultural Sociology. His latest publications include "Successful Icons of Failed Time: Rethinking Post-communist Nostalgia" (*Acta Sociologica* 2011). His dissertation thematizes the "iconic turn" as a new epistemological framework for sociological research and examines iconicity in the context of transitional urban landscapes of Berlin and Warsaw after 1989. He works in the areas of cultural sociology and social theory. His interests include sociology of knowledge and intellectuals, visual sociology, urban studies, and symbolic anthropology.

Miranda Christou is a lecturer in Sociology of Education at the University of Cyprus. Her research work has explored the role of educational systems in shaping questions of history and collective memory, the pedagogical function of the media in representations of human pain and suffering, and the cultural implications of globalized educational systems.

Nicolas Demertzis is professor at the Faculty of Communication and Media Studies, Athens University, Greece. He has written and edited ten books. He has published extensively in Greek and English journals and volumes. His current academic and research interests include political sociology, political communication, and the sociology of emotions.

Shai M. Dromi is a PhD student at the Department of Sociology at Yale University and a junior fellow at the Center for Cultural Sociology. His research interests include the sociology of emotions, urban sociology, the sociology of morality, and cosmopolitanism. His dissertation project is concerned with the interface of space, culture, and helping behavior.

Ron Eyerman is professor of sociology and co-director of the Center for Cultural Sociology at Yale University. His latest publications include *The Cultural Sociology of Political Assassination, From MLK and RFK to Pim Fortuyn and Theo van Gogh* (Palgrave MacMillian 2011), "Harvey Milk and the Trauma of Assassination" (*Cultural Sociology* 2011) and "Intellectuals and Cultural Trauma" (*European Journal of Social Theory* 2011). His current research concerns the impact of Hurricane Katrina and transitional justice in Argentina.

Rui Gao is a PhD candidate in sociology and a junior fellow at the Center for Cultural Sociology at Yale University. She got her MA degree in sociology from Yale University and her BA degree in English and English Literature from Beijing Foreign Studies University. Her fields of interest include cultural sociology, sociological theory, critical studies in media communication, gender and feminist studies, and China studies. Her latest publications include "Remembrance of Things Past: Cultural Trauma, the 'Nanking Massacre' and Chinese Identity" (*The Oxford Handbook of Cultural Sociology*, forthcoming). She recently submitted her PhD thesis, which traces the configuration and transformation in the representation of the War of Resistance against Japan in the public sphere of PRC since 1949.

Akiko Hashimoto teaches sociology at the University of Pittsburgh. She has published *Imagined Families, Lived Families: Culture and Kinship in*

Contemporary Japan (SUNY Press 2008, with J. Traphagan), *The Gift of Generations: Japanese and American Perspectives on Aging and the Social Contract* (Cambridge University Press 1996), and *Family Support for the Elderly: The International Experience* (Oxford University Press 1992, with H. Kendig and L. Coppard). She is now at work on a book, *War Stories Peace Stories: Cultural Trauma, Memory and Identity in Japan.*

Volker Heins is a senior researcher at the Institute for Social Research, Goethe University, Frankfurt, and a faculty fellow at the Center for Cultural Sociology, Yale University. His recent books include *Rethinking Ethical Foreign Policy* (co-edited with David Chandler, Routledge 2007), *Nongovernmental Organizations in International Society* (Palgrave Macmillan 2008) and *Beyond Friend and Foe: The Politics of Critical Theory* (Brill Academic 2011).

Andreas Langenohl is a professor of sociology at Justus Liebig-University (Giessen, Germany). His research covers collective memory, modernization theory, social studies of finance, and the epistemology of the social sciences. Recent publications include "How to Change Other People's Institutions: Discursive Entrepreneurship and the Boundary Object of Competition/Competitiveness in the German Banking Sector" (*Economy and Society* 2008) and "Modernization, Modernity, and Tradition: Sociological Theory's Promissory Notes" (in: Kim/Calichman, eds., *Rethinking Cultural Difference: Around the Work of Naoki Sakai,* Routledge 2010).

Ari Sitas is a writer and a sociologist. He currently holds a professorial chair at the University of Cape Town and is the director of the Ministry of Higher Education's Task Team for the future of the Humanities and Social Sciences in South Africa. He is also a fellow at the Institute of Advanced Studies, Jawaharlal Nehru University, New Delhi. His latest books include *The Ethic of Reconciliation* (Madiba Press 2008) and *The Mandela Decade: Labour, Culture and Society in Post-Apartheid South Africa* (University of South Africa Press and Brill Academic Publishers 2010).

Ivana Spasić is professor of sociology at the University of Belgrade and a faculty fellow at the Center for Cultural Sociology at Yale University. She has published extensively on social theory, everyday life, collective memory, and cultural aspects of Serbia's postsocialist and postwar transformation. Her publications include several books (in Serbian), among them *Politics of Everyday Life: Serbia 1999–2002* (Institut za filozofiju i drustvenu teoriju 2003), *Sociologies of Everyday Life* (Zavod za udzbenike 2004), and *The Legacy of Pierre Bourdieu* (Filip Visnjic 2006).

Carlo Tognato is currently affiliated with the Hawke Research Institute at the University of South Australia in Adelaide and is a faculty fellow at the Center for Cultural Sociology at Yale University. He has been the director of the Center for Social Studies and associate professor of Sociology at the National University of Colombia in Bogotá. His research focuses on symbolic communication in the economic arena and on the functioning of the public sphere in deeply divided societies.

61234350R00184